D0934825

Cardinal Gasparo Contarini, Museo Civico Correr, Venice.

Gasparo Contarini

The publisher gratefully acknowledges the contribution provided by the Gladys Krieble Delmas Foundation.

Gasparo Contarini

Venice, Rome, and Reform

Elisabeth G. Gleason

UNIVERSITY OF CALIFORNIA PRESS

Berkeley / Los Angeles / Oxford

University of California Press
Berkeley and Los Angeles, California

University of California Press, Ltd.
Oxford, England

Library of Congress Cataloging-in-Publication Data

Gleason, Elisabeth G.
   Gasparo Contarini : Venice, Rome, and reform / Elisabeth G.
Gleason.
       p.   cm.
   Includes bibliographical references and index.
   ISBN 0-520-08057-2
   1. Contarini, Gasparo, 1483–1542.   2. Venice (Italy)—Foreign
relations.   3. Statesmen—Italy—Venice—Biography.   I. Title.
DG678.24.C66G54   1993
945′.31—dc20   92-25925
                                                            CIP

Printed in the United States of America
9   8   7   6   5   4   3   2   1

The paper used in this publication meets the minimum requirements of
American National Standard for Information Sciences—Permanence of
Paper for Printed Library Materials, ANSI Z39.48-1984. ∞

For John

Contents

CONTENTS

Preface

The standard but hagiographic biography of Cardinal Gasparo Contarini appeared in 1885. Franz Dittrich, its author, was an assiduous scholar who managed to gather much documentary material during a stay of only five months in Italy and working under difficult conditions. His hefty volume has established Contarini's physiognomy, as it were, and many of his judgments have gone unchallenged for over a hundred years. Dittrich interpreted his subject primarily as an orthodox and exemplary Catholic. In fact, the vindication of Contarini's Catholicism is the underlying theme of the entire work. A learned and political Catholic himself, influenced by events of the German nineteenth-century *Kulturkampf*, Dittrich chose the Italian sixteenth-century cardinal as an example and, one suspects, an inspiration for readers at a time when heroes of their faith were particularly appreciated by Catholics in Germany.

Contarini has had a good press ever since. In scholarly literature his name has come to be identified with exceptional moderation and reason in an age of increasingly sharp religious controversy. Protestant writers have generally found him one of the few respectable members of the Roman curia and thought him more sympathetic with their theology than he actually was. Catholic historians have frequently exaggerated his role in the movement for church reform. Thus Contarini has been portrayed, on the one hand, as almost Lutheran in his theology of justification and, on the other hand, as staunchly Catholic despite a temporary lapse into theological "unclarity" in Regensburg in 1541.

This book is the result of my attempt to understand the thought of a good and devout man after I found many previous interpretations unconvincing. I came to realize that Contarini was emblematic of many Catholics not just in Italy but in all of Europe during the turbulent years of the Reformation, and I wondered about the nature of beliefs he held that prevented him from becoming another Gianpietro Carafa, a persecutor of those with whom he disagreed. It won't do simply to put him into a slot labeled "party of the middle" or "Erasmians," as if these terms explained his stand. The inquisitors have been given undue prominence because they had the power of coercion; what about those, like Contarini, who had only the power of conviction?

Reading Contarini's letters and works, placing them in their historical context, and meditating on their meaning has been a slow and at times frustrating process. Of course I am not sure that I have found the one "key" to his mind. But at least I can offer the reader a fresh interpretation of a figure who continues to excite interest and stimulate disagreement. That he was one of the leading churchmen of the pre-Tridentine period is certain. Equally important is the fact that he was a Venetian noble. But here we enter a hall of mirrors: Did he internalize the ethos of actual or ideal Venetian patricians? By extension, did he see in Paul III, that enigmatic pontiff so difficult of access to the historian, an actual or an ideal pope? Was reform a practical matter for him, to be pursued in the face of the Lutheran threat, or something to which he was committed on principle?

Venice, Rome—meaning the Rome of Popes Clement VII and Paul III—and reform are three intersecting and inextricably linked themes in Contarini's thought. I hope that I have made sense of their connection, and that my book has wider implications not only for the sixteenth century but for our own time as well.

Acknowledgments

My debts for assistance received from institutions and individuals are many, and it is a pleasure to acknowledge them. A grant from the Gladys Krieble Delmas Foundation enabled me to spend a semester in Venice, and a fellowship from the National Endowment for the Humanities made possible another semester's work in Rome. A sabbatical leave from the University of San Francisco facilitated the completion of research in Italy. The American Philosophical Society gave me a grant for microfilming documents in Italian archives. The Delmas Foundation made a generous grant in aid of publication. To all these organizations I am deeply grateful.

I want to thank Deans Carl Naegele and Stanley Nel of the University of San Francisco for their constant support, and the librarians of that institution's Gleeson Library for their helpful responses on the innumerable occasions when I asked for their assistance. The reference librarians, in particular, often went out of their way to answer my queries. I must also single out Hille Novak, head of acquisitions, who never refused a single request I made. She even found funds for the fifty-eight volumes of Sanuto's *Diarii* with which she surprised me one day.

In Italy, too, I received many courtesies and kindnesses in libraries and archives. I want to thank the staff of the Archivio di Stato in Venice, especially Dott.ssa Francesca Cavazzana Romanelli. Among the staff of the Biblioteca Correr I owe special thanks to Signor Pasquon, who most kindly assisted me in the early stages of my research. In the Archivio di Stato in Florence, Dott.ssa Paola Peruzzi was especially helpful, as was Monsignor Hermann Hoberg in the Vatican Archive. Rev. Leonard Boyle, O.P., Prefect of the Vatican Library, graciously permitted me to use the library after closing hours, greatly facilitating my research there.

Among my friends, my greatest debt is to William Bouwsma, the best of mentors and challenging partner in an ongoing dialogue all these years. He generously read the entire manuscript and offered penetrating criticism, as always. Gene Brucker gave me much support, good practical advice, and offered me warm hospitality in Florence. To Contarini I owe my friendship with Gigliola Fragnito. Ever since our first meeting she has kept me abreast of her own work by sending me numerous offprints and publications, and proved a delightful as well as incisive colleague from whom I have learned much. Another student of Contarini, JB Ross, gave me her own microfilms and notes at an early stage of my book; I have profited from her generosity. Aldo Stella has supplied me with much bibliographical information, as well as offprints and books, making me the beneficiary of his thorough knowledge of Italian religious history. Massimo Firpo sent me transcripts of several documents before they were published in his magisterial *Processo Morone*, and has included me among the recipients of his offprints and books. Paolo Simoncelli has been a faithful friend whose encouragement has meant—and continues to mean—very much to me. I am grateful for his articles and books, his challenging comments, and his participation in many a long and sometimes sharp debate about "our" *spirituali* as well as about wider historiographical problems. Anne Schutte has helped me in many ways, not the least of which was in arranging for photographs of the Contarini chapel in the church of the Madonna dell'Orto in Venice. Ronald Delph, Frederick McGinness, Laurie Nussdorfer, and Cornelis Augustijn have generously given me unpublished copies of their papers. My cousins Marco and Edda Giachery have repeatedly been my affectionate hosts in Venice. To all of them I owe sincere thanks, as I do to my editors, Tony Hicks and Anne Geissman Canright.

My family has been my greatest source of support. I cherish the memory of my father's loving encouragement of my intellectual development and proudly remember his death in the cause of freedom from political tyranny. My courageous mother has been an enormous and patient help in ways too numerous to mention. But the greatest help while writing this book I received from my husband, who has supported my work fully and selflessly from the beginning. By his example he set a high standard for me to follow. What I owe him can be said to him alone, and then only inadequately. This book is dedicated to him.

Elisabeth Gregorich Gleason
10 September 1992

Abbreviations

ASF	Archivio di Stato, Florence
ASM	Archivio di Stato, Mantua
ASV	Archivio di Stato, Venice
ASVat	Archivio Segreto Vaticano
BAV	Biblioteca Apostolica Vaticana
Beccadelli, "Vita"	Ludovico Beccadelli, "Vita di Monsignor Reverendissimo et Illustrissimo Messer Gasparo Contarino Gentilhuomo Venitiano et Cardinale della S. Romana Chiesa," *Monumenti Beccadelli* (q.v. below), vol. 1, pt. 2, 9–59
CSPV	*Calendar of State Papers and Manuscripts Relating to English Affairs, Existing in the Archives and Collections of Venice, and in Other Libraries of Northern Italy*, ed. Rawdon Brown, vols. 3–4 (London, 1869–71)
CT	*Concilium Tridentinum: diariorum, actorum, epistularum, tractatuum nova collectio*, ed. Societas Goerresiana, 13 vols. (Freiburg i.B.: Herder, 1901–38; reprint 1963–67)

DBI   *Dizionario biografico degli Italiani*, 37 vols. to date (Rome: Enciclopedia Italiana, 1960–)

Dispatches, Charles V   Contarini's dispatches from his embassy to the Emperor Charles V: VBM (q.v.), MS It., Cl. VII, 1009 (=7447)

Dispatches, Papal Court   Contarini's dispatches from his embassy to Pope Clement VII: VBM, MS It., Cl. VII, 1043 (=7616)

Ducali   Instructions from Doge Andrea Gritti to Gasparo Contarini, in VBC (q.v.), Cod. Cicogna 3477

Ep. Poli   *Epistolarum Reginaldi Poli S.R.E. Cardinalis et aliorum ad ipsum collectio*, 5 vols., ed. A. M. Querini (Brescia, 1744–57)

F. Contarini, Dispatches   Francesco Contarini's dispatches from Regensburg, 1541, in VBM, MS It., Cl. VII, 802 (=8219)

GC   Franz Dittrich, *Gasparo Contarini, 1483–1542: eine Monographie* (Braunsberg, 1885)

Jedin, "Contarini und Camaldoli"   Hubert Jedin, "Contarini und Camaldoli," *Archivio italiano per la storia della pietà* 2 (1959): 59–118; also published separately (Rome: Edizioni di Storia e Letteratura, 1953)

Jedin, Trient   Hubert Jedin, *Geschichte des Konzils von Trient*, 4 vols. in 5 (Freiburg i.B.: Herder, 1951–75)

Monumenti Beccadelli   *Monumenti di varia letteratura tratti dai manoscritti di Monsignor Lodovico Beccadelli*, ed. Giambattista Morandi, 2 vols. (Bologna, 1797–1804)

NB   *Nuntiaturberichte aus Deutschland nebst ergänzenden Aktenstücken*, 1st ser., 7 vols. (Rome: Königliches Preussisches Historisches Institut, 1892–1912)

Opera   *Gasparis Contareni Cardinalis Opera* (Paris, 1571)

PRO   Public Record Office, London

Reg.   *Regesten und Briefe des Cardinals Gasparo Con-
            tarini*, ed. Franz Dittrich (Braunsberg, 1881)

"Relazione"   Contarini's final report to the Senate, in Eugenio
              Albèri, *Relazioni degli ambasciatori veneti al
              Senato* (Florence, 1839–63), 1st ser., 2:1–73

Sanuto, *Diarii*   Marino Sanuto, *I Diarii*, 58 vols. (Venice,
                   1879–1903)

VBC   Venice, Biblioteca Civica Correr

VBM   Venice, Biblioteca Nazionale Marciana

CHAPTER ONE

In the Service of Venice

The Decision to Serve the State

The Contarini family was at the center of Venice virtually from the beginning of the city's existence. According to Venetian tradition, the first doge, Paolo Lucio Anafesto, was elected in the early eighth century. The families who later claimed descent from his electors took great pride in their putative ancestry, regarding themselves as superior to others in both dignity and devotion to the state.

One of these families was the Contarini, whose many branches were prominent in Venetian history for centuries. Like many noble clans, the Contarini constructed more or less imaginary genealogies linking them to important ancestors. One version traces the family back to a Roman official supposedly in charge of defending the area where the river Reno flows into the Po—the "Conte di Reno," whence the name Contarini.[1] Other versions of the family legend mention that the first Contarini came from Constantinople via Capo d'Istria,[2] from Concordia to Torcello and then to Venice,[3] or from Concordia via Loreto.[4]

---

1. One such genealogy is Venice, Biblioteca Civica Correr (hereafter cited as VBC), Cod. Cicogna 2327: "Portione de Huomeni Illustri della Famiglia Contarini di Venetia."

2. Archivio di Stato, Venice (hereafter cited as ASV), Marco Barbaro, *Arbori de' patritii Veneti*, vol. II, fol. 437.

3. VBC, Cod. Cicogna 1613: "Tute le caxade de zentilhomeni de Venetia dal principio fin al presente, MDVII," fol. 9r.

4. VBC, Cod. Cicogna 2330 (without title or page numbers), gives brief summaries of family histories together with their coats of arms.

The last two accounts inform us that the Contarini were tribunes characterized by a particular faculty for acquiring possessions.[5] In historical
times the clan gave the Republic eight doges, the first of whom,
Domenico, is remembered for supporting the start of the construction
of St. Mark's basilica in the eleventh century. There were Contarini
among holders of every Venetian political and ecclesiastical office, including twenty-two bishops and four patriarchs of Venice. By the sixteenth century the Contarini had far more members in the Great
Council than any other clan,[6] and their genealogy in the detailed *Arbori* by Barbaro runs to almost eighty pages.[7]

The branch of the family to which Gasparo Contarini belonged was
neither the wealthiest nor the best known. Its palazzo stood distant
from the center of the city, indeed at its very edge, facing the islands of
San Michele and Murano. Far from resembling the graceful Contarini
Fasan or the imposing Contarini degli Scrigni on the Grand Canal, the
palazzo was a large, plain building in a compound of warehouses, artisans' quarters, and smaller rented dwellings. Its distinction still derives
from a garden that is unusually large by Venetian standards and from a
small mid-sixteenth-century building constructed at its farthest corner,
which has come to be known by the romantic name of "il casino degli
spiriti."[8] The proximity of the church of the Madonna dell'Orto gave
this branch of the Contarini the name by which it continued to be

---

5. The term *tribunes* was used as the title for late Roman administrative officials, and
later became an honorific title signifying elevated social status; see Ernst Rodenwaldt,
"Untersuchungen über die Biologie des venezianischen Adels," *Homo: Zeitschrift für die
vergleichende Forschung am Menschen* 8 (1957): 4, who thinks that the Contarini possibly
had Germanic ancestors, since a document of 1116, preserved in Venice, was signed by a
Berengarius Guntarenus and a Peter Guntarinus, from whom the family name might
have originated.

6. In 1513, 147 families were represented among 2,622 members of the Great
Council, of whom 188 were Contarini; the next most numerous were the Morosini with
85; Venice, Biblioteca Nazionale Marciana (hereafter cited as VBM), MSS It., Cl. VII, 90
(=8029). In June 1527, among 2,708 male members of Venetian noble families in the
Great Council listed by Marino Sanuto in his diary, the Contarini had 172, followed by
the Morosini with 102 and the Malipiero with 81; Sanuto, *I Diarii* (Venice, 1879–
1903), 45:569–72 (all references to Sanuto, *Diarii*, are to vol. and col. nos.).

7. ASV, Barbaro, *Arbori*, vol. II, fols. 437–516.

8. The derivation of the name is not certain. The explanation given by Giulio
Lorenzetti, *Venice and Its Lagoons* (Trieste: Edizioni LINT, 1975), is attractive: the building was "at one time the site of merry parties and literary gatherings" (405), and "the
meetings and literary discussions held in the nearby garden overlooking the lagoon in
the Casino degli Spiriti ... were well known" (408). But there is no evidence for such
meetings, presumably linked with the fame of Gasparo Contarini as a writer and thinker.
The Contarini family must have constructed the casino between 1537 and 1566: it appears in the tax declaration of the latter date only. See below, note 15.

known until its extinction in the male line in 1688.[9] A small, elegant chapel there with an altar painting by Tintoretto, busts of family members (including that of Gasparo), and funerary inscriptions remains as a memorial to the Contarini "della Madonna dell'Orto" (see figs. 1 and 2).[10]

Gasparo, born in 1483, was the eldest of seven sons and four daughters of Alvise Contarini and Polissena Malipiero. Alvise also had two illegitimate children, a daughter whose name is not mentioned in the documents (daughters were often anonymous in the records: "a girl") and a son, Angelo. Probably all grew up together, since Contarini's later references to his "fratel natural" and "nostra sorella natural" show the same affectionate concern that he extended to other members of his family.[11] Three of his sisters and his half-sister married Venetian patricians,[12] while one became a nun. Of the brothers, only

9. Emmanuele Antonio Cicogna, *Delle inscrizioni veneziane* (Venice, 1824–53), 2:250; ASV, Barbaro, *Arbori*, vol. II, fol. 466; VBC, MS Gradenigo Dolfin 131, fols. 293–294.

10. For the church, see Ashley Clarke and Philip Rylands, eds., *Restoring Venice: The Church of the Madonna dell'Orto* (London: Elek, 1977); V. Zanetti, *La chiesa della Madonna dell'Orto in Venezia* (Venice, 1870); Giuseppe Bigaglia, *La chiesa della Madonna dell'Orto in Venezia* (Venice: A. Vidotti, 1937); and Lino Moretti, *La chiesa della Madonna dell'Orto in Venezia* (Turin: Scaravaglio, 1981).

11. His illegitimate sister was married to Vincenzo Belegno, a Venetian nobleman, in 1514; ASV, Avogaria di Comun, Reg. 106, *Cronaca Matrimoni*, fol. 1; VBC, Cod. Cicogna 2171, fol. 29. Contarini writes about the wedding festivities celebrated by the family, and mentions that "the whole house was topsy-turvy"; Hubert Jedin, "Contarini und Camaldoli," *Archivio italiano per la storia della pietà* 2 (1959): 59–118; also published separately as a preprint by Edizioni di Storia e Letteratura (Rome, 1953), spanning pp. 3–67, which version I use; see p. 27. His interest in her and her family continued, as can be seen in a letter to his sister Serafina, nun in the convent of S. Chiara in Murano (n.d., but probably 1540 or 1541), in which he asks her to treat their niece Belegnia, daughter of Vincenzo Belegno, as a daughter. She was about to enter the convent, and Contarini wished that she be shown the same courtesy and kindness that would be extended to himself: Archivio Segreto Vaticano (hereafter cited as ASVat), A.A., Arm. I–XVIII, 6461, fol. 65r–v.

Contarini's illegitimate brother Angelo is the subject of several letters by the cardinal in 1541 to diplomats and the papal legate at the French court; see ibid., fol. 58r; and ASVat, Fondo Borghese, ser. I, 409–10, fols. 200r–v, 201v–202r; *Monumenti di varia letteratura tratti dai manoscritti di Monsignor Lodovico Beccadelli*, ed. Giambattista Morandi (Bologna, 1797–1804), 1(2):94–95 (hereafter cited as *Monumenti Beccadelli*). Although he had lived in Turkish lands for twenty-three years and had a Turkish wife and a son, Angelo was imprisoned by the Turks when war with Venice began, and all his goods were confiscated. Presumably he traded for the family: Contarini writes of "roba sua" and "roba nostra." He asks his correspondents to urge King Francis I to intercede with the Turks and obtain his half-brother's release.

12. Contarina married Matteo Vitturi in 1502, Laura married Nicolò Grimani in 1511. See ASV, G. Giomo, *Indice dei matrimoni patrizii per nome di donne*. For Paola's marriage, see below, note 17.

GASPARI CONTARENI
S

CVIVS ADMIRANDAM INTEGRITATEM,
DOCTRINAM, AC ELOQVENTIAM, IN
VTRAQ. REP. ET APVD SVMMOS REGES,
GESTA, ET SCRIPTA, TESTANTVR.
BONONIAE LEGAT PONTIF
NATVRAE CESSIT
M · D · X L I I ·
VIXIT ANNOS LIX·
A OYSIVS AEQVES ET GAS
FRA E N

1. Monument to Cardinal Contarini, Contarini Chapel, Madonna Dell'Orto, Venice. Photo by Sam Habibi Minelli.

2. Detail: Bust of Cardinal Contarini by Alessandro Vittoria, in the Contarini Chapel, Madonna dell'Orto, Venice. Photo by Osvaldo Böhm.

two married; they also had illegitimate offspring, as did two of the unmarried ones.[13]

The brothers seem to have been a closely knit group. After the death of their father in 1502 they continued to live together, forming a

13. See James C. Davis, *A Venetian Family and Its Fortune, 1500–1900* (Philadelphia: American Philosophical Society, 1975), 93–106; and Rodenwaldt, "Untersuchungen," 18–19, for the Venetian custom of having only some brothers in a family

fraterna, a family economic unit in which each was a full partner.[14] They held real property in common, both in Venice and in the country, as shown by their tax declarations of 1514, 1537, and 1566.[15] In addition to their own dwelling in Venice, inherited from their father, they owned rental property that in 1537 brought an income of about one thousand ducats, shops, and several hundred *campi* of land (about eight-tenths of an acre each) in the Po Valley consisting of fields, meadows, pastures, and woods. In Piove di Sacco near Venice the family had a country villa that was the favorite retreat of Gasparo Contarini.[16] The extent of their commercial wealth is not easy to ascertain, but it must have been considerable, at least in the mid-1530s. The

marry. Regarding evidence for illegitimate children: Contarini's brother Tommaso mentions in his will a bequest to "Felicita, mother of Bianca, my deceased daughter"; ASV, Arch. notarile, *Testamenti*, Atti Ziliol, C., busta 1261, no. 885. The will of Gasparo, son of Contarini's brother Vincenzo, mentions "my dearest brother" Hieronymo Contarini, to whom no bequest is made; ibid., busta 1258, no. 409. Hieronymo is not included in any genealogy, since only legitimate descendants were shown. The third brother who fathered an illegitimate child was Ferrigo. His son Giulio became Contarini's successor as bishop of Belluno in 1542 after receiving a papal dispensation from the impediment due to his birth; ASVat, Fondo Concistoriale, *Acta Camerarii*, vol. V, fol. 64r. Contarini's fourth illegitimate nephew was Don Placido, monk of S. Giustina in Padua, son of his brother Zuan Antonio; Ludovico Beccadelli, "Vita di Monsignor Reverendissimo et Illustrissimo Messer Gasparo Contarino Gentilhuomo Venitiano et Cardinale della S. Romana Chiesa," in *Monumenti Beccadelli* 1(2):50 (hereafter cited as Beccadelli, "Vita").

14. Frederic C. Lane, "Family Partnerships and Joint Ventures," in *Venice and History* (Baltimore: Johns Hopkins University Press, 1966), 36–55; and Davis, *A Venetian Family*, 7–8. Sanuto, *Diarii*, repeatedly mentions "Gasparo Contarini et fradelli" as an economic unit: for example, 46:383, 417–18 ["figlioli" mistakenly for "fradelli"]; 47:305; 49:318.

15. ASV, Dieci Savi alle Decime, *Redecima* 1514 (S. Marco, Castello, Canareggio, S. Polo), Reg. 363, no. 46; *Redecima* 1537 (S. Croce, S. Polo), Reg. 366; and *Redecima* 1566 (Canareggio), BI, 133, no. 763. The first is in the name of Gasparo Contarini and his brothers, the second in that of Tommaso Contarini and his brothers, and the third in that of Tommaso Contarini and his nephews Alvise and Gasparo, sons of Vincenzo. The 1566 declaration is especially informative and detailed. It is briefly discussed by Bernardo Canal, "Il Collegio, l'Ufficio e l'Archivio dei Dieci Savi alle Decime in Rialto," *Nuovo Archivio Veneto* 16 (1908): 143, who points out the usefulness of the declarations for our knowledge of the everyday life of Venetian families.

16. The villa is described in the tax declarations as entailing only expenses for the family, unlike their other country property, which was rented. Contarini mentions it in letters to his friend Tommaso Giustiniani; Jedin, "Contarini und Camaldoli," 55, 56, 59. The Contarini also owned land near the villa together with Daniele Dandolo; see *Redecima* 1514 as cited in preceding note. It was later divided; Jedin, "Contarini und Camaldoli," 61, 62. In 1518, the Contarini owned at least 445 *campi*; Robert Finlay, *Politics in Renaissance Venice* (New Brunswick, N.J.: Rutgers University Press, 1980), 166.

brothers traded in Apulia, Cyprus, Alexandria, the eastern Mediterranean, and Spain,[17] and had one or more galleys of their own.[18] The commercial involvements of the family declined as brothers died off without leaving sons to carry on the business in their stead. By 1549 only Tommaso, Gasparo's next younger brother, was alive, and his main occupation during the remainder of his long life until 1578 was officeholding.[19] It is likely that the Contarini gradually concentrated their wealth in land rather than commerce, following the pattern of many Venetian noble families in the sixteenth and seventeenth centuries.[20]

Of Gasparo's education little is known. Lodovico Beccadelli, his secretary and biographer, states that his precocious intellectual gifts were recognized and encouraged by his father.[21] Presumably the other sons were given a more practical education as apprentices in the family

17. The Contarini della Madonna dell'Orto were well off in 1515, when they offered to lend the state 3,000 ducats at a time when the usual amount of loans was under 1,000; Sanuto, *Diarii* 21:85, 86, 186, 188. They financed two expensive embassies of Gasparo in 1521–25 and 1528–30. In 1521 their sister Paola was married to Matteo Dandolo (ASV, Avogaria di Comun, Reg. 106, *Cronaca matrimoni*, 1; and VBC, Cod. Cicogna 2171, fol. 87) with a dowry of 8,000 ducats; see Sanuto, *Diarii* 30:29. The legal limit on dowries was 3,000 ducats in 1505 and 4,000 in 1535. Even if "official limits bore no relation to reality," as Brian Pullan maintains in "The Occupation and Investments of the Venetian Nobility in the Middle and Late Sixteenth Century," in *Renaissance Venice*, ed. J. R. Hale (London: Faber & Faber, 1973), 389, the sum of 8,000 ducats was very large. See also Stanley Chojnacki, "La posizione della donna a Venezia nel Cinquecento," *Tiziano e Venezia: convegno internazionale di studi* (Vicenza: Neri Pozza, 1976), 69.

On the other hand, some evidence points to the opposite conclusion for the later 1530s: Contarini as cardinal had a small household in Rome, in marked contrast to those of his fellow Venetian cardinals Grimani and Pisani, for example; also, at the time of his death, the Venetian Senate petitioned the pope on behalf of the family, referring to it as "ruined" and "poor"; VBC, Cod. Cicogna 1540, fols. 113–114: "1542. Die 26 Aug^{ti}. Oratori in Curia Gabrieli Venerio. Raccomandazione per la famiglia del Card^{le} Contarini." The involvement of the family in overseas trade is mentioned also by their brother-in-law Matteo Dandolo in a sketch of Contarini's life, published by Gigliola Fragnito in *Memoria individuale e costruzione biografica: Beccadelli, Della Casa, Vettori alle origini di un mito*, Pubblicazioni dell'Università di Urbino, Serie di lettere e filosofia (Urbino: Argalìa Editore, 1978), 174.

18. Sanuto, *Diarii* 40:595; 46:357, 383, 417–18.

19. Renzo Derosas, "Contarini, Tommaso," in *Dizionario biografico degli Italiani* (Rome: Enciclopedia Italiana, 1960–), 28:300–305 (hereafter cited as *DBI*). I wish to thank Dr. Derosas for kindly allowing me to see the typescript of his article before publication.

20. See Pullan, "Occupation and Investments," 379–408, esp. 381; also Ugo Tucci, "The Psychology of the Venetian Merchant in the Sixteenth Century," in Hale (ed.), *Renaissance Venice*, 346–78, esp. 357–59.

21. Beccadelli, "Vita," 10.

business. After receiving instruction in grammar, Gasparo studied at the schools of San Marco and Rialto, where his teachers included the humanist Giorgio Valla, the historian Marcantonio Sabellico, and Antonio Giustinian, who eventually left teaching for a diplomatic career.[22] At the age of eighteen, in 1501, Contarini entered the faculty of arts at the University of Padua. His stay there lasted eight years,[23] with one brief interruption in 1502, occasioned by the death of his father and the need to settle family affairs. He returned to Venice without a degree in 1509 when the university was closed because of the War of the League of Cambrai.[24]

Little material about Contarini's years at Padua has come to light.[25] His studies seem to have centered on the works of Aristotle. Bernardo Navagero, one of his friends, declares hyperbolically that Contarini knew Aristotle's works so well that if all of them were lost he would have been able to write them again from memory.[26] He also studied theology, which at Padua included the traditions of both St. Thomas and Scotus;[27] however, it is not possible to determine the extent of his

22. On the two schools, see Bruno Nardi, "La scuola di Rialto e l'umanesimo veneziano," in *Umanesimo europeo e umanesimo veneziano,* ed. Vittore Branca, Civiltà europea e civiltà veneziana, Aspetti e problemi 2 (Florence: Sansoni, 1963), 93–139; and idem, "Letteratura e cultura veneziana del Quattrocento," in *La civiltà veneziana del Quattrocento* (Florence: Sansoni, 1957), 101–45. Very useful are James Bruce Ross, "Venetian Schools and Teachers, Fourteenth to Early Sixteenth Century: A Survey and a Study of Giovanni Battista Egnazio," *Renaissance Quarterly* 39 (1976): 521–60, with bibliography; and Fernando Lepori, "La scuola di Rialto dalla fondazione alla metà del Cinquecento," *Storia della cultura veneta,* ed. Girolamo Arnaldi and Manlio Pastore Stocchi (Vicenza: Neri Pozza Editore, 1980), 3(2):539–605.

23. See Gigliola Fragnito, "Cultura umanistica e riforma religiosa: il 'De officio boni viri ac probi episcopi' di Gasparo Contarini," *Studi veneziani* 11 (1969): 82n.29, for Contarini's presence in Padua; also Franz Dittrich, *Gasparo Contarini, 1483–1542: eine Monographie* (Braunsberg, 1885), 13–21 (hereafter cited as *GC*).

24. The university was not reopened until October 1517; see Sanuto, *Diarii* 23:562; 25:30, 69.

25. *GC*, 13–21, discusses Contarini's teachers and the subjects he studied. The evidence for these years is sketchy, and much of what Dittrich suggests is inferred from general works about the university and the curriculum of that period, like A. Favaro, "Lo studio di Padova al tempo di Niccolò Copernico," in *Atti del R. Istituto Veneto di scienze, lettere ed arti* 6 (1880): 285–356. For more recent works, consult the bibliography of Lucia Rossetti in *Quaderni per la storia dell'Università di Padova* 1 (1968): 179–311; 2 (1969): 109–88. See also François Dupuigrenet Desroussilles, "L'Università di Padova dal 1405 al Concilio di Trento," in Arnaldi and Stocchi (eds.), *Storia della cultura veneta* 3(2):607–47.

26. Giuseppe De Leva, "Della vita e delle opere del cardinale Gasparo Contarini," *Rivista periodica dei lavori della I. R. Accademia di scienze, lettere ed arti in Padova* 12 (1863): 53.

27. For a survey, see Antonino Poppi, "La teologia nell'Università e nelle scuole," in Arnaldi and Stocchi (eds.), *Storia della cultura veneta* 3(3):1–33.

training in theology, in which he seems to have been essentially self-taught. Greek, under Marco Musuro, who held a chair from 1503 on, was a subject Contarini took up seriously, as were mathematics and astronomy;[28] but he did not acquire unusual proficiency in these studies.

The Paduan period saw the establishment of a network of continuing friendships.[29] The deepest bonds tied Contarini to two Venetian nobles, Tommaso Giustiniani and Vincenzo Querini: "At the center of Contarini's affective life before 1514 there lay, one might say, a triangle, the apex representing Giustiniani, his spiritual mentor and elder by seven years, the other angles himself and Querini, his *alter ego*, about four years older than himself."[30] Querini left Padua in 1502 and obtained the doctorate in philosophy in Rome; Giustiniani stayed on at Padua until 1505, when he returned to Venice. Upon his own return to Venice in 1509 Contarini resumed contact with his two friends. To his inner circle belonged also Niccolò Tiepolo, Sebastiano Zorzi, Giovanni Battista Egnazio, and Trifone Gabriele.[31]

One finds frequent mention of this group of young aristocrats (Egnazio being the only commoner), this "generation" of Venetian *nobili* who shared experiences of religious crisis at a time of political

28. *GC*, 13, 16. On Musuro, see Martin Lowry, *The World of Aldus Manutius* (Ithaca, N.Y.: Cornell University Press, 1979), 164–67 and passim; Francesco Foffano, "Marco Musuro, professore di greco a Padova ed a Venezia," *Nuovo Archivio Veneto* 3 (1892): 453–73; and Deno J. Geanakoplos, *Greek Scholars in Venice: Studies in the Dissemination of Greek Learning from Byzantium to the West* (Cambridge, Mass.: Harvard University Press, 1962). For the teaching of mathematics, see Carlo Maccagni, "Le scienze nello studio di Padova e nel Veneto," in Arnaldi and Stocchi (eds.), *Storia della cultura veneta* 3(3):135–71.

29. For these friendships and biographical notices of individuals who were close to Contarini during this early period of his life, see James Bruce Ross, "Contarini and His Friends," *Studies in the Renaissance* 17 (1970): 192–232. See also Beccadelli, "Vita," 11–12; and Eugenio Massa, "Gasparo Contarini e gli amici, fra Venezia e Camaldoli," in *Gaspare Contarini e il suo tempo: atti convegno di studio*, ed. Francesca Cavazzana Romanelli (Venice: Comune di Venezia, Assessorato Affari Istituzionali, and Studium Cattolico Veneziano, 1988), 39–91.

30. Ross, "Contarini and His Friends," 195. On Giustiniani, see Eugenio Massa, "Paolo Giustiniani," in *Bibliotheca Sanctorum* (Rome: Istituto Giovanni XXIII della Pontificia Università Lateranense, 1966), 7, cols. 2–9, with bibliography. Also useful is Jean Leclercq, *Un humaniste érémite: le bienheureux Paul Giustiniani (1476–1528)* (Rome: Edizioni Camaldoli, 1951). There is no modern biography of Querini. See Cicogna, *Delle inscrizioni veneziane* 5:62–73; for bibliography, Jedin, "Contarini und Camaldoli," 7n.1; and idem, "Vincenzo Querini und Pietro Bembo," in *Miscellanea Giovanni Mercati* (Vatican City: Biblioteca Apostolica Vaticana, 1946), 4:407–24, reprinted in Jedin, *Kirche des Glaubens—Kirche der Geschichte: ausgewählte Aufsätze und Vorträge* (Freiburg i.B.: Herder, 1966), 1:153–66.

31. Ross, "Contarini and His Friends," 195nn.9–12, for bibliography on these men; also Ross, "Venetian Schools and Teachers," for Egnazio.

disorder and war.[32] In fact, however, little specific information exists about the circle that supposedly formed around Giustiniani and met at his house on Murano. The meetings are thought to have taken place between 1505 and 1510, when he left Venice to become a hermit at Camaldoli.[33] Perhaps we should think of these young men simply as a loosely structured group of friends rather than a more formal "circle." Giustiniani may have played an important role among them not only because he was the oldest but also because of his intense intellectual and spiritual travails during these years, which touched sympathetic chords in the minds and emotions of the others.

The stages of Giustiniani's passage from a Venetian patrician, by his own admission a sensuous and passionate man,[34] to an ascetic reformer of his order and an advocate of church reform have yet to be told fully.[35] Judging from the available evidence, he was a charismatic figure

32. For the first use of the term *generation* in this sense, see Carlo Dionisotti, "Chierici e laici nella cultura italiana del primo Cinquecento," in *Problemi di vita religiosa in Italia nel Cinquecento: atti del Convegno di storia della chiesa in Italia (Bologna, 2–6 settembre 1958)* (Padova: Antenore, 1960), 176. The essay appears in a fuller version under the title "Chierici e laici" in his *Geografia e storia della letteratura italiana* (Turin: Einaudi, 1967), 55–88; the passage on the Venetian group is on 78. Roberto Cessi, "Paolinismo preluterano," *Rendiconti dell'Accademia dei Lincei: classe di scienze morali, storiche e filologiche* 12 (1957): 3–30, sees (p. 8) the group consisting of Giustiniani, Querini, Egnazio, and Contarini as among the "best interpreters" of a mystical awakening in early sixteenth-century Venice.

33. Giustiniani himself describes his life on Murano thus in a letter of 20 July 1518 to "two gentlemen, his friends": "I remember my wanting to try the solitary life in a house I had on Murano, and experience showed me that such a life was that of a pagan philosopher rather than of a religious Christian soul. In it there was no drowning out of the world, no mortification of one's own will, no virtue of obedience, no true poverty, while instead there were countless dangers to chastity" (Johannes Benedictus Mittarelli and Anselmus Costadoni, eds., *Annales Camaldulenses Ordinis Sancti Benedicti* (Venice, 1755–73), 9, col. 595. Of course it is possible that this statement eight years after he left Venice did not reflect his feelings at the time. But it is significant that in thinking back he says nothing about the "circle of Murano." Neither is it mentioned in the extracts from his writings between 1505 and 1509 quoted by Leclercq, *Un umaniste érémite*, 22–34, or in the letters of Contarini to Giustiniani and Querini. Fragnito speaks of the "group" of which Giustiniani was the "spiritual director," adducing as evidence his later letters, written after he entered Camaldoli, and stating that "they also throw some light on the themes and subjects that were discussed at the meetings of the 'group' itself"; but no exact reference pointing to the existence of this group is given; see "Cultura umanistica," 86. Massa casts doubt on the existence of the "Murano circle" in "Gasparo Contarini e gli amici," esp. 39–53. See also his *L'Eremo, la Bibbia e il medioevo in umanisti veneti del primo Cinquecento* (Naples: Liguori Editore, 1992), 15–23.

34. See Leclercq, *Un humaniste érémite*, 17–22.

35. His writings and letters are in course of being published in a modern edition by Eugenio Massa. Thus far two volumes of a projected multivolume edition have appeared under the general title *Trattati, lettere e frammenti* (Rome: Edizioni di Storia e Letter-

whose opinions strongly influenced his friends. Gradually detaching himself from the social and political activities expected of a young man in his milieu, he repudiated civic life for monastic withdrawal and his humanistic education for Christian learning. His search for a life of solitude led him to consider and reject the Camaldolese monastery of San Michele in Isola, which his friend Paolo Canal had entered shortly before his death in 1508.[36] Like a latter-day St. Jerome, Giustiniani traveled to the Holy Land in 1509 but did not find there the sort of peaceful retreat he envisioned. Finally, in 1510, he decided to enter the Camaldolese hermitage near Arezzo, not as a layman, as he had at first wanted, but as a monk, assuming the name Paolo. He was joined a year later by Vincenzo Querini, who left Venice and a public career to become Fra Pietro. Contarini called their departure a "loss"[37] that left him suddenly alone without his "brothers and friends."[38]

New light on Contarini's inner life at this juncture was shed by the discovery in 1943 of thirty of his autograph letters to Giustiniani and Querini,[39] which were published by Hubert Jedin ten years later.[40] The letters begin in 1511, when Contarini was twenty-eight, and span the twelve-year period until 1523, when he turned forty. In them we catch glimpses of Contarini's ideology at a crucial period of his life during which he established his own identity through his choices in religion and career along lines that were to remain characteristic of his thought.[41]

If it is true that "human nature can best be studied in a state of conflict,"[42] then these letters provide a unique source for understanding

atura, 1967–74). Volume 1 bears the title *I manoscritti originali del Beato Paolo Giustiniani custoditi nell'Eremo di Frascati*; volume 2 is entitled *I primi trattati dell'amore di Dio*. The work by Leclercq, *Un humaniste érémite*, while based on the original manuscripts, remains a sketch.

36. Giustiniani writes that he hopes to find Canal in heaven, and calls him his "friend beyond compare . . . who, if it is permitted to speak like this, showing one's love, was half and more than half of myself"; Giustiniani to all his friends, Dec. 1510, in Mittarelli and Costadoni (eds.), *Annales Camaldulenses* 9, col. 476. For a bibliography on Canal, see Fragnito, "Cultura umanistica," 87n.48.

37. Jedin, "Contarini und Camaldoli," 25 (letter 7).

38. Ibid., 37 (letter 11).

39. Ross, "Contarini and His Friends," 192n.3.

40. Ibid., 193n.3.

41. I am using the term *ideology* here in Erik H. Erikson's sense, as an "unconscious tendency underlying religious as well as political thought: the tendency at a given time to make facts amenable to ideas, and ideas to facts, in order to create a world image convincing enough to support the collective and the individual sense of identity" (*Young Man Luther: A Study in Psychoanalysis and History* [New York: W. W. Norton, 1962], 22).

42. Ibid., 16.

Contarini's complex personality. They have attracted considerable attention from scholars, and their interpretation has become almost a subtopic of sixteenth-century Italian religious history.[43] On the simplest level, they evoke a sense of immediacy through their candor and lack of stylistic pretension. To their first commentator, Jedin, the letters seemed to reveal above all Contarini's deep religious crisis and his struggle to find a merciful God, made more acute by his uncertainty about his own vocation, which prompted him to consider whether he too should not embrace the monastic life and join his two friends.[44] Jedin saw Contarini's crisis as culminating in a religious insight on Holy Saturday 1511, strongly reminiscent of Luther's later "experience in the tower."[45] While Jedin could not determine the precise moment when Contarini solved his doubts concerning his vocation, he thought that it had happened by the fall of 1515.[46]

Although most later scholars do not share Jedin's view that Contarini seriously considered entering a monastery,[47] there is less agree-

43. In addition to Jedin's "Contarini und Camaldoli," 3–10, see also his "Ein 'Turmerlebnis' des jungen Contarini," *Historisches Jahrbuch der Görresgesellschaft* 70 (1951): 115–30; and idem, "Gasparo Contarini e il contributo veneziano alla riforma cattolica," in *La civiltà veneziana del Rinascimento* (Florence: Sansoni, 1958). See further Heinz Mackensen, "Contarini's Theological Role at Ratisbon in 1541," *Archiv für Reformationsgeschichte* 51 (1960): 3–57; Cessi, "Paolinismo preluterano"; Felix Gilbert, "Religion and Politics in the Thought of Gasparo Contarini," in *Action and Conviction in Early Modern Europe: Essays in Memory of E. H. Harbison*, ed. T. K. Rabb and J. E. Seigel (Princeton: Princeton University Press, 1969), 90–116; Fragnito, "Cultura umanistica," esp. 97–115; Innocenzo Cervelli, "Storiografia e problemi intorno alla vita religiosa e spirituale a Venezia nella prima metà del '500," *Studi veneziani* 8 (1966): esp. 466–67; Ross, "Contarini and His Friends," 192–232; Delio Cantimori, "Le idee religiose del Cinquecento: la storiografia," in *Storia della letteratura italiana*, ed. Emilio Cecchi and Natalino Sapegno, vol. 5: *Il Seicento* (Milano: Garzanti, 1967), 7–87; Giuseppe Alberigo, "Vita attiva e vita contemplativa in un'esperienza cristiana del XVI secolo," *Studi veneziani* 16 (1974): 177–225 (the somewhat shorter French version appeared as "Vie active et vie contemplative dans une expérience chrétienne du XVIᵉ siècle," in *Théologie: le service théologique dans l'église. Mélanges offertes à Yves Congar pour ses soixante-dix ans* [Paris: Cerf, 1974], 287–321); and Giovanni Miccoli, "La storia religiosa," in *Storia d'Italia* (Turin: Einaudi, 1974), 2(1):947–55.

44. Jedin, "Contarini und Camaldoli," 9.

45. Jedin, "Ein 'Turmerlebnis,'" does not give sufficient weight to conversion experience as a topos, and makes no reference to what Heiko A. Oberman calls "Turmerlebnistradition." See Oberman's "Wir sein pettler. Hoc est verum: Bund und Gnade in der Theologie des Mittelalters und der Reformation," *Die Reformation: von Wittenberg nach Genf* (Göttingen: Vandenhoeck & Ruprecht, 1986), 93.

46. Jedin, "Contarini und Camaldoli," 10.

47. For example, Felix Gilbert thinks that "Jedin's assumption that Contarini intended to become a monk is erroneous," since it "cannot be reconciled with [his] repeated declarations that he was not suited to a monastic life" ("Religion and Politics," 94). Similar views are expressed by Innocenzo Cervelli, *Machiavelli e la crisi dello stato veneziano* (Naples: Guida, 1974), 15; and Fragnito, "Cultura umanistica," 99.

ment on the central thrust of this correspondence between Contarini and his two friends.[48] The main reason is the variety of themes touched on or implicit in his unsystematic and at times emotional letters.[49]

Almost at the very beginning of the correspondence we find the account of Contarini's Holy Saturday experience.[50] Despite his affirmation of love for Giustiniani and gratitude for his friend's affection, Contarini confesses his inability to follow Fra Paolo's example; he knows that he is not cut out for the monastic life. He must have arrived at this conviction before the date of the first letter,[51] since from the outset he is not arguing with himself as to whether to become a monk. He firmly announces the position from which he does not depart in the entire course of the correspondence: he must seek a way in the world for himself, as a layman, "among the multitude of the city" and among his friends and relatives.[52] Several references to his hardened heart[53] sound an almost formulaic note; maintaining that it is preventing him from following the way of truth, Contarini has offered his friend at least an initial reason for his decision.

48. Ross, "Contarini and His Friends," has discussed the correspondence of Contarini, Giustiniani, and Querini in a sensitive manner as showing "the spiritual crisis" of Contarini between 1511 and 1514, followed by its resolution between 1514 and 1516, and states that her analysis "differs from Felix Gilbert's recent treatment ... in tracing more fully the stages of his affective experience and relating them causally to the bonds of intimacy with Querini and Giustiniani rooted in their earlier Paduan comradeship" (205n.58). Alberigo, "Vita attiva," interprets the letters as revolving not so much around the problem of an active or contemplative life for Contarini as around the question of Querini's monastic vocation and Contarini's refusal to see monastic withdrawal as a privileged state of Christian life. They have been called "letters of confession" that show Contarini's personal and emotional interiority by Miccoli, "Storia religiosa," 948. Cantimori, "Idee religiose," 17, considers them as evidence of a passionate element, mystical in quality, in the religious preoccupations of Contarini, Querini, and Giustiniani, and as Contarini's affirmation of the priority of man's will and emotions over the intellect. Cessi, "Paolinismo preluterano," 17, uses them to argue for a mystical component in Contarini's thought. Eugenio Massa, "Paolo Giustiniani e Gasparo Contarini: la vocazione al bivio del neoplatonismo e della teologia biblica," *Benedictina* 35 (1988): 429–74, uses the letters as evidence for Contarini's Aristotelian, traditional philosophical and theological attitudes in contrast to the Neoplatonic thought of Giustiniani, less constrained by scholastic presuppositions.

49. That they lack literary polish was already stressed by Jedin, who stated that Contarini wrote his friends "no epistles with the possibility or explicit intention of eventual publication in mind ... [but] rather always out of the immediate experience of the moment, frequently in haste because a courier was already waiting, at times on torn-off pieces of paper, since nothing better was handy, in one sitting, as was his habit. What was lost to literary form through this was made up for by a gain in the content" ("Contarini und Camaldoli," 9).

50. Ibid., 12–15 (24 Apr. 1511).   51. Ibid., 11–12 (1 Feb. 1511).

52. Ibid., 13, 15.

53. Ibid., 11, line 19; 13, line 35; 14, line 42.

The real reason, however, is profoundly personal. Alluding to a now lost letter of Giustiniani, Contarini summarizes what his friend had written him—that even after leading a life of self-abnegation Giustiniani was troubled by fears of not being able to do sufficient penance for past sins. "I see you persisting in this idea and this fear,"[54] writes Contarini in what is a key phrase for understanding the almost pathological anxiety and depression he himself was enduring.[55] If someone like his friend, who not only embraced an austere eremitical life but also persistently urged others to do the same, still felt such fear, the problem of finding a way to God's mercy and forgiveness naturally became even more acute for Contarini, determined as he was to remain in the world. Giustiniani's avowal of his fears obviously made a strong impression on Contarini, who repeatedly states that he is comparing his own life with that of his friend. Perhaps on some level he even welcomed these fears as a quasi-logical reason for not becoming a monk himself.

Against this background his confession on Holy Saturday took place. He describes it in a measured, almost dry fashion: "I spoke for quite a while with a monk full of sanctity, who among other topics, almost as if he knew my difficulties, began to tell me that the way of salvation is broader than many people think. And, not knowing who I was, he spoke to me at length."[56] No sudden illumination occurred during this confession. Only afterward, as Contarini was mulling over the discussion, did his thoughts turn to the human condition before God and to the question of what constitutes man's happiness. "And, in truth, I understood that even if I did all the penance I could, and more, it would not suffice in the least to merit happiness or even render satisfaction for past sins."[57] From this basic insight flowed Contarini's belief that God loves man with a love beyond human understanding, since he wanted "to send his only-begotten son who through his passion would render satisfaction for all those who desire to have him as their head and want to be members of the body whose head is Christ....Only we must strive to unite ourselves with [Christ] our head in faith, hope, and the little love of which we are capable. As for the satisfaction for past sins and those into which human frailty continually falls, his passion has been enough and more than enough."[58] Contarini

---

54. Ibid. 13, line 27.
55. He describes himself as "poco men che quasi disperato" (ibid., 13, line 33).
56. "Contarini und Camaldoli," 13–14.
57. Ibid., 14.   58. Ibid.

concluded that it was licit for him to live in the world, in the midst of the city, since justification before God was not a matter of doing penance in a hermitage but of believing firmly in the merits of Christ's sacrifice on the cross. He restates that he has known fear from experience, especially fear of the day of judgment, to which someone who loves a solitary life would be particularly susceptible. Obviously he is thinking here of Giustiniani, his spiritual guide and mentor in the past. Now a new moment occurs in their friendship, and it is Contarini who gives Giustiniani spiritual advice: "Let all your thoughts be focused on that perfect love [which is Christ], with hope and absolute faith that if we approach him with even a little love, no other satisfaction is necessary because he has rendered satisfaction out of the depth of his charity for the love of us."[59]

This, the most famous letter in the correspondence, has frequently been singled out for special comment. Contarini's insight has been likened to Luther's and used to explain, at times too mechanically, Contarini's later thought.[60] In spite of apparent similarities to Luther's "Turmerlebnis," as recounted by the old reformer, Contarini's experience was structurally different. It neither occurred during a specific, definable crisis, nor was it a sudden conversion experience.[61] Rather, the event of confession to which he went in a somewhat uncertain frame of mind, followed by discussion with the unknown monk, was an emotional stimulus that led to a profoundly significant religious reorientation.[62] Contarini had felt the inadequacy of his own insecure position when confronted with Giustiniani's clear choice and was seeking

59. Ibid., 15.

60. I am thinking here especially of Mackensen's affirmation in "Contarini's Theological Role at Ratisbon," 53: "This then was the experience and time from which sprang Contarini's doctrine of justification, which came to full flower thirty years later at Ratisbon and received its final formulation in *The Epistle on Justification*." Such a view slights the sweep of Contarini's intellectual development between 1511 and 1541, using an inadequate analogy that does not consider what other factors could have helped Contarini to persist in his original insight, and to deepen it.

61. I am using the term here in William James's sense: "To be converted, to be regenerated, to receive grace, to experience religion, to gain an assurance, are so many phrases which denote the process, gradual or sudden, by which a self hitherto divided, and consciously wrong inferior and unhappy, becomes unified and consciously right superior and happy, in consequence of its firmer hold upon religious realities" (*The Varieties of Religious Experience* [New York: New American Library, 1958], 157).

62. See Gordon W. Allport, *The Individual and His Religion* (New York: Macmillan, 1950), 38, who distinguishes three forms of religious awakening: that brought on by a definite crisis, that triggered by a single event or stimulus, and that which occurs gradually without a specific crisis or event.

a rationale for his rejection of the monastic life. His insight on Holy Saturday had both emotional[63] and intellectual aspects that testify to the intensity of his search for a way to be accepted by God and to resolve his own uncertainties. His belief in justification by faith was arrived at by a process which William James considered as conscious in part only, for it was also the result of "subconscious incubation and maturing of motives deposited by the experiences of life."[64]

Without giving the episode a purely psychological explanation, one can see that Contarini is rationalizing a position to which he is already committed. He is not simply adding another chapter to the old debate about the relative merits of the active and the contemplative life,[65] and opting in the end for the former. Rather, he is using his religious insight to construct a model for Christian life different from that of the late medieval church, which taught that the active life of the layman in the world had less value before God than the contemplative withdrawal of the cleric. In his effort to justify himself before Giustiniani, Contarini underscored the validity of Christian vocations both in the world and in the cloister, different though they were. He did not attack Giustiniani's life of contemplation; indeed, he thought that the ability to lead such a life was a privilege granted to only a few truly heroic Christian souls. Yet although he admired contemplative devotion, he insisted on the acceptability and dignity in the eyes of God of his own choice of the life of a Christian layman, the choice made by the vast majority of those belonging to the *corpus Christianorum*.[66]

63. Cantimori, "Idee religiose," 11–17, stresses the "predominance, in those who experienced religious problems, of passionate and sentimental elements, permeated by subjective psychological reactions" (15) and notes the emotional fervor with which Contarini, Querini, and Giustiniani express themselves in their letters of this period.

64. James, *Varieties of Religious Experience*, 186. Ross, "Contarini and His Friends," 208n.63, has pointed out the relevance of James's chapters 9 and 10 for an understanding of what Contarini describes in these letters. Also useful is James's chapter 8: "The Divided Self, and the Process of Its Unification." See also Gordon W. Allport, *Becoming: Basic Considerations for a Psychology of Personality* (New Haven: Yale University Press, 1955), 95–96, for a discussion of man's "ultimate presuppositions" and the "creative pressure" exerted by them on conduct.

65. Christopher Cairns states that "Contarini was . . . a result of the Venetian political tradition in which . . . the distinction [between active and contemplative life] is perhaps no longer meaningful" (*Domenico Bollani, Bishop of Brescia: Devotion to Church and State in the Republic of Venice in the Sixteenth Century* [Nieuwkoop, Neth.: B. De Graaf, 1976], 239n.18). On this subject see also Gilbert, "Religion and Politics," esp. 105–7; and Antonino Poppi, "Il prevalere della 'vita activa' nella paideia del Cinquecento," in *Rapporti tra le università di Padova e Bologna: ricerche di filosofia, medicina e scienza*, ed. Lucia Rossetti (Trieste: Edizioni LINT, 1988), 97–125.

66. Alberigo develops this point fully in "Vita attiva," and rightly thinks that Contarini denied the automatic relationship between a given state of life and personal perfec-

In expressing his newfound belief in justification by faith, Contarini did not dissociate his own experience from the life of the church, nor did he reduce it to a purely personal level.[67] His point of departure was traditional: reception of the sacrament of penance at Easter. Just as traditional was his willingness to accept his confessor's spiritual counsel. It is only in the light of subsequent interpretations of *fides sine operibus* and the momentous implications of this formula that Contarini's description of the hoped-for solution to his religious problems acquires a more radical tinge.

In 1511, Contarini is writing to a friend who shared his insight. Giustiniani, too, had declared that he could reach heaven only through the merits of Christ's passion, not through his own works.[68] In fact, belief that salvation was a gratuitous gift of God was common among serious Christians at the time.[69] It would be a mistake to regard these serious young men as proto-Lutherans simply because they expressed that belief. Contarini and his friends shared a Christocentric spirituality that emphasized the vast reach of God's love compared with the limited powers of man to merit it in any way. Striking in Contarini's case was, first, his unwillingness to follow his friends in seeking closeness to God in the cloister and, second, the unusual combination of a strong commitment to ecclesiastical and political institutions with an absolute conviction that man is justified by faith. Without in any way withdrawing from the institutional church of his time, Contarini sensed that it failed to offer him the ethic of the secular life for which he was groping. He had to formulate this ethic alone, seeking a way through lengthy uncertainty and anguish, but convinced of the validity of his choice of a Christian vocation in the world.

The insight of Holy Saturday 1511 did not suddenly resolve all of Contarini's perplexities, nor could it have done so. While answering

---

tion (223). However, I do not fully share his view that Contarini refused to recognize the existence of a privileged "state" of Christian life. Alberigo's wide-ranging article includes a full bibliography on the history of the distinction between the lay and clerical state in the Western church.

67. The otherwise thoughtful analysis of Contarini's letters by Miccoli, "Storia religiosa," 948–51, makes the contrary points too strongly.

68. Giustiniani to all his friends, Dec. 1510, in Mittarelli and Costadoni (eds.), *Annales Camaldulenses* 9, col. 476.

69. "It seems difficult to find during these years men seriously concerned with the search for their own salvation who fail to express vigorously and absolutely their conviction of the total gratuitousness of that salvation," Alberigo rightly observes in "Vita attiva," 187. Besides Giustiniani, Querini also several times mentions his acceptance of the central importance of Christ's suffering for man's salvation; see, e.g., Mittarelli and Costadoni (eds.), *Annales Camaldulenses* 9, cols. 460, 475, 476.

the question "How shall I be saved?" it left open a correlative question, "What shall I do with the life I will live in the world?" Over the next three years expressions of doubt about finding his way recur in Contarini's correspondence. He describes his condition as ranging from passivity before God, in which he is ready to "receive that impression which seems right to His Majesty,"[70] to almost pathological states of extreme melancholy and affliction of spirit accompanied by disgust with the mere reading of Scripture.[71] Yet while his dejection, even depression, persists as an undertone in his letters until 1515, it did not prevent him from exploring new lines of thought.

The second of Contarini's close friends, Vincenzo Querini, entered Camaldoli in the fall of 1511.[72] Our knowledge of Querini's thought and character is incomplete; as in the case of Giustiniani, no modern work on him exists, and much of his correspondence remains to be published.[73] Those letters that are available, however, show him to be a much more complex figure than Giustiniani, whom he regarded as his spiritual guide.

After a promising early start in public life as Venetian ambassador to the court of Burgundy and to Emperor Maximilian, he decided to follow in the footsteps of Giustiniani. Yet despite his deep religious zeal, Querini showed a remarkable degree of uncertainty and ambivalence even after he became a Camaldolese hermit on 22 February 1512. His available letters are evidence that he was an emotional, high-strung man who cherished deep affective bonds with friends and family. Often moved to tears, he was not afraid to weep,[74] and seems to have agreed with Giustiniani that "not weeping does not show strength of mind."[75] His debate about choices forms the substance of his correspondence with Giustiniani published thus far. His unusually intense, almost relentless self-examination reveals how difficult leaving Venice was for him. In unfolding his thoughts to Giustiniani he signs several letters

70. Jedin, "Contarini und Camaldoli," 18 (letter 4).

71. Ibid., 37–38, 39 (letters 11 and 12). Massa argues that the reason for this disgust was Contarini's inability to read the Bible without employing the "logical-scientific" system he had learned at Padua, whereas Giustiniani could, because he belonged among the "progressives of the human spirit" ("Giustiniani e Contarini," 470).

72. For bibliography, see above, note 29.

73. It is among the manuscripts belonging to the Camaldolese of the Sacro Eremo Tuscolano, near Frascati.

74. See, for example, Querini to Giustiniani, Dec. 1510, in Mittarelli and Costadoni (eds.), *Annales Camaldulenses* 9, col. 498; and again 15 July 1510, col. 457.

75. Giustiniani to Niccolò Tiepolo and Contarini, Mar. 1517, in ibid., col. 590, where Giustiniani writes at some length about his own weeping.

not with his own name but with "Licenope,"[76] as if that were someone else participating in the debate. Licenope is in essence his better self, who would like to follow Giustiniani into the hermitage and who tries to overcome Vincenzo's doubts, weaknesses, and hesitations. As a professed Camaldolese monk, Querini still expressed views that were closer to those of Contarini rather than of Giustiniani when he wrote:

Let us perform holy works of piety, and walk in this world like pilgrims....Only with help from above and not otherwise, this can be done equally well in solitude, in the city, among people, while engaged in public administration, or with wife and children....We should consider only that man to be on the true path of salvation who feels himself loving Jesus Christ from his heart, and who acts in accordance with His will and through Him. If you remain in your fatherland, among your family, who knows? Maybe you will reach your goal before many who go to live in solitude.[77]

Even as a hermit who, in fact, had gone to live in solitude, he continued to be attracted to Florentine humanist circles and the court of Leo X, where he helped to conduct diplomatic negotiations between Venice and the Holy See in 1514.[78] At the time of his death shortly afterward, his nomination to the cardinalate was expected, which would have meant a very different stage in his restless life.

With Querini's departure from Venice the second group of Contarini's letters begins, an exchange that continued until Querini's death.[79] Discussing above all the question of Querini's monastic vocation and then the possibility of his cardinalate, the letters show new dimensions of Contarini's thought. His ideas about the nature of the

76. For example, in Querini's long letter of 1511 to Giustiniani (no closer date given), ibid., cols. 496–509, he uses "Licenope," probably a play on the Latin form of his name, Quirinus, in the phrase "I said to myself" (col. 505) and as his signature. He signs himself the same way in two letters of 15 July (cols. 454 and 461), a letter of 13 August (col. 517), and a letter of 15 September (col. 518). Throughout the letter to Giustiniani of 1 August 1510 (cols. 461–67) he writes of "Licenope" in the third person.

77. Nelson H. Minnich and Elisabeth G. Gleason, "Vocational Choices: An Unknown Letter of Pietro Querini to Gasparo Contarini and Niccolò Tiepolo (April, 1512)," *The Catholic Historical Review* 75 (1989): 18.

78. Jedin, in "Vincenzo Querini und Pietro Bembo," seeks to explain Querini's behavior and defends him against the accusation of hypocrisy and self-seeking made by Vittorio Cian, "A proposito di un'ambasceria di Pietro Bembo (dicembre 1514)," *Archivio veneto* 30 (1885): 355–81.

79. Jedin, "Contarini und Camaldoli," 19–48 (letters 5–15, from the end of November 1511 to 11 July 1514). To them should be added Contarini's letter to Querini written after 22 February 1512, in Mittarelli and Costadoni (eds.), *Annales Camaldulenses* 9, cols. 539–43.

Christian life are stated with increasing clarity and firmness, and one can discern that he is beginning to solve the second of his pressing problems, that of the nature of his own vocation.

Following Aristotle,[80] Contarini writes to Querini that "solitary life is not natural to man, whom nature has made a sociable animal." He warns that anyone who wants to embrace the eremitical life must possess a "perfection which is almost beyond human nature," attained by extremely few men.[81] Contarini distrusts Querini's attempt to force his monastic vocation by sheer willpower and sounds a recurring caution: one cannot do violence to one's own nature without running serious risks.[82] The second argument he uses with Querini is the pull of human affections. Citing his obligations to friends and family, including his grandmother,[83] Contarini touches a sensitive chord with his warm-hearted and effusive friend, who by his own admission keenly felt the force of human love.[84] The third theme struck by Contarini is that of civic duty. In a rather formal Latin letter he informs Querini that many say he has left his homeland in the hour of need, like a soldier who deserts his unit or a sailor who jumps ship. They think that no republic can last if its citizens behave as Querini did. Contarini reports that his attempts to defend his friend fall on deaf ears; his countrymen roundly condemn what they see as Querini's selfishness. The letter closes with a summary of other criticisms leveled at Querini and Contarini's rather stiff admonition to his friend to defend his honor and his name.[85]

Not Querini but Giustiniani replied to Contarini's attempts to dissuade Fra Pietro from the monastic life.[86] Apparently Niccolò Tiepolo had written to Querini in a similar vein, for Giustiniani addresses both friends in a bitter letter that calls them instruments of the devil, miserable Antichrists, wretched souls, and even persecutors of Christ. In their letters "all is falsity, ignorance, impiety, and manifest heresy."[87]

---

80. Ross, "Contarini and His Friends," passim, esp. 210–13.

81. Jedin, "Contarini und Camaldoli," 23 (letter 7).

82. He cites the telling example of a monk whose presumption in wanting to lead an extremely ascetic life ended in death; see ibid., 24.

83. Ibid., 25.

84. For example, see especially the letter of Querini to Giustiniani, ca. 1511, in Mittarelli and Costadoni (eds.), *Annales Camaldulenses* 9, cols. 496–509.

85. The letter was written in 1512; see ibid., cols. 539–43. To Jedin's doubt that it was sent ("Contarini und Camaldoli," 30n.29), Fragnito offers a convincing reply; see "Cultura umanistica," 94n.73.

86. Giustiniani to Contarini and Niccolò Tiepolo, Feb. 1512, in Mittarelli and Costadoni (eds.), *Annales Camaldulenses* 9, cols. 544–50.

87. Ibid., col. 548.

The heresy mentioned here could only refer to Contarini's denial of the superior value of the monastic life, since Giustiniani does not attribute specific doctrinal errors to Contarini or Tiepolo.[88] Contarini's reply to this torrent of accusations is an impressively gentle letter, reminding Giustiniani that he should not judge everyone by his own example.[89] But he stands firm in his conviction that everyone has to follow his own way to salvation in accordance with his nature and that the eremitical life is for only the very few. He thinks that Querini "was perhaps presumptuous" in wanting to reach such a rare state of perfection immediately, without prior experience, and shrewdly surmises that Querini's nature "is not much inclined to solitude."[90] Giustiniani's reply expresses regret for his verbal violence. Apologizing to Tiepolo and Contarini, whom he calls "not only good . . . but most kind," he promises to be more careful in future and to speak more circumspectly with friends and others.[91] The exchange about Querini's vocation terminates with Contarini's perfunctory acceptance of his friend's choice, accompanied by routine exclamations like "O happy Querini, on what service are you embarked!"[92] But his own way is different; although his "most beloved friends" are his exemplars, he will go only so far as to come for a visit, but he will not imitate them.[93]

The letters spanning the period from July 1512 to February 1514 deal more directly with Contarini's state of mind. He barely mentions the upheavals that the War of the League of Cambrai brought to Venice and makes no allusion to his own participation in it.[94] Rather, he focuses on what he calls his melancholy disposition and states that he is

88. See Alberigo's informative discussion in "Vita attiva," 206–13 and bibliography in 218n.82.

89. Jedin, "Contarini und Camaldoli," 32 (letter 9).

90. Ibid., 31.

91. Giustiniani to Tiepolo and Contarini, 18 Apr. 1512, in Mittarelli and Costadoni (eds.), *Annales Camaldulenses* 9, col. 561.

92. Jedin, "Contarini und Camaldoli," 34 (letter 10).

93. Ibid., 35.

94. Sanuto, *Diarii* 21:85, states that Contarini was at the siege of Padua in September 1509 with his brothers and twenty men. In 1513, he sent one of his brothers with fifteen men to the defense of Padua; Sanuto, *Diarii* 17:257, 300. Ross's references should be corrected: "Contarini and His Friends," 205n.51, mentions two men of the same name as if they were one. Sanuto, as usual, refers to our Contarini in *Diarii* 21:85 as "Gasparo Contarini, *qu.* sier Alvise"; the Contarini in 9:146, in contrast, who was sent to Padua on 8 September 1509, is "Gasparo Contarini, *qu.* sier Francesco Alvise." The latter is mentioned among the defenders of Padua in 12:327, 353. Besides these two, there was also a third Gasparo Contarini, son of sier Hironimo, grandson of sier Luca (Sanuto, *Diarii* 12:326, 327). For the defense of Padua, see Frederic Lane, *Venice, a Maritime Republic* (Baltimore: Johns Hopkins University Press, 1973), 242–45.

again restless, depressed, tormented by dark thoughts, and unable to proceed with a planned program of studies. Even reading the Scriptures is of no help; on the contrary, it causes him vexation.[95] While holding fast to his belief in the merits of Christ, Contarini tries to understand what is happening to him, and arrives at the conclusion that God permits his afflictions so that he can learn to trust the divine mercy completely, without illusions about his own power to will inner peace or arrange his life according to his own plans.[96]

Unlike Giustiniani and Querini, Contarini never mistrusted human learning or wanted to turn away from it in order to devote himself entirely to Christian knowledge.[97] A good case can be made that his inner turmoil and uncertainty about his vocation were caused by conflicting values he accepted both from humanistic culture and late medieval spirituality.[98] But it is also possible that a medical reason, the exact nature of which we may never know, was at least partly responsible for his anxiety, despondency, and inaction during these years. He began to resolve the inner tensions not by embracing one set of values and rejecting the other, but by seeking to harmonize them as much as possible through the intellect, while leaving also an ample role to the will. This incipient resolution may have coincided with improved health.

Two letters, dated 26 November 1513 and 26 February 1514,[99] help to establish the time of Contarini's turning point, when he started the process of "unification of a personality sorely divided."[100] In the first, Contarini indulges in a bit of rhetoric by alluding to the first

95. Contarini to Giustiniani and Querini, in Jedin, "Contarini und Camaldoli," 37 (letter 11).

96. Mittarelli and Costadoni (eds.), *Annales Camaldulenses* 9:38; and Contarini to Giustiniani, in Jedin, "Contarini und Camaldoli," 39 (letter 12).

97. On Giustiniani's and Querini's attitudes toward humanist learning, see Felix Gilbert, "Cristianesimo, umanesimo e la bolla 'Apostolici regiminis' del 1513," *Rivista storica italiana* 79 (1967): 976–90.

98. So Cessi, "Paolinismo preluterano," 8; reemphasized by Fragnito, "Cultura umanistica," 109.

99. Jedin dates letter 8 in "Contarini und Camaldoli," 26–29, to 1512. It should be dated 1514 and arranged so as to follow letter 13 (40–43). Contarini writes on 26 February 1514 about the marriage of his illegitimate sister to Vincenzo Belegno, son of Beneto Belegno, which took place "on the day after the feast of the Purification of Mary," that is, on 3 February. Two sources confirm 1514 as the correct year of the marriage: ASV, Avogaria di Comun, Reg. 126: Cronaca Matrimoni, 1; and VBC, Cod. Cicogna 2171, fol. 29. The departure of Querini, mentioned by Contarini (p. 27) and discussed by Jedin (27n.8), probably refers to Querini's trip to Rome; see Jedin, "Vincenzo Querini und Pietro Bembo," 156–57.

100. Ross, "Contarini and His Friends," 217.

canto of Dante and comparing himself, lost and wandering in the deep valley, to his two friends who have reached the top of the mountain. He affirms that he cannot follow them but must remain content with his lowliness (*bassezza*). At the same time, and in a different vein, he states that he has begun to read St. Augustine's work *On the Trinity* and *The Republic* of Plato, recently published in Greek.[101] Philosophy and theology continued to occupy him, and he did not perceive them as antithetical. While he occasionally experienced "vain and mad fears" and perturbations, he was nevertheless able to pursue his studies in a more systematic fashion. He acknowledged, however: "I have to be content [with the study] of that morality which the philosophers have grasped by natural light, also a great gift of God."[102] For the rest, he entered into the speculations of St. Thomas to the extent that he was able. He is not comfortable with the writings of "older" prescholastic theologians who interpret Scripture in a mystical key or counsel a way of life he cannot follow, and states that reading some of their writings is actually harmful to him, since they hold up an ideal of Christian life that he cannot embrace.

This is a new note struck by Contarini. He has arrived at some certainties and gained the courage to state his own convictions clearly. If monastic life is not for him, neither is the striving after perfection according to patristic precepts. He mentions the pleasure he takes in music, the company of friends, and social occasions with relatives.[103] While he still is not entirely sure about God's will for him, his tone suggests much greater inner peace than he had enjoyed since 1511.

Contarini's focus of attention soon shifts from himself to the possibility of Querini's cardinalate. Having heard the rumor that Querini might be appointed by Pope Leo X, Contarini urges his friend not to refuse but to become an instrument of the pope for the good of the church. For the first time Contarini explicitly mentions his long-standing concern with church reform, writing that the news rekindled in his heart a desire he had harbored for many years: "to see God in his goodness turn his eyes finally to this poor little ship of his which is being buffeted by so many storms."[104] A conviction is expressed here that will recur many times—that it is necessary for good men to accept the burden of high office for the benefit of the whole church[105] and to

---

101. Fragnito, "Cultura umanistica," 110, thinks that Contarini's simultaneous reading of St. Augustine and Plato is a sign that he is overcoming his crisis.

102. Jedin, "Contarini und Camaldoli," 27 (letter 8).

103. Ibid., 28.   104. Ibid., 44 (letter 14).   105. Ibid., 45.

become active movers of reform. He appeals to Querini to set a good example to other prelates who as a result might change their way of life. While Querini should not actively seek the cardinalate, he should accept it as God's will. And here Contarini unexpectedly reveals his own dreams: he hints at his desire to live together with Querini, to whom he remained deeply attached, as a member of his household and to resume their former intimacy.[106] The emotional intensity of these idealistic young men's friendship flared up again here, almost for the last time.

Querini's death in Rome on 23 September 1514 shattered this dream. No letter written by Contarini during the following seven months has come down to us. The last group of his letters, fifteen in all, runs from 1515 and 1516, plus one each from 1518 and 1523. A number are merely brief notes sent to Giustiniani shortly after Contarini visited Camaldoli in 1515. For the most part they report Contarini's activities or deal with visitors and family affairs. Obviously he continued to be linked by ties of close friendship to Giustiniani, but the fervent, emotional expressions of the past have almost entirely given way to a calm, more matter-of-fact writing style. There are still echoes of old themes: not only does he have ups and downs, but he also characterizes himself as having moments when, "seized by a certain frenzy," he would like to ascend to the heavens, only falling soon afterward to the level of brute animals.[107] But these states are transitory. Finally there is the avowal that God has gradually led him "to see a little light, and to discern the right way."[108]

That way is Contarini's acceptance for himself of the traditional role of a Venetian patrician. He mentions his interest in government service for the first time in November 1515, recounting to Giustiniani how his brothers and friends urged him to become a candidate for the post of *avogador di comun*, or public prosecutor and state attorney.[109] Contarini admits that he was "excited by the stimulus of ambition,"[110] but professes somewhat lamely to have been glad that he lost the election,

---

106. Ibid., 47 (letter 15).

107. Ibid., 52 (letter 20). This is an echo of Contarini's reading of Neoplatonic works to which he may have been led by his Florentine friends mentioned in letter 19 (51).

108. Ibid., 53 (letter 20).

109. There were "three *avogadori*, elected to sixteen-month terms by the Great Council; they were the state prosecutors in the three supreme courts or *Quarantie*, and at least one state attorney was required to be present in all councils to guard against violations of the law" (Finlay, *Politics in Renaissance Venice*, xvi–xvii).

110. Jedin, "Contarini und Camaldoli," 55 (letter 22).

since he could then return to his studies and the quiet life of a "friar without a hood." Lest he be misunderstood, he makes it clear that he is not contemplating a monastic vocation. On the contrary, in the strongest statement yet on this subject he professes to feel horror at the very thought of it, since he is neither called nor inclined to such a life.[111]

As if to underline that point, Contarini describes his deep enjoyment of life in his country villa and his interest in agriculture. This may mean simply that he was reading the few classical works on the subject,[112] but it may be that, like Machiavelli in the same years, he went himself to inspect the work in the fields. Family affairs, property matters, and his brothers are mentioned several times. Contarini saw himself as part of a family group and took keen interest in its well-being. The last letter to his Camaldolese friend is written after a break of three years in the correspondence, and exactly twelve years after his insight of Holy Saturday. Contarini affirms his belief in justification by faith in a clear, strong statement that seems like an epilogue to this period of his life:

Truly, I have arrived at the firm conclusion which, though I had already read it, nevertheless I now can understand very well in my [own] mind: that nobody can become justified through his own works or cleansed from the desires in his own heart. We must have recourse to divine grace which we obtain through faith in Jesus Christ, as St. Paul says, and we too must say with him: happy the man to whom God does not impute his sin, irrespective of his works [Rom. 4:6]…having experienced it, and seeing what I can do, I have taken refuge in this alone. All the rest seems nothing to me.[113]

These words were written in Valladolid, when Contarini was Venetian ambassador to Emperor Charles V. Despite the rhetorical dismissal of "all the rest," the writer in actuality was embarked on a public career that was to involve him intimately in the inner circles of the Venetian ruling elite. His letters alone do not suffice to give us a picture of the young Contarini, nor do they reveal the full extent of his participation in public life. Other evidence might help us to understand him during this period.

By modern standards Contarini's inner troubles and turmoil occurred late, when he was almost thirty, and continued past the point where he might have been expected to have made his choices. But while the reason for his vacillations is hidden in the makeup of his

111. Ibid., 56.   112. Ibid., 59 (letter 24).   113. Ibid., 67 (letter 30).

personality and in his medical history, contributing circumstances can be adduced for his late entrance into public life. First of all, by Venetian criteria he was relatively young for the holding of office.[114] If he entered the Great Council in 1508, at the usual age of twenty-five, he would most likely have spent the next few years attending meetings and voting on candidates for office rather than competing for office himself. A patrician theoretically could be elected to the Senate at thirty-two, or to the Council of Ten at forty; however, "deference to the elderly pushed the age of de facto eligibility to councils some ten to twenty years beyond the legal requirement."[115] A period of political apprenticeship lasting ten to twenty years was not uncommon; during it one would be regarded as young in politics, even though by the usual standards of the time one could be approaching old age. "From the age of twenty-five to about forty-five, a patrician found high offices closed to him, although a host of minor positions, in the city and abroad, introduced him to government."[116]

The first extant record of Contarini's candidature for an office is from 23 January 1512, when his name was included among those from whom the ambassador to Hungary was to be chosen.[117] He was then twenty-eight years old, a typical age for being considered for this minor office (though his precocious friend Querini was already ambassador to Duke Phillip of Burgundy in his mid-twenties). Contarini's candidacy implies previous active participation in the Great Council; and though he lost by the sizable margin of 48 yes to 128 no votes, he was apparently willing to serve Venice in a post that would have entailed a financial outlay by his family. His famous letter to Querini, written less than a year before, thus acquires additional value as a personal document. When he reported Querini's detractors as castigating him for deserting Venice in her hour of need, he was probably expressing also some of his own thoughts and feelings.[118] They were formu-

---

114. For a discussion of the age at which early-sixteenth-century Venetians assumed higher offices, see Robert Finlay, "The Venetian Republic as a Gerontocracy: Age and Politics in the Renaissance," *Journal of Medieval and Renaissance Studies* 8 (1978): 157–78; and his *Politics in Renaissance Venice*, 124–41. For an illuminating contrast, see David Herlihy, "Vieillir à Florence au Quattrocento," *Annales: E.S.C.* 24 (1964): 1338–52 (reprinted in *Cities and Society in Medieval Italy* [London: Variorum Reprints, 1980]).

115. Finlay, *Politics in Renaissance Venice*, 126.

116. Ibid., 139.

117. Sanuto, *Diarii* 13:408. The lists of the times Contarini was proposed for office given by Fragnito, "Cultura umanistica," 99n.94, and by Ross, "Contarini and His Friends," 219n.114 and 221n.126, should be supplemented; see n. 120 below.

118. Mittarelli and Costadoni (eds.), *Annales Camaldulenses* 9, col. 541.

lated more clearly nine years later when, in a letter to his friend Niccolò Tiepolo, newly appointed ambassador to England, he wrote this about the career of a Venetian diplomat: "Such a life is most beautiful and honorable, most similar to a life of studies; or rather, it is more important."[119] The very period when Contarini's letters were full of his inner vacillations and uncertainties was also when his name appears frequently on lists of men to be considered for offices.[120] His identity as a Venetian patrician was being forged in a conventional, seemly fashion, and he was embarking upon a *cursus honorum* that would lead him to ever greater responsibilities until 1535. In a sense, then, he was a "young man" in the Venetian political milieu until 1516, when he was elected as one of three arbitrators to settle differences that had arisen in a patrician family over property matters,[121] and 1518, when he finally obtained his first office as *provedador sora la camera de imprestidi*,[122] one of three officials elected by the Senate for a two-year term whose task was to reduce the public debt.[123]

Between 1518 and 1520 he was in charge of surveying and measuring reclaimed land in the Po delta before it was put up for sale by the government. He was also responsible for drainage and irrigation

---

119. Letter of 25 April 1521, in Franz Dittrich, ed., *Regesten und Briefe des Cardinals Gasparo Contarini* (Braunsberg, 1881), 252 (Inedita, no. 1) (hereafter cited as *Reg.*); also Sanuto, *Diarii* 30:217.

120. After January 1512 the chronology of Contarini's nominations for offices, all unsuccessful, is as follows (parenthetical references are to Sanuto, *Diarii*, except as otherwise specified): 2 Oct. 1512: ambassador to Florence (15:161); 15 Oct. 1512: ambassador to the duke of Urbino (15:232); 4 Nov. 1512: ambassador to the doge of Genoa (15:315); 5 Sept. 1514: ambassador to France and England (19:21); 2 Sept. 1515: *avogador di comun*, after his brother offered the government a loan of 3,000 ducats (21:15, 16, 181; and Jedin, "Contarini und Camaldoli," 55–56); 16 Sept. 1515: *avogador di comun* (21:85, 86, 186, 188) (Contarini lost despite the offer of 500 ducats to be added to the existing loan, already among the largest listed; usually loans were under 1,000 ducats; see 21:182, 183, 185, 188, 190); 17 Jan. 1516: ambassador to Milan (21:460); 20 Jan. 1516: *avogador di comun* (21:464); 7 May 1516: ambassador to Rome (22:198); 24 Aug. 1516: one of six councillors to the Senate (22:465); 22 Jan. 1517: ambassador to the king of Castile (23:516); 14 May 1517: ambassador to France (24:236); 19 Nov. 1517: ambassador to England (25:90); 3 July 1518: ambassador to Hungary (25:516); 3 Sept. 1518: ambassador to Rome, followed on the same day by voting for ambassador to Spain (26:12–13); 12 Sept. 1518: one of two censors (26:39); 29 Sept. 1518: *savio di terra ferma* (26:71); and 2 Oct. 1518: ambassador to Verona (26:90).

121. The family was the Premarin; see Sanuto, *Diarii* 22:11.

122. He was elected on 17 October; see ibid., 26:129. The commission is in ASV, Collegio, Secreta, Commissioni, 1513–1559, fol. 37r–v. It specifies that Contarini is to be in charge of measuring land belonging to the Republic in the Polesine, that he is to determine its exact character and use, and that he is to draw a salary of not more than 1 ½ ducats per day.

123. Marin Sanuto, *Cronachetta*, ed. R. Fulin (Venice, 1880), 148–49.

projects and had to deal with complaints and disputes, some of which reached the Senate.[124] According to a contemporary, Contarini and his brothers made an important investment in the reclaimed land, acquiring twenty thousand *campi*. Tax records do not substantiate this figure, however; the actual investment was probably smaller.[125] Still, it shows a respectable level of family wealth, especially after the forced loans of the War of the League of Cambrai.

Contarini discharged the duties of his first office well, if we can believe Agostino da Mula, Venetian *podestà* and captain of Rovigo, who praised him in the *collegio* for his work in surveying and measuring land. The doge, too, recognized that work by giving him the customary thanks upon completion of a charge.[126] More importantly, Contarini's willingness, even his eagerness, to be nominated for other offices argues for his growing interest in a public career, setting him apart from many nobles who shirked the burdens of office in any way they could.[127] Contarini himself stated that he was ambitious and able

124. Sanuto, *Diarii* 28:120, 137, 197, 236, 237, 270, 549, 620–21.

125. Marcantonio Michiel in his *Diarii,* which span the period 1511–20, asserts that Contarini and his brothers bought that amount of land; VBC, Cod. Cicogna 2848, fol. 300. See also Lane, *Venice,* 257, 472. Such a figure seems unlikely, however. One *campo* was approximately 0.3 hectare or 0.8 acre, and according to Michiel was sold for 70 to 76 ducats. But see Ugo Tucci, "Pesi e misure nella storia della società," in *Storia d'Italia* (Turin: Einaudi, 1973), 5(1):606. The size of *campi* varied from province to province in the Veneto. An unsavory side of the Contarini acquisition of land, at least for modern sensibilities, emerges from a document of 1528, when the "nuntio et commisso," or agent, of Gasparo Contarini and his brothers bought on their behalf two *campi* of land in Campolongo Maggiore in the Saccisica for 20 ducats. The small landowner and his son who sold the plot were forced to do so in order to survive: "volentes sibi ipsis subvenire in hac tam magna penuria victus ne fame pereant" (quoted by Paolo Sambin, "Altre testimonianze [1525–1540] di Angelo Beolco," *Italia medioevale e umanistica* 7 [1964]: 231–32). I am indebted to Professor Linda Carroll for this reference. Michiel goes on to say that the Contarini were important creditors of the state, having previously bought shares in the *monte nuovo* or funded debt. They probably received at least some of the land in lieu of repayment of their loans. In later tax declarations the figure of 445 *campi* owned by Gasparo Contarini is mentioned; ASV, Dieci Savi sopra le Decime, Condizione de' nobili e cittadini veneti per beni in Padova e territorio, 1518–1523, Reg. 418, no. 957.

126. Sanuto, *Diarii* 29:381.

127. See Donald E. Queller, "The Civic Irresponsibility of the Venetian Nobility," in *Economy, Society, and Government in Medieval Italy: Essays in Memory of Robert L. Reynolds,* ed. David Herlihy, Robert S. Lopez, and Vsevolod Slessarev (Kent, Ohio: Kent State University Press, 1969), 223–36; and idem, *The Venetian Patriciate: Reality Versus Myth* (Urbana: University of Illinois Press, 1986). Contarini continued to be nominated for office without being elected: on 4 Dec. 1518 for ambassador to France (Sanuto, *Diarii* 26:241); 29 Dec. 1518 for *savio di terra ferma* and ambassador to France (26:319); 4 Jan. 1519 for *savio di terra ferma* (26:337); and 24 Jan. 1519 for the same

to take pleasure in competition for office.[128] Moreover, his brothers supported him and were willing to invest money in his career, in the hope of gaining prestige and benefits for the family through him. Contarini remained involved in public life during the seventeen years following his initial success. The question of how to lead his life in the world had been fully answered. He assumed wholeheartedly the duties of a Venetian patrician.

Venetian Ambassador

Contarini was elected to his first major post as ambassador to the young Holy Roman Emperor Charles V on 24 September 1520.[129] He left Venice on 16 March 1521 and arrived in Germany in April.[130] His commission opened with conventional phrases, then proceeded to instruct him to establish connections with the French ambassador at the imperial court, "as is fitting to the indissoluble league and alliance which we have with his Most Christian Majesty."[131] Here, in one sentence, was the root of countless awkward moments Contarini would have to face, since in the conflicts between Charles V and Francis I Venetian sympathies, especially under the doge Andrea

---

(26:395). On 22 February Contarini wrote to the Senate about his surveying of public land near Rovigo (Sanuto, *Diarii* 26:483). He is mentioned as having surveyed land in the Polesine (27:111, 154). In April he was nominated three times for ambassador to Rome (27:180, 205, 316), and proposed for *savio di terra ferma* (27:429) and *savio del consiglio* (27:461). He spent forty-five days in the area of Bassano supervising the construction of drainage and irrigation ditches (27:462, 466), and was spokesman for the Venetian government in response to local complaints (27:625). On 26 September he was nominated for ambassador to France (27:682) and *savio di terra ferma* (27:688, 28:392).

128. Jedin, "Contarini und Camaldoli," 55 (letter 22).

129. Sanuto, *Diarii* 29:202. The Mantuan ambassador Giambattista Malatesta characterized him in a dispatch of 30 October 1520 as "a very learned man, though not very expert in matters of state" (quoted in Finlay, *Politics in Renaissance Venice*, 222).

130. Sanuto, *Diarii* 30:29, mentions that Contarini delayed his departure on account of his sister Paola's marriage to Matteo Dandolo (whose name is erroneously given as Marco). See also col. 128; and ASV, Avogaria di Comun, Reg. 106, Cronaca matrimoni, 1, where the marriage is listed under March 1521; also VBC, Cod. Cicogna 2171, fol. 87.

131. ASV, Collegio, Secreta, Commissioni, 1513–1559, fol. 53r; the commission is dated 18 March 1521. For a narrative account of Contarini's embassy, see *GC*, 26–124. Orestes Ferrara, *Gasparo Contarini et ses missions* (Paris: A. Michel, 1956), adds no substantive material or interpretation.

Gritti, were with the latter. The emperor was feared because of his interests in Italy, above all in Milan and Naples, and the Venetians preferred to side with the French, considering them a lesser threat to the maintenance of peace. One of the principal tasks of the Venetian ambassador was to steer Charles V away from Italy as much as possible.

Accompanied by his younger brother Tommaso, who probably was in charge of the practical details of the household,[132] Contarini lived for the next four years at the imperial court, moving with it to the Low Countries, England, and then Spain. His meticulous and lengthy dispatches deal with important personages he encountered, events at the court, conversations with Charles V and various members of the imperial suite, and transmit much information about politics and economics.[133] He was in Worms during the momentous diet of 1521, and at the imperial court in the late summer when the Spanish *comuneros* rose, with effects on Charles V that Contarini observed closely. In Bruges, Contarini met Thomas More, whom he described as "uno cavalier Englese molto letterato." Unfortunately for the modern reader, his report of their dinner together tells very little more than that he tried in vain to get information from More about negotiations between Cardinal Wolsey, in whose suite More was traveling, and Charles V.[134] A series of dispatches describes in detail the ceremonies

132. The Senate granted Contarini 730 ducats for his expenses on 29 September 1520 (Sanuto, *Diarii* 29:215), and he was given 400 ducats when he departed (29: 669). Tommaso's surviving letters, all addressed to relatives, show that he enjoyed the journey and that he took special delight in jousts, dances, and pageants at the imperial court. He describes ball games, bullfights, and other festivities and writes in admiring terms about the knightly qualities of Charles V (33:67). See also 32:270–71, 34: 356–58, 36:543–44. Tommaso later had a long and distinguished career in the Venetian public service; see Derosas, "Contarini, Tommaso," in *DBI* 28:300–5.

133. Contarini's dispatches to the Senate from his embassy to Charles V are preserved in VBM, MS It., Cl. VII, 1009 (=7447), copied by his secretary Lorenzo Trevisani (hereafter cited as Dispatches, Charles V); their translation by Rawdon Brown is accompanied by valuable marginal notes: London, Public Record Office (hereafter cited as PRO), MSS. 31/14/70, 31/14/71, and 31/14/91. Extracts and summaries focusing on English affairs were published by Brown in *Calendar of State Papers and Manuscripts Relating to English Affairs, Existing in the Archives and Collections of Venice, and in Other Libraries of Northern Italy*, vols. 3–4 (London, 18691–71) (cited hereafter as *CSPV*). Copies of many letters are included in Sanuto, *Diarii*, vols. 31–39 passim. Eight dispatches from Worms are printed in *Deutsche Reichstagsakten*, Jüngere Reihe, vol. 2 (Gotha, 1896). The dispatches would merit detailed analysis and fuller discussion than they receive in *GC*, sec. 2. For political events of these years, see especially Karl Brandi, *The Emperor Charles V*, trans. C. V. Wedgwood (London: Jonathan Cape, 1939), 134–77, 181–236.

134. Bruges, 19 Aug. 1521; in Dispatches, Charles V, fol. 79v; and *CSPV* 3, no. 302.

accompanying the emperor's visit to England and his meetings with Henry VIII. Contarini's special interest was directed to Cardinal Wolsey, at that point a powerful and influential figure at the English court.[135] Finally, Contarini's long sojourn in Spain from June 1522 to August 1525 coincided with the Habsburg-Valois wars, which culminated in the battle of Pavia and the capture of the French king.[136]

Contarini's strategy from the outset was to emphasize the necessity of peace between Christian rulers in the face of the formidable challenge posed by the Turks. He hoped to move Charles V to lead a crusade against the Ottomans. On the emperor's side there was considerable distrust of Venice, reinforced by Mercurio Gattinara, who became grand chancellor upon the death of Chièvres on 27 May 1521. Gattinara was strongly anti-French; he used his position of increasing importance as advisor to Charles V to press Contarini for an alliance of Venice with the imperial side.[137] After Henry VIII joined the emperor against the French king in August 1521, the English ambassadors also began to urge that Venice follow suit.

Contarini was at once personally liked, politically mistrusted, and repeatedly embarrassed. Not only did he have to defend Venetian unwillingness to change sides, but it was also his duty to try to explain away the intelligence received at the imperial court that his government was actively helping the French king with a loan of 25,000 ducats.[138] On another occasion, when the emperor learned that Venice had invited Francis I to come to northern Italy and that a Turkish force of ten thousand men besieging Postoina, a town in the Archduke Ferdinand's domains, had marched through Venetian territory without eliciting any protest from the Republic, Contarini's position became extremely uncomfortable.[139] The emperor was visibly upset. Pedro Ruiz de la Mota, bishop of Palencia, even observed to Contarini, "You Venetians are not just French, but arch-French [*francesissimi*]!"[140]

135. For example, Canterbury, 31 May; and London, 6 June 1522; in Dispatches, Charles V, fols. 235v–237v, 240r–v; and *CSPV* 3, nos. 463, 466.
136. Contarini visited Francis I when the latter was a prisoner in Madrid; see *GC*, 104–5.
137. See John Headley, *The Emperor and His Chancellor: A Study of the Imperial Chancellery Under Gattinara* (Cambridge: Cambridge University Press, 1983).
138. Brussels, 30 Mar. 1522; in Dispatches, Charles V, fols. 208–210v; and *CSPV* 3, no. 438.
139. Brussels, 28 Apr. and 16 May 1522; in Dispatches, Charles V, fols. 221v–222v, 227v–228r; and *CSPV* 3, nos. 448, 458.
140. Bruges, 20 May 1522; in Dispatches, Charles V, fol. 229v; and *CSPV* 3, no. 460.

Eventually Venice did change sides under pressure from the emperor, whose old tutor, elected Pope Hadrian VI on 9 January 1522, now also supported imperial policy in Italy. Doge Andrea Gritti, despite his known pro-French sympathies, was too astute a politician to persist in a course that could be ruinous for Venice, only recently emerged from the costly War of the League of Cambrai. On 29 July 1523, an alliance was concluded among Charles V, his brother Ferdinand, Henry VIII, the pope, and Venice.[141] During his involvement in the negotiations leading to that agreement, Contarini had ample opportunity to see how little room Italian states had for maneuvering between the two great powers in European affairs. Essentially, they could support one side or the other in the continuous conflicts but could not hope to develop an independent foreign policy.

A brief but more pleasant period for Contarini personally followed the conclusion of the alliance between the emperor and Venice. In this accord, however, the Venetians proved to be less than half-hearted partners, vacillating and delaying in fulfilling their obligations almost from the start. Contarini took every opportunity to divert Charles's attention from Italy, and at the same time exerted himself to keep Venice from antagonizing the emperor. This meant defending the reputation of Venice against charges of duplicity, even treason, or continually apologizing for the actions of the Venetian government, which remained pro-French even to the extent of signing a nonaggression clause with Francis I while allied with the emperor.

After the French invaded Italy in 1524 and occupied Milan, Contarini resigned himself to the prospect of war in Lombardy and spent the next months trying to find excuses for Venice's failure to support Charles V in accordance with the terms of the treaty of the preceding year. When at the beginning of February 1525 news of the imperial victory at Pavia and the capture of Francis I reached Spain, Contarini's position was awkward indeed. The Venetians had not supported Charles, and Gattinara told Contarini that their conduct was inexcusable. Contarini appealed in vain to the chancellor as one Italian to another, asking his help and protection for all Italian states, which were in a difficult situation.[142] The emperor seemed to be overmighty, without effective counterbalance to his power. The papal nuncio Baldassare Castiglione, who arrived in Madrid in March 1525, was in an

141. GC, 74.
142. Madrid, 12 Mar. 1525; in Dispatches, Charles V, fol. 422r; and CSPV 3, no. 956.

equally unpleasant position, having to defend Clement VII's separate peace with France. In fact, all the Italian states that had not supported the emperor were in a similarly difficult situation.

Another task of the Venetian ambassador was to protect the interests of his compatriots, as when both the Spanish and English governments confiscated Venetian galleys in 1521 and 1522.[143] The English called their action "borrowing"; yet despite many efforts, Contarini was unable to free the galleys. To add to his discomfort, he had to cope with the repercussions of reports that Venetians were denying imperial troops passage through their territory. Contarini's appeals to Wolsey met with no success, and eventually he and Antonio Surian, the Venetian ambassador to England, had to resign themselves to their powerlessness.[144] Venice was not strong enough to enforce the restitution of her galleys when diplomatic means failed, and in the end Contarini, in a revealing joint dispatch with Surian, wisely counseled his government to accept the inevitable:

We know that these parties chuse at any rate to have the gallies aforesaid, wherefore we are of opinion that it is much better they should take them, apparently with the good will and approval of your serenity, than on the contrary, to their displeasure; and considering the nature of the present times, and the business on the carpet, we intend, when an opportunity presents itself for conferring with the Emperor, to offer them to him ourselves and thus make a present of what we are unable to sell.[145]

During his years at the Spanish court Contarini received the training of an expert diplomat. His dispatches are good examples of thorough, professional reporting by a Venetian ambassador at one of the centers of European political life. Naturally they focus on external events and offer only glimpses of Contarini's own thoughts and attitudes. Yet from the rare instances where a personal note can be detected, it is

143. In Cadiz the *Boschaina* was seized. On receipt of letters from the Venetian government about this incident Contarini immediately took up the matter with Gattinara, who obtained the emperor's directive to the Council of Castile to free the ship (dispatches from Worms, 7 May [Dispatches, Charles V, fol. 8r–v;] and 14 May 1521 [Dispatches, Charles V, fols. 11r–12r]). The *Donata*, belonging to the Donà family, was seized as well (dispatch from Ghent, 9 Jan. 1522 [Dispatches, Charles V, fols. 158r–160r; *CSPV* 3, no. 388; and Davis, *Venetian Family*, 24]). The Spanish suspected the galleys of aiding the French (dispatch from Ghent, 11 Jan. 1522 [Dispatches, Charles V, fols. 160v–161r; *CSPV* 3, no. 391]).

144. Hampton Court, 13 and 19 June 1522; in Dispatches, Charles V, fols. 244r–245r, 247r–248v; and *CSPV* 3, nos. 474, 484.

145. Contarini's and Surian's dispatch, Canterbury, 31 May 1522, translated by Rawdon Brown; PRO, MS. 31/14/71, 388.

possible to see something of his development. During the first months of his embassy Contarini was above all anxious to please the Senate. He wrote like a novice, loading his reports with peripheral detail.[146] Gradually, however, he acquired self-confidence, and on occasion even showed more enterprise than ambassadors were expected to display.[147] He also became a shrewd observer of men and developed a sound strategy for dealing with important persons at the court, foremost among them Gattinara. In a revealing dispatch describing his efforts to keep Charles V out of Italy, Contarini gave his assessment of the chancellor's character:

I urged the chancellor strongly to maintain the friendship with England, and made use of many arguments which the chancellor admitted; so I believe him now to be better disposed than he was formerly. It is requisite above all to sustain the fancies of the chancellor, and then adroitly to dispel them, because he is a man of very small brains, and when he once takes an impression he becomes obstinate. The path on which he was entering seemed very perilous. . . . I therefore deemed it necessary to pursue the abovementioned course, which has not proved fruitless.[148]

Actually, Contarini's personality was so pleasing to Gattinara that he continued to like the ambassador despite his strong disapproval of Venetian political decisions—about which the chancellor did not mince words.[149]

In the course of fifty-two months[150] spent in the emperor's entourage, Contarini had ample opportunity to observe the change in Charles V from the shy young monarch at the Diet of Worms to the self-assured victor over the French in 1525. Contarini generally spoke of the emperor without warmth but with respect. He praised the Habsburg ruler's seriousness, habits, and willingness to work long

146. For example, the minute description of the king of Denmark's dress and hair in a dispatch from Brussels, 4 July 1521 (Dispatches, Charles V, fol. 41r–v; *CSPV* 3, no. 248).

147. E.g., Hampton Court, 4 July 1522 (Dispatches, Charles V, fols. 250v–251v; *CSPV* 3, no. 492), in which Contarini justified himself after being reproved by the government for his independence.

148. Valladolid, 16 Aug. 1524; Dispatches, Charles V, fol. 370v; and *CSPV* 3, no. 860; also Contarini's final report to the Senate, in Eugenio Albèri, *Relazioni degli ambasciatori veneti al Senato* (Florence, 1839–63), 1st ser., 2:55–56 (hereafter, this report specifically [whose full page span is 1–73] is cited as "Relazione"), on Gattinara.

149. One of the worst moments of Contarini's mission was a six-hour session with Gattinara in which the latter demanded a decision as to whether Venice would become an ally of Charles V; dispatch from Valladolid, 26 October 1522; in Dispatches, Charles V, fols. 269v–273v; and *CSPV* 3, no. 571.

150. Contarini says fifty-six: "Relazione," 73. He may have reckoned the time from his appointment, but then it would have been fifty-eight.

hours, gave him credit for his devotion to the Catholic religion, and quoted the emperor's confessor to the effect that Charles's most negative trait was nothing worse than an inability to forgive injuries readily.[151] Charles V, for his part, was favorably impressed by Contarini, to whom he was courteous throughout the entire embassy. Nevertheless, as Contarini observed the Habsburg court and government, he developed no admiration for it. While he could not write about his reservations in his dispatches, he did express them in the report on his mission that he eventually read before the Venetian Senate, as was customary for returning ambassadors.[152] In it he noted that the Habsburg lands were scattered, that their lines of political authority were not clear, and that the working of the government was cumbersome; he remarked with obvious disapproval on their civil unrest and the institution of the inquisition.

Contarini's reflections on the Habsburg possessions form a sharp contrast with his view of Venice. In the former he saw a loosely structured agglomerate of territories held together only by a dynastic bond, while in the latter he admired, and idealized, a well-ordered state.[153] An important revelation of Contarini's private thoughts can be found in his comments on the Spanish Inquisition. In January 1525, in the port of Almazarón, the inquisition seized three masters of Venetian vessels, one of whom was his brother Andrea. They were suspected of having sold a Bible with texts in Hebrew, Latin, and Chaldaean and annotations by a rabbi, and they were brought to Murcia for interrogation. Officials of the inquisition demanded the surrender of all books carried by the galleys, threatening to board the vessels and search for any writings that might be against the faith. One of the captains protested in vain, declaring that he could not permit anything so contrary to Venetian laws. Andrea Contarini, for his part, sent a plea for help to his brother Gasparo.[154] The latter immediately spoke to the emperor, his

151. Ghent, 27 July 1521; in Dispatches, Charles V, fols. 61v–62r. See also "Relazione," 60–61. Tommaso Contarini, who enjoyed the diversions at the court, expressed great admiration for the emperor's prowess in tourneys and *corridas* (cf. note 132 above).

152. For a different view from mine, see Federica Ambrosini, "Immagini dell' impero nell'ideologia del patriziato veneziano del '500," in *I ceti dirigenti in Italia in età moderna e contemporanea: atti del Convegno Cividale del Friuli, 10–12 settembre 1983*, ed. Amelio Tagliaferri (Udine: Del Bianco, 1984), 70. She argues that Contarini considered a universal monarchy of Charles V not a threat but a possible advantage to Italian states.

153. See the discussion of his treatise on Venice in the following chapter.

154. Copy of letter from Andrea Contarini to Gasparo Contarini, Murcia, 28 Jan. 1525; in Sanuto, *Diarii* 38:200–201.

council, and the grand inquisitor, and then sent his brother Tommaso to take charge of the galleys. Contarini attempted to secure freedom for his compatriots by addressing the entire council of the inquisition on 4 February: "I spoke for a long time, explaining to them that the practice in Italy as well as in the whole Catholic church was to tolerate any infidel author, such as Averroes and many others, although, as it seemed to them, he contradicted the faith. I adduced many reasons why it would be wrong not to permit our adversaries to be heard and read. . . . In brief, I believe that I omitted little that could be said." Contarini heard that the Venetians had sold Lutheran books, but claimed not to believe it. Although the accused were soon freed, Contarini became convinced that "the inquisition in this kingdom is a most terrible thing, and not even the king has power over it. As far as the New Christians are concerned, what appears to us insignificant seems serious to the inquisition."[155]

In this incident and its echoes in the later report to the Senate it is possible to see a significant side of Contarini, a man who never advocated or approved of the use of force and coercion in matters of religion. On the contrary, he had faith in human reasonableness, and the necessity of calm debate on disputed issues was one of his firmest convictions. While it is not possible to say whether Contarini read Erasmus while he was in Spain, he certainly was in an environment where the views of the Dutch humanist were known.[156]

The nearly four hundred dispatches Contarini wrote during his embassy would repay close study not only as diplomatic documents illustrating the complexities of the Habsburg-Valois wars, but also as evidence for customs and ceremonies at the court of Charles V and for the rapid changes in the image of the world with which European intellectuals were confronted at that period. For example, Contarini showed keen interest in Central America and acquired remarkably accurate knowledge of its geography (which was probably incorporated into his lost work *Geographia*).[157] He also astonished the Spanish court by offering an explanation for the seeming loss of one day in the carefully kept log of Magellan's voyage around the world.[158] Through dis-

155. Letter of Gasparo Contarini to Federico Contarini and his other brothers, Madrid, 7 Feb. 1525; in ibid., 38:202–3. A faulty copy is in *Reg.*, 257 (Inedita, no. 3). See also Contarini's comments on the inquisition in "Relazione," 40.

156. Cf. Marcel Bataillon, *Erasme et l'Espagne* (Paris: Droz, 1937).

157. See Paola Mildonian, "La conquista dello spazio americano nelle prime raccolte venete," in *L'impatto della scoperta dell'America nella cultura veneziana*, ed. Angela Caracciolo Aricò (Rome: Bulzoni Editore, 1990), 118n.9.

158. Ibid., 117n.6.

cussions with Pietro Martire d'Anghiera, an Italian humanist and teacher at the court who later became an administrator, a member of the Council of the Indies, and the author of *De orbe novo decades III*, a history of Spanish discoveries, Contarini obtained a good deal of knowledge about the native peoples and their customs.[159] He was familiar with Cortés's reports of the conquest of Mexico and saw some of the treasures that were sent back to Spain. But although he admired the skill of Mexican artisans, whose feather-work he called "miraculous" and "finer than the finest embroidery," he had on the whole a conventional attitude toward the people who were conquered.[160] As a Venetian he was concerned with ascertaining the quantity of spices and gold imported from the Spanish and Portuguese overseas possessions, a subject he knew to be of particular interest to his government. Yet strangely, he showed little interest when approached by Sebastian Cabot with a plan, whose details were not spelled out, for launching an enterprise that could be "of great use" to Venice. Contarini duly reported his conversations with the navigator, but did not conceal his skepticism, which was shared by enough Venetian senators to cause Cabot ultimately to offer his services to England instead.[161] Cautious and conservative, Contarini had no sympathy for untried schemes in unknown lands.

It is surprising how rarely Contarini's dispatches mention Luther and the religious situation in Germany. Although he discussed the Lutheran movement as a political problem for Charles V,[162] he gave no sign of a personal interest in the German reformer's theology. Official correspondence, of course, was hardly the place for expressing personal views on religion; still, it is striking how little Contarini reported to Venice about the Reformation and how dry his reports on that subject are. Among his few surviving private letters of the period, at least three convey some interest in Luther as well as his reflections on the impact

159. Pietro Martire's work was published in three installments, in 1511, 1516, and (first complete edition) 1530. See also Giovanni Stiffoni, "La scoperta e la conquista dell'America nelle prime relazioni degli ambasciatori veneziani (1497–1559)," in Caracciolo Aricò (ed.) *L'impatto*, 356.

160. "Relazione," 53. He may have seen the pieces that are now preserved in the Museum für Völkerkunde in Vienna. His letter about the conquest of Mexico City is printed in Sanuto, *Diarii* 33:501–3. See also Federica Ambrosini, "Echi della conquista del Messico nella Venezia del Cinquecento," in Caracciolo Aricò (ed.), *L'impatto*, 7–23, esp. 10–11.

161. Giorgio Padoan, "Sulla relazione cinquecentesca dei viaggi nord-atlantici di Nicolò e Antonio Zen (1383–1403)," in ibid., 234n.45.

162. Toledo, 26 June 1525; in Dispatches, Charles V, fols. 456v–457r; and *CSPV* 3, no. 1049.

of Lutheranism.[163] But he did not perceive the Reformation as directly touching Venetian interests; instead he concentrated on the minutiae of the Franco-Spanish wars into which Venice, too, was being drawn.

In June 1525, to Contarini's considerable relief, his designated successor, Andrea Navagero, arrived in Toledo. After inducting Navagero into the conduct of affairs, Contarini finally left for Venice on 11 August. The leisurely return trip took him through southern France and northern Italy.[164] Not until 16 November did he make his formal report to the Senate, in accordance with the provisions of a law of 1268.[165] Marin Sanuto has left a vivid picture of Contarini and Lorenzo Priuli, who accompanied Navagero and then spent two months with Contarini in Spain, as the two appeared before Venetian dignitaries.[166] Priuli, the younger, was dressed in crimson velvet and spoke first. Contarini addressed the Senate after dinner. Sanuto does not fail to mention that he was clad in the solemn black velvet robe of a Venetian noble. He spoke for three and a half hours, presenting an informative description of the countries he had visited, their people, cities, and governments, and of Charles V and his court. The summary of Contarini's report can still be read with profit, especially where it deals with the emperor's family and advisors. How his report struck his audience is hard to say, since we are told that he spoke "in a very soft voice which could not easily be heard."[167] Apparently he lacked the oratorical ability that would have brought him to the fore in a large group like the Great Council, a fact that may partly account for his slow start in public life. Later, however, he seems to have become a more effective speaker, for Sanuto praised his "wise and good speeches."[168] Contarini's biographer Giovanni della Casa reports that Contarini spoke

163. To Niccolò Tiepolo, Worms, 25 Apr. 1521 (*Reg.*, 252–53 [Inedita, no. 1]); to his brother-in-law Matteo Dandolo, Worms, 26 Apr. 1521 (*Reg.*, 254–57 [Inedita, no. 2]) and Brussels, 3 Feb. 1522 (Sanuto, *Diarii* 32:473).

164. For Contarini's description of the homeward journey, see "Relazione," 66–73.

165. In 1268 the Great Council ordered that all reports of embassies be made in writing. This order was reaffirmed in 1425, but the oldest extant reports date from the end of the fifteenth century. On 15 November 1524, the Senate issued a decree that every report had to be presented in writing two weeks after it was delivered, and registered by the chancery; see Angelo Ventura, "Scrittori politici e scritture di governo," in Arnaldi and Stocchi (eds.), *Storia della cultura veneta* 3(3):553–54. See also Donald E. Queller, "The Development of Ambassadorial Relazioni," in Hale (ed.), *Renaissance Venice*, esp. 184–87. Contarini's *relazione* is printed in Albèri, *Relazioni*, 1st ser., 2:1–73; and in Luigi Firpo, ed., *Relazioni di ambasciatori Veneti al Senato*, vol. 2: *Germania, 1506–1554* (Turin: Bottega d'Erasmo, 1970).

166. Sanuto, *Diarii* 40:284, 286.   167. Ibid., 286.

168. Ibid., 55:348, 536; 56:667.

calmly, in a simple direct way that carried authority, so that his audience remembered what he said,[169] while an eighteenth-century biographer even makes his eloquence exemplary.[170] The latter two sources are not reliable, but Sanuto's testimony to Contarini's increasing effectiveness as a speaker is important because it comes from a contemporary who saw him in action. It is certain, however, that Contarini never developed the charismatic qualities necessary for an outstanding public speaker; he remained most effective in small groups.[171]

Contarini's embassy had an unpleasant epilogue. He stated before the Senate that he had spent more than four thousand ducats "of his, that is of his brothers' property" on it.[172] While he did not ask directly for any financial relief, a proposal was made by some of the highest Venetian officials that he be allowed to keep one thousand ducats that the emperor had given him as a parting present. Two votes were taken, but the motion failed to pass:[173] nobles simply were expected to draw on their own resources in the service of the state. Despite the length of the embassy and its attendant high costs, the senators were not moved to grant Contarini even partial compensation. The ambassador's reaction to this setback is characteristic. We are told that, far from displaying any resentment, "he wanted to rest awhile, and to see whether he could be elected on Sunday to the Council of Ten in the place of sier Andrea Badoer, ... who had died"[174]—a clear indication of Contarini's ambition to enter the inner circle of Venetian government. While he did not succeed in so doing at this date, another lower office was open to which he had been elected while still on his embassy, that of *savio di terraferma*, one of five officials charged with overseeing affairs of the Venetian mainland, especially regarding war and defense.[175] He was

169. Giovanni della Casa, "Gasparis Contareni Vita," in *Gasparis Contareni Cardinalis Opera* (Paris, 1571), [4] (hereafter cited as *Opera*).

170. "... Sic sententiam dicebat, ut neminem magis prudenter, magisve composite locutum unquam fuisse constaret" (Card. Angelo Maria Quirini, *Tiara et purpura veneta* [Venice, 1761], 147).

171. It is interesting to note that one generation after Contarini, Agostino Valier, the reforming bishop of Verona, in a tract addressed to Contarini's nephew Alvise, attached little importance to oratorical skills, thinking that ornate rhetoric was not in keeping with the traditions of a Venetian patrician; see Valier, *Memoriale ... a Luigi Contarini Cavaliere sopra gli studi ad un senatore veneziano convenienti*, ed. G. Morelli (Venice, 1803), 46–47.

172. This was in addition to the 730 ducats that the Senate had voted for his expenses on 29 September 1520; Sanuto, *Diarii* 29:215.

173. Ibid., 40:308.   174. Ibid.

175. Contarini received the news of his election in letters from his family, and replied in a dispatch from Brussels on 5 March 1522: "I thus know my obligation to

also elected *capitano* of Brescia, or military governor charged with the fortifications and defense of the city.[176] On 20 November 1525, thus, he assumed the post of *savio*, which had been reserved for him until his embassy was concluded.[177] But he never actually held the position at Brescia and indeed resigned it two years later. The reason is uncertain, for members of his family regarded the post as important; a period of poor health may have been the determining factor.[178]

Despite his efforts as ambassador, the mission to Charles V did not immediately result in election to higher office but was followed only by a series of short-term, often ad hoc appointments. He was, for example, on several committees convoked to settle disputes involving

be as great as any ever incurred by any other son and servant of that most illustrious state. . . . After my duty to God [I am] bound to spare no labour in the service of the State, and besides my fortune to place my life itself, if necessary, at the disposal [of] your Highness" (PRO, MS. 31/14/70, 299). Brown notes in the margin that "the appointment implied that members of the Grand Council were well satisfied with their ambassador at the Imperial Court."

176. Oliver Logan, *Culture and Society in Venice, 1470–1790* (London: Batsford, 1972), 25, has a succinct paragraph on the hierarchy of Venetian offices and the place of the military governorship of Brescia in it. He considers it "at the summit of the *cursus honorum*," along with the civil and military governorships of Padua, the lieutenancy of Friuli, and full ambassadorships. Contarini was elected by the Great Council on 19 March 1525 (Sanuto, *Diarii* 38:106). There was disagreement over holding the post of *capitano* open for him until he could assume it. On 19 June 1525 a motion was made and passed by the Senate over the objections of Niccolò Malipiero, Contarini's maternal uncle, to elect another *capitano* of Brescia at the expiration of whose term of office Contarini could assume the post (ibid., 39:89). His brothers complained to the public prosecutors (*avogaria di comun*), and the motion was annulled (ibid., 95). It was decided that a substitute should be elected until Contarini could take up the post (ibid., 105). See also J. R. Hale, "Terra Ferma Fortifications in the Cinquecento," in *Florence and Venice: Comparisons and Relations* (Florence: La Nuova Italia, 1980), 2:168–69.

177. Sanuto, *Diarii* 39:484, 40:316.

178. Cicogna, *Inscrizioni* 2:229, states that Contarini did not accept the position because he fell ill with quartan fever and because he wanted to avoid the tumults of war. The anonymous "Portione di Huomeni Illustri della Famiglia Contarini di Venetia," VBC, Cod. Cicogna 2327, fol. 82r–v, gives the same reasons but is more explicit: the news of the sack of Rome, which reached him as he was about to take up his position at Brescia, together with his poor health, was the reason for his refusal. Neither source mentions that all through 1526 Contarini intended to assume the position though he never actually did so. On 24 April 1526 (the vigil of St. Mark's), for example, he accompanied the doge to solemn vespers carrying a sword, the symbol of his captaincy in Brescia (Sanuto, *Diarii* 41:214). On 5 October 1526, he stated in a letter that he was beginning to think about his post (*Reg.*, 260 [Inedita, no. 5]), while in September 1527 he mentioned that his possessions had been loaded on board a ship and he was ready to depart when he fell ill and renounced the appointment on the advice of family and friends (to Giustiniani, *Opera*, 94). One wonders whether he underwent another period of listlessness or depression.

cities, individuals, and a monastery.[179] In January 1527, he and Lorenzo Priuli were appointed censors by the three heads of the Council of Ten and charged to examine a book that Franciscans in Venice claimed contained libelous and heretical material. Contarini and Priuli presented their report on this book, Alvise Cinzio's *Libro della origine delli volgari proverbi*,[180] on 18 March 1527, as a consequence of which the author had to modify his text. This seemingly minor episode was to have significant consequences. On 29 January 1527, while the matter was still pending, the heads of the Council of Ten issued a regulation providing that no book could be printed in Venice unless they first licensed it after examination by two censors. This requirement of an *imprimatur* marked the beginning of official press censorship in Venice.[181]

In September 1527 Contarini was elected one of the advisors to the Senate[182] and in the following month was sent as envoy to Duke Alfonso d'Este of Ferrara.[183] His mission was to help secure the duke's adherence to the anti-imperial League of Cognac concluded in May 1526 among France, England, Pope Clement VII, Venice, and Milan.[184] After the terrible sack of Rome by the troops of Charles V in May 1527—atrocious even by the standards of sixteenth-century

179. Between Verona and Vicenza (Sanuto, *Diarii* 42:472), between Diana d'Este and a monastery about water mills (43:57), and problems among the Benedictines of S. Giustina in Padua (43:68).

180. The book is scarce. A fine copy, which probably belonged to Cinzio himself, is in the Biblioteca Marciana in Venice; it contains some manuscript poems by the author in the back; Degli Fabritii, Alvise Cintio, *Libro della origine delli volgari proverbi* (Venice: Bernardino & Matheo Vitali, 1526) [Cod. Ital. Cl. IX, 648 (=11942)]. On the flyleaf is the following note: "J'ai cherché ce livre pendant 30 ans, et le hasard seul me l'a procuré. Il a été bruslé par l'inquisition et recherché avec tant de soins qu'il est presque introuvable. Je l'ay payé fort cher. La pièce MS qui est à la fin écrite de la main de l'Auteur semble annoncer que cet exemplaire lui a appartenu." An attached letter is dated 1 May 1784. The Franciscans objected to a commentary on the proverb "Ciascun tira l'acqua a suo molino" (Everyone diverts the water to his own mill, clxxv^v–clxxix^r). It castigates Franciscans who tolerate and perpetuate abuses in their order and no longer follow the teachings of their founder.

181. Sanuto, *Diarii* 43:26, 748. Horatio Brown, *The Venetian Printing Press* (London, 1891), 67–71, discusses this incident more fully; as does Cicogna, *Inscrizioni* 5:586–88. Paul Grendler, *The Roman Inquisition and the Venetian Press, 1540–1605* (Princeton: Princeton University Press, 1977), 74, mentions it only in general terms.

182. He was elected to the *zonta de pregadi*, an advisory body of the Senate; Sanuto, *Diarii* 46:122.

183. Ibid., 239–40.

184. Sanuto (ibid., 42:78) describes its publication and celebration in Venice on 8 July 1526.

warfare[185]—the league decided to take action against the overmighty emperor. Together with the envoys of the other member-states and Florence, Contarini persuaded the duke to join the anti-Habsburg allies[186] and signed the resulting treaty in the name of the Republic. He stressed that the duke had housed him in his palace, had come twice to his rooms to consult with him, and had "done him great honor."[187] While these outward manifestations were meant to show Duke Alfonso's respect for Venice rather than for the person of the ambassador, Contarini's emphasis on them demonstrates that he was an ambitious man who wanted to make his successes known. His first allegiance clearly was to the Council of Ten, and only then to the Senate, as Sanuto tells in a revealing passage.[188] It comes as no surprise, therefore, that Contarini was soon proposed as a candidate for the Council of Ten.[189] Although he was not elected on this occasion, his star definitely was in the ascendant.[190]

In January 1528 a new ambassador to Pope Clement VII was elected. Although the respected old Marco Dandolo received the most votes, he did not accept the office, and the Senate chose Contarini in his stead.[191] Contarini's willingness, even eagerness, to accept the post was evidence of his keen desire for a public career. In a sense, it was a gamble: he and his brothers had to bear the heavy expenses of the embassy, which, however, might then open the door to higher offices in the Venetian government. The mission, moreover, was an especially difficult one. While the pope was confined to Castel Sant'Angelo following the sack of Rome, Venice, though his ally, had taken advantage

185. Recent works dealing with the sack of Rome and containing bibliographies of earlier literature are Judith Hook, *The Sack of Rome, 1527* (London: Macmillan, 1972); Eric R. Chamberlin, *The Sack of Rome* (London: Batsford, 1979); and André Chastel, *The Sack of Rome, 1527* (Princeton: Princeton University Press, 1983).

186. For the most important provisions of the treaty, see Sanuto, *Diarii* 46:336–38.

187. Only a summary of Contarini's report is extant; see ibid., 321–22. Also see p. 302 for a partial summary of additional provisions of the treaty.

188. Contarini had been sent on his mission by the Council of Ten, to whom he reported while there. Sanuto repeatedly states that he was not informed of the contents of Contarini's letters (which have not survived): ibid., 275, 280, 284. Some senators "murmured" at their being left in the dark concerning Contarini's mission, and a motion was passed requiring that Contarini's oral report be made before the Senate (312). Nevertheless, Contarini reported first to the Council of Ten and only on the following day to the Senate (319).

189. On two occasions, 24 November and 15 December 1527, Contarini was one of four candidates for the Council of Ten; ibid., 323, 376.

190. As shown, for instance, by his being chosen as one of eight senators who accompanied the papal legate during his ceremonial visit; ibid., 459.

191. This occurred on 16 January 1528; see ibid., 492.

of the situation by unilaterally reestablishing its right to make ecclesiastical appointments in all territories of the Republic[192] and occupying the papal cities of Ravenna and Cervia on the pretext of protecting their inhabitants.[193] Thus, upon the pope's liberation from detention in December, the Venetian government was faced with the necessity of sending a particularly skilled envoy to the Holy See for what were bound to be protracted negotiations over the two occupied cities and the recurrent problem of jurisdictional rights. At the same time, it was the ambassador's task to draw Clement VII into the anti-imperial league.

Under these pressing circumstances it at first seems strange that Contarini did not leave on his embassy until late May. The explanation for the delay lies at least partly in the unsettled conditions of the papal court at Orvieto, where the pope had moved from Rome, as well as in the uncertainties of the war in southern Italy and in Lombardy, in which Venice was involved on the side of the league and against the emperor.[194] But the most important factor was the lack of agreement among the members of the Venetian government about whether an ambassador should be sent at all. On 6 May the *collegio*, the initiative and executive body of the Republic, discussed making a motion in the Senate to send Contarini on his embassy.[195] When such a motion was in fact made two days later it was opposed by Lunardo Emo, one of the *savi del consiglio* (a high-level advisory committee of six), and attacked by Alvise Mocenigo on the grounds that "nothing good could come of it" and that the Florentines and the duke of Ferrara would be alienated. Others spoke in the opposite sense, and at length the matter was tabled for lack of agreement.[196] On 10 May discussion was resumed,

192. The Republic had had to relinquish this right to the pope in 1510 during the War of the League of Cambrai. In August 1527, when the bishopric of Treviso fell vacant, the Venetian government reasserted its right to appoint a successor. See Heinrich Kretschmayr, *Geschichte von Venedig* (Gotha: Perthes, 1905–34), 3:16–17. For relations between the Venetian government and the church following the War of the League of Cambrai, see Paolo Prodi, "The Structure and Organization of the Church in Renaissance Venice: Suggestions for Research," in Hale (ed.), *Renaissance Venice*, esp. 412–13.

193. On the economic importance of Cervia in the production of salt, see Jean-Claude Hocquet, "Monopole et concurrence à la fin du moyen âge: Venise et les salines de Cervia (XIIᵉ–XVIᵉ siècles)," *Studi veneziani* 15 (1973): 21–133; and idem, *Le sel et la fortune de Venise*, 2d ed. (Lille: Publications de l'Université de Lille, 1982), 1:95, 246–47, and passim. On Venetian relations with Ravenna, still useful is Pietro Desiderio Pasolini, *Delle antiche relazioni fra Venezia e Ravenna* (Florence, 1874).

194. F. Bennato, "La partecipazione militare di Venezia alla Lega di Cognac," *Archivio veneto*, 5th ser., 58 (1956): 70–87.

195. Sanuto, *Diarii* 47:364.

196. Ibid., 392, 393.

and a long list of speakers stated their views for or against Contarini's mission. Among the former we find the doge Andrea Gritti, and among the latter the irascible Alvise Mocenigo, who was not in the habit of mincing words and wanted to treat the seizure of Ravenna and Cervia as an accomplished fact rather than a matter for negotiation. Yet despite opposition, the motion to dispatch Contarini carried. An additional delay was caused by the death of his brother Andrea before Contarini finally left on or shortly after 19 May.[197]

The surviving documentation for this embassy is unusually full, making possible an insight into the highest councils of the Venetian government and giving a far better picture of Contarini's personality than do the surviving dispatches from Spain.[198] His experience, self-confidence, and knowledge of psychology are mirrored in the reports, which also document the growth of a friendship between the pope and the ambassador. Whereas Contarini's dispatches from Spain were almost invariably the straightforward accounts of an observer rather than an actor, and the emperor remained a figure described only from the outside, the dispatches from the papal court have a much more personal quality, revealing their author's character and shedding new light on his thought.

On 11 May Contarini was voted money for his expenses and staff,[199] and on the twenty-third he was given a commission with detailed instructions.[200] The Senate spelled out the arguments he was to use

197. Sanuto (ibid., 470), without mentioning the name, reports simply that "one of his brothers died." That it was Andrea can be seen from ASV, Barbaro, *Arbori*, vol. II, fol. 466. Andrea Contarini participated in the family trading ventures in North Africa; Barbaro adds after his name, "fu in Barberia." *GC*, 127, should be corrected on the date of Contarini's departure, which according to Sanuto was the twentieth; Contarini's final report to the Senate mentions the eighteenth as his departure date, but since it was written several years later it was probably in error: see Albèri, *Relazioni*, 2d ser., 3:260.

198. Contarini's dispatches are in VBM, MS It., Cl. VII, 1043 (=7616). *CSPV*, vol. 4; and *Reg.* give extracts and summaries from them (the latter is not always reliable because the author used copyists). VBC, Cod. Cicogna 3477 (hereafter cited as *Ducali*), contains thirty *ducali*, or instructions, from Doge Andrea Gritti to Contarini. Written on parchment, they are badly damaged, and several can no longer be read. Expert restoration in 1976 has made it possible to use portions or all of twenty-one of them. The *ducali* were published in part by Domenico Urbani, "Lettere ducali a Gasparo Contarini," *Raccolta Veneta* 1 (1866): disp. 1, 19–34, and disp. 3, 7–25.

199. ASV, Senato Terra, Reg. 25 (1528/29), fol 44v; and Sanuto, *Diarii* 47:405. Contarini was given 400 ducats, although on 10 May a proposal was made to give him an initial sum of 600 ducats; see ASV, Senato, Delib. Secreta, Reg. 53 (1528/29), fol. 54v.

200. ASV, Senato, Delib. Secreta, Reg. 53 (1528/29), fols. 68r–70v. There was disagreement in the Senate about what Contarini should say to the pope, especially regarding Ravenna and Cervia; Sanuto, *Diarii* 47:501.

both in the initial public audience and in the subsequent private one. Contarini was ordered to express above all the sorrow of his government at the pope's plight, to stress Venetian obedience to the Holy Father, and to emphasize the great danger the Spanish posed for Italy and all Christianity. Only in the private interview was the envoy to broach the question of Ravenna and Cervia by expressing the surprise of the Republic at hearing that there existed some misunderstanding on the part of Clement VII regarding the two cities, which Venice had saved from imperial occupation at great cost to herself and which had formerly been in her possession with the acquiescence of many popes. To Clement's predictable reaction at this point Contarini was to use another approach by urging the pope to consider the insignificance of the cities in comparison with the benefits he could derive from Venetian help and support. The tactics become clear: without arguing about legal matters but falling back on his skill and pleasant manner,[201] Contarini was to deflect the pope's interest away from Ravenna and Cervia; instead he was to turn the pope against Charles V as the cause of all his sufferings, thus drawing him closer to Venice and France as his true allies.

The persuasiveness of Contarini's arguments depended not only on the Senate's well-laid plans but also on the political and military situation in Italy. Shortly before Contarini's departure, Andrea Doria, the French and papal captain-general, had been victorious over a Spanish fleet near Amalfi. The anti-imperial allies were on the offensive: Marshal Lautrec's army was besieging Naples, and Venetian forces had taken several cities in Apulia, including Trani and Manfredonia. The affairs of the allies were going well in the north also: the Senate even hoped that all Lombardy might be taken.[202] But the situation began to change abruptly when Doria shifted his allegiance from Francis I to Charles V.[203] This defection was followed by a further setback for the

201. There are several references to the tone Contarini was to adopt, for example: "Et vederai de redur sua Beatne in quella bona dispositione che devemo desiderar, come speramo seguira mediante la dexterita del ingegno tuo" (ASV, Senato, Delib. Secreta, Reg. 53 [1528/29], fol. 69r). Or again: "Et vederai de addolcirla, mitigarli l'animo, et aquietarli lanimo quanto piu potrai" (ibid., fol. 69v).

202. Ibid., 22 Sept. 1528, fol. 105r.

203. Contarini's dispatches of 12 July 1528, in which he reports that Doria and Francis I are said to have ironed out their disagreements (VBM, MS It., Cl. VII, 1043 [=7616], fol. 27r); of 19 July (fol. 31v); of 21 July (two), when the first news of Doria's change of sides reached the papal court (fols. 32v–34r); and of 23 July (fols. 34v–35r) show the anxiety of the pope, his advisors, and Contarini himself. Henceforward I quote from the corrected text of the *Regesten*, collated with the originals. The latter will be cited as Dispatches, Papal Court, and used to supplement the *Regesten* where their summaries are too brief.

anti-imperial camp: an outbreak of disease among French troops and the death of Lautrec made it necessary to raise the siege of Naples on 30 August. The anti-imperial forces were now disunited and poorly led. This was the atmosphere in which Contarini was to persuade the pope to join what was clearly becoming the losing side.

Contarini entered on his embassy with no very favorable opinion of Clement VII's statecraft. While still in Spain he had come to the conclusion that the pope was too timid to be relied on.[204] This verdict was only confirmed by a year at the papal court, when he wrote in blunt words to the Council of Ten: "Your Excellencies should know that the pope is by nature extremely timid and cowardly."[205] The final report to the Senate on his embassy, in March 1530, again makes a point of Clement's indecisiveness and irresolution; Contarini had found no reason to change his view.[206] Yet despite their antagonism in political matters and Contarini's critical attitude, the two men developed a warmer relationship than the usual one of a ruler and an ambassador, marked by the pope's expressions of trust in Contarini.

Their first long private interview in Viterbo, where the pope now resided, set the tone for subsequent audiences. The pope recalled how badly Venice had treated him, showing great perturbation and raising his voice as he spoke. In obedience to the Senate's instruction Contarini reiterated that the Venetians had saved Ravenna and Cervia from falling into enemy hands, and then proceeded to portray an idealized Venice: "Could a better occasion than this be found to gratify the [Venetian] Signoria, which would be most obliged to [Your Holiness]? In the past we have been the church's front line of defense against the Turks. So we are still, [only] now on the sea against the Turks and on land against Lutheran Germans who are greater enemies of the Holy See than the Turks!" To this the pope replied coldly, "Much though you personally please me, your embassy displeases me equally."[207] He pointed to the practical reality of the salt pans of Cervia, which produced annually seventy thousand sacks of salt, the tax on which would constitute an important source of revenue for the depleted papal treasury,[208] and refused even to consider the Venetian side

204. Toledo, 7 May 1525: "Dio voglia, che questa timidità sua non sii causa de la ruina d'Italia. Certo è, che molto ha pegiorata la conditione di quel eccellentissimo stato [Venice] et ha diminuita la reputatione d'Italia" (*Reg.*, 23 [no. 57]).

205. Rome, 31 July 1529: "V. Serenità sappia, che la natura del Pontefice e supra modum timida et vile" (*Reg.*, 60 [no. 191]).

206. Albèri, *Relazioni*, 2d ser., 3:265.

207. Viterbo, 7 June 1528; *Reg.*, 29 (no. 86).

208. Dispatches, Papal Court, 7 June 1528, fol. 7r.

of the case.[209] He had other complaints against Venice as well, primarily its heavy taxation of the clergy and its interference in ecclesiastical jurisdiction.

To his surprise and even frustration, Contarini came to realize that the pope's indecisiveness did not extend to the subject of the papal state and that Clement was unwilling to engage in any negotiations regarding the two disputed cities. The French and English ambassadors supported him in his demands for their restitution.[210] Contarini had to hear repeatedly that Venice was a stumbling block to the success of the anti-imperial forces; indeed, while the French agent, Joachim Passano, went so far as to curse Ravenna and Cervia several times as the cause of all the mischief, the pope was overheard cursing Venice.[211] Clearly, Contarini's diplomatic finesse was a necessity in this difficult situation.

That he possessed the needed abilities is beyond doubt. His dispatches show that he was successful in winning the pope's goodwill despite his unwelcome charge. Clement took a liking to Contarini from the first, and the ambassador knew how to make the most of this liking. Less than three weeks after his arrival Contarini was already on easy terms with the pope, who discussed various subjects with him as they walked together. Contarini mentioned in passing the Venetian expenses during the war but then went on to other things; he reported that he did not wish to make himself odious and thus endanger Venetian affairs, "which must be treated with all possible delicacy and skill."[212] The pope and the ambassador could even adopt a bantering tone about serious issues, showing that both were masters of that art of conversation so highly admired in their society.[213] Time after time Contarini reports that he had sought to calm the pope, or "soothe and appease his mind," always aware that he must not exceed certain limits lest he irritate the pontiff.[214] Sometimes he tried to move the issues onto a philosophical plane, but the pope was uniformly unresponsive,

209. Second dispatch of the same date, ibid., fols. 8v–9r; and 8 June 1528, fols. 9v–10r.

210. The English ambassador, Stephen Gardiner, is described as "caldissimo ad far ogni opera adcio Ravenna et Cervia siano restituite al Pontefice" (ibid., 14 June 1528, fol. 11v).

211. Ibid., 28 Sept. 1528, fol. 87r; and 18 July 1528, fol. 29v.

212. Ibid., 10 June 1528, fol. 10v.

213. Contarini describes how the pope and he made rather barbed remarks to each other "while laughing" (*ridendo*); *Reg.*, 14 June 1528, 31 (no. 89). There is a faint reminder of the conversations in the *Cortegiano* in this dispatch, with phrases like "Io ridendo…dissi," or "proferendo tale parole cum riso."

214. *Reg.*, 31 (no. 89).

and Contarini took refuge in resigned platitudes about the divine will.[215] Clement VII, like many weak people, had a stubborn side, especially when he thought his dignity had been offended. He never swerved from his contention that the Venetians had not only taken his lands but also injured his honor. He put his case plainly to Contarini: the Signoria had shown openly, "so that everyone can see, that you Venetians take little account of me. . . . You behave without proper respect in taking my lands, conferring [ecclesiastical] benefices, levying imposts"; and on another occasion the pope cried, "I want my lands, and you do not want to give them to me!"[216]

Try as he might, however, Contarini did not succeed in moving the pope, though he was aware that Clement thought highly of him personally. "I continually seek to placate the mind of His Holiness by various means. Therefore I sometimes try to be in his presence, seeing that I am not displeasing to him. In this way I can always drop some word or make some courteous and appropriate gesture, which certainly does no harm. In my judgment it is necessary to proceed step by step in this business, and to use all [possible] skill."[217] The Senate in response praised its ambassador's dexterity and prudence, granting him discretion in further talks.[218] But despite Contarini's entreaties, it put no pressure on the Venetian cardinals Corner and Grimani to rejoin the papal court and help counteract anti-Venetian sentiment in the pope's entourage.[219] Thus Contarini was left to answer for Venetian actions alone, as a resourceful and intelligent man in an increasingly intractable situation.

His dispatches from this embassy can be read on several levels. Most report how the complex political situation during an intense phase of the Habsburg-Valois struggles looked from the perspective of the

215. Dispatches, Papal Court, 18 July 1528, fols. 29v–30r.

216. *Reg.*, 16 June 1528, 31 (no. 91), and 27 June 1528 (no. 93). Clement could also be subtle: he realized that he had a strong card to play by threatening to seek the aid of the emperor, both for the restoration of the Medici in Florence and for the restitution of church lands. Appealing to Venice to return his cities he added ominously, "Perhaps you do not know the difference between the mad and the wise. The mad and the wise both do the same thing—the difference between them does not lie in that. But the wise do it at the right time and the mad at the wrong time, and therein lies the difference" (*Reg.*, 30 July 1528 [date should be corrected], 33 [no. 100]).

217. *Reg.*, 16 June 1528, 31 (no. 91).

218. ASV, Senato, Delib. Secreta, Reg. 53 (1528/29), 27 June 1528, fol. 83v.

219. This despite Contarini's report to the Council of Ten (12 July 1528, ASV, Capi del Consiglio dei X, Lettere di ambasciatori, busta 22 [Roma, 1515–38], fol. 170) about the desirability of their coming; and to the Senate in the same sense (Dispatches, Papal Court, 15 July 1528, fol. 27v).

papacy and illuminate the diplomatic intricacies of the papal court.[220] Contarini is a keen observer who creates a sense of immediacy, at times even of tension, in the reader. Then, the letters and instructions from the Senate and Doge Andrea Gritti together with Contarini's replies give a good idea of how Venice attempted to deal with the new political realities of an Italian peninsula whose fate was increasingly determined by the large European territorial states. Gritti, despite his pro-French views, was a political realist. His *ducali*, or letters to Contarini, written between 27 July 1528 and 21 January 1530, range from, at the start, urging the ambassador to draw Clement VII into firmly supporting the anti-Habsburg forces,[221] to a final realization that the best course of action for the Venetians would be to come to terms with Charles V and the pope and work for a general peace.[222] Differences of opinion about this change of direction existed within the Venetian ruling group.[223] The fear of Habsburg power runs through the entire correspondence of the Senate with Contarini, together with an at times pathetic trust in Francis I, who certainly did not deserve it.[224] Not only did Francis show no concern for his former allies when concluding the Peace of Cambrai with Charles V; he also subsequently offered to subsidize the emperor in a war against Venice and to divide the Venetian territory with him in return for the cession of Milan to France.[225] For the Venetians this was a hard blow indeed, and for Contarini personally a bitter political lesson.

His dispatches also offer a wealth of information about his personality. We meet in them a Venetian patrician, proud of his standing, well versed in court etiquette, and moving with ease in the world of princes. Beyond his role as ambassador he filled the more personal one of

220. *GC*, 125–203, presents a detailed discussion of the main political events reported on by Contarini.

221. *Ducali*, 30 Aug. and 31 Oct. 1528; 19 Apr. and 23 July 1529.

222. Ibid., 26 Sept. and 22 Oct. 1529.

223. Sanuto, *Diarii* 48:413–14 and 49:222, shows that there was no general agreement about how to instruct Contarini.

224. News of Charles V's planned trip to Italy greatly worried the Venetian Senate, which deliberated about asking Francis I to come: ASV, Senato, Delib. Secreta, Reg. 53 (1528/29), 2 Apr. 1529, fol. 166r. Contarini, too, had faith in Francis I's promises to Venice and rejected the possibility that the French king could think of concluding a separate peace with Charles V; see Dispatches, Papal Court, 9 Apr. 1529, fols. 222v–223r. Without regard for the Italian states, and to the great consternation of Contarini, Francis I did precisely that; ibid., 14 Aug. 1529, fols. 288v–290v. Contarini tersely records in his final report to the Senate that "the Republic and all other allies were excluded from this peace" (Albèri, *Relazioni*, 2d ser., 3:263).

225. Albèri, *Relazioni*, 2d ser., 3:199.

the pope's frequent confidant,[226] at times even of his conscience. Most striking is Clement VII's exclamation to Contarini, made after only seven months of acquaintance: "I trust you to such an extent, that if you were not the Venetian ambassador and a nobleman of that city, I would place all my disagreements in your hands."[227]

The welfare of Italy was a theme often brought up by Contarini in his conversations with Clement, only to elicit the justified response that Venice, having seized the cities of its neighbor, was hardly the model of a state concerned with the common good. One senses Contarini's frustration as he replied to the pope on one such occasion: "Holy Father, this is not the time to dwell at length on the problems of Ravenna and Cervia. If you do not wish to hear me as orator of the illustrious Signoria of Venice, then listen to me as an Italian speaking to you only for the common good of Italy and for the Holy See, which will certainly be ruined entirely if the plans of its enemies succeed!" When the pope replied that he was interested only in the good of the church, that he had done too much for Italy already with no other result than his own defeat, Contarini became disturbed indeed, fearing the ruin of Italy.[228] That the good of Italy was not merely a convenient diplomatic counter but genuinely dear to Contarini can be seen from his impassioned letter to Carlo Cappello, the Venetian ambassador to Florence, written immediately after reports of the accord between Charles V and Clement VII, made public in Barcelona on 29 June 1529, reached Rome. Passing on the bad news that now emperor and pope would collaborate against the Florentine Republic, Contarini declares that men with noble hearts should have little concern for their own lives, property, or wealth in the defense of freedom. If the

226. Brief remarks show that Contarini continued to be on friendly personal terms with the pope; for example: "Doppo pranso retiratese [Clement VII] cum me solo ne la sua camera intrassemo in ragionamento de le presente ocorentie" (Dispatches, Papal Court, 4 Oct. 1528, fol. 90r); or 10 June 1528, fol. 10v; and 14 Oct. 1528, fol. 98r—both of which mention Contarini's walking with the pope. On one occasion the pope sent his secretary, Sanga, to tell Contarini that he would see him as his friend: "Et cosi heri da sera preditto secretario mi fece intender, che hoggi a 21 hora dovesse andar perche seria admesso non gia come oratore, ne per parlarli de facende alcune, ma solum come privato amico suo" (ibid., 7 June 1529, fol. 252v).

227. Reg., 4 Jan. 1529, 44 (no. 126).

228. Reg., 5 Sept. 1528, 34 (no. 103). The pope's reply should be corrected to read: "Io non voglio procurar se non il ben de la chiesia; troppo ho io fatto per Italia et a bon fine, siche mi ho ruinato" (Dispatches, Papal Court, fol. 66v). See also, e.g., Reg., 7 June 1529, 55 (no. 173); or 14 Aug. 1529, 61 (no. 196), where Contarini asserts what he takes to be best for Italy.

Florentines comprehend this and make the necessary preparations for their defense they will withstand their enemies: "Thus, they will preserve themselves and Italy to their eternal glory, and [their enemies] will be baffled in their designs."[229] The Senate, too, had expressed concern at the rumor that the emperor was actually to come,[230] only reinforcing Contarini's anxiety. He was in a position to see how little room for maneuver the Italian states really had, and his concern for Italy and desire to speak as an Italian went far beyond mere rhetoric. Unfortunately, however, the pope thought neither as an Italian nor even as a Florentine but as the head of the house of Medici, on whose restoration he was single-mindedly bent.

The greatest theoretical interest attaches to the arguments Contarini used with Clement VII and reported to the Senate in a dispatch of 4 January 1529, the most lively and personal dispatch in his entire diplomatic correspondence.[231] In a private audience with the pope Contarini explained that this time he had not come to convey an official instruction from his government, but to be heard as an Italian, a private person, and a Christian. Encouraged by Clement to continue, he appealed to the pope to act in a manner different from other rulers who pursued only their own interests. Contarini called on the pope to put the interests of all Christians first and to become a peacemaker among European states. He argued that what distinguished the pope's position from that of other princes was his twofold appointment by Christ: as his vicar, the holder of the highest spiritual authority in the *respublica Christiana*, and as the magistrate primarily responsible for the well-being of the Christian commonwealth, who for that very reason must give an example of unselfish behavior. In answer to

---

229. *Reg.*, 16 July 1529, 58 (no. 183), should be corrected to read: "Et cosi cum immortal gloria si conserverano loro et Italia et costoro rimanian inganati del pensier loro" (Dispatches, Papal Court, fol. 273r). In a dispatch of 31 October 1529 Contarini is more explicit: "All of Italy can be regarded as a body composed of several members. It is not possible for one of them to suffer without harm to the others" (*Reg.*, 70 [no. 227]).

230. ASV, Senato, Delib. Secreta, Reg. 53 (1528/29), 2 Apr. 1529, fol. 166r. Kretschmayr, *Geschichte von Venedig* 3:14, thinks that during its whole history Venice had rarely concerned itself with the idea of Italy as much as it did during the period of the League of Cognac.

231. Dispatches, Papal Court, fols. 148r–154r, should be used to correct the long extracts in *Reg.*, 41–46 (no. 126). See *GC*, 146–51; Ludwig von Pastor, *Geschichte der Päpste seit dem Ausgang des Mittelalters*, vol. 4, pt. 2 (Freiburg i.B., 1956), 347–49; and Giuseppe De Leva, *Storia documentata di Carlo V in correlazione all'Italia* (Venice, 1863–94), 2:503–5.

Clement's declaration that in pursuing the return of Ravenna and Cervia he was acting only for the good of the church, Contarini made a sharp reply:

Your Holiness should not think that the welfare of Christ's church is comprised in this little temporal state which she has acquired. Even before this state existed there was a church, and a most excellent one. The church is the community of all Christians. This state is like the state of an Italian prince, joined to the church. But Your Holiness should above all be concerned with the welfare of the true church, which consists in peace and tranquillity among all Christians, and for the present relegate to second place the interests of this temporal state.[232]

For Clement VII Contarini's words must have lost some of their sting because they were spoken by a Venetian in the service of his state.[233] Yet the pope responded to this serious plea by admitting its truth, though still assuming the attitude of a political realist: "Don't you see that the world has reached a point where it is the most cunning schemer who reaps most praise, is esteemed and extolled as an admirable man, whereas he who acts in opposite fashion is thought of as good but worthless and is left only with the name of 'a good man'?" In his reply Contarini raised the issue to a higher plane: "Holy Father, if [you] search through the whole of Sacred Scripture, which cannot lie, you will see that there is nothing stronger or more powerful than truth, virtue, goodness, and right intention. I have found this to be true and have experienced it in many of my private affairs; let Your Holiness take heart and proceed with honorable intention, and God will undoubtedly send his help and render you most glorious!"[234] Contarini's words made an impression on the pope,[235] who however did not change his mind either about the disputed cities or about the political stand that half a year later culminated in the alliance with Charles V.

This letter, striking for its reported dialogue, is also important for revealing Contarini's thought. His primary purpose was to convince Clement VII to embrace the cause of the anti-imperial side, but Ludwig von Pastor, the historian of the popes, has judged Contarini's

232. *Reg.*, 43 (no. 126).
233. Already in the late fifteenth and early sixteenth centuries there was Venetian insistence on the pastoral rather than political role of the pope; see Gaetano Cozzi, "I rapporti tra stato e chiesa," in *La chiesa di Venezia tra riforma protestante e riforma cattolica*, ed. Giuseppe Gullino (Venice: Edizioni Studium Cattolico Veneziano, 1990), 17.
234. *Reg.*, 44 (no. 126).
235. Contarini reports, "Io non credo inganarme, vedeva, che le parole mie li facevano impressione" (*Reg.*, 45 [no. 126]).

motives too harshly in asserting that the Venetian ambassador in this instance confused what was advantageous for the Republic and the lost cause of the independence of Italy with the welfare of Christendom.[236] Contarini's dispatch touches on two themes to which he was often to return: that of an idealized, spiritual papacy, and that of the crucial importance of experience and example. Of course he was speaking to the pope as a Venetian; but that fact should not cast into doubt Contarini's own convictions about the papacy, which he was to elaborate in later tracts, or the important place he gave to emotion in his understanding of human nature. In this dispatch we see not ad hoc arguments but ideas that had become a permanent part of Contarini's thinking, and which he shared with other Venetian patricians who dreamed of a reformed, spiritual church removed from the sordidness of money, possessions, and political deals. Beyond the inadequacies of the individual pope he discerned the ideal papacy instituted by Christ, just as beyond the world of contention, whether in politics or religion, there was for him the power of human goodness and charity to move men's hearts. In this famous audience Contarini spoke as a Venetian deeply imbued with reform ideas current among his friends, as an expert diplomat, and as a concerned Christian who expressed his vision of what the papacy might become if the pope were to take reform seriously.

The doge on several occasions praised Contarini's conduct of affairs and expressed trust in him.[237] The *collegio*, too, was most pleased with his dispatches.[238] After receiving the report of 4 January, the Senate wrote to express its great satisfaction with his handling of matters and sent him a mandate to engage in negotiations for a universal peace.[239] This did not mean, however, that he had much scope for initiative or that he could conclude any agreement on his own. One little episode, insignificant in itself, shows that even a trusted ambassador like Contarini was expected to be above all the obedient servant of the

236. Pastor, *Geschichte der Päpste* 4(2):349.
237. *Ducali*, 10 Nov. 1528, 30 Oct. 1529, and 28 Dec. 1529.
238. ASV, Collegio, Lettere Secrete, 30 Dec. 1528.
239. ASV, Senato, Delib. Secreta, Reg. 53 (1528/29), 15 Jan. 1529, fol. 141v: "Abbiamo per quelle [Contarini's letters of 2, 4, and 5 January] inteso il longo, et fiducial conferimento per voi havuto cum la Santᵃ del Pontefice circa le occorentie delli importantissimi presenti tempi. Nelche invero vi havete si ben, et accomodamente disporta, che di tal officio vostro et noi [the Signoria] et il Senato nostro habbiamo sentita cumulata satisfattion, et vi attribuimo merite, et condigne laude." The mandate is on fols. 142v–143r.

state. When rumors reached Venice that the pope was ill and that the emperor might come to Italy, but no letter arrived from Contarini for several days, he was sharply reminded of his duty to keep an anxious Signoria and Senate promptly informed. The doge lectured him, the experienced diplomat, in no uncertain terms about transmitting not only facts but also hearsay and rumors, adding pedantically that of course Contarini should specify which was which.[240]

During the first half of 1529 Contarini continued to work in vain against a rapprochement of pope and emperor, aided for a time by Gian Matteo Giberti, bishop of Verona as well as former secretary and leading counselor of Clement VII, who had left the papal court after the sack of Rome.[241] Giberti was strongly pro-French, and both the doge and Contarini had high hopes that he could influence the pope at least to remain neutral. Giberti, however, who knew Clement well, realized there was little he could do and returned to his diocese despite Contarini's annoyance and efforts to detain him.[242] Contarini was again left to look after Venetian interests alone. He could neither prevent Clement from signing an accord with the emperor[243] nor do more than wait passively to learn what Charles V and Francis I would determine about Italy and Venice in the Peace of Cambrai.[244] After July his dispatches become increasingly reports of what he had learned at second hand. Charles V landed in Genoa on 12 August; meanwhile, the pope was preoccupied with the impending meeting with the emperor, for which Bologna was chosen. Contarini found that Clement did not want to tell him anything specific about his dealings with the emperor,[245] which meant that he had to operate from rumors—such as that Clement might consent to the present state of Ravenna and Cervia, which proved groundless.[246] One can sense his frustration when he complains at finding himself "in deep darkness," not knowing how to proceed since he had heard nothing from Venice in three weeks.[247] No

240. *Ducali*, 17 Feb. 1529. The instruction to write is repeated in ASV, Collegio, Lettere Secrete, 1528 (dated 7 Feb. 1528) (*more Veneto* = 1529).

241. For Giberti, see the excellent study by Adriano Prosperi, *Tra evangelismo e controriforma: G. M. Giberti (1495–1543)* (Rome: Edizioni di Storia e Letteratura, 1969).

242. *Reg.*, 14 Apr. 1529, 52 (no. 159).

243. *Reg.*, 28 July 1529, 59 (no. 189). The treaty had been negotiated in Barcelona, and agreed upon on 29 June.

244. Dispatches, Papal Court, 7 Aug. 1529, fol. 285r.

245. Ibid., 10 Sept. 1529, fol. 306v.

246. Ibid., 5 Sept. 1529, fol. 304v.

247. Ibid., 19 Sept. 1529, fol. 311r. Contarini's tone is almost sarcastic: "Pero la [the Signoria] prego instantemente che la si degni qualche volta per sue lettere darmi qualche pocco de lume."

wonder that he asked for the appointment of a successor, alleging that he could no longer support the burden and expense of his mission. Yet despite his discouragement he continued in his embassy, reaching the high point of his Venetian diplomatic career in his personal contributions to the Peace of Bologna in 1530.

In 1529 the Venetian government began preparing for a general peace. After the conclusion of separate treaties between the pope and the emperor and between the emperor and the French king, it was obvious that the anti-imperial league had crumbled and that the Italian states were on their own. Venice naturally tried to preserve her territories. But an equally important objective for her was to prevent Milan, her neighbor to the west, from becoming a Spanish dependency. Over and over Contarini was sent instructions to work for the restitution of Milan to Duke Francesco Sforza, a difficult task since the duke's anti-imperial stand had made him unpopular with Charles V and his advisors.[248] Contarini urged the pope to make sure than the Milanese ruler was an Italian,[249] but became perturbed when he suspected that the emperor might grant Milan to the pope's nephew Alessandro de' Medici, admittedly an Italian but pro-imperial and therefore undesirable from the Venetian point of view. A tone of growing unease appears in Contarini's reports about the pope's Italian policies, especially his attitude toward Florence. Despite Clement's assurances, the envoy was worried about the destiny of Florence and took every opportunity to put in a good word for the Florentines, urging the pope to work for the liberty and the good of his native city. At one point he provoked Clement into exclaiming, "Do you think I do not realize what it would mean to place Florence at the mercy of Spaniards and Germans? I have many women relatives there. Do you think I want them to go—to use his own words—to the bordello with Spaniards and Germans?"[250] Ironically, despite these disclaimers, one of the clauses in the agreement between the emperor and the pope specified that they would collaborate in reducing Florence to a Medici dependency, and Contarini's fears proved justified when the last Florentine republic fell in 1530.

The Venetian Senate and Signoria had no choice but to adapt to the reality of the emperor's power. After Charles V arrived in Italy the

248. *Ducali*, 26 Sept. and 5 Dec. 1529, reiterate that Venice stood by the duke of Milan. See also ASV, Senato, Delib. Secreta, Reg. 53 (1528/29), 19 Nov. 1529, fols. 267v–270r.

249. *Reg.*, 10 Aug. 1529, 61 (no. 196).

250. *Reg.*, 13 July 1529, 60 (no. 190).

instructions to Contarini change tone: now he was to stress above all Venice's desire for peace, with no reference to the role Venice had played in the anti-imperial league.[251] In October, Contarini accompanied the papal train on its journey to Bologna. He received a mandate from the doge as well as credentials from the Senate to negotiate in the name of the Republic with both emperor and pope.[252] While realistic about the necessity of restoring to Charles V cities conquered in Apulia, the Venetians were still hoping against hope for some agreement that would leave Ravenna and Cervia in their hands. Contarini was told to use "all the strength and quickness" of his mind, and even ordered to engage the good offices of the emperor to persuade Clement VII if necessary.[253] This was no easy task for the Venetian ambassador, for it meant petitioning the emperor to help a state that only very recently had been his enemy. Predictably, Charles V was not willing to put pressure on the pope in this matter. Despite Contarini's best efforts in the course of several meetings, Clement VII remained adamant about regaining possession of the two cities,[254] and finally the majority in the Venetian Senate realized that the cities would have to be returned to the pope.[255]

The emperor made a splendid entrance into Bologna on 5 November.[256] Contarini's pleasant and gentlemanly manner came to his aid at the awkward moment of meeting Charles V face to face. Saying nothing about Venice's war against him, the emperor greeted Contarini not as the orator who was an agent of the Republic, but as Messer Gasparo Contarini, with whom he had been on very friendly terms while the latter was ambassador to him in Spain; "and he received him

251. *Ducali,* 26 Sept. and 22 Oct. 1529. In the former a striking change of tone in regard to the emperor occurs, and Contarini is told that Venice is "most inclined" toward His Majesty. See also ASV, Senato, Delib. Secreta, Reg. 53 (1528/29), 31 Aug. 1529, fol. 225r; 5 Oct. 1529, fol. 239r–v.

252. Dispatches, Papal Court, 22 Oct. 1529, fol. 247r.

253. Ibid., 2 Nov. 1529, fol. 252r.

254. *Reg.,* 26 Oct. 1529, 68–69 (no. 224); 27 Oct. 1529, 69 (no. 225); and 5 Nov. 1529, 71 (no. 230). In early November Contarini still tried in vain to appeal to the pope "non come oratore dei miei signori, ma come Gasparo Contarini, privato e sviscerato servitore della Santità Vostra" (Albèri, *Relazioni,* 2d ser., 3:160).

255. ASV, Senato, Delib. Secreta, Reg. 53 (1528/29), 10 Nov. 1529, fols. 253v, 254r. This decision provoked intense debates. Hardliners in the Senate like Girolamo Pesaro, Alvise and Pietro Mocenigo, and Lunardo Emo did not favor the restitution of the cities; see Albèri, *Relazioni,* 2d ser., 3:171–72. See also Sanuto, *Diarii* 52:212.

256. Dispatches, Papal Court, 5 Nov. 1529, fols. 338r–340r, describes the emperor's entry into the city with about eight hundred horse and three to four thousand infantry, and his gracious reception of Contarini.

with such kind words and courteous actions that all who were present marveled."[257] Contarini later replied with a masterful speech to the effect that Venice had gone to war against the emperor only for defensive reasons but now welcomed him as a bringer of peace.[258]

The documents of the peace negotiations show Contarini to be a skilled, intelligent statesman who knew how to smooth over difficulties with his genial manner.[259] He could speak informally to emperor and pope, assuming the persona of a "private person," and get a ready hearing. Clement VII solicited his advice,[260] while Charles V accepted it when it was offered. In the latter case Contarini stressed that he was approaching the emperor "not as the Venetian orator" but as a faithful servitor who allowed himself to suggest that neither Charles V nor his counselors understood the nature of Italians. He argued deftly against the Spanish plan to retain fortresses in Milanese territory as a pledge of the duke's loyalty, saying that if that were to occur the people would think the Spaniards were the real masters of Milan and would not pay taxes to the duke; as a result, the latter would be unable to pay the indemnity he was required to give to the emperor, and in the end no solid result would be achieved.[261] With great diplomatic skill and tact Contarini won Charles V's high opinion.[262] He was instrumental in persuading the emperor to return Milan to Duke Francesco Sforza as a means of keeping peace in northern Italy, even though the duke had been an enemy. This victory of Venetian diplomacy kept direct Spanish power out of northern Italy for the time being. Contarini also managed to whittle down the payment demanded of Venice to one

257. Albèri, *Relazioni*, 2d ser., 3:162.

258. Ibid., 173.

259. The judgment of Horatio F. Brown, "Cardinal Contarini and His Friends," in *Studies in the History of Venice* (London: John Murray, 1907), 2:128, to the effect that Contarini had no "grain of humor," should be qualified. See, for example, the quick reply Contarini made "sorridendo" to Clement VII's complaint that the Venetians had not paid him interest on the value of the salt from Cervia while the city was in their hands: "Your Holiness might with more justification ask for the interest on what you suffered during the siege and sack of Rome, in which so many silver objects, crosses, chalices, relics, together with churches, were robbed and destroyed!" (Albèri, *Relazioni*, 2d ser., 3:188).

260. The pope asked Contarini, "Ditemi il vostro parer, non come ambasciatore, ma come Messer Gasparo Contarini privato" (Albèri, *Relazioni*, 2d ser., 3:191).

261. Ibid., 207. See also *Ducali*, 17 Dec. 1529.

262. Charles V was convinced of Contarini's goodwill toward him. During the peace negotiations he remarked, "Domine orator, ... although you can be accused of doing everything for your homeland, still we know that next to it you have always loved the person of the emperor" (Albèri, *Relazioni*, 2d ser., 3:178).

hundred thousand ducats in addition to what was still owed the emperor after the peace treaty of 1523.[263]

While Contarini in Bologna was using his good offices also for the dukes of Ferrara and Urbino, considerable dissent erupted in the Venetian Senate. Besides the disagreements regarding the restitution of Ravenna and Cervia, there was discord about a proposed defensive league of Italian states with Charles V and his brother Ferdinand. The emperor pressed for the league, but the Venetians hesitated to enter it for fear of provoking the Turks, who had only recently lifted the siege of Vienna and were still at war with the Habsburgs.[264] In the Senate the relations of Venice with the emperor, Francis I, and the Turks were hotly discussed.[265] To Contarini's annoyance, some senators leaked the content of the debates to the papal nuncio in Venice, who promptly wrote to Clement VII. Thus the pope was sometimes informed of what was going on in Venice before Contarini himself received official letters. Other potential problems for Contarini were caused by senators like Alvise Gradenigo and Girolamo Pesaro, who proposed that Venice send an ambassador to the Turks to apologize for treating for peace with the emperor and explain that she did so only because otherwise she would remain isolated, all other Italian states having agreed to peace. Alvise Mocenigo, who frequently opposed Contarini, this time rose in his support. He declared that if Charles V heard that such an ambassador was sent, the peace negotiations would certainly suffer a setback.[266] His view prevailed, and Contarini's labors were made easier.

On 23 December the peace treaty of Bologna was concluded, and by the twenty-eighth the news had reached Venice, causing great joy in the whole city.[267] On New Year's Day 1530 the treaty was solemnly proclaimed in the cathedral of San Petronio in Bologna. Venice, besides having to return to the pope Ravenna and Cervia, and to the emperor Trani, Monopoli, and other towns in southern Italy, was also constrained to join a defensive league that included Charles V, Ferdinand of Austria, Clement VII, and the duke of Milan.[268] The Venetians

263. Ibid., 217.

264. ASV, Senato, Delib. Secreta, Reg. 53 (1528/29), 26 Nov. 1529, fols. 264v–265r.

265. Alvise Mocenigo delivered a long and clever anti-French speech; see Albèri, *Relazioni*, 2d ser., 3:195–96.

266. Ibid., 211–12.

267. *Ducali*, 28 Dec. 1529; and ASV, Senato, Delib. Secreta, Reg. 53 (1528/29), fols. 282v–283r. The Senate swore to uphold the treaty on January 11; see fol. 293r–v.

268. For the provisions of the treaty, see ASV, Senato, Delib. Secreta, Reg. 53 (1528/29), fols. 265r–267r; and Albèri, *Relazioni*, 2d ser., 3:217–18.

elected four ambassadors for the ceremonial mission to congratulate both pope and emperor on the peace.[269] Clement VII's intimation that he wished to receive formal obeisance from Venice provoked a long debate in the Senate, including a lengthy speech by the anti-papal Alvise Mocenigo.[270] Regrettably, the sources do not tell us whether Mocenigo was elected as one of the four ambassadors because of his speech or in spite of it.[271] Contarini was instructed to remain in Bologna for the emperor's coronation on 24 February; thereupon his request to be relieved of his post was granted, with Antonio Soriano elected to succeed him.[272] After the splendid ceremonies of the imperial coronation, described in detail by his brother-in-law Matteo Dandolo,[273] Contarini finally returned to Venice.

On 4 March he made the customary final report on his mission before the Senate. A short summary, not written until at least five years later, is all that survives.[274] In it he briefly discusses the pope and his advisors, the emperor and his advisors, and the duke of Milan. There is nothing not contained in his dispatches, and one looks in vain for any personal reflection on the diplomatic background of the Peace of Bologna. One of the few noteworthy phrases concerns Clement VII, whose attitude to church reform Contarini sums up pithily: "He manifests his desire to see the abuses of the Holy Church curbed, but nevertheless he does nothing to put any such idea into practice, nor does he decide to issue any regulations."[275] Contarini's perfunctory summary is no substitute for the full report, which was described as "very specific but contained nothing superfluous; it was unanimously praised by the whole Senate, which listened to it most attentively for more than two hours."[276]

269. ASV, Senato, Delib. Secreta, Reg. 53 (1528/29), 29 Dec. 1529, fol. 286v.

270. Albèri, *Relazioni*, 2d ser., 3:231–34.

271. The other ambassadors were Marco Dandolo, Alvise Gradenigo, and Lorenzo Bragadin. Their commission is in ASV, Senato, Delib. Secreta, Reg. 53 (1528/29), fols. 294v–295r, with a characteristic touch at the end: Juan Dolfin was sent along to supervise expenses and make a daily accounting.

272. Ibid., fol. 289r–v.

273. Sanuto, *Diarii* 52:628–38, 639–79, gives other descriptions of the coronation and associated festivities.

274. Albèri, *Relazioni*, 2d ser., 3:259–74. The summary was written after Pope Paul III's election in 1534 (260). Albèri mistakenly reports Sanuto as dating Contarini's speech to 7 March and saying that it lasted three hours; Sanuto, *Diarii* 53:16, says two hours.

275. Albèri, *Relazioni*, 2d ser., 3:265.

276. Ibid., 247. Niccolò da Ponte summarized twenty-two years later what Contarini said, basing himself on letters he had written to his father in 1530. His recapitulation omits details that would flesh out Contarini's report.

For Venice, the peace provided a welcome breathing spell after the war and the expenses of the unsuccessful alliance against Charles V. But it also underlined her political decline, which had begun during the War of the League of Cambrai. Venice was increasingly forced to perceive herself as a small state whose fate was, if not determined, at least decisively influenced by the great European monarchies. For Contarini personally, the peace was the culmination of twenty months of patient and determined work. While he did not achieve his main objective, the retention of Ravenna and Cervia in Venetian hands, he did contribute to making the situation of the northern Italian states easier than it would have been had the Spanish established themselves in Milan at that point. The embassy had also given him insight into the affairs of the church, stimulating his reflections on its structure and the nature of the papacy. At the papal court he had become a well-known figure, among others to Cardinal Alessandro Farnese, who as Pope Paul III was to appoint him cardinal. Contarini had also won the respect of Charles V and his advisors; it was Charles who requested Contarini's presence as papal legate at the Diet of Regensburg eleven years later.

The most immediate impact of Contarini's success and prestige was on his career in the service of the state. On 31 December 1529 he was elected in absentia by the Senate *savio grande* (or *savio del consiglio*), a member of the committee of six that constituted one of the highest levels of the Venetian government.[277] Because he was still in Bologna, a supplementary motion was passed to elect another *savio* while Contarini was on his diplomatic mission but to give him the first vacant position on the committee after his return.[278] His status was further enhanced by a letter to the Senate from the Mantuan ambassador to Bologna, Giovanni Battista Malatesta, who praised Contarini as an outstanding emissary who would be greatly missed at the papal court; "it is impossible," he declared, "to express in what a praiseworthy manner, giving satisfaction to all, he behaved during his embassy."[279]

Yet Contarini also had enemies among his peers, most notably Francesco Foscari, who managed to invoke a procedural technicality to

---

277. The six *savii del consiglio* (or *savii grandi*), together with five *savii di terra-ferma* (in charge of mainland affairs) and five *savii agli ordini* (in charge of naval affairs), formed the *consulta*, which was a part of the *pien collegio*, the initiative and executive body of the government. See Appendix 2. For Contarini's election, see Sanuto, *Diarii* 52:401; and Albèri, *Relazioni*, 2d ser., 3:237.

278. Sanuto, *Diarii* 52:448.   279. Ibid., 478.

prevent the ambassador from keeping the emperor's parting present of 1,500 gold ducats. Though the doge urged the Senate to grant Contarini the money, and a motion was made to award it to him "in recompense for the expenses he incurred, and in recognition of his praiseworthy work," the necessary four-fifths of votes could not be mustered. That Contarini's pride was hurt can be seen from his unwillingness to have the matter voted on again. Even a motion to grant him one-half the sum was defeated, and Contarini had to hand over his gift to the treasury.[280]

More humiliating for Contarini was a sharp attack on him on 11 March by the same Francesco Foscari for having signed the peace treaty of Bologna without noticing that it contained a phrase against the Turks. After Contarini explained that the offending words were inserted owing to an oversight of his secretary Antonio Mazzaruolo, the heads of the Council of Ten proposed sending instructions to the new ambassador, Antonio Soriano, to have the phrase removed. The Venetian government was unwilling to antagonize the Turks in any way, but neither the doge nor most of the *collegio* thought this was a crucial matter. Piero Mocenigo and then Foscari, however, turned it into a major issue; the latter moved that Contarini be handed over to the public prosecutors for investigation and trial, "as such a great disorder demands," since he had not followed his instructions exactly. Contarini's brother Tommaso came to his defense, "shouting that if his brother did wrong he should be punished, but first he must be heard; he is without guilt!" Others thought the same, even Contarini's old enemy Alvise Mocenigo, who defended him in this instance, and Foscari's motion was defeated.[281] This bitter epilogue to Contarini's

280. This episode shows that although Contarini was generally well liked, he had enemies among the Venetian nobles. Francesco Foscari, in 1530 one of the ducal councillors, seems to have felt a strong personal hostility toward Contarini. Knowing that the Contarini family had paid all the expenses of the embassy to Clement VII, he still opposed even the motion to let Contarini keep the 1,500 ducats. When the motion he opposed was put to the vote he invoked the absence of Alvise Gradenigo, one of the four ceremonial ambassadors to the emperor, as the reason no final decision should be taken. He insisted that senators be reminded of legislation forbidding gifts to ambassadors and managed to sway enough senators so that the motion lost. See ibid., 53:16, 17, 19; ASV, Senato Terra, Reg. 26 (1530/31), fols. 1v, 2r–v; Albèri, *Relazioni*, 2d ser., 3:249–50. Other nobles in high government positions were more likely to oppose Contarini on specific issues, for example the pro-imperial Alvise Mocenigo, Girolamo Pesaro, Pietro Mocenigo, and Lunardo Emo; but at times they attacked him personally as well; see Sanuto, *Diarii* 53:24, 126; 56:667, among other instances.

281. Sanuto, *Diarii* 53:24–25; ASV, Senato, Delib. Secreta, Reg. 54 (1530/31), fols. 6r–v, 7r; Albèri, *Relazioni*, 2d ser., 3:251–53.

embassy reveals not only the divisions among the ruling elite, but also Venice's keen sensitivity to the Turkish danger in its political calculations[282] and the extreme circumspection with which it approached any issue involving the Ottoman Empire.[283]

In the Inner Councils of Venice

The five years following the return from the embassy to Clement VII are the least-known portion of Contarini's career. In Franz Dittrich's 880-page biography, the period from March 1530 to May 1535 receives only a single short paragraph, and for his compilation of Contarini's *Regesten* comprising 407 pages the same scholar found only material enough from these five years to fill not quite two pages.[284] Several factors help to explain the neglect of this crucial epoch in Contarini's career. One is the scattered nature of the documentation, almost all of it archival, which his biographer did not know or to which he did not have access. Even more significant is the perspective of most scholars writing on Contarini after Dittrich. For them he was primarily the cardinal and advocate of church reform, not the Venetian statesman.[285] But the two cannot be separated, for a remarkable continuity ran through Contarini's life. As churchman he regularly drew on

282. For a thorough study, see Paolo Preto, *Venezia e i Turchi* (Florence: Sansoni, 1975).

283. See, for example, the eloquent response given to Gian Matteo Giberti, sent to Venice by Pope Clement VII to ascertain the Venetian attitude toward the Turks. Giberti was given to understand the need for extreme caution, since Venice had the Turks as her neighbors; ASV, Senato, Delib. Secreta, Reg. 54 (1530/31), fol. 105r–v. However, some Venetians saw the Turks as a useful counterpoise to the power of Charles V in Italy; see Contarini's dispatch from Bologna, 17 Feb. 1530, in ASV, Capi del Consiglio dei X, Lettere di ambasciatori, busta 22 (Roma, 1515–38) (incorrectly dated in *Reg.*, 48 [no. 143]). Through an ambassador the Turks applied pressure on Venice in 1529 not to sign a peace or enter into a league with the emperor; see G. Romano, *Cronaca del soggiorno di Carlo V in Italia* (Milan, 1892), 158–59.

284. Even in the one paragraph he devotes to this five-year period Dittrich confuses our Contarini with a namesake, Gasparo Contarini qu. Francesco Alvise, despite Cicogna's note in *Inscrizioni* 2:227. Rawdon Brown also confuses the careers of the two men, in *CSPV* 3:xiv.

285. Important exceptions are the discussions of Contarini's secular thought by Felix Gilbert, both in "Religion and Politics" and in "Gasparo Contarini as a Venetian Gentleman," paper delivered at the XVIII International Congress of Medieval Studies, Kalamazoo, Michigan, May 1983; and the essays by Gigliola Fragnito in *Gasparo Contarini: un magistrato veneziano*.

the experience he had acquired in Venetian politics, and in his theoretical considerations he united the secular and ecclesiastical spheres.

The period of Contarini's participation in the highest levels of the Venetian government began with his assumption of the office of *savio grande* on 1 April 1530.[286] A term of office in the Council of Ten, which began in September 1530 and continued through August 1531,[287] followed by another from September 1533 to August 1534,[288] showed that he had entered the inner circle of the political elite. Until his elevation to the cardinalate in 1535 he continued to hold important offices both successively and simultaneously. He was one of the three *capi*, or heads, of the Council of Ten for October and December 1530, March and June 1531, October and December 1533, and March 1534,[289] and he also served five times as one of the council's inquisitors.[290] Two yearlong terms as one of the doge's six councillors

286. See note 277 above. Contarini held that office twice more, in 1532 and 1534; see Sanuto, *Diarii* 55:308; and ASV, Segretario alle voci, Elezioni dei Pregadi, Reg. 1531–54, fols. 1v, 26v.

287. ASV, Consiglio dei X, Comuni, Reg. 1530, fol. 78; and Sanuto, *Diarii* 53:483.

288. ASV, Consiglio dei X, Reg. 1533, fol. 109v. Between his two terms on the Council of Ten, Contarini was a substitute for members in cases where they could not vote because of a conflict of interest: thus in September 1531 (ASV, Capi del Consiglio dei X, Criminali, busta 7 [1531–34]), in August 1532 (ibid., Reg. 4 [1525–34], fol. 128v), in October and December 1532 (ibid., fols. 131v, 133r). In July 1533 he was elected to a replacement position on the Council of Ten until the next regular election; see Sanuto, *Diarii* 57:520.

289. For October 1530, see ASV, Consiglio dei X, Secreta, Reg. 3 (1529–32), fols. 73v–74r; Capi del Consiglio dei X, Lettere, filza no. 30; and Sanuto, *Diarii* 54:5. For December 1530: ibid., 143; Consiglio dei X, Comuni, Reg. 1530, fol. 103r; Consiglio dei X, Criminali, Reg. 4 (1525–34), fol. 88r. For March 1531: ibid., fol. 95v; Consiglio dei X, Comuni, Reg. 1531, repeatedly in entries for that month; Sanuto, *Diarii* 54:318. For June 1531: ibid., 454; Consiglio dei X, Comuni, Reg. 1531, repeatedly listed. For October 1533: Capi del Consiglio dei X, Criminali, busta 7 (1531–34); Consiglio dei X, Secreta, Reg. 4 (1533–39), fol. 21v; Consiglio dei X, Comuni, Reg. 1533, fol. 109v. For December 1533: ibid., fol. 135r and ff.; Consiglio dei X, Criminali, Reg. 4 (15251–34), fol. 154r. For March 1534: ibid., fol. 159v; Consiglio dei X, Comuni, Reg. 1534, fol. 2v and ff.

290. For Contarini's terms as inquisitor of the Council of Ten for January 1531, see ASV, Capi del Consiglio dei X, Criminali, busta 6 (1525–30); Consiglio dei X, Criminali, Reg. 4 (1525–34), fol. 90v. For April 1531: ibid., fol. 97r; Capi del Consiglio dei X, Criminali, busta 7 (1531–34). For July 1531: ibid.; Consiglio dei X, Criminali, Reg. 4 (1525–34), fol. 101v. For November 1533: ibid., fol. 153r; Capi del Consiglio dei X, Criminali, busta 7 (1531–34), repeated entries. For January 1534: Consiglio dei X, Criminali, Reg. 4 (1525–34), fol. 155v. The inquisitor concerned himself in the broadest sense with the welfare of the state, and his charge remained different from that of officials of the later inquisition into religious matters; see Grendler, *Roman Inquisition*, chap. 1; Rinaldo Fulin, "Gl'inquisitori dei Dieci," *Archivio veneto* 1 (1871): 1–64, 298–313; 2 (1871): 357–91.

increased his prestige further.[291] He continued to be elected to divers other posts as well: he was one of the supervisors of finances;[292] one of the three officials in charge of the University of Padua;[293] deputy public prosecutor (*vice avogador di comun*);[294] member of the *collegio delle acque*, the board that planned and supervised Venice's perennial war against the sea;[295] and supervisor of artillery supplies and distribution.[296] Nor was the diplomatic ability he had shown at the imperial and papal courts forgotten by his peers. When Charles V passed through Friuli in the fall of 1532, Contarini was elected to be one of the four ceremonial orators who met the emperor in the name of Venice and paid him the customary respects.[297] Likewise, following the election of Cardinal Alessandro Farnese to the papacy in the fall of 1534, Contarini was chosen as one of eight Venetian orators to congratulate the new Pope Paul III.[298]

Contarini had now risen through almost all the stages of the Venetian *cursus honorum*, and between 1530 and 1535 was part of "an elite which, in practice, held the reins of government in its hands."[299] But while it is possible to list the offices he held, it is much more diffi-

291. ASV, Segretario alle voci, Elezioni del Maggior Consiglio, Reg. 1529–40, fols. 1v–2r. The terms to which he was elected ran from 1 June 1532 to 31 May 1533, and 1 February 1535 to 31 January 1536. After he became cardinal in May 1535, and therefore could not complete his second term, a successor was chosen; see ibid., fol. 2r.

292. *Revisore delle casse*; see ASV, Consiglio dei X, Comuni, Reg. 1530, fol. 78r. Sanuto liked Contarini personally and obviously felt at ease with him (see, for example, his account of how the two of them went together in a boat to watch the palace of Giorgio Corner burn [*Diarii* 56:753]). Yet this did not prevent him from making a biting comment after Contarini and Andrea Trevisan were elected to the above positions: "They are not going to do anything, since neither of them is capable of examining accounts or books" (54:12).

293. From March 1531 until September 1533 Contarini was one of the *riformatori dello Studio di Padova*; see ASV, Senato Terra, Reg. 26 (1530–31) and 27 (1532–33), passim; Sanuto, *Diarii* 54:178.

294. Sanuto, *Diarii* 55:380.

295. Ibid., 341.

296. *Provveditore sopra le artellarie*; see ASV, Consiglio dei X, Comuni, Reg. 1533, fol. 109v. He held the office from November 1533 until 22 April 1534; see ibid., Reg. 1534, fol. 20v.

297. Contarini could not go on this mission because Marc'Antonio Contarini was ambassador to Charles V and the law forbade more than one man from any one family on the same legation; see Sanuto, *Diarii* 57:39.

298. ASV, Segretario alle voci, Elezioni dei Pregadi, Reg. 1, fol. 26v. Contarini was elected on 19 October but did not go on the embassy.

299. Gaetano Cozzi, "Authority and Law in Renaissance Venice," in Hale (ed.), *Renaissance Venice*, 298. Felix Gilbert's essay in the same volume, "Venice in the Crisis of the League of Cambrai" (reprinted in his *History: Choice and Commitment* [Cambridge: Belknap Press of Harvard University Press, 1977], 269–91), argues that the War of the League of Cambrai completed the formation of a bloc of rich nobles who held high

cult to determine his political stance, for he acted through and within committees and groups. Still, the policies with which he agreed, the measures for which he voted, and his few recorded personal statements enable us to get at least a sense of his views.

Most important is his support of the growing power of the Council of Ten in the years following the Peace of Bologna, an evolution that was to culminate in the 1570s.[300] During Contarini's first term as a member of the council, indeed while he was one of its three heads in March 1531, the Council of Ten took a remarkable step to extend its power over the Venetian noble class by passing a law that prohibited more than eight of its male members, unless related, from meeting together in a private house.[301] While the prevention of political plots was no doubt its main motive, the council acted here as a legislative body that arrogated sweeping authority to itself. It tightened its own internal discipline as well by decreeing that any member absent for three weeks or any head absent for one week would be replaced; Contarini himself had to receive permission to go to his country villa for two weeks.[302]

As a *capo*, in December 1530 Contarini supported prior censorship by the Council of Ten of letters to be shown to the Senate,[303] thus agreeing that at times the council should be a decision-making body superior to the Senate, virtually exercising the functions of a *princeps*.[304] "The Council of Ten has supreme authority among Venetians,"[305] Contarini wrote in his treatise on the Venetian government, completed during these years of his political service.[306] While affirming that "the entire task of governing the Republic belongs to the Senate,"[307] he was realistic enough to see that the Council of Ten had extended its

---

office: "The institutions of Venice were not changed by the war but in these critical years the final step was made in establishing as rulers of Venice a small, closely united group, which kept in its hands all decisions about the life of the inhabitants and the policy of the Republic" (290).

300. For the Council of Ten in this period, see the magisterial pages of Cozzi, "Authority and Law," 305–9, and especially the section entitled "Il Consiglio dei X e l'autorità suprema' (1530–83)" in his *Repubblica di Venezia e stati italiani: politica e giustizia dal secolo XVI al secolo XVIII* (Turin: Einaudi, 1982), 145–73.

301. ASV, Consiglio dei X, Comuni, Reg. 1531, fol. 13r.

302. Cozzi, "Il Consiglio dei X," in *Repubblica di Venezia*, 151; and Sanuto, *Diarii* 54:372.

303. ASV, Consiglio dei X, Secreta, Reg. 3, fols. 79r, 104v, 106r.

304. Cozzi, "Authority and the Law," 306, quoting Domenico Morosini.

305. "De magistratibus et republica Venetorum," in *Opera*, 295.

306. Felix Gilbert, "The Date of the Composition of Contarini's and Giannotti's Books on Venice," *Studies in the Renaissance* 14 (1967): 172–84.

307. "De magistratibus et republica Venetorum," in *Opera*, 292.

authority in recent years, a development for which he, too, was partly responsible. During his first term as a member the council decreed that it would resume its authority over the elections of the *savii alle acque* after having delegated it to the Senate sixteen years earlier. Thus it reasserted control over a most important magistracy, of which Contarini was a member in 1532, a magistracy empowered to issue broad regulations to protect the city against the ever-encroaching water. Soon the council added another key office to its competence by taking over the elections of the magistrates in charge of grain supplies.[308] Also while Contarini was one of its *capi* the council tangled with the *Quarantia criminal,* a law court that sought to reclaim from the Ten its traditional prerogative concerning appointments to lesser bureaucratic posts, something akin to what we should now call patronage. From this controversy it became clear that the Council of Ten aspired to control of the entire bureaucracy.[309]

Contarini's support for the council's growing power meant that despite his description of the Senate as the heart of Venetian government he actually endorsed a strict hierarchy that confined supreme executive authority to a small elite of thirty-two men: the Council of Ten, its advisory board (*zonta*) of fifteen, the doge, and his six councillors. Contarini's stand shows that he prized efficiency and order in the day-to-day workings of the government and did not fear that the Council of Ten might become tyrannical. In practice, therefore, he supported a ruling group of thirty-two at the expense of the two hundred and more senators, and therefore a marked tilt in the constitutional balance.

The theoretical picture of a static harmony between the Senate and the Council of Ten that he painted in his treatise must be set alongside the much more dynamic conception he actually held—and put into practice—as a member of the inner circle of Venetian statesmen. A significant example of his real view occurred in December 1533 when the council, with Contarini as one of its heads, declared that only it, in association with its *zonta,* could interpret, alter, or grant exemptions from its own laws. The reason was clearly stated: "to prevent problems that ensue as a result of interpretations of the laws of this council, so that no oversubtle ingenuity will find new forms or means to break

---

308. On the election of three *savii sopra le ague,* see Cozzi, "Il Consiglio dei X," in *Repubblica di Venezia,* 150; and ASV, Consiglio dei X, Comuni, Reg. 1530, fols. 108v–109v.

309. Cozzi, "Il Consiglio dei X," in *Repubblica di Venezia,* 151.

these laws in indirect ways."[310] Similarly, the Ten set themselves above the *avogadori di comun*, the public prosecutors and attorneys, by forbidding them under any circumstances to propose measures to the *Quarantia criminal* for remitting or abbreviating sentences of banishment.[311] Further examples were the council's creation of new magistracies in 1537 and 1539, as well as the conclusion of a peace with the Turks in 1540 following secret negotiations of which the Senate was not informed.[312] Although these measures date from the time after Contarini became a cardinal, nevertheless, the evidence suggests that had he continued to exercise his political offices he would have approved these developments.

His years as a member of the Venetian ruling elite exposed Contarini to a wide variety of issues and problems. In dealing with them daily he not only gained insight into almost all aspects of the government, but he also gathered formidable political experience. As one examines the routine business of the Council of Ten during Contarini's years in its service, one notices the large number of letters directed to Venetian rectors and *podestà* in the mainland cities. The majority deal with economic matters, commerce, and directives to Venetian officials; others deal with benefices, individual petitions, or licenses and permits of all sorts, ranging from permission to cut wood in certain forests to granting Pietro Bembo access to official documents in order to prepare for his task as official historiographer of the Republic.[313] Contarini came into contact with criminal cases of the most varied kind, involving murder, violence, rape, peculation, theft, counterfeiting, and bearing concealed arms.[314] He had to deal with regulating confraternities and, more important, the problems of convents, where disorders repeatedly occurred. As a head of the Ten in December 1530 he

310. ASV, Consiglio dei X, Comuni, Reg. 1533, fol. 135r: "Inconvenienti che seguono in le interpretacione de le parte prese per questo cons.o che per sotilitia de inzegni non vengino ritrovate nove forme, et modi per vie indirette de contravenire a ditte parte."

311. ASV, Consiglio dei X, Comuni, Reg. 1553, fol. 143v. See also Cozzi, "Authority and Law," 306–9, for a discussion of the conflicts between the Council of Ten and the Avogaria di Comun.

312. Cozzi, "Authority and Law," 153, 155.

313. ASV, Capi del Consiglio dei X, Lettere, Filza 30, includes a large number of letters on these subjects. The grant of access for Bembo is dated 18 December 1530, a month when Contarini was one of the heads. On Bembo as historian of Venice, see Franco Gaeta, "Storiografia, coscienza nazionale e politica culturale nella Venezia del Rinascimento," in Arnaldi and Stocchi (eds.), *Storia della cultura veneta* 3(1):85ff.

314. Contarini's two terms on the Council of Ten are within the time frame of the cases in ASV, Consiglio dei X, Criminali, Reg. 4.

supported the election of three nobles to supervise convents and assure their good order.[315] Ironically, one of the chief troublemakers in the convent of Corpus Domini was a sister Felicita Contarini, and Contarini himself with two other officials was sent to investigate her convent in February 1533.[316] They apparently did not succeed in settling the controversies, for Sister Felicita and her convent continue to appear in the documents of the Council of Ten for the remainder of that year and into the next,[317] providing a vivid illustration of the difficulties that faced officials trying to regulate religious houses, or control their own refractory relatives.

Another recurring problem confronting the Council of Ten was how to ensure adequate supplies of wheat in Venetian territories. Contarini participated in the efforts to prevent speculation and hoarding and in the many attempts to supervise the grain trade. His name appears, for example, as a head of the council in a letter to the *podestà* of Verona, ordering that anyone caught exporting wheat from the Venetian state should be hanged.[318] Since shortages of grain could lead to popular unrest, the Council of Ten closely monitored the commodity's supply and distribution in the interests of maintaining good order, and its documents show the great importance attached to this matter.

These same documents also now and then give us a glimpse of seemingly trivial incidents that nevertheless could have serious consequences for Venice. One such incident occurred in December 1530, when it came to the council's attention that a certain Florentine merchant, one Francesco Corboli, had made a bet that Charles V would

---

315. ASV, Consiglio dei X, Comuni, Reg. 1530, fols. 82v–83r. This measure was reiterated in 1533; see ibid., Reg. 1533, fols. 116v–117r, again during a month when Contarini was one of the heads. For conditions in convents of nuns during the earlier decades of the sixteenth century, see Pio Paschini, "I monasteri femminili in Italia nel Cinquecento," in *Problemi di vita religiosa in Italia nel Cinquecento*, 42–60; Gabriella Zarri, "Monasteri femminili e città (secoli XV–XVIII)," in *Storia d'Italia, Annali 9: La chiesa e il potere politico dal medioevo all'età contemporanea*, ed. Giorgio Chittolini and Giovanni Miccoli (Turin: Einaudi, 1986), 357–429. Innocenzo Giuliani, "Genesi e primo secolo di vita del Magistrato sopra monasteri (Venezia, 1519–1620)," *Venezie francescane* 28 (1961): 42–68, 106–69, thinks that the committee of three to supervise convents became a permanent magistracy already in 1528.

316. Sanuto, *Diarii* 57:494.

317. ASV, Consiglio dei X, Secreta, Reg. 4, fols. 22r, 25v–26r, 27r, 29v, 49r.

318. This letter reaffirmed a law of the Council of Ten of 18 July 1501; see ASV, Consiglio dei X, Comuni, Reg. 1534, fol. 6r–v. In the same source there is frequent mention of the wheat supply and related matters while Contarini was on the council; ibid., Reg. 1530 and 1533. For wheat prices, see Gigi Corazzol, *Fitti e livelli di grano: un'aspetto del credito rurale nel Veneto del '500* (Milan: Franco Angeli, 1980).

not be alive one year hence. The emperor's ambassador to Venice was furious and insisted on speaking to the doge. Contarini's diplomatic skill was called upon to soothe the ambassador. The Venetian government was anxious to preserve good relations with Charles V and certainly did not want to seem to condone conspiracies against his life. Even though it turned out that Corboli was merely betting with another Florentine according to their habit and that the matter had no political implications, Corboli was apprehended and had to post high bail. The Venetian ambassador to the Spanish court was instructed to explain the whole affair to the emperor in order to clear the Republic of any suspicion of harboring his enemies.[319]

On certain issues the records enable us to see clearly Contarini's personal position. He was, for instance, consistent in advocating a cautious and moderate attitude toward the Turks, giving them no grounds for complaint against Venice[320] but also careful not to bend too far in their direction.[321] Similarly, his experience of European rulers had made him chary of Venetian involvement in their affairs or plans. He steadily advocated peace as a necessity for Venice, and in 1533 he strenuously opposed a possible new league for the defense of Italy; he made "a wise speech that changed [the minds of] many senators," according to Sanuto, whereas his opponent Sebastiano Giustiniani "spoke badly."[322]

The conception of peace as an absolute good was the cornerstone of Contarini's generally dovish position in foreign policy. At the same time, he never favored surrendering what he considered legitimate Venetian rights for the sake of peace, as can be seen from the stand he took on matters involving the relations of Venice with the papacy. His branch of the Contarini did not belong to the *papalisti*, the families who because their members held important ecclesiastical benefices supported policies favorable to the Roman court. He was not programmatically either pro-papal or anti-papal but sought to judge issues on their merits. At the very beginning of his term as *savio del consiglio*, in

319. Sanuto, *Diarii* 54:183, 184; ASV, Consiglio dei X, Secreta, Reg. 3, fols. 81r–v, 82r.

320. While Contarini was a head of the Council of Ten, in March 1531, instructions were issued that in Venetian territories the pope's orders to bishops and heads of orders to preach against the Turks should not be carried out; ASV, Consiglio dei X, Secreta, Reg. 3, fol. 86r–v. Contarini agreed to the sending of presents to the Turkish governor of Bosnia in order to keep the Turks on the borders of Dalmatia well disposed toward Venice: ibid., fols. 75v–76r.

321. Sanuto, *Diarii* 53:150, 159; 55:373; 56:667.

322. Ibid., 57:430.

April 1530, he crossed swords with the consistently anti-papal Alvise Mocenigo over Pope Clement VII's right to make appointments to benefices in Venetian territory. At issue was Clement VII's appointment of an admittedly good prelate from a Venetian family, Jacomo Coco, to the bishopric of Corfu. When Mocenigo objected, Contarini replied that Venice should not irritate the pope, whom he had persuaded not to insert a clause insisting formally on his rights of appointment by the assurance that the Signoria would take account of the pope's wishes. This provoked an outburst from Mocenigo, who maintained that Contarini had no right to promise anything and turned on him with the sarcastic question, "Messer Gasparo, perhaps you would like to be pope and nobleman, like Pope Clement?"[323] To Mocenigo a jurisdictional principle was involved, whereas Contarini in this case was primarily the practical diplomat interested in good relations with the pope and willing to compromise in a matter where a suitable Venetian had been appointed and Venice stood to lose nothing by acceding to the pope's choice.

In instances involving significant change in the relations between church and state, however, Contarini was not at all willing to compromise. In October 1530, for example, when he was one of its heads, the Council of Ten had to deal with a jurisdictional issue involving the patriarch of Venice, Girolamo Querini. The latter had obtained a papal brief excommunicating members of the clergy who appealed to the government to support the old custom of election of parish priests. The Council of Ten instructed Venice's ambassador in Rome, Antonio Soriano, to explain carefully the Venetian custom to the pope and to obtain a revocation of the papal brief.[324] Simultaneously, Contarini was deputed together with a colleague to speak with the patriarch, who proved adamant.[325] Contarini was equally so, presenting the views of the Venetian government. On this occasion Clement VII did issue a bull recognizing the Venetian system of election of the parish clergy, as the government had requested. But in June 1531, again at a time when Contarini was a head of the Council of Ten, the patriarch refused to recognize the election of the prior of the hospital of San Lorenzo,

323. Ibid., 53:125–26. For Coco's career, see Anna Foa, *DBI* 22:537–39; Giuseppe Alberigo, *I vescovi italiani al Concilio di Trento (1545–1547)* (Florence: Sansoni, 1959), 54–56, 71–72, 351–52, 438.

324. ASV, Consiglio dei X, Secreta, Reg. 3, fols. 73v–74r, 83v–84v. See also the brief summary of the issues in Prodi, "Structure and Organization," 419–20, and pertinent bibliography in 428nn.59, 62.

325. Sanuto, *Diarii* 54:36.

appointing his own man instead. This time the council firmly ordered the patriarch's appointee to renounce his post immediately and instructed the Venetian ambassador to report events to the pope. Furthermore, all priorates of hospitals were declared to be lay matters, and on 10 June the Council of Ten confirmed that no one might accept appointment to a Venetian church unless elected by its chapter, specifically referring to the papal bull approving this practice.[326] In this dispute over jurisdictional rights attached to the Venetian church Contarini unequivocally supported the government's defense of tradition against the encroachments of the patriarch.

But he never espoused the position of those who championed Venetian jurisdictional rights at all costs, as can be seen in the 1534 Senate debate concerning a forced loan from the clergy. Sebastiano Foscarini argued that imposing such a burden without any consultation was entirely within the sphere of the state's jurisdiction. His supporters in the Senate agreed that the pope need not be consulted, since he was to be obeyed only "in materia fidei et sacramentorum." Girolamo Aleandro, the papal nuncio in Venice, ascribed to Contarini's influence the eventual decision to petition the pope first.[327] Here again Contarini's diplomatic skills were brought into play to make the loan, which was inevitable anyway, more acceptable to the touchy Clement VII by not seeming to slight his authority. Contarini had a clear sense of when to take a stand and when to compromise, as well as a grasp of what each issue involved for the Venetian government. He was fair-minded and moderate, intent whenever possible on securing peace.

Different kinds of issues confronted Contarini in yet another of his offices, as one of the three *riformatori dello studio di Padova*. In this office, which he held from early 1531 to September 1533, he shared responsibility for the supervision and regulation of the only university in Venetian territory.[328] He participated in numerous decisions regarding

---

326. ASV, Consiglio dei X, Secreta, Reg. 3, fol. 89r–v.

327. Franco Gaeta, ed., *Nunziature di Venezia*, vol. 1: *12 marzo 1533–14 agosto 1535* (Rome: Istituto Storico per l'Età Moderna e Contemporanea, 1958), 210 (letter 77). Contarini was on the Council of Ten at the time of this dispute.

328. See Desroussilles, "L'Università di Padova," 634–39, for a succinct account of the role played by the *riformatori* in university affairs during the 1530s. His statement that after 1519 "no trace of new elections [of the *riformatori*] can be found until 1532" (634–35) should be corrected. Contarini was elected on 15 December 1530, together with Marino Zorzi; see Sanuto, *Diarii* 54:178. From this entry it is clear that there had been a previous election and that the terms of two members of the committee were completed: "Fu fatto scrutinio di do Riformatori dil Studio di Padoa, in luogo di sier Sebastian Foscarini el dottor et sier Lorenzo Bragadin, hanno compido li soi anni." The third

faculty appointments and salaries, which showed a remarkable range from a low of fifty florins a year to a high of one thousand florins for the illustrious law professor Mariano Sozzini, whom the *riformatori* were anxious to keep at Padua.[329] In general they were working toward reestablishing good order at the university, where enrollment had declined because of the wars in the second and third decades of the sixteenth century.[330] Restoration of order involved curbing violence among students, an issue of particular concern to the Council of Ten, and a prohibition against carrying arms, which the *podestà* at Padua was expected to enforce. Rowdiness could be a prelude to sedition, and the Ten were determined to nip such displays in the bud. Thus they handed down a sentence of five years' banishment to Capodistria for a student from Vicenza who had publicly deplored that "so many noble gentlemen of Padua, Vicenza, and Treviso are subject to these [Venetian] boatmen."[331] Contarini favored tightening discipline regarding student dress, behavior, and institutional organization, as seen in the revision of the statutes first of the arts faculty and later of the law faculty, which came before the *riformatori* in 1531 and 1532, respectively.[332] During these years the Council of Ten strengthened its authority over the university, but the government remained careful not to alienate the students from other parts of Europe and continued to listen to their concerns and complaints.[333] Contarini's combination of diplomatic ability and concern for Venetian institutions stood him in good stead while he was one of the *riformatori*.

He certainly was not a programmatic conservative who unquestioningly supported whatever already existed. At times he was willing to bend the law, as in the case of one Angelo Gabriel, elected as an *avogador di comun* but unable to take up the office because of illness. Contarini joined several senators in moving that the position be reserved for Gabriel notwithstanding laws of 1471 and 1481 prohibiting that

---

member, whose term had not yet expired, was Marco Minio. Contarini's name appears for the first time as a *riformatore dello Studio di Padova* on 3 May 1531 in ASV, Senato Terra, Reg. 26, fol. 109v. Desroussille's erroneous citation to Sanuto at 635n.249 should also be corrected. It refers to an entry of 29 September 1530 in "vol. XLIX, col. 577," whereas that volume goes only from 1 October 1528 to 28 February 1529.

329. ASV, Senato Terra, Reg. 26, fol. 110.

330. For figures see Desroussilles, "L'Università di Padova," 631.

331. Ibid., 637.

332. ASV, Senato Terra, Reg. 26, fols. 195r, 223r; Sanuto, *Diarii* 55:106, 433–34.

333. For example, when French students complained that the Piedmontese had preempted their nation (or organization), the two groups were separated: ASV, Senato Terra, Reg. 26, fol. 110r.

practice. However, Zuan Francesco Mocenigo, one of the avogadori and a strict constructionist, demanded that the text of the old laws be read, and the vote in the Great Council went overwhelmingly against the motion Contarini had supported.[334] In this instance he ranged himself with those taking the liberal view, being willing to adapt the law to circumstances. In other instances, though, he espoused a conservative position. While a ducal councillor, for example, he supported a long motion requiring strict and harsh punishment for theft or misuse of public money. Sanuto, among others, spoke against the motion, although he admired Contarini. When the motion did not come to a vote but was sent back to committee for further study, Sanuto expressed great personal satisfaction.[335]

A little vignette recounted by Sanuto aptly summarizes Contarini's conception of a Venetian noble's obligations in the political service of the state. After a night and morning of continuous snowfall, only three ducal councillors appeared for a scheduled meeting; one of them was Contarini.[336] Undaunted by the unusual weather that kept even the doge away, Contarini put his duties first with the sort of devotion ideally expected of his class. His career from 1530 to 1535 was that of a securely established member of the governing elite, who dealt confidently with the many and varied issues that came before the councils and committees on which he sat. He had sought public office avidly and was an ambitious man who regarded such service an honor for himself and his family. His brothers supported his efforts from the time he first tried to win a post, and they continued their financial subsidies through two costly embassies. Several eventually held government offices themselves,[337] as did his brothers-in-law Matteo Dandolo and Matteo Vitturi.

Contarini was above all a pragmatic politician whose aim was to resolve conflict, keep peace, and contribute to the proper functioning of the form of government he considered best: that of a well-run republic. His admiration for Venice was genuine. Not only his treatise

---

334. Sanuto, *Diarii* 57:411.

335. Sanuto took the whole matter much to heart, considering the motion too sweeping and himself as defender of his class. When the motion was not voted on he wrote, "Et fo grandissimo honor mio" (ibid., 395).

336. Ibid., 301.

337. Notably his younger brother Tommaso, who had a long and distinguished government career; see Derosas, "Contarini, Tommaso," in *DBI* 28:300–5. See also ASV, Segretario alle voci, Elezioni del Maggior Consiglio, Reg. 1529–40, fols. 17v, 18r, 21v, 22r–v, 23r, 24v, 25r, 58v, 59r, for offices held by his brothers Vincenzo and Federigo.

on the state but also his private letters and dispatches show the depth of his devotion to the state. But he was also a realistic observer of European politics on whom the "lesson of events" was not lost. By the time of the peace negotiations at Bologna he knew how little scope for maneuver Venice had in actuality, and he adapted himself to the changed circumstances. His vast experience of day-to-day government affairs in the years following, his understanding of the internal and external problems Venice faced, and his ability to deal with men all made him a seasoned statesman.

When the news of his appointment to the college of cardinals reached Venice on a Sunday in May 1535, he was standing by the ballot box in the hall of the Great Council. Even amid the commotion and excitement that followed, Alvise Mocenigo, who had so often opposed Contarini, was heard to call loudly from his seat, which he could not easily leave because of his gout: "These priests have robbed us of the foremost gentleman our city has."[338] Friends and opponents alike knew that it was no inexperienced outsider who now entered the court of Rome, but a highly finished diplomat, a statesman, and above all, a Venetian gentleman.

338. Beccadelli, "Vita," 21.

CHAPTER TWO

Concepts of Order
in Church and State

Philosophical Foundations

The first edition of Contarini's works appeared in 1571 in Paris; it was seen through the press by his nephew Alvise and dedicated to Cardinal Alessandro Farnese, who had first known Contarini thirty-six years before. Alvise Contarini divided his uncle's career into three stages. He thought of the first as having been devoted to the study of philosophy, the second to the service of the Venetian state, and the last to the service of the church. Accordingly he divided the works into three parts by grouping them as philosophical, political, and theological writings.[1] While Alvise implied a progression on Contarini's part from philosophy to theology, the actual picture is less schematic. Contarini's most important philosophical works were written during the period of service to Venice, as were two of his theological treatises, while a third belongs to the period before he entered political life.[2] Philosophy remained his favorite field of study, and on

---

1. *Gasparis Contareni Cardinalis Opera* (Paris, 1571). Alvise Contarini's dedication is on the first unnumbered page. For the background and printing history of this edition, see Gigliola Fragnito, "Aspetti della censura ecclesiastica nell'Europa della Controriforma: l'edizione parigina delle opere di Gasparo Contarini," *Rivista di storia e letteratura religiosa* 21 (1985): 3–48.

2. The *Compendium primae philosophiae* was written between 1522 and 1526, during Contarini's embassy to Charles V, and then corrected and revised in 1526–27. *De elementis et eorum mixtionibus libri V* was written between 1530 and 1535, while

several occasions he expressed regret that the pressure of affairs left him little time for its pursuit. During his seven years as cardinal he took a stand on many disputed questions dealing for the most part with theology. But whatever the topic, all his works bear a strong family resemblance since they proceed from the same presuppositions.

Several modern studies have been devoted to Contarini's theological writings,[3] chiefly because of the interest inhering in his role at the colloquy at Regensburg in 1541. His political thought has not fared so well, and less attention still has been given to his philosophical works, on which we have but a single thirty-year-old article and no book-length study.[4] Although the philosophical writings are technical and for the most part derivative, they are an invaluable key to understanding the structure of Contarini's thought on politics and religion. This thesis was argued persuasively more than twenty years ago, yet there has been no further progress in the systematic study of Contarini's philosophy.[5]

His literary activity began in 1517 with two tracts. One dealt with the duties of a bishop, while the other was written in answer to the famous *On the Immortality of the Soul* by his teacher Pietro Pomponazzi, who sent his treatise to Contarini shortly after its publication in Bologna in November 1516. Contarini's reply was his only work published during his lifetime.[6] Pomponazzi answered with an *Apologia* in February 1518, to which Contarini in turn made a response that was

---

Contarini was actively serving the Venetian government. To the same period belong his *Confutatio articulorum seu quaestionum Lutheranorum* and *De potestate pontificis quod divinitus sit tradita*, while *De officio episcopi* goes back to 1517.

3. The most useful are Fragnito, "Cultura umanistica," 75–189; Hanns Rückert, *Die theologische Entwicklung Gasparo Contarinis*, Arbeiten zur Kirchengeschichte (Bonn: A. Marcus & E. Weber, 1926); Mackensen, "Contarini's Theological Role at Ratisbon"; Hubert Jedin, *Kardinal Contarini als Kontroverstheologe* (Münster i.W.: Aschendorff, 1949), 5–18; Friedrich Hünermann, Introduction to Gasparo Contarini, *Gegenreformatorische Schriften (1530c.–1542)* (Münster i.W.: Aschendorff, 1923), xi–xxiv; idem, "Die Rechtfertigungslehre des Kardinals Gasparo Contarini," *Theologische Quartalschrift* 102 (1921): 1–22; Aldo Stella, "Spunti di teologia contariniana e lineamenti di un itinerario religioso," in Cavazzana Romanelli (ed.), *Gaspare Contarini e il suo tempo*, 147–66.

4. Carlo Giacon, "L'aristotelismo avicennistico di Gasparo Contarini," *Atti del XII Congresso internazionale di filosofia*, vol. 9 (Florence: Sansoni, 1960), 109–19.

5. Gilbert, "Religion and Politics," 102, rightly thought that Contarini's works of the decade 1516–26, especially those dealing with philosophy, "represent the application of the same general system of thought to different aspects of life and nature" and thus cannot be viewed in isolation from his later writings.

6. *Opera*, 179–209. Originally it was entitled *Tractatus contradictoris* and published in part by Pietro Pomponazzi together with his own *Apologia* (Bologna, 1518), then in complete form following the text of the *Apologia* (Venice, 1525). Eventually it became Book I of Contarini's *De immortalitate animae*. Fragnito, "Cultura umanistica,"

printed only much later as Book II of his own *De immortalitate animae*.[7] This exchange between the noted philosopher,[8] certainly the most original mind with which Contarini came in contact during his years at Padua, and his former student belongs to the vehement debate about two topics of the late fifteenth and early sixteenth centuries, both discussed in the third book of Aristotle's *De anima*: the unity of the intellect and the immortality of the soul. A thinker was considered an Averroist, a Thomist, or an Alexandrist depending on the position he took as to whether the human intellect (*intellectus possibilis*), common to all men, retained an identity after death or became united with a higher active intellect (*intellectus agens*). If the former, did it continue to exist in union with the mental faculties of the individual, or did it attain its end in the Thomistic *visio beatifica*? Further, was there such a close union of the soul and the body that the soul could not be conceived of as immaterial or separable from the body—in short, that it was incapable of immortality? These questions and related controversies with long historical antecedents became especially acute in Padua during the later fifteenth century as a result of increasing acquaintance with the works of Greek and Roman philosophers. One of Pomponazzi's teachers, Nicoletto Vernia, was himself deeply involved in the arguments for and against the immortality of the soul, and brought to his students' attention such lesser-known Greek commentators as Themistius and Simplicius, on whom he drew in his own writings, thus widening the scope of the debate.[9] That the extent and

---

176n.375, argues for a date between July and November 1517. See Etienne Gilson, Appendix 1 to "L'affaire de l'immortalité de l'âme à Venise au début du XVIᵉ siècle," in Branca (ed.), *Umanesimo europeo e umanesimo veneziano*, 31–136; and idem, "Autour de Pomponazzi: problématique de l'immortalité de l'âme en Italie au début du XVIᵉ siècle," *Archives d'histoire doctrinale et littéraire du moyen âge* 28 (1961): 163–279.

7. *Opera*, 210–31.

8. The bibliography on Pomponazzi is extensive. Among the most pertinent works in the present connection are Paul Oskar Kristeller, *Eight Philosophers of the Italian Renaissance* (Stanford: Stanford University Press, 1964), chap. 5; Bruno Nardi, *Studi su Pietro Pomponazzi* (Florence: F. Le Monnier, 1965); John H. Randall, *The School of Padua and the Emergence of Modern Science* (Padua: Antenore, 1961), 69–115; idem, "The Development of Scientific Method in the School of Padua," *Journal of the History of Ideas* 1 (1940): 177–206; Antonino Poppi, *Saggi sul pensiero inedito di Pietro Pomponazzi* (Padua: Antenore, 1970); Cesare Oliva, "Note sull'insegnamento di Pietro Pomponazzi," *Giornale critico della filosofia italiana* 7 (1926): 83–103, 179–90, 254–75; and Erich Weil, "Die Philosophie des Pietro Pomponazzi," *Archiv für Geschichte der Philosophie* 41 (1932): 127–76.

9. Edward P. Mahoney, "Nicoletto Vernia on the Soul and Immortality," in *Philosophy and Humanism: Renaissance Essays in Honor of Paul Oskar Kristeller*, ed. Edward P. Mahoney (New York: Columbia University Press, 1976), 144–45.

ramifications of the dispute caused concern to the ecclesiastical authorities can be seen from a decree of 1489 by Pietro Barozzi, bishop of
Padua, forbidding public discussion of the unity of the intellect as
interpreted by Averroës.[10]

During the period when Contarini was a student, Pomponazzi was
working out the ideas he expressed more fully in his later writings. He
came increasingly to assent to the mortality of the individual soul as
held by Alexander of Aphrodisias,[11] and to see man as an integral whole
comprising a body and a not entirely immaterial soul. Man was therefore a creature of this world, whose happiness could not be attained
after death through the gratification of one element of his nature
only.[12] Pomponazzi contended that virtue was an end in itself, quite
apart from the conventional notions of reward and punishment after
death. Thus he adopted essentially Stoic principles. When Contarini
first knew Pomponazzi the latter had not yet openly expressed these
ideas but was moving toward them.[13] Pomponazzi also advocated
the separation of both science and philosophy from theology on the
ground that the former two depended on reason, the latter on will—
a position that "is widely, and somewhat crudely, referred to as the
theory of the double truth."[14] Actually, Pomponazzi never taught
this doctrine in the exaggerated form in which it is sometimes presented. Contarini accepted his master's view that a truth in the realm
of faith, though it may not be susceptible of rational proof, is not
thereby cast into doubt. [15]

The existence of a bond between master and pupil is already attested by Pomponazzi's dedicating a philosophical tract to Contarini in
1515, and by Contarini's signing a notarial document on behalf of

10. Ibid., 149.

11. Paul Oskar Kristeller, "Two Unpublished Questions on the Soul of Pietro Pomponazzi," *Medievalia et humanistica* 9 (1955): 83.

12. Weil, "Philosophie des Pietro Pomponazzi," 138–39. See especially chap. 9 of
Pomponazzi, *On the Immortality of the Soul*, in *The Renaissance Philosophy of Man*, ed.
Ernst Cassirer and John Herman Randall, Jr. (Chicago: University of Chicago Press,
1948), 313–30.

13. From lecture notes of a student in 1504 it is possible to see how Pomponazzi's
ideas then differed from his more mature conceptions, and to get an idea of the Pomponazzi who taught Contarini; see Paul Oskar Kristeller, "A New Manuscript Source for
Pomponazzi's Theory of the Soul from His Paduan Period," *Revue internationale de
philosophie* 5 (1951): 144–57.

14. Kristeller, *Eight Philosophers*, 84.

15. But see M. Pine, "Pomponazzi and the Problem of 'Double Truth,'" *Journal of
the History of Ideas* 29 (1968): 174–76, for the view that Pomponazzi ultimately came
down on the side of the superiority of reason over revelation.

Pomponazzi in 1516.[16] This teacher who deeply influenced Contarini was a complex, undogmatic person, unconcerned with clinging to a given philosophical position or any one school. He is credited with maintaining that "in philosophy, one must be a heretic,"[17] in the sense of having confidence in one's own intellectual powers, and he ultimately entertained a very exalted view of man's reasoning abilities.[18] Even when Contarini disagreed with Pomponazzi, he spoke of him with a respect and reverence that go far beyond what was required by convention. Contarini's own undogmatic, open attitude toward questions of philosophy carried over to theology and was probably fostered by his contact with his teacher. Though Contarini thought primarily in Aristotelian terms, he felt free to range eclectically. Indeed, one of the most attractive qualities of his philosophical and theological writings is their frequently provisional nature and openness to reconsideration. He was often quite literally thinking as he wrote, so that his writings show a freshness but also a lack of stylistic finish.

Contarini's *De immortalitate animae* is a case in point. A commentary on Pomponazzi's treatise, neither revised nor polished, it was not intended for publication. In the first part Contarini musters proofs for the immortality of the individual soul, refutes Pomponazzi's arguments in favor of the opposite view, and adduces reasons for believing that Aristotle considered the soul immortal. Book II further explains many of the points made in the first part, to which it is really a more vigorous supplement. That Pomponazzi took Contarini's views seriously can be seen from the fact that he replied to only two of his many critics, Contarini and the Dominican Agostino Nifo. While Contarini's piece primarily illustrates contemporary reaction to Pomponazzi's ideas, it also reveals a good deal about Contarini's own attitudes and ways of thinking.

Contarini approached the problem of the soul's immortality neither as an abstract philosophical question nor as a dogma of the church, but above all as an issue with profound implications for personal ethics.

16. The tract was *De reactione*; see Oliva, "Note," 266. For the document, see Nardi, *Studi su Pietro Pomponazzi*, 229.

17. Oliva, "Note," 275.

18. John H. Randall characterizes "the Paduan doctrine of man" thus: "The Paduans were not merely secularists, they believed in a rational science attainable by the human mind. In the act of knowing, man seemed to them to lift himself above the limitations of an animal body and to see What Is with a transparency and clarity that no merely biological creature has any right to possess" ("Paduan Aristotelianism Reconsidered," in Mahoney (ed.), *Philosophy and Humanism*, 277.

Because he thought that one's way of life and the choices one made depended directly on the position one took regarding the soul's immortality, he spent years examining the matter.[19] As a student he initially agreed neither with Averroës nor with Aristotle on this topic, but preferred Alexander of Aphrodisias to both, following the lead of his teacher. Even before 1516, however, he changed his mind and came to espouse a position similar to that of Avicenna, holding that the incorruptible possible intellect specific to each person survives death, while the active intellect is distinct and single.[20] Contarini's main argument against Pomponazzi is that individual immortality is capable of rational proof because it can be shown that the soul is immaterial.[21] He disagrees strongly with Pomponazzi's psychology and epistemology according to which the soul cannot perceive, think, or will without the body and therefore is incapable of existing wholly apart from it or surviving physical death intact because it is partly mortal and partly immortal.[22] Contarini sets out to demonstrate the immortality of the soul through reason alone, adducing a series of propositions which culminate in the argument that Pomponazzi's dictum "intelligere non est sine phantasia" is mistaken since concepts are in fact grasped without images, and that only the immaterial part of man can understand abstract ideas that do not depend on sense impressions. He goes on to argue that reason does not suffice to illuminate the status of the soul after death: faith alone can do that.[23] Contarini's arguments were ostensibly based on reason alone. Yet as he came to see that reason alone could not guarantee the only conclusion acceptable to him—that the soul was truly immortal—he casually called in the fundamentally different authority of faith. He liked to philosophize, but he was not a philosopher.

Another issue on which Contarini differed from Pomponazzi was the relation between faith and reason. Unlike his teacher, Contarini was at pains to insist that there was harmony between what man knew

19. *Opera*, 179, 192. In 1513 the Fifth Lateran Council proclaimed the immortality of the soul a dogma; see Johannes Dominicus Mansi, *Sacrorum Conciliorum nova et amplissima collectio*, ed. J. B. Martin and L. Petit (Paris: Welter, 1899–1927), 32:842.

20. *Opera*, 204; Giacon, "L'aristotelismo avicennistico," 116–19.

21. *Opera*, 198.

22. For a descriptive summary of each man's central arguments, see Giovanni Di Napoli, *L'immortalità dell'anima nel Rinascimento* (Turin: Società Editrice Internazionale, 1963), 277–97. There is, however, no analysis of the issues.

23. *Opera*, 192.

from "the light of natural reason" and through faith, because both were ways toward one truth.[24] He thought they should not be kept separate, since reason acted as a check on speculation while faith gave answers unattainable through reason.[25]

What emerges from the exchange between Contarini and Pomponazzi is a picture of the young Venetian patrician that supplements the evidence for his attractive character drawn from other sources. He was open-minded and flexible enough to change his views on issues of crucial importance to himself and did not mind admitting his own uncertainties,[26] yet possessed enough independence to disagree with a major philosophical thinker of his time. In his arguments he was careful, dispassionate, and professional, stating repeatedly that he had no intention of merely quoting authorities, since he sought to rely on reason alone.[27] That he held man's rationality in high esteem appears also from other works he wrote in different contexts, most notably the *Confutatio articulorum seu quaestionum Lutheranorum*. Believing firmly that human beings were amenable to persuasion by means of clear logical arguments, he saw man very much as St. Thomas Aquinas had, as a creature whose well-ordered faculties, properly exercised, enable him to rise to great heights of understanding through the use of his intellect and his will. Although Contarini drew on St. Thomas, as did Pomponazzi, he did not simply recapitulate Thomistic arguments but turned also to other philosophers for aid in formulating his own ideas.[28] In theology Contarini followed St. Thomas to a considerable extent, yet in philosophy he was quite eclectic, working out from an Aristotelian foundation but showing familiarity with Plato and Neoplatonic thought as well.

Contarini's treatises on the immortality of the soul, besides revealing some of his basic attitudes, make clear that he was learned and

24. Ibid., 229.   25. Ibid., 157.

26. Ibid., 180. See the perceptive remarks about the exchange by Ross, "Contarini and His Friends," 227.

27. Ross, "Contarini and His Friends," 181, 212, for example. Beccadelli, "Vita," 41, stresses Contarini's dislike of simply quoting authorities in arguments: "He [Contarini] used to say that studying the theories advanced by others meant understanding the reasons that made them hold them, and that basing oneself only on authorities was not knowing but believing." Beccadelli also underlines Contarini's common sense: "Because he had good judgment, he always accepted the real senses [of philosophical writings]."

28. For example, Contarini had recourse to the epistemology of Albert the Great; see *GC*, 224.

sensible but unoriginal in philosophy.[29] Although he had confidence in his own judgment, his philosophical ideas at no point broke new ground. Arguably it is precisely because of this basic unoriginality, his conservative bent and balanced personality, that he belonged to the mainstream of the Venetian ruling class. He was well attuned to the conservative categories of thought he encountered in the circles in which he was reared, and also of the church in which he had grown up. The absence of eccentricities or novel ideas characteristic of exceptional minds makes his a nondistorting mirror of the world he knew both in Venice and in Rome.

Contarini's major philosophical work, the *Compendium primae philosophiae*,[30] gives a better insight into his thought than do the treatises against Pomponazzi. Composed during the Spanish embassy, the *Compendium* was dedicated in September 1527 to his friend Giustiniani, who had requested it. Since "no subject of philosophy was treated more scantily by Aristotle" than metaphysics, according to Contarini,[31] he hoped to offer fuller discussions of certain key concepts on which others could build further. He emphasized to Giustiniani his distrust of eloquence for its own sake: "I took the work in my hands, read it again, and took care that it was copied for you with little change. In this work many who have more delicate literary tastes than I will probably reprove me for not troubling myself about any ornamentation of language or splendor of eloquence, or for using words or phrases that do not belong to the Latin language but rather seem taken from the barbarous middle ages."[32] Contarini was not troubled about such criticism; he did not want to distract the reader's attention from his meaning by employing a style that could obscure it. Here we see some of the same consistent lack of interest, not to say defensiveness, regarding

29. Gilbert, "Religion and Politics," 102, finds that "Contarini was not a thinker of great originality." This is a far more accurate assessment than the hyperbole of Giovanni Di Napoli: "Il Contarini ... è quasi ignoto come cultore di studi filosofici; il poco che egli ci ha lasciato rivela un intuito speculativo di prim'ordine, dal quale molto il pensiero cristiano avrebbe potuto ottenere, se il nobile veneziano si fosse dato agli studi ... [egli] si formò una cultura filosofica varia e mantenne una grande indipendenza di giudizio" (*Studi sul Rinascimento* [Naples: Giannini, 1973], 300). Dittrich bypasses the question of Contarini's originality by overstressing his independence as a thinker; see *GC*, 231 (contrasting Nifo, who depended on Averroës, with Contarini, who "mehr als selbstständiger Philosoph vorgegangen war") and 257: "überall tritt Contarini als selbstständiger Philosoph auf."

30. *Opera*, 93–176.   31. Ibid., 95.

32. Ibid., 94. For a similar emphasis on his disdain for eloquence, see Fragnito, "Cultura umanistica," 185; and the opening section of *De elementis*, in *Opera*, 2.

literary studies as such that made his speeches before large groups pedestrian and lackluster. For him, the *gravitas* proper to a Venetian patrician required no support from "mere" oratorical skills. At the same time, he was confident enough to use Latin as it suited him, in a lively personal manner, without allowing his style to be forced into a Ciceronian mold. The *Compendium* is written in a more relaxed, less technical manner than *De immortalitate animae*; it is easy to believe that Contarini enjoyed working on it as a change from the stream of dispatches he was obliged to send from Spain, and that the work brought back memories of his student days in Padua.

The *Compendium* is not an orderly commentary on Aristotle's *Metaphysics* but rather a sort of anthology of ideas about the main topics of that work drawn from philosophers ranging from Plotinus, St. Augustine, pseudo-Dionysius the Areopagite, St. Thomas, Avicenna, Al-Farabi, and Averroës down to Contarini's own Paduan teachers. To these Contarini adds the ideas at which he himself had arrived as a result of "constant reflection."[33] While the thought of Aristotle is basic to Contarini's treatise, he does not simply summarize it. Often he argues with its emphases or supplements it with Platonic or Neo-platonic explanations for the great questions he examines: being, the one, truth, goodness, act and potency, the first cause and the relation of all created beings to it, the heavenly bodies, and finally the realm of coming-to-be and passing-away.[34]

No surprises are in store for the reader, who will find in the *Compendium* simply the result of a reasonably solid philosophical education. Its most basic motif is Contarini's belief in the reality of a comprehensible, orderly universe. He seems to have had not even an inkling of such disquieting alternatives as those proposed by Nicholas of Cusa, a man not far removed from him in time, whose notion of an infinite universe, without a center where God is located, breaks new ground in philosophy.[35] For Contarini, all in the universe is order and hierarchy, beginning with God and the spiritual beings closest to him and descending to the lowest of the four elements, earth.[36] Contarini

33. "...Nonnullaque assidua cogitatione harum rerum mihi assequutus esse viderer, quae alios fortasse praeterissent" (*Opera*, 95).

34. *Opera*, 95–96.

35. See Pauline Moffitt Watts, *Nicolaus Cusanus: A Fifteenth-Century Vision of Man* (Leiden: E. J. Brill, 1982), 61–74.

36. See *Opera*, 170–72, for Contarini's exposition of creation arranged in hierarchical order. Felix Gilbert has rightly stressed the importance of this in Contarini's thought: "The feeling that an ordered world meant a hierarchically organized world was extremely

embraced the Neoplatonic concept of divine emanation, interpreting this to mean that the entire graduated universe derived its being from the first being.[37] Man, partly spiritual and partly material, can come close to the celestial intelligences by the use of his reason[38] and is capable of grasping that the bond moving all of creation closer to its creator is love: "Inasmuch, then, as all that exists emanates from the first being in proportion as it has being, but of itself tends toward nonbeing, it is clear that if anything that exists is to be as perfect as its own capacity permits, there must be a force implanted in it by nature by means of which it turns back again toward that being from which it derives. In this manner it describes an unbroken and perfect circle."[39] Contarini's emphasis here is on a dynamic universe suffused with desire of and love for its creator and moving toward him in harmony symbolized by the circle. He was convinced that the goodness of everything that was created is manifest to the rational faculties of man, who can understand that the primary force in creation is love, which in turn has for its object the good.[40] This love is active and outflowing, causing every being to seek to overcome impediments to its own perfection and thus "to divest itself of matter as far as possible and to realize its own form."[41]

The terminology of the *Compendium* may be that of metaphysics, but the specific accents in the treatise reflect Contarini's own deeply held views. There is a strikingly direct and down-to-earth quality about his refusal to be drawn into the debate over universals or to become sidetracked into combating radical positions. He explains his own moderate realism in a straightforward manner,[42] choosing a solution that appeals to his common sense. It is little wonder that Aquinas was particularly congenial to Contarini, who called him "that most excellent man, who can never be praised enough."[43] Contarini's views

---

strong in Contarini and permeated his entire thinking" ("Religion and Politics," 105). For a succinct discussion with an extensive bibliography of works on ideas of hierarchy and order, and the important distinction between the two, see C. A. Patrides, "Hierarchy and Order," in *Dictionary of the History of Ideas*, ed. Philip P. Wiener (New York: Scribner, 1973), 2:434–49.

37. *Opera*, 107.

38. "...Inter substantias inferiores homo supremum locum obtinet, qui suprema sui parte etiam coelestes mentes quadam ratione attingit" (*Opera*, 169).

39. Ibid., p. 174.

40. "Appetitus vero huius primus motus ac praecipuus est amor, cuius obiectum est bonum" (ibid., 163).

41. Gilbert, "Religion and Politics," 105.

42. *Opera*, 100–101.

43. Ibid., 160; and *De elementis*, 13, where he calls St. Thomas "vir item doctissimus et nunquam satis laudatus." Beccadelli, "Vita," 40, writes that Contarini moved away

regarding the relation between faith and reason, like those of St. Thomas, do not contemplate the possibility of their ultimate conflict. Nature has set limits on the human ability to know, Contarini argues, which man must accept in the realization that many things will remain obscure and hidden from him.[44] Repeatedly he asserts that the final answers to the deepest questions about God and man's destiny come through revelation and are nonrational, and thus not amenable to philosophical analysis. There comes a point where words and reasoning power fail: "If we are to approach the Godhead as it is in itself, then we must be all but silent. For no one has words or concepts by which adequately to express it or speak of it."[45] Contarini here restates conclusions at which he had already arrived in the course of his own religious development. But though man must accept the limits set to reason, it does not follow that he should slacken his efforts to use that reason to the fullest extent possible. For it is precisely reason that shows him the perfect order of the universe and the ideal order in state and church. Disorder in either is due to material, not spiritual, causes, and to evil seen as the absence of the good and defined by Contarini in essentially Augustinian terms.[46]

By the time he finished writing the *Compendium* Contarini's most important and characteristic philosophical views were fully formulated. He saw himself as already serving God through an active life of service to Venice and his fellow man, secure in the knowledge that God had created an orderly universe and given everything in it an ideal, perfect form. This deep conviction, expressed most fully in the *Compendium*, was the foundation on which his political thought rested and on which his ideas concerning reform of the church were to be built. Contarini was a fortunate man in whom the ethos of commitment to a specific social class, political commitment to a state, personal religious convictions, and a good education combined in a harmonious way. After the resolution of his religious and emotional difficulties, his world of thought was ordered and consistent. His philosophy was cut from the same cloth as his political and theological writings, since according to him they all addressed aspects of the same reality.

Contarini's preoccupation with philosophy can also be seen in another lengthy treatise belonging to the period 1530–35, *De elementis*

---

from Averroism toward St. Thomas: "As it seemed to him that St. Thomas was the more learned doctor, he applied himself to [St. Thomas] and always took him into account, especially in theology."

44. *Opera*, 157.   45. Ibid., 142–43; cf. also 106.   46. Ibid., 127–28.

et eorum mixtionibus libri V.[47] It was dedicated to his brother-in-law Matteo Dandolo, to whom Contarini was closely tied by friendship and kindred intellectual pursuits.[48] Again, this work concerning physical science contains nothing unexpected. Like the *Compendium* it, too, begins with a more or less superfluous disclaimer of literary merit, stylistic gloss, or verbal ornamentation.[49] Then Contarini sets himself to discuss in brisk readable Latin that part of natural philosophy which examines the four elements and their combinations. He summarizes prevailing views on the nature of the physical world, adding his own comments, based largely on Aristotle but also on scholastic thinkers. While the work makes no contribution to sixteenth-century physics, it testifies to Contarini's Aristotelian and Galenic opinions about physical reality, and the delight he took in returning to philosophical questions in the midst of his *vita activa*.

His conventional explanations of natural phenomena are interspersed with many details of personal experiences from his travels. He was fascinated by topography and especially the question of what causes tides,[50] and avidly sought information from navigators' reports of newly discovered lands.[51] As we have seen, he knew Pietro Martire d'Anghiera, the Italian author of *De orbe novo decades*, which described Spanish discoveries and conquests in the New World.[52] The fresh knowledge of new lands and peoples is integrated by Contarini into old thought patterns, as was generally the case with Europeans of the first generation or two who received descriptions of America.[53] Contarini's views of the physical world were not structurally altered by new infor-

---

47. Ibid., 1–90. For a summary, see Lynn Thorndike, *A History of Magic and Experimental Science* (New York: Columbia University Press, 1923–58), 5:552–55.

48. That they discussed philosophical issues together is evident from Contarini's remarks in *Opera*, 2. Beccadelli, "Vita," 57, says that Contarini "loved [Dandolo] not only because he was related to him but because of the prudence and knowledge of letters and the goodness he saw in [him]."

49. Beccadelli, "Vita," 43, remarks that "it is true that in his writing style he paid little attention to the refinements of the Latin language, concentrating more on the knowledge of things than on words; yet one can see that he was not uncouth, but came quite close to the style of the ancients."

50. *Opera*, 30–36.   51. E.g., ibid., 39–40.

52. For Contarini's acquaintance with Pietro Martire, see "Relazione," 50 (16 Nov. 1525).

53. See John H. Elliott, *The Old World and the New, 1492–1650* (Cambridge: Cambridge University Press, 1970); Antonello Gerbi, *The Dispute of the New World: The History of a Polemic, 1750–1900*, new enlarged ed., trans. Jeremy Moyle (Pittsburgh: University of Pittsburgh Press, 1973); Federica Ambrosini, *Paesi e mari ignoti: America e colonialismo europeo nella cultura veneziana (secoli XVI–XVII)* (Venice: Deputazione Editrice, 1982).

mation, but he had great curiosity about details, which he worked into his writings as illustrations of general propositions.[54] *De elementis*, in fact, shows that Contarini was as conservative in physics and geography as he had been in cosmology. In another and minor work of the same period, he opposed the theory of epicycles, calling it a deformity and ugly disgrace, and disagreed strongly with explanations of planetary motion that had recourse to epicycles.[55] His biographer is right in pointing out that Contarini looked at the physical universe from a purely theoretical standpoint and "saw the world primarily in the form of an esthetic idea."[56] Therefore he could admit no modification of its consummate order and perfect circular motion. One can only wonder how he would have reacted to the ideas of Copernicus, his fellow student at Padua, had he known of them. But Contarini's *De elementis* must have struck his own age as having greater merit than modern readers are inclined to grant it, for part of it, translated into Italian, was plagiarized and printed at Venice by Paolo Manuzio under his own name at the Aldine Press. Strangely enough, this version was translated back into Latin a year later by a French writer, without any reference to either Manuzio or Contarini.[57]

A more intimate idea of Contarini's personality than his writings on metaphysics, cosmology, and physics afford us can be found in two letters to the Venetian patrician Trifon Gabriele, Contarini's friend since youth. As philosophical minitreatises revealing some of Contarini's cherished convictions, they deserve to be read with care.[58] They were written at Gabriele's request as meditations on topics the two men had been considering in the course of their frequent discussions of philosophical questions. The first, dated 10 January 1531 (*more Veneto* = 1532), asks: "Since God is true and good, why is it that one reaches him more readily with the will than the intellect, notwithstanding that as truth he is the object of the intellect [in the same way that] as goodness he is the object of the will?"[59]

54. E.g., *Opera*, 414, where he discusses the idea that religion is natural and ingrained in mankind, using evidence from ancient history and also from newly discovered peoples.

55. "De homocentricis ad Hieronymum Fragastorium," in *Opera*, 238.

56. *GC*, 278.

57. Thorndike, *History of Magic* 5:555–56.

58. These two letters were preceded by another to Gabriele, a general treatment of the mind and the intellect, that is published in *Delle lettere volgari di diversi nobilissimi huomini et eccellentissimi ingegni scritte in diverse materie* (Venice, 1560), 110–14, and was written on Christmas night 1530.

59. "A Messer T. G. Risposta," in *Quattro lettere di monsignor Gasparo Contarino* (Florence, 1558), 9–20.

Behind this rather clumsily phrased question lie specific issues close to Contarini's heart, which he approaches, as was his habit, through general considerations. He first asks in what our chief happiness consists, answering that for some thinkers it is the intellectual knowledge of God reached through the understanding of his creation,[60] while for others it lies in the motion of the will toward that love by which we love God perfectly.[61] (That a person's chief happiness could be this-worldly was a notion not even worth refuting.) Citing from pseudo-Dionysius the Areopagite's *On Divine Names* to the effect that both approaches are necessary, Contarini proposes a third solution consisting in the union of the soul with divine goodness and truth in such manner that it loses itself and becomes that with which it is united. He echoes St. Paul in 2 Corinthians that tongue cannot express such felicity nor intellect apprehend it: "Thus he who has reached that center and that repose ceases his own action, or rather transcends his every action of intellect and will, but is absorbed in peace, truth, and divine being."[62]

As in the *Compendium*, Contarini stresses that the deepest recognition of unutterable truth is in the silence that lies beyond the operations of human faculties. In other contexts he was to repeat that God is ultimately known in a wordless way, in the silence that transcends all human understanding. This conviction forms a prominent element in Contarini's religious thought and was rooted in his own experience of God's ineffability. More important, it made him uninterested in splitting hairs over theological definitions and impelled him to look at wider, more fundamental issues beyond terminological differences. What to some of his critics seemed unnecessary accommodation to the Protestants in 1541 was actually another instance of Contarini's lack of trust in the ability of words to express fully the mysteries of faith, and thus his unwillingness to stake everything on verbal constructs.

The letter to Gabriele is of interest for another reason as well. Contarini is not the impartial examiner of the question posed at the outset, but argues that if we want to know God by joining ourselves to him and becoming similar to him, then the will is especially powerful, because knowledge and intellect do not cleanse the stains that make us most unlike God, whereas love does. It draws us out of ourselves toward God.[63] Thus a good but unlearned man can arrive at the knowledge of God better than a man learned but not good.[64] Contarini's

---

60. Ibid., 13.   61. Ibid., 16.   62. Ibid., 17.   63. Ibid., 20.
64. Ibid., 19.

emphasis on the importance of the emotions is deeply personal. It was his experience that love and trust brought him close to God, and that love was ultimately the only response man can properly make to the sacrifice of Christ on the cross. Indeed, he had already dealt with these issues in the letter describing his confession of Holy Saturday 1511.[65] Although the ideas are here recast in different language, they still had the same reality for him as they had had twenty years earlier.

Like the first letter to Gabriele, the second begins by considering general topics but soon comes to echo Contarini's personal experience. The introduction gives an attractive picture of him and Gabriele engaged in philosophical discussion during a boat trip to the charterhouse near Padua. They considered whether the speculative sciences are nobler and more perfect than the moral virtues, and then asked whether, if one had to choose, one should choose knowledge or innocence. Somewhat wistfully Contarini reports that he is now so busy with other matters that he has lost touch with the study of philosophy,[66] though he had always taken pleasure in it and indeed "joyfully spent time on such inquiry."[67] In reply to Gabriele he first resorts to Aristotle's *Ethics* to define virtue and clarify the difference between science and moral virtue. This becomes something akin to a textbook exercise until Contarini reaches his third point, a discussion of whether innocence or knowledge is to be preferred.

Suddenly the tone changes and life is infused into the little treatise. It is obvious that for Contarini the question is no longer simply theoretical. First he demonstrates that science is nobler than moral virtue because together with contemplation it belongs to man, "insofar as there is in him something of the divine," whereas "the moral virtues guide man in the active life which is proper to him."[68] He uses the example of the captain of an armed fleet in relation to his second-in-command as a parable of the intellect and will. But lest one conclude from this that the choice of science (which Contarini calls the virtue of the intellect) is preferable, he adds that the particular good that is most noble and perfect on an absolute scale need not be chosen by everyone in every case. "Everyone should choose that good which is most appropriate and most in accordance with his own nature, his condition, and his time, and should take into account all other circumstances, because for everything the greater good is that which is suitable to it, not that which may suit others, even though in absolute

65. Jedin, "Contarini und Camaldoli," esp. 14–15.
66. *Quattro lettere*, 40. Contarini's letter is dated 13 December 1532.
67. Ibid., 20.   68. Ibid., 31.

terms the second may be more perfect than the first."[69] Contarini's conclusion is that if one must choose between intellectual knowledge and science, on the one hand, and moral virtue, on the other, the latter is preferable even though it is less perfect than the former. He adds that everyone must choose that good "which is appropriate to his nature rather than a good that [might entail] some loss for his nature. Moral virtue is the active life which is proper to man, the contemplative life is beyond man."[70]

When read against the background of the earlier letters to Giustiniani and Querini, this little treatise is impressive testimony to the remarkable continuity of Contarini's thought regarding the respective merits of the active and the contemplative life. His commitment to the active life has deepened, and there is no sense of regret about the choice he made as a young man except for his having little time for philosophical studies. At the time he composed this letter to Gabriele he was deeply involved in the work of the Venetian government as one of the six ducal councillors who participated ex officio in the meetings of numerous councils and committees. The letter is evidence of Contarini's inner calm and certainty, but also of his humanity. Far from prescribing schematically what people should do, he is capable of accepting the fact that vast differences exist among individual characters and temperaments; thus, he understands that the choices people make cannot be governed by formulas but must arise from specific circumstances.

This way of thinking gave him what was for his time an unusually wide tolerance for others. No wonder that his friendships were many and lasting, and that he had the reputation of being unusually gentle. This reputation he consciously cultivated. Beccadelli records how Contarini kept his occasionally quick temper successfully in check so that he appeared mild even though he was in fact inclined to be irascible.[71] He was an emotional man with deep feelings, loyalties, and commitments. These appear even in his philosophical works, sometimes as *obiter dicta* and sometimes expressly, as in the two letters to Gabriele. For Contarini, the universe was hierarchical, hence orderly and understandable, and man's life in it was purposeful. Because all was God's creation, man could move toward him with a love that defied logical analysis and expression in words. Contarini's thought and actions rested on these convictions.

69. Ibid., 37.   70. Ibid., 38.   71. Beccadelli, "Vita," 48–49.

Order in the Church

Contarini's Christianity was profound and personal. As a young man he had experienced uncertainty, dryness of heart, and list-lessness while in quest of a vocation that would be pleasing to God. As a mature man he had acquired inner certainty, yet his religion does not strike the reader of his works and letters as static. For him, being a Christian meant commitment. He accepted the visible church as founded by God, with the pope as his vicar who ruled over a hierarchi-cal structure that embraced all men. There is no trace of the conciliarist model of church government in Contarini's writings; his mention of the Council of Constance is so cursory that from it no reader could realize the importance of its decrees.[72] But acceptance of the church's hierarchical government did not preclude criticism of its shortcomings. His ideal of the church made him chafe all the more at the toleration of abuses, and he championed reform with conviction. Contarini com-bined great loyalty to the institutional church and its doctrines, in-cluding the Eucharist as defined by the Fourth Lateran Council, the Petrine supremacy, and the conventional teaching on the seven sacra-ments, with an undogmatic spirit of freedom and openness. Just as he was eclectic in philosophy, he demonstrated a willingness to take seriously the views of others in religious matters and give them full consideration. This attitude, so intimately a part of his personality, nevertheless remained incomprehensible to many who knew him, and eventually it became suspect.

Apart from the letters to Giustiniani and Querini, the earliest evi-dence for Contarini's interest in church reform is found in a short note he wrote on Savonarola. Giustiniani, having been consulted by Pope Leo X in connection with the reexamination of the friar's case,[73] asked Contarini for his opinion.[74] In his reply of 18 September 1516

72. "... Celebrata fuit synodus Constantiensis tempore magni schismatis: quo tres Pontifices erant Benedictus, Gregorius et Joannes vigesimus tertius. Opera Sigismondi Imperatoris, qui multum laboris, et industriae impendit, ut schisma illud tolleretur, fuit coacta synodus Constantiae ... electus fuit Martinus Columna vir egregius, et pius. Post Constantiense consilium, ut seruaretur Decretum de congregatione conciliorum, indic-tum fuit concilium, quod fuit Basileae coactum" (*Conciliorum magis illustrium summa*, in *Opera*, 563).

73. Felix Gilbert, "Contarini on Savonarola: An Unknown Document of 1516," *Archiv für Reformationsgeschichte* 59 (1968): 145–46.

74. For the text, see ibid., 147–49.

Contarini wrote that he had been reading Savonarola's works, including sermons preached after the friar's excommunication. The fact that Savonarola did not obey the pope was for Contarini insufficient reason to declare him a heretic, for "the vicar of God used the power given to him against God and charity; . . . therefore he did not have to be obeyed."[75] Another accusation against Savonarola was that he had declared himself a prophet. Again, Contarini defends the friar by arguing that it is not contrary to faith to think that prophets could still arise in the church: "To enter a definitive judgment in this matter seems to me very presumptuous and dangerous. I say the same about the interpretation of Scripture according to his prophecies. I know that renewal of the church [is necessary], not because of prophecies but because natural and divine reason tell me so. . . . Divine reason also tells me that sometimes God must order his church, which is to be fervently desired by all Christians."[76]

Despite his sympathy with Savonarola's call for reform, Contarini ends his letter by submitting himself in all respects to the decision of the church. Though he freely asserts that no vicar might use the power committed to him for purposes contrary to those which that power was intended to serve, he balances this declaration by accepting the need for church discipline. It is telling of Contarini's way of thinking that he could admire both the visions of Savonarola and later the methodical spirituality of Ignatius of Loyola, with its emphasis on the necessity of "sentire cum ecclesia," or thinking with the church.[77] For Contarini, membership in the church entailed subjection to legitimate papal authority. He felt free to speak against its arbitrary exercise precisely because he accepted the principles on which it was founded. But Contarini's declaration of submission to the ecclesiastical authorities in this particular instance could also be explained at least in part by his realization that he was unfamiliar with the technical arguments used by the friar's opponents. His diffident handling of the Savonarola case points to a real weakness in his academic preparation for his later career in state and church: a lack of familiarity with civil and canon law.[78]

75. Ibid., 149.   76. Ibid., 149.

77. A. Suquía, "Las reglas para sentir con la iglesia en la vida y en las obras del cardenal Gaspar Contarini (1483–1542)," *Archivum historicum Societatis Iesu* 25 (1956): 380–95.

78. Fragnito, "Cultura umanistica," 120–25, discusses Contarini's letter fully and gives useful bibliographic information. She mentions Contarini's "insufficiente preparazione teologica e canonistica" (124, 178); nevertheless he appreciated the importance of legal education for the bishop; see *Opera*, 411.

Here, knowledge of the latter might have sharpened his argumentation considerably and given him a better grasp of the legal issues involved.

In the following year, 1517, Contarini wrote one of his best-known treatises, *De officio viri boni ac probi episcopi*,[79] the first part of which describes the formation of the ideal bishop, and the second his exercise of the office entrusted to him.[80] It has received thorough examination by Gigliola Fragnito.[81] She points out that the work owes much to the example of Pietro Barozzi, bishop of Padua from 1487 to 1507, whom Contarini knew, as well as to the ideas of his friends Giustiniani and Querini, and possibly also to Contarini's reading of Savonarola's sermons during the summer of 1516.[82]

The immediate occasion for the composition of *De officio episcopi* was the accession of the teenaged Pietro Lippomano to the bishopric of Bergamo as successor to his uncle, in flagrant contravention of canon law, which established a minimum age of thirty for bishops.[83] Contarini makes no allusion to the bishop-designate's youth or the law that was flouted in this treatise intended for Lippomano's guidance. Indeed, the work eludes neat categorization, although it is generally ranged among Contarini's theological writings.[84] It includes philosophical reflections, discussion of moral issues, ideas on education and psychology, criticism of prevailing practices, even specific suggestions for the bishop's everyday life down to such details as his meals, the kinds of music he should listen to, and the kinds of books he should read.[85] The treatise lacks the theological and legal dimensions of other works in the "mirror of the bishop" literature. A portrait reflecting Contarini's own wishes and preferences, it does not touch on theoretical issues of episcopal power, its nature, or origin. Neither does it dwell on concrete matters of diocesan administration, about which its young lay author probably knew little. But it is more than the work of "a

---

79. *Opera*, 401–31.

80. Silvio Tramontin, "Il 'De officio episcopi' di Gaspare Contarini," *Studia Patavina* 12 (1965): 295, thinks the work is divided into three distinct parts discussing the virtues of the bishop, his duties, and the bishop's day.

81. Fragnito, "Cultura umanistica," 75–189.

82. Ibid., 126–33. For Barozzi as model, see also Hubert Jedin, "Das Bischofsideal der katholischen Reformation: eine Studie über die Bischofsspiegel vornehmlich des 16. Jahrhunderts," in *Kirche des Glaubens* 2:86.

83. Fragnito, "Cultura umanistica," 179n.386.

84. *GC*, 283.

85. For a detailed summary of the contents, see Fragnito, "Cultura umanistica," 138–75; and *GC*, 283–96.

sensitive observer,"[86] since its main ideas are rooted in Contarini's own religious experience and foreshadow his later, more fully elaborated views.

The author of an otherwise thoughtful study finds the first book of the treatise "academic in the worst sense, unoriginal and uninspiring. It was most surely the concrete programme of action enunciated in the second book that gave the treatise its reputation."[87] Yet it is the first book that reveals significant aspects of Contarini's way of thinking. As was his custom, he opens the treatise with general considerations, in this case of the nature of the two societies to which men belong, the secular and the ecclesiastical. It soon becomes obvious that Contarini takes a hierarchical view of both. Just as the ruler by virtue of his position in the body politic enforces order in that realm, so the bishop must be responsible for order in the church on the diocesan level. The two societies, however, do not exist side by side; the ecclesiastical is superior to the secular because its charge is the transmission of the Christian message and instruction in Christian living, responsibilities that confer on the bishop greater dignity than the secular ruler possesses.[88] By virtue of his office the bishop has a special position: he "is between the divine spirits and the human race" and must participate in both the angelic and the human nature.[89] Contarini's extravagant exaltation of the bishop follows from his conviction that the moral and religious foundation of the Christian people is a higher endeavor than the task of secular government, because their eternal salvation depends on their acceptance and understanding of the Christian message. In keeping with his own preferences, he stresses repeatedly that the best instruction is through the bishop's good example, not through the rules and regulations he might make. As he himself had learned from "living books," as he called his friends, so the bishop's flock would learn from seeing in his behavior the way to conduct themselves as good Christians.

Given these premises, it is understandable that Contarini designs an ideal education for the formation of the youth who is to rise above the level of ordinary men by his position as bishop in the church. To be sure, the rather dry listing that follows of what such a man must know and what virtues he must possess is heavily indebted to Aristotle's

86. Jedin, "Bischofsideal," 86.

87. Oliver Logan, "The Ideal Bishop and the Venetian Patriciate: c. 1430–c. 1630," *Journal of Ecclesiastical History* 29 (1978): 429.

88. *Opera*, 402.   89. Ibid., 403.

Ethics. Nevertheless, the choice of virtues that the bishop needs is Contarini's own: amiability and kindness, fortitude, magnanimity, simplicity of living, humility, justice, and prudence, in addition to the three theological virtues of faith, hope, and charity.[90] The stress on justice and especially on prudence gives Contarini's treatise an unmistakably Venetian character. If it is true that "the Venetian political temperament was characterized by compromise, consensus, conciliation, and expediency,"[91] then Contarini was arch-Venetian. He prized all the virtues but gave pride of place to prudence, that peculiarly Venetian virtue[92] without which a man in a responsible position could not be effective, whether in church or state. Contarini here assigns many of the same specifically Venetian virtues associated with secular rule to the man in charge of the fundamental unit of church administration, the diocese.

His ideal bishop has the quality that Contarini himself thought basic to the government of men in a Christian society: moral probity. Thus the bishop's education centers on the formation of a morally principled good man rather than on the perfect gentleman. The study of moral theology and philosophy is the best preparation for the future bishop, not the pursuit of worldly wisdom, poetry, or eloquence. Here again we find distrust of eloquence in itself, disjoined from nobler, higher purposes. We have found this distrust in the letters to Trifon Gabriele a dozen years earlier; it no doubt goes back to the period of Contarini's close association with Giustiniani and Querini, who were so convinced of the perils inherent in secular learning that they recommended to Pope Leo X that priests be instructed in Latin only to the extent necessary for understanding the Scriptures.[93] Giustiniani and Querini's *Libellus* might have been the basis for the decree of the Fifth Lateran Council of 19 December 1513. Felix Gilbert has argued persuasively that this decree not only condemns philosophical debates about the immortality of the soul, but also testifies to a profound suspicion of the secular tendencies in humanistic studies.[94]

90. Ibid., 405–10. I do not agree with A. D. Wright's summary of the purpose of this treatise, that the "central and characterisic concern of Contarini" was "to encourage an underage boy, of the patrician elite, not so much in the practical duties of the episcopal office as in the private pursuit of God-fearing but unsuperstitious virtue" (Review of *Gasparo Contarini*, by Gigliola Fragnito, *Journal of Modern History* 63 [1991]: 405).

91. Robert Finlay, "Politics and Family in Renaissance Venice: The Election of Doge Andrea Gritti," *Studi veneziani*, n.s., 2 (1978): 107.

92. See the fine observations on prudence as "an aspect of the Venetian collective sensibility" by Cervelli, *Machiavelli*, 321.

93. For a discussion of their views, see Gilbert, "Cristianesimo," 984–85.

94. Ibid., 978.

Contarini's sympathy with his two friends' view appears clearly in his treatment of the bishop's education, where he expressed reservations regarding the effects of a humanist education on the moral development of the young.[95] He never condemned humanistic studies as sweepingly as his two friends did.[96] Like them, he was sensitive to basic tensions between secular learning and Christian principles;[97] yet he was also well aware that such tensions had been a constant in the life of the church. In his sensible, balanced way Contarini issued no blanket condemnations of humanist education but sought to limit its potentially harmful effects. This is why twenty years later he agreed to the recommendation that the reading of Erasmus's *Colloquies* be forbidden in the grammar schools, since they "contain many things inciting uneducated minds to impiety."[98] What was forbidden to boys, however, he thought useful to adults. It is certain that he himself had read some Erasmus, though there is no evidence that he ever had personal contact with the great Dutch humanist.[99]

Several other themes in *De officio episcopi* are especially useful in illuminating Contarini's conception of order. He posits a close cooperation between secular and ecclesiastical authorities. The ideal bishop would supervise carefully the applicants for admission to holy orders, making sure that the church never served as an asylum for criminals; he would respect the state and its laws and not shield guilty clerics, who should be committed to the secular jurisdiction save in exceptional cases wherein he personally would act as judge.[100] Here Contarini incorporates into his ideal diocese the same relation to secular authority that characterized Venice. A reflection of Venetian practice is his

95. Fragnito, "Cultura umanistica," 129–32. See also *Opera*, 426.

96. For Giustiniani and Querini's views, see the references in Fragnito, "Cultura umanistica," 130.

97. For arguments for a particular sensitivity to these issues in the generation to which Contarini belonged, see Cessi, "Paolinismo preluterano," 18–19.

98. In the "Consilium de emendanda ecclesia," *Concilium Tridentinum: diariorum, actorum, epistularum, tractatuum nova collectio*, ed. Societas Goerresiana (Freiburg i.B.: Herder, 1901–38), 12:141 (hereafter cited as *CT*); translated in Elisabeth G. Gleason, *Reform Thought in Sixteenth-Century Italy* (Chico, Calif.: Scholars Press, 1981), 96. Fragnito, "Cultura umanistica," 138n.266, suggests that Contarini may have had to compromise on this point with Carafa and Aleandro.

99. See Contarini's references to his familiarity with Erasmus's "De libero arbitrio" in the "Confutatio articulorum ... Lutheranorum," *Gegenreformatorische Schriften*, 7. For Contarini's possible indirect contact with Erasmus, see Fragnito, "Cultura umanistica," 137. For the larger question of Erasmus's influence on Italian contemporaries, see Silvana Seidel Menchi, *Erasmo in Italia, 1520–1580* (Turin: Bollati Boringhieri, 1987).

100. *Opera*, 422, 426.

recommendation that the secular government be called upon, where necessary, to end disorders in nunneries and root out the terrible conditions prevailing in many of them. In his view, the state should concern itself also with heresy, for heresy, like civil crime, endangered both societies and undermined the foundations of all government.[101] Contarini did not diverge from contemporary thinking on the nature and danger of heresy; in fact, he repeated the stock arguments against it. Just how conventional his view was can be seen by comparing it with the somewhat later work of Mino Celsi, for example. Celsi introduced new and original elements into the debate about heresy by arguing that heretics cannot be treated as criminals since the necessary condition for any crime is the will to commit it. Heretics, however, were misguided and impaired, and therefore, like mentally ill persons, they had no consciousness of wrongdoing.[102]

Another personal note in Contarini's tract is the fervent expression of a desire for reform of the church. Although his denunciation of absentee bishops at the end of Book I adds no new dimension to the topos of the shepherd who abandoned his flock to the hireling, its passionate tone is reminiscent of Protestant attacks on abuses in the Catholic church.[103] Contarini's misgivings about excesses in devotion to the saints led him to recommend that the bishop teach his people to love God above all and to impress on them that without God the saints are nothing. These recommendations were later censured by ecclesiastical authorities; though printed editions of the treatise contained passages on this topic, they were greatly toned down in comparison with the manuscript original, where Contarini's indignation at the laxity and abuses on the diocesan level had been expressed forcefully, even vehemently.[104]

It has been pointed out that Contarini failed to mention such obvious and proven means of reform in a diocese as episcopal visitations and diocesan synods.[105] One explanation for the omission may be his lack of knowledge of diocesan administration at the time he wrote the treatise. A more important reason for the neglect of these practical steps is likely to be Contarini's focus on the individual: reform in *De*

101. Ibid., 425; and Gilbert, "Religion and Politics," 110.

102. Mino Celsi, *In haereticis coërcendis quatenus progredi liceat,* ed. Peter G. Bietenholz, Corpus Reformatorum Italicorum (Naples: Prismi Editrice/Chicago: Newberry Library, 1982), 346.

103. *Opera,* 413.

104. Fragnito, "Cultura umanistica," 77–79, 187–89.

105. Ibid., 180.

officio episcopi has no collective or communal dimension. Contarini's moral radicalism is uncluttered by institutional and legal asides. He was convinced that the bishop's example was of fundamental importance for a diocese; the bishop would bring about change not so much by laws and regulations as by what he himself was. There is, of course, an appealing simplicity about such an approach. But Contarini's design of the ideal bishop was not simpleminded. His treatise affirmed in yet another mode what he had experienced and interiorized—that change of heart in the individual was the necessary first step toward reform of the church. Good men were "living books" impelling others to learn from them. In the last analysis Contarini's good bishop touches men's emotions and will rather than their intellect, moving them to the love of God and charity toward their neighbors and kindling in them the desire to lead Christian lives based on the precepts of the Gospels.

The weakness of Contarini's treatise lies in the absence of a thorough and precise examination of the nature and limits of the bishop's power in the church, its theoretical underpinnings, and a clear sense of how he could initiate or advance institutional reform. Its strength is in the vision of a church whose order depends on the observance of the gospel precepts by its shepherds, the bishops. Contarini's ideal has just enough concrete touches to prevent his bishop from becoming a cardboard figure and to bring him into the realm of the thinkable and desirable, if not always the possible. By the perfection of his virtues the bishop was to be a potent critic of those who in actuality fell far short of the obligations of their office. In that sense one can agree with Dittrich that *De officio episcopi* was Contarini's "first reformatory deed."[106]

Contarini's first exclusively theological work, of great significance for the understanding of his thought, is the *Confutatio articulorum seu quaestionum Lutheranorum*, written between 1530 and 1535 (probably closer to the earlier date).[107] In it he summarizes and comments on sixteen of the twenty-eight articles of the Augsburg Confession for the benefit of an unnamed correspondent. The treatise is notable for the serious consideration Contarini gives to Philip Melanchthon's accommodating formulations of basic Protestant teaching, quite unlike the

106. *GC*, 296
107. The edition in *Opera*, 564–80, is superseded by that in *Gegenreformatorische Schriften*, 1–22. For a German translation, preceded by a useful introduction, see Jedin, *Kardinal Contarini als Kontroverstheologe*. For the most plausible dating, see Rückert, *Theologische Entwicklung*, 6n.2.

later Catholic theologians who rejected the document for the very reason that it toned down differences with Catholic doctrine.[108]

Contarini's interest in Luther and the German religious situation was of long standing. During his embassies to the Spanish and papal courts he was well informed of events in Germany. His brother-in-law Matteo Dandolo, Venetian ambassador to the Diet of Augsburg in 1530, may have given him a copy of the Augsburg Confession.[109] That Contarini mulled over its articles can be seen in the fact that he rearranged their order so as to give them a tighter structure than the original document did. Articles on which there existed actual or potential agreement were omitted, such as that on God (art. 1), the Son of God (art. 2), baptism (art. 9), or the Second Coming of Christ (art. 17). He thought it appropriate to begin with the fourth article of the Augsburg Confession because it deals with justification by faith, the subject "on which Luther chiefly dwells." Contarini follows St. Thomas closely in considering the infusion of divine grace as the formal cause of justification, which he calls a spiritual rebirth that allows man to participate in divine nature.[110] He also accepts the Thomist proposition that although the justified continue thereafter to entertain an inclination to sin, this inclination is not itself culpable in God's eyes but is rather a punishment for past sins.[111] The first step toward justification is the *dispositio*, man's acceptance of the infusion of grace given freely by God. Contarini defines this disposition as "credulitas qua in Deum tendimus,"[112] and thus a dynamic, living, active faith rather than passive assent. In this specific sense the beginning of justification is by faith alone. But by its very nature this faith brings forth good works, since it is united to love in a single harmonious whole. Because of this intimate connection it is possible to say that "for that reason and in that sense man is justified by works, not only by faith. Not that we

108. Jedin, *Kardinal Contarini als Kontroverstheologe*, 11.

109. Dittrich, *GC*, 305, thinks that Contarini relied on detailed reports by others rather than on the text of the *Confession*. Neither Hünermann (Introduction to Contarini, *Gegenreformatische Schriften*, xii, n. 2) nor Jedin (*Kardinal Contarini als Kontroverstheologe*, 10–11) commits himself on the question of whether Contarini worked from the actual text. I agree with Rückert, *Theologische Entwicklung*, 30n.1, that Contarini was unlikely to write an entire work about a text he had not read, especially since he makes specific references to details of the Augsburg Confession and is obviously familiar with many of its arguments.

110. *Gegenreformatorische Schriften*, 2.

111. Rückert, *Theologische Entwicklung*, 19.

112. *Gegenreformatorische Schriften*, 3.

merit justification by our works (that idea has been rejected above), but because a faith that remains without works is not that faith by which we strive toward God and through which we are disposed to receive grace; it is therefore dead, as St. James says."[113] We find here no hint of Contarini's later theory of double justification, but rather a marked dependence on St. Thomas and a characteristically sensible approach to Lutheran paradoxes, which led him to deemphasize the reformer's ideas of concupiscence and preserve the importance of both faith and works.

The further examination of their relation logically follows as Contarini looks at article 20. He agrees with the Lutheran idea that good works are necessary to "destroy the body of sin which we have inherited from Adam" and to purify the soul. But he argues against the assertion that good works are of no avail in gaining for us eternal life. His main point is that because good works after justification are done by God's grace they have their origin in his being, in which men participate through divine goodness and generosity, and for this reason they do merit for us eternal life and happiness.[114] The careful scholar Hanns Rückert noticed Contarini's divergence here from St. Thomas but was at a loss to understand it. He tentatively attributed it to the effect of Reformation ideas about faith and works upon Contarini's independent thought. In the last analysis, however, Rückert thought Contarini incapable of formulating these ideas clearly, for he did not reach definite conclusions.[115] But Rückert wrote before Contarini's letters to Querini and Giustiniani were discovered, and thus could not know how deeply personal this whole issue was for him. Contarini was no systematic theologian; his own experience of justification and closeness to God is at the root of his idea that man participates in the divine nature and that God's grace brings forth good works in us. His personal conviction is the key to understanding what otherwise seems an idiosyncratic view that neither agrees with Luther nor depends clearly on St. Thomas.

In his treatment of original sin Contarini went out of his way to minimize difficulties, but in fact he misinterpreted the Lutheran position. Twice in a few lines he appeals to "those among the Lutherans who are more reasonable"—presumably meaning Melanchthon and other moderates who were willing to enter into discussion with Cath-

---

113. Ibid.; cf. James 21:7.   114. *Gegenreformatorische Schriften*, 4.
115. Rückert, *Theologische Entwicklung*, 32.

olics.[116] After summarizing articles 2 and 4, Contarini suggests some improvement in wording and interpretation that would make Lutheran teaching about the necessity of the law acceptable. By correcting the definition of original sin, Contarini makes it essentially Thomistic in spirit if not in words, calling it "carentia gratiae et iustitiae Dei" (privation of God's grace and justice).[117] Significantly, he does not come to terms with the Lutheran concept of concupiscence in all its rigor, and his version of it cannot be reconciled even with the "soft" expression of the Augsburg Confession, let alone with Luther's words.

Willingness to accept what to him seemed right and well expressed in Protestant thought characterizes Contarini's brief discussion of free will. He states that he has not read Luther's *De servo arbitrio*, which he knows only from Erasmus's *De libero arbitrio* and from what he has heard from others.[118] His arguments are directed against what he takes to be the Lutheran position that God is the cause of our good as well as our bad works, and concludes that man can fall into perdition by his own power but cannot be saved without the grace of God, which, however, he can choose to accept or reject. Seeking to agree with as much of the Protestant position as possible, he accepts what Luther has said "in a beautiful and excellent way," that we must have recourse to grace in order to do good and that we cannot be justified through the Mosaic law.[119] This discussion, though, is quite unsatisfactory, leaving no doubt that he was unfamiliar with the logic of Luther's views on the bondage of the will. Contarini's irenic temperament made him seek to reconcile God's overwhelming grace with man's freedom of the will, yet he does not manage to do so in any convincing way.

The last major article of faith that Contarini singles out for discussion deals with the sacrament of penance. Again he interprets the Lutheran position in less than its full austerity, an easy enough error given the brevity of article 11 and the broadly general nature of article 25 of the Augsburg Confession. In principle he finds acceptable the Protestant position that only those serious sins that oppress the conscience

---

116. *Gegenreformatorische Schriften*, 5. Contarini here writes of "illis ex Lutheranis qui melius sentiunt."

117. *Gegenreformatorische Schriften*, 6. Cf. *Summa theologiae* I^a II^{ae}, qu. 82, art. 1. Contarini simplified the Thomistic definition and came close to that of Cochlaeus: "Carentia seu privatio originalis iustitiae, quam Adam protoplastus lapsu suo perdidit" (Hugo Laemmer, *Die vortridentinisch-katholische Theologie des Reformationszeitalters* [Berlin, 1858], 107).

118. *Gegenreformatorische Schriften*, 7.   119. Ibid., 10.

should be confessed. Nevertheless, he prefers to see the old practices retained for the sake of simple Christians who frequently find it impossible to distinguish serious from venial sin.[120]

Contarini's next four articles deal with disciplinary matters or long-established liturgical practices: the invocation of saints, monastic vows and the celibacy of priests, the mass, and fasting on Fridays and during Lent. Without advancing new ideas, he confirms the old practices, but his tone and spirit differ significantly from the tack taken by such other Catholic controversialists as Johannes Eck.[121] Contarini's sincere attempt to understand the Protestant position notwithstanding his frequent inability to share it stands out, as does his willingness to admit errors and abuses in the Catholic church. Granting that a misunderstood cult of saints can lead to flagrant superstition, Contarini repeats what he wrote in *De officio episcopi*, that reform in this area is an urgent matter to be undertaken by zealous bishops.[122] Similarly, he makes no excuses for the deplorable conditions in many monasteries and nunneries. While defending monastic vows and celibacy in principle, he calls for energetic reform.[123] He would also do away with another evil of which Lutherans made much: masses said too frequently in private houses without regard to their sacred character.[124] He singles out for treatment the laws of fasting and the widespread misunderstanding of their purpose, even though the Augsburg Confession contains no separate article on them. In themselves these laws do not affect man or his soul, nor are they divinely instituted, yet obedience to them shows obedience to the church and the pope. With this last consideration Contarini returns briefly to the necessity that there be one head and one authority for all Christians. In this he was arguing implicitly against the final article of the Augsburg Confession but avoiding a thorough treatment of papal power and its relation to that of bishops and councils. He contents himself with saying that these questions are still being debated: "Many say many things."[125]

The *Confutatio* is the first work in which Contarini grapples with the great issues raised by the Protestant reformers. As a theological treatise it is not remarkable, and its minor place in the history of

120. Ibid., 11.

121. A comparison of Contarini's *Confutatio* with Eck's *Enchiridion locorum communium adversus Lutheranos* (1526) shows the mildness and willingness of the former to give Lutheran opinions serious consideration. Eck, by contrast, calls Lutherans "haeretici" and polemicizes sharply against them; he devotes chap. 27 to cautioning Catholics not to dispute with them.

122. *Gegenreformatorische Schriften*, 14.   123. Ibid., 16.

124. Ibid., 18.   125. Ibid., 20.

sixteenth-century religious controversy is justified. Contarini had not read enough of Luther at the time he wrote it to understand clearly the difference separating the reformer's views on such crucial topics as justification, freedom of the will, or authority in the church from his own views. Nor did he know Melanchthon's *Apologia*, which would have made some of his optimism about the Augsburg Confession impossible. Neither did he make reference to the *Confutatio* issued on 3 August 1530 by Catholic theologians. The importance of Contarini's treatise, rather, comes from the light it sheds on the future cardinal's mind regarding questions of reform and order in the church.

A striking feature of the *Confutatio* is its dependence on St. Thomas. In the first five sections there is hardly an idea not derived from Aquinas's *Summa*, though Contarini abridges and simplifies,[126] presumably in the interest of the unknown addressee and other laymen ignorant of philosophy. Unlike his earlier philosophical treatises, this work is written in nontechnical language. At this stage of his life Contarini was firmly convinced of the validity of Thomistic thought in explaining the mysteries of faith. [127]

Another evident quality of the *Confutatio* is the desire to be fair to the Lutherans. Contarini does not dig in to defend indiscriminately everything then regarded as forming part of Catholic faith. Equally remarkable is the fact that he writes from the standpoint of a Venetian aristocrat even when he is dealing with critical issues of Reformation theology. Repeatedly we find theological points illustrated by reference to Venetian civic order, so pervasive and self-evidently correct was the political and social world of his *patria* in Contarini's mind. For example, in discussing original sin he uses the analogy of a foreigner given citizenship and patrician status through the generosity of the

126. This is repeatedly stressed by Rückert, *Theologische Entwicklung*, 8, 46. Mark Burrows argues in his paper "Converging Themes in a 'Counter-Reformation' Debate: A Study of the Pastoral Foundations of Contarini's *Confutatio articulorum seu quaestionum Lutheranorum* and the *Confessio Augustana*," presented at the Princeton Theological Seminary in September 1984, that common pastoral concerns underlie both Contarini's and Melanchthon's thought, and that they are united in their antipathy to late medieval nominalism. I would like to thank Mr. Burrows for allowing me to read his paper.

127. Beccadelli was struck by Contarini's agreement with St. Thomas: "[Contarini] fù studiosissimo d'Aristotile, il quale haveva tutto più di una volta con diligenza visto, et perchè varie sono le vie de gli espositori, fu prima Averroista, la cui dottrina a quel tempo era maestra nelle scuole; di poi parendoli che San Thomaso d'Aquino fosse più reale Dottore, a lui s'applicò, et gran conto ne fece sempre, et maxime nella Theologia" ("Vita," 40). Also: "Nella Theologia ... fu molto dotto, et tenne principalmente la via di San Thomaso, del qual Dottore imitava non solo la dottrina, ma li costumi anchora, et haveva ... tutta la Summa di quel Santo Dottore alla mente" (43).

Senate. This man's posterity would inherit his newly acquired status, but if he were to commit an act against the state not only would he lose that status himself, but so would his descendants, "who, though they may not themselves have transgressed against us, are shoots from a bad plant, from him who committed an offense against us. Let this suffice for describing original sin."[128] Here Contarini's identification with the ruling elite of Venice is complete: it is obvious that "we" who are offended can deprive the offender and his descendants of the status "we" have conferred on them. So we have a wonderfully Venetian touch: the Senate watches over justice in the state just as God watches over justice among mankind.

Venetian thinking appears again in the discussion of the sacrament of penance. Contarini argues against the Lutheran idea that satisfaction for past sins performed after absolution is of no avail by using the example of a murderer's punishment. Like all men, the murderer is subject to the laws of God, nature, and civil society. Therefore, even after his reconciliation with God he is not freed from the sanctions of the state. In Contarini's mind, the state's laws must be upheld without question.[129] Later on, writing about invocation of the saints, he calls the saints "citizens of the city of God" who pray for us, their fellow citizens.[130] For Eck, by contrast, saints are "friends of God who should be asked to intercede for us."[131] In justifying celibacy and arguing that not everyone need be married, Contarini reaches for another interesting parallel from civil society. God's command to increase and multiply, he argues, was given to mankind as a whole rather than to each individual singly. Those who remain celibate for the sake of the kingdom of heaven benefit the community of believers much as do their counterparts in a state threatened by overpopulation, whose decision not to have children benefits the body politic:

Generation is for the good of the [human] species, so that it can endure, as agriculture is good because it gives the food to nourish us. However, it does not follow that any given person has to take it upon himself to beget children. In fact, since man is a political animal and an excessive number of citizens militates against the good of the city, as philosophers agree, so the celibacy of some men contributes not a little to the happiness and goodness of human life.[132]

The church, as the body of all Christians, would be excellently ordered, he maintains, if it became more like a well-governed city or state.

128. *Gegenreformatorische Schriften*, 6.   129. Ibid., 12.   130. Ibid., 13.
131. Eck, *Enchiridion*, fol. 56.   132. *Gegenreformatorische Schriften*, 16.

The *Confutatio* reveals also Contarini's profound belief in the rationality of men. We have noticed this aspect of his thought in his philosophical writings, but in this tract it is indeed remarkable. Time after time he invokes natural reason as arbiter of theological differences, most notably when considering freedom of the will and arguing against Luther, who, "if we can believe Erasmus, and if I am repeating correctly what I have read, makes God the author of both our good and our bad works. . . . This position of Luther goes so much against natural reason and Scripture that one cannot imagine anything more incongruous. Who in his right mind would say that God is the author of our bad works? . . . Only a madman can say that God causes our bad works; it goes against natural reason."[133] Contarini makes such arguments again when he discusses good works, satisfaction after forgiveness of sins, and the authority of popes and bishops.[134] At times the appeals to reason as arbiter in theological disputes are simply substitutes for rigorous debate. They mask his impatience with long-drawn-out discussions and the technical language of theology—in which he did not particularly shine—and make him glide rapidly over basic differences between Catholics and Protestants, most notably on original sin.

Older Catholic authors, writing when contrasts between Lutherans and Catholics were more rigorously maintained than they are at present, studied the *Confutatio* to show Contarini's unexceptionable Catholicism.[135] More recent readers of the treatise are likely to single out his irenic orientation and his willingness to seek common ground between the two confessions, emphasizing similarities rather than differences. His ideal of peaceful solutions to difficulties encouraged him to take too sanguine a view of the Augsburg Confession and see more points of agreement between it and Catholic doctrine than existed in reality. More important for the future was Contarini's erroneous conception of the nature of Luther's attacks on the Roman church: he believed that once disciplinary reforms were effected in the church, the other obstacles to concord would fall away of themselves.

Some of Contarini's convictions on the subject of church reform emerge clearly from the *Confutatio*. They can be summed up in one phrase: restoration rather than change, let alone revolution. Aware

133. Ibid., 7.   134. Ibid., 4, 11, 20.

135. Dittrich, *GC*, 308, 310, writes of Contarini's "correct" views concerning Catholic teaching on original sin and good works. Laemmer, *Vortridentinisch-katholische Theologie*, 137–69, repeatedly seeks to show that Contarini's thought on justification, faith, and works was in agreement with that of Catholic theologians; as also does Friedrich Lauchert, *Die italienischen literarischen Gegner Luthers* (Freiburg i.B.: Herder, 1912), 375.

of the spread of abuses throughout the hierarchy of the church, Contarini distinguished between the ideal and actuality, clinging always to the former. The tightening of discipline everywhere, the doing away with superstitious practices, and the abandonment of luxurious living emerge as prerequisites for any meaningful reform, be it disciplinary or doctrinal.

Ultimately, he said, concord will come not from papal or conciliar decrees but from charity and humility. He interrupts his discussion of article 24 of the *Confession* (his own eighth section) with this aside:

If only Christians who profess to be followers of Christ and firm believers in him would preserve charity and humility! Christ commends these virtues as superior to all others. Then it would be easy to obviate all controversies. Since we now make a verbal show of love of God and neighbor and of humility of soul, while we are actually puffed up with arrogance and pride and everyone wants to appear wiser than others and not to have accused his neighbor without cause, it has come about that, blinded by pertinacity, we consider nothing more important than to defend our own views and refute those of our adversaries. Let us preserve humility of soul; then it will be easy to settle this controversy![136]

This passionate appeal to the power of love and humility leaves altogether out of account the reality of the situation that prevailed between the two religious groups in Augsburg in 1530. Contarini closed his eyes to the political and economic struggle in which the Catholic princes were involved in Germany and to the defensive stance of the old church in the face of Lutheran attacks. But it is of utmost importance to realize that he did not do this because he was ignorant of the gravity of the situation in Germany or because he was simpleminded. There is remarkable consistency in his thought. When he held the image of the ideal papacy before Clement VII or drew the portrait of the ideal bishop, he appealed to the highest and noblest idea one could entertain of the men in charge of the church. In the *Confutatio* he again presents an ideal, that of the conceivable outcome of religious controversy if both sides took their professions as Christians seriously. There is a radical, uncompromising strand in Contarini's thought that can easily be missed if it is considered merely utopian. Contarini the critic held up to Catholic theologians and controversialists a mirror when he closed his *Confutatio* with this vision:

No councils, battles of words, syllogisms, or biblical citations are needed to quiet the unrest of the Lutherans, but good will, love of God and one's neigh-

136. *Gegenreformatorische Schriften*, 17.

bor, humility of soul in order to do away with avarice, luxury, large households, and courts, and to limit oneself to that which the Gospels prescribe.
This is what is needed to overcome the tumults of the Lutherans. Let us not
move against them with masses of books, Ciceronian orations, subtle arguments, but with an exemplary life, humble mind, without luxury, only desiring
Christ and the good of our neighbor. With these weapons, believe me, not
only the Lutherans but also the Turks and Jews could be converted without
difficulty. In this the duty of Christian prelates consists, and to this they should
direct all their ambition. If they fail to do so, seeking support instead in the
favor of princes, in reasons and authorities and masses of books, their efforts
will be of no avail. This is my firm conviction.[137]

One brief phrase reveals the heart of his program: limiting oneself
to "that which the Gospels prescribe" meant personal, internal reform.
As in his earliest extant letters to his friends, so now he sees this sort
of self-correction as the beginning of church reform. The systematic
weaknesses of his position are balanced by the fervor of his convictions.
Reform would begin with an act of the will and proceed to an affective,
interior response to the gospel by the individual.

Reflection on proper order in the church led to consideration of the
papacy. Of Contarini's three tracts on the power of the pope, one was
written while he was a layman: the brief treatise *De potestate pontificis
quod divinitus sit tradita.*[138] The occasion for its composition was a
series of debates in the Venetian Senate during the early 1530s regarding forced loans that the Republic intended to levy on ecclesiastical
property. Some senators, notably Sebastiano Foscarini, held that it was
unnecessary to consult the pope first on such a matter, for he was to be
obeyed only "in materia fidei et sacramentorum"—in questions involving faith and the sacraments. As we have seen, however, Contarini's
opposing view prevailed, and according to the report of Girolamo Aleandro, then the papal nuncio to Venice, it was Contarini's influence,
notwithstanding the views of prominent anti-papal senators who mistrusted the pope as the destroyer of republican government in Florence, that persuaded the Senate to consult the pope before levying
the loans.[139] In this context Contarini wrote *De potestate pontificis* in a
single sitting at the request of a friend.

The brief treatise seems intransigent in tone, out of keeping with his
statements as ambassador to Clement VII, indeed simply an echo of
conservative views concerning the divine institution of the papacy. It

137. Ibid., 22.
138. The best text is in ibid., 35–43; also *Opera*, 581–87.
139. Gaeta (ed.), *Nunziature di Venezia* 1:210 (letter 77).

adduces proof from Scripture, reason, and history, without any reference to exegetical work by Protestant theologians, some of whose
arguments Contarini certainly knew by that time. He affirms that the
keys were given to Peter alone, whose successor possesses the *plenitudo
potestatis* of judging, binding, and loosing, and through whom bishops
receive their power. Two other powers were also given by Christ to
the pope: to be the supreme shepherd of the Christian flock, and to
instruct it in true doctrine, with authority to make the final decision
on matters of dogma and faith.[140]

The second line of argument proceeds from a philosophical basis as
Contarini states that no human group can be united without a head.
Rejecting the Lutheran belief that Christ leads the church without an
intermediary, Contarini argues human nature is such that without a
visible head chaos would soon ensue.[141] Turning to the history of the
early church, he seeks to show that from the beginning the authority of
Peter was greater than that of James, and that the see of Rome took
precedence over all others. He closes with a paragraph reaffirming the
divine institution of papal authority.[142]

Despite first impressions, a careful reading will show the links between this little treatise and the ideas Contarini expressed earlier about
the papacy. Above all, he strongly affirms the hierarchy of the church
culminating in the pope. He was never to deviate from this position or
to entertain other conceptions of church structure and governance.
Moreover, he stresses throughout that the fullness of power belongs
properly to the pope but that its misuse has grievous consequences
for both the church and secular society. Long ago he had written to
Querini that the principal cause of temporal and spiritual evils in the
church was "lack of religious feeling and the example of the lack of
devotion in persons who in past years governed the church of God."[143]
Contarini believed that the pope must understand clearly not only
the immense power given him by God but also its precise limits and
the proper sphere for its exercise if the church was to see meaningful
change. These ideas were developed further after he became a cardinal,
as we shall see.

Before that time, however, his ideas on order in the church were
neither novel nor systematic. He did not envision new possibilities of

---

140. *Gegenreformatorische Schriften*, 40.

141. Ibid., 41.   142. Ibid., 42–43.

143. "...Il pocho religioso affecto et exemplo de quelli che ne li passati anni hanno
governato la Chiesia di Dio" (Jedin, "Contarini und Camaldoli," 44).

organizing the Christian people or conceive of administrative structures that differed substantially from existing ones he considered adequate. In Contarini's works there is no image of a golden age of the church to which he wanted to return; he knew church history well enough to realize how many practical difficulties and theological disputes had arisen in the past. Instead, his view of order puts first the observance of norms and regulations already enacted by ecclesiastical authorities but no longer properly enforced. In advocating the reaffirmation of existing laws that would ensure good government in the church, Contarini was of course looking backward. Yet his stance was not simply that of a conservative intent on preserving whatever already existed; rather, it was that of an intelligent Christian living in the world who knew that laws alone do not suffice to maintain order throughout the church.

It is precisely for this reason that the figure of the bishop assumes such importance in Contarini's writings. The bishop can become the key to good order on the local level through his moral force and example to the priests and people of his diocese, making the Christian message a living reality to them. But as a good shepherd he also enforces the laws of the church in a reasonable manner. He is the visible link between the spirit of prophecy in the church and the spirit of order, of the fervent, visionary aspect of Christianity and the necessary structures designed to transmit the Christian religion from generation to generation. Contarini was only too aware of how difficult it would be to reform the whole church, and he had no detailed blueprint for change. On the local level, a good and appropriately educated bishop could conceivably bring about a turn for the better. Notwithstanding the seemingly utopian character of Contarini's tract on the office of the bishop, it arguably has its practical side too. After all, its author confined himself to the level of the church where there was most hope for change, rather than tackling the entire hierarchy.

One quite specific Contarinian concept is the need for cooperation between the bishop and the secular authorities. Here the author's Venetian outlook again shows itself. Contarini envisions church and state working harmoniously in their separate spheres for the good of society. Order in the church entails the recognition that there are limits to the competence of ecclesiastical rulers in deciding issues concerning their Christian flock, including deference to the state in such matters as criminal justice. Though Contarini did not use the image of the two swords, he unquestioningly accepted a theory that saw both church and state as God's agents in bringing about and preserving peace, order, and justice in this world.

Finally, order in the church, in Contarini's view, excluded coercion or violence. That his was not an inquisitorial mentality can be seen from the *Confutatio*. Unlike Gianpietro Carafa, his future close associate in efforts at reform, Contarini never considered the battle against heretics of prime importance for the church. Christians were to be like the light shining on the mountain, impressing the sinful and the indifferent by their example. Here a side of Contarini emerges that is almost Erasmian: his firm belief in the teachability and rationality of human beings, who will respond to what is good, true, and noble when it is set before them. Again, Contarini should not be interpreted as an impractical dreamer in the conclusion to the *Confutatio*. Open to persuasion and utterly unfanatical himself, he had no difficulty in imagining men who held different, even antithetical, opinions, without seeing in them adversaries to be extirpated. The strength of his position came from the inner certainty he himself had attained. It made him willing to discuss and debate other views without fear of compromising his own. The ideal ecclesiastical hierarchy in the *Confutatio* is in reality a projection of Contarini's own ideal. He saw Christians as reasonable persons whose spirit of charity precluded undue attachment to their own opinions; they would be willing to listen even to Lutherans, and to see in them brothers.

Just as he had called on the pope in 1529 to be a father and keeper of peace among nations, so Contarini in his theological works of the early 1530s called on the governors of the Christian people to set them the example of good shepherds. He saw charity and humility, not coercion or sanctions, as the key to a revitalized church.

Order in the State

Contarini's literary fame in the sixteenth century rested not so much on his philosophical or theological writings as on his book dealing with the government of Venice, which remains even today the best-known treatise on the subject. Begun between 1523 and 1525 and finished in the early 1530s,[144] *De magistratibus et republica Vene-*

---

144. Gilbert, "Date of Composition," 175–77.

torum was first published in Paris in 1543, with French and Italian translations appearing in the following year and an English translation in 1599.[145] The only modern monograph devoted to the book[146] needs to be updated by recent contributions that have deepened our understanding of what has been called "the great source that fed republican thought in monarchical centuries"[147] and underlined the significance of the work for European political thought. Although one of the treatise's principal purposes was to reinforce the so-called myth of Venice as the perfect state,[148] a close examination of the text reveals a number of other purposes as well. But no consensus has emerged concerning its ultimate intent or the readers for whom it was intended.

One intriguing suggestion is that the book may have originated in a dinner-table conversation between Contarini and Thomas More in Bruges in 1521.[149] More's *Utopia* had appeared five years earlier, and Contarini could easily have read it. Yet Contarini makes no mention of the book and remarks merely that More was a very learned gentleman. A more likely candidate than More as a stimulus to reflection on the nature of republics is Giovanni Corsi, the Florentine ambassador to Spain from 1522 to 1525. Corsi had belonged to the group that met in the Orti Oricellari, with which Contarini became briefly acquainted in 1515, and the two ambassadors were friends at the Spanish court.[150] Inevitably they discussed the governments of their own states, in

145. The first Latin edition was published by M. Vascosani, the French translation of 1544 by Galiot du Pré in Paris, and the Italian translation of the same year by Girolamo Scotto in Venice. The English translation by Lewis Lewkenor was published in London in 1599 (facsimile reprint, Amsterdam and New York, 1969); see David McPherson, "Lewkenor's Venice and Its Sources," *Renaissance Quarterly* 41 (1988): 459–66. Numerous editions of the Italian and French versions attest to the continuing interest in Contarini's book well into the seventeenth century. The manuscript is in Florence, Biblioteca Nazionale, Cod. Magliab., cl. XXX, N. 146, fols. 1r–78r.

146. Hermann Hackert, *Die Staatsschrift Gasparo Contarinis und die politischen Verhältnisse Venedigs im sechzehnten Jahrhundert* (Heidelberg: Winter, 1940).

147. Gilbert, "Date of Composition," 184. For a comprehensive view of the work, see the observations of William J. Bouwsma, *Venice and the Defense of Republican Liberty* (Berkeley and Los Angeles: University of California Press, 1968), 145–53; and the more debatable treatment of J.G.A. Pocock, *The Machiavellian Moment* (Princeton: Princeton University Press, 1975), 320–30. See also Elisabeth G. Gleason, "Reading Between the Lines of Contarini's Treatise on the Venetian State," *Historical Reflections/Réflexions historiques* 15 (1988): 251–70.

148. James S. Grubb, "When Myths Lose Power: Four Decades of Venetian Historiography," *Journal of Modern History* 58 (1986): 46.

149. Gilbert, "Religion and Politics," 115.

150. Fragnito, "Cultura umanistica," 114n.165. On Corsi, see P. Malanima, "Corsi, Giovanni," in *DBI* 29:567–70.

contrast both to each other and to the Habsburg Empire, which they were observing at its administrative center. During his stay in Spain Contarini had the leisure to put his thoughts on paper, an occupation that may have assuaged the yearning for Venice he occasionally expressed in his dispatches.

The years following the Spanish embassy were crucial for the final shape of the book. The sack of Rome, the mission to Clement VII, participation in the negotiations leading to the Peace of Bologna, and finally immersion in Venetian government affairs all gave Contarini an insider's understanding of Venetian, Italian, and European politics. *De magistratibus* is written without illusions about the new realities of political power after Charles V's triumph in 1530. Contarini knew that Venice had descended to the rank of one of the lesser European states. His book thus does more than merely reflect views held by Venetian patricians after the War of the League of Cambrai[151] or the "interpretation of history and politics formulated by Venetian humanists of the post-Cambrai generation."[152] It is marked first of all by Contarini's realization of what the Peace of Bologna meant for Venice, and only secondarily is it his response to the Cambrai crisis.

The work is divided into five books. The first deals with the location and origins of the city of Venice and its basic political institution, the Great Council. Book II treats the office of the doge, followed in the next by a discussion of the Senate, the Council of Ten, and the main judicial tribunals. Book IV continues the description of the various magistracies, while the last discusses the government of the Venetian *terraferma*. Along the way the author offers numerous reflections about the past, pointed and at times poignant *obiter dicta*, and glimpses of his own views, all of which contribute to infuse life into the book as well as to make its texture more intricate than it at first appears.

On the surface, *De magistratibus* is written for strangers coming to Venice, predictably full of admiration for the beautiful and splendid city in its improbable setting. Contarini sets out to help his readers see a less obvious aspect of the city's remarkable nature: its excellent government, which surpasses even the dreams of philosophers who created imaginary commonwealths.[153] His intention thus seems clear. Yet even

151. Myron Gilmore, "Myth and Reality in Venetian Political Theory," in Hale (ed.), *Renaissance Venice*, 434.

152. Lester J. Libby, Jr., "Venetian History and Political Thought After 1509," *Studies in the Renaissance* 20 (1973): 8.

153. *Opera*, 264. If Contarini is including More's *Utopia* here, the reference remains very general.

a cursory reading reveals that he went far beyond his announced intention by writing a treatise that at crucial points speaks to members of his own patrician class much more forcefully than to even the most admiring foreigner, who after all had little personal concern with many of the issues Contarini raised. The book in fact has several levels of meaning: first, the description of institutions and magistracies; then, well-chosen and pedagogically effective examples from the Venetian past meant to illustrate the philosophical basis of the Republic's form of government; and finally, subtle but pointed references to aspects of the Venetian state which Contarini regarded as needing reform so that Venice could take her due place in a greatly changed Europe. The new international order had left her diminished in military, political, and economic significance, but Contarini believed that the Venetian state could still contribute much to contemporary European culture and political understanding.[154]

Contarini's treatise is neither a faithful portrait nor a utopian tract, but a combination of the actual and the ideal, the descriptive and the prescriptive, which blend to form the portrait of good and just government.[155] Enlarging on his statement that he is addressing his work to foreigners, he adds that he hopes to enable "anyone to determine easily whether [the Venetian Republic] is ordered well or wrongly."[156] For this purpose an exposition of the principles on which the government is based is as important as a discussion of its various organs and

154. William A. Bouwsma, "Venice and the Political Education of Europe," in Hale (ed.), *Renaissance Venice*, 451, discusses the "particular advantages" of Venice "for bringing into focus the political conceptions of modern Europeans" and remarks that the Venetian achievement "corresponded to the emerging needs of the European nations."

155. Zera S. Fink, *The Classical Republicans*, 2d ed. (Evanston, Ill.: Northwestern University Press, 1962), 39, briefly but correctly notes that Contarini "performed the extraordinary feat of bringing the real and the ideal together." But I have reservations about the notion that Contarini thought he was describing a "miracle." Gilbert, "Religion and Politics," 110n.70, points to Hackert's misunderstanding of Contarini's idealizing of Venice. Unless one reads the work as both descriptive and idealizing, it is possible to accuse Contarini of hypocrisy and "the smugness of Venetians" (Hackert, *Staatsschrift*, 113) and to miss what he was really doing. Dittrich, *GC*, 238, in my opinion overstates the importance of philosophical elements in Contarini's book, thereby missing some of its most significant dimensions. While stating that it describes "the actual circumstances of the Venetian constitution at the beginning of the sixteenth century," he nevertheless decides that it should properly be reckoned among Contarini's philosophical works.

156. "Quamobrem dum de hac nostra Republica scribere instituerim, ut quilibet facile dignoscere queat, rectene an perperam se habeat, hinc mihi potissimum exordium sumendum reor" (*Opera*, 264).

magistracies. The state, according to Contarini, exists to ensure that through its institutions its citizens can lead happy lives in the exercise of virtue. He thinks that Venice has been more successful in this than any of the states of antiquity, including Athens, Sparta, and Rome, and the whole of his book supports this central thesis.

Interestingly, Contarini makes no flat assertion that republics are inherently superior to monarchies. His comparison of the two forms of government is more cautious and more subtle than that. Not only would many of his presumed readers come from states governed by princes or kings, but even his fellow nobles in Venice, who in general were convinced of the incompatibility of principalities and republics, included open admirers of Charles V and his empire.[157] If not outright advocates of a *pax Habsburgica*, these men at least contemplated with equanimity Venice's close cooperation with the emperor and his brother Ferdinand. To this group belonged Alvise Mocenigo, Contarini's inveterate enemy, whose pro-imperial stand was notorious.[158] Thus Contarini did not challenge the proponents of monarchical government, acknowledging that all things being equal the rule of one man exercised in accordance with reason might be best. Yet he thought that this possibility remained open only in the realm of philosophy, for in actuality human nature is inclined to baseness, and the brevity of human life makes government by a larger number of men preferable for civil society, as "experience, the mistress of all, so excellently teaches us."[159] Venice is the paradigm of a state in which experience has tempered theory to produce a perfect government. In this pronouncement we catch an autobiographical note: for Contarini, experience was a critical contributor to the development of living organisms, whether individual or collective.

Contarini's reconstruction of the Venetian past reveals first of all that he fully accepted the ethos of his patrician class. The establishment of perfect political order was due to noble ancestors, "maiores nostri," who are repeatedly spoken of as having possessed all but superhuman virtue—wisdom and goodness together with complete selflessness—

157. Ambrosini, "Immagini dell'impero," 67–68. I do not think that the prospect of Charles V's universal monarchy seemed to Contarini a good thing for independent Italian states, as the author does (69).

158. For his deportment during the negotiations at Bologna in 1529–30, see Sanuto, *Diarii* 53:51, 65, 68, 132. He consistently supported Habsburg political objectives; see, for example, Aldo Stella, "Die Staatsräson und der Mord an Michael Gaismair," *Der Schlern* 58 (1984): 309–10.

159. *Opera*, 266–67.

which made them willing to subordinate their private good to the public good.[160] From the beginning of the city's existence aristocrats had been the shapers of her destiny, since the first inhabitants, refugees from Attila who had settled with their families in the lagoon after being forced to abandon their mainland homes, "excelled others in nobility and wealth." Although the makers of Venice were God's instruments, their superior social status did not derive from that fact. They brought nobility with them when they first reached the site of the future city: "The noblest people of the province of Venetia, fleeing the violence of the barbarian and the destruction of all Italy, withdrew to our estuaries and founded this most splendid city. They gave it the name of Venetia so that posterity should know that the flower of the nobility of all towns in the region of Venetia were assembled together there."[161]

Nobles had shaped the city, and only they possessed the fullness of citizenship. The founders in their wisdom had decreed that the common people could not share in this privilege, since "a citizen is a free man," unlike those who perform servile work.[162] Nobility of birth alone enabled men to participate in government; the mere amassing of wealth was no argument in favor of admission to noble status. Contarini is aware that new names had been inscribed in the rolls of Venetian nobility, most notably after the War of Chioggia in the fourteenth century, but he touches on this fact only briefly in mentioning foreigners whose high rank or exceptional service to the Republic had made them eligible for admission to its patriciate.[163] These cases were so rare as not to mar Contarini's general picture of the hereditary nobles as "the eyes of the city." Using the analogy of the human body, Contarini points out that members who lacked eyes necessarily obeyed those who did have eyes and saw what needed to be done. This is the order that harmonizes with nature. Contarini concludes that "if in any state—as happens in many—the citizens should get to the point of folly, and the people should want to exercise the power of sight and claim for themselves the function of the eyes, that entire state will necessarily be in continuous turmoil."[164] To prevent that from happening Venice had guardians of order, the nobles, whom God used to preserve

160. E.g., ibid., 264: "Certissimum hoc reor argumentum esse, non ambitionis ventosaeque famae maiores nostros studiosos fuisse, sed patriae tantum bono, communique utilitati consuluisse. Hac ergo incredibili virtute animi, maiores nostri hanc Rempublicam instituere, qualem post hominum memoriam nullam extitisse." Similarly, p. 263.

161. Ibid., 307.

162. Ibid., 268. Here Contarini echoes Aristotle, *Politics*, 3.5.

163. Ibid., 269.   164. Ibid., 326.

justice and minister to the general good.[165] Contarini believed that the nobles were a superior class even when they were impoverished, and argued elsewhere that they had a special claim on assistance should they need it.[166] As Venice's preeminent element, the nobles had created an orderly society that in turn reflected hierarchical cosmic order;[167] they were the mind and soul of the Venetian state, which originated from the political genius of their class.[168] Thus Contarini's book, while it continues the long tradition of exalting aristocracy that is found in Venetian humanist literature,[169] is also the supreme literary monument to what he considered the political achievement of the Venetian nobility: a just state and a just society. Although governed by nobles, the state existed by the consent of the governed and their love of those who guided them.[170] Ultimately, the system worked because of the moderation of the nobility,[171] on whose virtue Venetian greatness rested and who wisely provided safeguards against disturbances by the people.

The most famous part of Contarini's book is his presentation of the Venetian state as a perfect balance of democracy, oligarchy, and monarchy. Elaborating the myth that Venice possessed a mixed constitution, Contarini sees the democratic principle operating in the Great Council; the aristocratic in the Senate, the Council of Ten, and the *savi*; and the monarchical in the doge.[172] At the conclusion of Book I

165. Contarini expressed similar thoughts in "Cardinali Polo de poenitentia," *Reg.*, 355–56: "Il medesimo ordine si vede nel governo delle famiglie fra li homeni et nel regimento delle cita, che dio usa per instrumento suo alcuni homeni, li quali sono causa di conservare la iustitia et il bene commune."

166. "De officio episcopi," in *Opera*, 430.

167. See the observations of Cervelli, *Machiavelli*, 315.

168. This point is stressed in Franco Gaeta, "L'idea di Venezia," in Arnaldi and Stocchi (eds.), *Storia della cultura veneta* 3(3):635.

169. For this tradition, see Margaret L. King, *Venetian Humanism in an Age of Patrician Dominance* (Princeton: Princeton University Press, 1986), esp. 92–150.

170. *Opera*, 321: the people of the Venetian mainland showed themselves always as loving and obedient to the Venetian nobility ("populus . . . semper amantissimum atque obsequentissimum nobilitatis se praestitisse").

171. Ibid., 326. Contarini closes his book with these reflections.

172. Ibid., 269. A vast literature exists on the myth of Venice as the perfect state in the sixteenth century. Among the most important studies are Gina Fasoli, "Nascita di un mito," in *Studi storici in onore di Gioacchino Volpe per il suo 80 compleanno* (Florence: Sansoni, 1958), 1:447–79; Felix Gilbert, "The Venetian Constitution in Florentine Political Thought," in *Florentine Studies*, ed. Nicolai Rubinstein (London: Faber & Faber, 1968), 463–500 (reprinted in *History: Choice and Commitment*, 179–214); Franco Gaeta, "Alcune considerazioni sul mito di Venezia," *Bibliothèque d'humanisme et renaissance* 23 (1961): 58–75; idem, "L'idea di Venezia," 565–641; Brian Pullan, "The Significance of Venice," *Bulletin of the John Rylands University Library of Manchester* 56 (1973–74): 443–62; August Buck, "Laus Venetiae," *Archiv für Kulturgeschichte* 57 (1975): 185–94. For further bibliography, see Grubb, "When Myths Lose Power."

and the beginning of Book III, Contarini repeats this idea, each time comparing the well-tempered constitution to the harmony of beautiful music, which comes to serve as a metaphor for the well-ordered state.[173] This analysis of the Venetian constitution depends primarily on Aristotle and Polybius, but it also carries on the Venetian tradition, reaching back into the Middle Ages, of stylized encomia of the excellence and balance of the Republic's government. It has been rightly suggested that Contarini's should be compared with earlier treatises in order to be bring out all its nuances.[174] His treatment of the mixed constitution is much more than "a masterpiece of intellectual play, full of elegance and taste."[175] Contarini believed that this constitution existed in reality as the basis of civil concord, since it assured that no single element could assume the dominant role in government. He did not, however, think that a mixed constitution in and of itself guaranteed good order and civic peace. The key to the latter was the political wisdom of the noble class. Because the government was the exclusive preserve of that class, Contarini actually was analyzing democratic, oligarchic, and monarchical elements within the ruling class alone. Jean Bodin's later observation that Contarini denied the aristocratic character of Venice is beside the point because Contarini made a basic distinction between mere inhabitants of the city and the nobles as its true citizens, to whom he confined his discussion.[176]

Although in Contarini's writings the identification of the ruling class and its *ratio* is complete, his personal solidarity with the actual nobility of his time is a more complex matter. *De magistratibus* reveals him as both the encomiast and critic of his class, conscious that some of its members have turned their back on the patterns of behavior laid down by the founders. He addresses himself to them in outlining the high ideals they must live up to in order to perpetuate the excellence of the state into which they were born. Choosing a few key instances from the past, Contarini uses them as mirrors for nobles whose departure from established practices has brought harm to the state.

173. See Ellen Rosand, "Music in the Myth of Venice," *Renaissance Quarterly* 30 (1977): 512–13; and Libby, "Venetian History and Political Thought," 19. For the wider implications of Contarini's analogy, see Leo Spitzer, *Classical and Christian Ideas of World Harmony* (Baltimore: Johns Hopkins University Press, 1963).

174. Daniel Robey and John Law, "The Venetian Myth and the 'De Republica Veneta' of Pier Paolo Vergerio," *Rinascimento*, 2d ser., 15 (1975): 13. Vergerio's work of the early fifteenth century already includes the idea of the Venetian political system as a mixture of aristocratic, democratic, and monarchical elements (ibid., 17).

175. Hackert's formulation of "ein meisterhaftes Spiel, voll Eleganz und Geschmack" (*Staatsschrift*, 99) is quite inept, for it touches only the surface.

176. Ibid., 98–99.

Foremost in his critique is the nature of their participation in maritime affairs. He recalls that in former times Venetians achieved many victories at sea because they were familiar with it and, owing to extensive training, inured to the hardships it posed,[177] whereas now young patricians no longer regularly went to sea.[178] In the past the Arsenal was more important than it now was, and its supervising magistrate held in higher esteem.[179] Similarly, the magistrates in charge of naval affairs, the *savi agli ordeni*, formerly were of great account, whereas now young and inexperienced men were often elected to those positions.[180] Contarini points regretfully to the decline of Venice as a maritime power, in the hope of seeing that decline reversed by the same class that originally had carved out a seaborne empire. Still, he knows that the reorientation of the ruling class away from the sea and toward the *terraferma* is an accomplished fact.

It has been argued recently, and I believe incorrectly, that "Contarini's traditionalist view of the sources of Venetian strength and greatness made him deeply hostile to the republic's policy of landward expansion, which he regarded as a dangerous innovation of recent times."[181] On the contrary, he paints an idealized picture of Venetian expansion that reconciles it with his theme of Venice as the perfect commonwealth. Venice manifested her greatness by coming to the aid of her neighbors when they appealed for help, even though the Republic was reluctant to become embroiled in the affairs of the *terraferma*:

Nevertheless after a long period the policy of the Senate yielded to the pleas of the neighboring peoples, all of whom suffered under the rule of petty kings whom they could endure no longer. The Senate turned its attention to the mainland. When it had driven out the tyrants, and the citizens everywhere gave it their adherence, it restored the whole region of Venetia to essentially its original state. Venetia now reverted gratefully to its native inhabitants after the foreign tyrants were ejected, those offscourings of the barbarians who had settled throughout the region and oppressed the conquered peoples with a harsh servitude.[182]

Contarini here employs a humanist historiographical scheme, portraying Venice as the restorer of order on the mainland as it had existed in

177. *Opera*, 317, 319.   178. Ibid., 320.
179. Ibid., 314.   180. Ibid., 293.
181. Libby, "Venetian History and Political Thought," 29. Cervelli, *Macchiavelli*, 324–26, gives a better assessment of Contarini's ideas regarding Venetian expansion.
182. *Opera*, 317.

classical times before the onset of the destructive barbarians. By acting as it did, the Senate in a sense built a bridge between the Republic and ancient Rome that spanned the valley of darkness and bondage into which the neighbors of Venice had been plunged for centuries.

In olden times there was a link between the sea, commerce, and the *virtù* of the nobility. That *virtù*, far from being lost, now maintained itself in a different setting. Venetian wisdom in modern times was revealed in the government of mainland cities. Each had an appointed *podestà* or governor who now functioned as judge, a *capitano* in charge of military affairs, a treasurer, and a castellan where there was a castle or fortress.[183] Despite the appointment of Venetians to the more important posts, the subject cities had been left undisturbed in the possession of their ancient laws and statutes. When dealing with legal issues the governors sat together with local experts in the law, deciding nothing without consulting them. Venetian nobles were not permitted to function as *iurisperiti*, or legal advisors,[184] in deference to local customs and traditions. Thus the uniquely high standards of Venetian justice forged an additional tie between city and *terraferma*, the solidity of which was shown in the mainland's loyalty to Venice during the dark days of the War of the League of Cambrai. Contarini sees the expanded Venetian state as benefiting the subject cities greatly, since they were assured of good order while still retaining a certain amount of autonomy and having their defence organized and paid for by Venice.[185] The city, then, was not only the center of the *terraferma* in every sense, but also the bringer and guardian of peace.

On this last point Contarini is eloquent, attributing to the founders of Venice a deep concern for harmony and peace. Unlike the Romans, who educated their young so completely in warfare that when Carthage was destroyed they turned upon one another, the Venetians did not gear their men for war but for defense. Venice never forgot the intention of the founders, who in their wisdom knew that warfare should be subordinated to peace and that wise government would ensure continued peace.[186] For Contarini peace is not the mere absence of conflict but a transcendent good. It benefits the entire state and society and must be pursued actively, even aggressively. His views

183. Ibid., 316.   184. Ibid., 325.

185. On this topic see also Gaeta, "L'idea di Venezia," 637–38, who regards Contarini's treatment of the harmony between the city and the mainland as "the most subtly seductive" part of the entire work.

186. *Opera*, 267.

cannot be explained simply as the product of a contemplative bent that made him dislike armed conflict, or by supposing that he and his contemporaries consciously rejected the turbulence of martial undertakings for the security of an ordered *cursus honorum* where one office led smoothly to the next with no risks entailed.[187] Contarini's exaltation of peace has more complex roots. His consistent preference for resolving conflicts by patient diplomacy reflects his own temperament, his reasoned conviction, and his experience as ambassador. He knew how dangerous further war would be for his homeland. By herself Venice could not hope to achieve military victories in Italy, but joining leagues was an alternative also fraught with problems, as recent experience had shown. Contarini is speaking to his fellow nobles when he praises peacekeeping as a specifically Venetian virtue. In this instance he ignores the fact of Venice's many previous wars in order to drive home to his readers the bitter lesson he himself had drawn from the involvement of his homeland in the League of Cambrai.

For Machiavelli, too, that lesson was clear. He saw in the defeat at Agnadello a proof of the deficiency of the Venetian state: "In one day they [the Venetians] lost the state which they had acquired during many years with infinite expense; although they recently have gained some of it back, they have regained neither their reputation nor their strength, and thus live at the mercy of others, like all the other Italian rulers."[188] That Machiavelli was no admirer of Venice is well known. He thought Venetians arrogant in prosperity but weak and cowardly in adversity, and he judged their state to have been a threat to the political stability of Italy before 1494 because of its expansionism and aspirations to the "monarchia d'Italia."[189] Agnadello only confirmed that underneath the blustering façade which Venetians presented to the world there lay the serious weakness of a state that relied on mercenary soldiers. To their chagrin they had to learn what St. Mark himself had

187. Hackert, *Staatsschrift*, 75, 96. He believes Contarini's encomium of peace masks his passive, contemplative side that makes him shrink from war, and compares Contarini's generation unfavorably with that of the great warrior Andrea Contarini, even seeing in the outlook of the former a sign of Venetian decadence.

188. *Istorie fiorentine*, Book I, 29. For an excellent description of the battle of Agnadello, see Piero Pieri, *Il Rinascimento e la crisi militare italiana*, 2d ed. (Turin: Einaudi, 1971), 455–69.

189. Machiavelli "represented Venice as an ungrateful friend, an unreliable ally, and a major threat to the peace of Italy before the coming of the French. Her populace he depicted as morally deficient, insolent in prosperity and abject in adversity" (Bouswsma, *Venice*, 69). See *Discorsi*, Book III, chap. 31; *Istorie fiorentine*, Book V, chaps. 19–21; *Il Principe*, chap. 2. For Agnadello, see *Discorsi*, Book I, chap. 6.

had to learn in order to be the symbol of effective Venetian domination of the mainland: "At his own cost, and perhaps to no avail, St. Mark realized too late that he needs to hold in his hand the sword and not the book."[190]

Contarini interprets the consequences of Agnadello quite differently. Though almost all the European rulers had conspired against Venice, she had withstood their assault with God's help, "and our state, which almost fell into ruin, is [now] restored undiminished."[191] While duly acknowledging that God had preserved the Venetian state from its enemies, Contarini leaves no doubt that it deserved to endure because of its fundamental justice. The period immediately following the defeat in the War of the League of Cambrai showed once and for all that the nobility and the state were one[192] and that the political virtue of the rulers had bound the entire dominion to its center not by force or fear, but by the love and devotion of the governed for their governors. No other state had ever achieved what Venice had:

> From the first beginnings until our own time [the Republic] has remained safe for one thousand two hundred years not only from the domination of strangers but also from civil sedition of any consequence. This was accomplished not by violence, armed might, or fortified strongholds, but by a just and temperate manner of ruling so that the people obeyed the nobility very willingly. They desire no change of government, but on the contrary are more strongly attached to the nobles.[193]

The recent war furnished proof that the Venetian state survived because of the reciprocity of right disposition and action on the part of the nobles and the other inhabitants. After the terrible defeat at Agnadello, when Venice was hard pressed on all sides, the people not only made no attempt to overthrow the nobility, but even, "weeping, offered their lives for the defense of the Republic, thereby preserving it." Their love for Venice was further demonstrated at the siege of Padua, when many plebeians voluntarily joined the nobles against the troops

---

190. Machiavelli, "Dell'ambizione," as quoted by Gaeta, "L'idea di Venezia," 607: "San Marco a le sue spese, e forse invano, / tardi conosce come li bisogna / tener la spada e non il libro in mano." For a fine discussion of Machiavelli's anti-Venetian attitude, see pp. 604–14.

191. *Opera*, 309.

192. Another Venetian patrician, Andrea Mocenigo, stressed the absolute solidarity of the state with the nobility in his history of the War of the League of Cambrai, written between 1515 and 1518; on this see Libby, "Venetian History and Political Thought," 33.

193. *Opera*, 325.

of Emperor Maximilian.[194] A most important argument barely surfaces here: that the Venetian state has continued to exist because of the consent of the governed. This idea, however, is not elaborated. Having given their actions his approval, Contarini has little more to say about the commoners, who as a class held no theoretical interest for him.

The most important lesson of Agnadello for Contarini was that Venetian nobles had built a state so solidly based that it survived a calamitous war, proof of the nobles' political and moral virtue. Yet Contarini is not complacent in his admiration of this supreme achievement of his class; rather, he voices his apprehension that the war may have strained the cohesion of the nobility. His book does not present the nobility as a monolithic unit, but as a complex class in which the interests of the young and the old or the rich and the poor members are at odds.[195] The best arguments against reading *De magistratibus* as a picture of static Venetian perfection is contained in certain significant passages, which, although their author does not stress them, illuminate his remarkable understanding of Venice's actual historical position.

In the first such passage he comments on an old law providing for relief of poor nobles. Each Venetian galley used to have eight young nobles assigned to it who were not only salaried but also allowed to carry a certain amount of trading merchandise exempt from tolls and taxes. The latter privilege could be transferred for a payment; thus nobles could profit from it even if they did not themselves engage in trade. By this means the state gave financial support to the nobles, who in turn learned the art of seafaring.[196] Contarini continues: "These ancient laws and customs endure even to our time, although certain young men, corrupted by ambition or luxury since the expansion of the empire, have neglected their country's institutions. In addition the number of citizens has so increased that through the inroads of war in our time and expenses at home, many more have become poor than can be provided for by this law."[197] Here is explicit admission that

---

194. Ibid.
195. Gilbert, "Venice in the Crisis of the League of Cambrai," 290, writes: "Of course the struggle of the young against the old, of the poor nobles against the rich, of the old families against the new has been a constant feature in Venetian history. Nevertheless it might be suggested that the formation of a firm bloc consisting of the traditional ruling families and of the newer families of great wealth distinctly separate from the rest of the nobility, achieved its completion and perfection in the times of the war of the League of Cambrai."
196. *Opera*, 319.
197. Ibid., 320 (translation from Bouwsma, *Venice*, 152–53).

change had occurred in both the values and the economic position of members of the noble class. Old laws were falling into desuetude not because of their inadequacy but because recent events had produced a new type of noble who no longer subordinated his own interests to those of his class or the state as a whole. Contarini's brief mention of two additional instances of the neglect into which old regulations had fallen acquires added poignancy: no longer observed is either the law forbidding a Venetian noble to command more than twenty-five men[198] or the law providing that no captain of an armed galley can return to the city without first paying and dismissing most of his crew in Istria.[199] These are but surface symptoms of a much deeper problem, the decline from the high standards to which the noble class formerly adhered.

Contarini touches this problem only briefly, as if reluctant to face the implication of his reflections on order and disorder in the state. A crack has opened in the harmonious structure he has been describing, and he is too honest to ignore it but too much the Venetian to face it squarely. A few pages from the end of the book we read:

For nature so works that nothing can be permanent among men, but all things, no matter how perfectly they seem to have been established at the beginning, require restoration after some years, since nature inclines toward the worse; just as the body, though sated with its midday meal, cannot long remain sound unless dinner follows some hours later. Thus in everything it is necessary to assist and renew declining nature. May God help us to follow reason in this too, and devise such a remedy that everything needful may be provided in our Republic.[200]

William Bouwsma has called attention to "the curious ambiguity in Contarini's appeal to nature" here, and his awareness "of some sense in which nature is far from stable."[201] But this passage also reflects Contarini's mainstream cosmological views dating from his Paduan years. In contrast to the supralunary sphere, where everything was in harmony and order, the sublunary sphere was thought to undergo continuous change. The Venetian state, for all its perfection, belonged to the sphere of generation and corruption; mutable nature made no exception for it. Contarini is not denying that Venice, too, is subject to change, but he is calling on the nobles to stem and deflect the course of "natural" events by summoning up those qualities that made the

198. Ibid., 318.   199. Ibid., 321.
200. Ibid., 320 (translation from Bouwsma, *Venice*, 153).
201. Bouwsma, *Venice*, 152. For ideas of nature as both disorderly and orderly, see George Boas, "Nature," in Wiener (ed.), *Dictionary of the History of Ideas* 3:346–51.

state extraordinary in the first place: the employment of reason, the exercise of political virtue, and total identification with the Republic. Remedy was possible only if the ruling class grasped the danger in which Venice found itself and the nobility looked once more to the ideal vision of Venice as inspiration for its political, social, and ethical actions. Just as the mind is nobler and more perfect than the body, so, Contarini asserts, right understanding can triumph over the obstacles posed by the material world. Agnadello and its aftermath, for all the humiliation it brought upon Venice, might prove the impetus for a vigorous renovation of the state, which in turn would depend on rekindling the once ardent *virtù* of the nobility and restoring consensus among its members.

Contarini might have been worried about the power of the *papalisti*, the families within the nobility that were closely linked with the papal curia through the holding of ecclesiastical preferments and whose clerical members were barred from state offices. The pursuit of their own interests at the expense of those of the state made families like the Grimani, Cornaro, and Pisani disruptive of harmony and concord. The danger that such divided allegiances posed for the Republic was an important reason for Contarini's call to respect the ideals of the past.[202] Certainly Contarini, who was in Venice from 1525 to 1528, between his two embassies, at a particularly difficult period of social tensions and economic problems, had no illusions about these matters. He knew at first hand of other disruptive potentialities of the nobility as well: the dangers of the so-called *svizzeri*, or poor nobles, willing to cast their votes wherever financial compensation was offered, and of the *broglio*, the maneuvers and deals that preceded elections.[203] He entered public life during the war period, when the government's need of money was so desperate that it broke with time-honored tradition and consented to the sale of offices.[204] There was no denying that the laws were not applied impartially to rich and poor nobles, rich transgressors often being able to escape punishment entirely. It would nev-

202. Gaetano Cozzi, "Lo stato veneziano nell'opera politico-religiosa di Gasparo Contarini a cavallo degli anni '30," paper read at the meeting commemorating the five-hundredth anniversary of the birth of Gasparo Contarini, Venice, 2 March 1986. On the *papalisti*, see also Grendler, *Roman Inquisition*, 30–31; and Pullan, "Occupations and Investments," 397–400.

203. See the masterly discussion of Venetian social, legal, and economic tensions during the 1520s by Gaetano Cozzi, "Authority and the Law," 293–345, esp. 321–35.

204. Ibid., 313–14; and Gilbert, "Venice in the Crisis of the League of Cambrai," 284–85.

ertheless be a mistake to regard *De magistratibus* as glossing over the lack of harmony among those who were "the eyes of the Republic." His strong practical sense, coupled with his expert understanding of how the government actually functioned, is attested by the careful description of offices and procedures throughout his treatise. Although with his insider's knowledge he could have expatiated on the realities of Venetian politics, he deliberately chose to dwell on the perfection of its ideal rather than the realities of corruption and degeneration that he knew disfigured it.

I suggest that he had two audiences in mind, and that he was addressing them on different levels. The first was the audience of educated foreigners for whose benefit he described the workings of the Venetian constitution. The second was his own class, which did not need description so much as reflection on Venice's tradition and values in a time of turmoil and uncertainty. Contarini, like his contemporaries, had passed through the crisis of Cambrai, and he belonged to a generation that had been deeply affected by then-recent events. He was therefore addressing himself primarily to the nobility in his muted admission of the need for reform in the state; he held before their eyes the vision of what Venice had been and ideally might be again, though he knew that a literal return to the past was impossible. The former position of Venice among European states could not be restored, but Venice's political virtue could once more flourish.

How he envisioned a restored Venice is not made explicit save perhaps in a few hints comprehensible only to insiders. One especially significant passage of this kind can be found at the beginning of the discussion of the Council of Ten. According to Contarini, "The Council of Ten has supreme authority among Venetians; it can be rightly asserted that it bears the responsibility for the safety of the state."[205] We have seen that in practice Contarini, as one of its members, supported the growing power of the Ten. His treatise shows his conviction that reform of the state would entail the tightening of the government by placing supreme authority firmly in the hands of a small elite. This inner circle was for Contarini the nerve center of the state, around which were arranged all the other parts of the governmental and administrative apparatus down to the most minor magistracies.

That Contarini favored an oligarchy of powerful men in control of the government can be seen further in his relations with Andrea Gritti,

---

205. "Decemvirum hoc collegium apud Venetos summae est autoritatis, et a quo non immerito quis asserat Reipub. incolumitatem praestari" (*Opera*, 295).

doge from 1523 to 1538. He judges Gritti to have been a senator of "outstanding wisdom and integrity,"[206] who brought these qualities to his ducal position. He does not, however, tell the reader that this doge, though admired for the strength and courage he had shown at Padua in 1509, was by and large not popular,[207] and that his election was due to a remarkable network of alliances among powerful Venetian families that formed an inside group within the nobility.[208] As doge, Gritti favored the *grandi*, a narrow oligarchy among the nobles.[209] During his two embassies, significantly, Contarini was in agreement with Gritti's political objectives. He shared the doge's pro-French sympathies, especially at the court of Clement VII, where he was the spokesman for Gritti's ideas. The thirty surviving letters from Gritti to Contarini between 1528 and 1530 reveal the close contact the two men maintained during this mission to Rome, the often minute instructions the doge personally sent to the ambassador, and the trust he had in Contarini's diplomatic abilities.[210] Between 1530 and 1535, while occupying ever higher offices, Contarini remained one of Gritti's close collaborators and supporters.

Recently, the period during which Gritti was doge has been the subject of several studies that have opened new perspectives on the man and his times.[211] It has become clear that membership in the Gritti circle meant espousing, or at the very least sympathizing with, a definite political and cultural program. Gritti championed the reform of the entire Venetian legal system in order to streamline laws and eliminate contradictory and confusing legislation. His schemes had far-

---

206. Ibid., 311.

207. Manfredo Tafuri, "'Renovatio urbis Venetiarum': il problema storiografico," in *"Renovatio urbis": Venezia nell'età di Andrea Gritti (1523–1538)*, ed. Manfredo Tafuri (Rome: Officina Edizioni, 1984), 11.

208. Finlay, "Politics and Family," 107ff.

209. Tafuri, "'Renovatio,'" passim; and idem, *Venezia e il Rinascimento: religione, scienza, architettura* (Turin: Einaudi, 1985), esp. 162–71.

210. VBC, Cod. Cicogna 3477; and Urbani, "Lettere ducali," disp. 1, 19–34; and disp. 3, 7–25. For an expression of Gritti's anti-imperial and pro-French views, see especially his letter of 23 July 1529 (Urbani, "Lettere ducali," disp. 3, 14–15).

211. Besides the two works of Manfredo Tafuri cited above (notes 207 and 209), see Antonio Foscari and Manfredo Tafuri, *L'armonia e i conflitti: la chiesa di San Francesco della Vigna nella Venezia del '500* (Turin: Einaudi, 1983); Leonardo Puppi, ed., *Architettura e utopia nella Venezia del Cinquecento: catalogo della mostra* (Milan: Electa, 1980). Gaetano Cozzi, "La politica del diritto nella Repubblica di Venezia" (1980), reprinted in his *Repubblica di Venezia*, 293–313, deals with Gritti's proposed reforms in masterly fashion.

reaching implications for the nobility, for their intent was that magistrates would become experts in the law and part of an efficient, specialized bureaucracy. In the end, opposition from nobles who closed-mindedly defended the status quo proved too strong for Gritti's designs to be realized. But Contarini's association with the doge demonstrates that his endorsement of the oligarchic tendencies within the Venetian ruling class was as much a matter of principle with him as it was personal preference. The Gritti circle prized order in the state even if that meant restructuring traditional relations among the Senate, the doge, and the Council of Ten in favor of the last-named. Contarini, too, believed that a vital, extremely powerful Council of Ten composed of experts who belonged to the most important families of the Republic and had the greatest stake in its welfare was needed for the revival of the state. Such a council, together with its *zonta* or advisory group, a doge who wielded wider discretionary powers than tradition assigned him, and the doge's six councillors were to be the thirty-two men who in reality governed Venice.

If the Gritti circle in fact had a distinct cultural program, as Manfredo Tafuri has argued convincingly, we can place Contarini's timeless-sounding views of Venice in their immediate cultural context. Tafuri thinks that the men around Gritti shared his vision of the state as a machine, the efficiency of which depended on speed in decision making and a reliable fund of specialized technical knowledge. He further believes that the ruling elite wanted to stimulate a reorientation of thought patterns among Venetians and launch a new image of Venice that would downplay the importance of military power. Venice was to become the cultural and intellectual center of Europe, the seat of philosophic wisdom, artistic excellence, and religious renewal.[212] For this program to succeed, Venice needed concord at home and peace abroad. In moving to achieve these goals the doge was also concerned with the less lofty but at least equally important task of assuring the grain supply that would keep Venice's own population content while the Republic's new image was diffused abroad.

The Venice of *De magistratibus* is a city of peace and concord. Time after time Contarini stresses the commitment to peace, a peace that is a positive moral excellence promoting good in the state and its people. While the treatise says nothing of art and touches on the city's archi-

212. Tafuri, "'Renovatio,'" esp. 23–42.

tecture only in the most general terms, it contributes to Venice's cultural revival in the Gritti period by constructing the ideal Venice as the model for present and future generations. Its constitution, as Contarini describes it, challenges its own ruling class to rise to heights of political wisdom, and invites those dwelling beyond its borders to emulate Venice's singular greatness. The Republic could truly be the education of Europe.

CHAPTER THREE

Venetian Reformer
at the Roman Court

Contarini's Rise to Prominence:
The *Consilium de emendanda ecclesia*

On 21 May 1535, for the second time in his pontificate, Paul III appointed new cardinals. They included John Fisher, bishop of Rochester, already imprisoned by Henry VIII; Guillaume du Bellay, archbishop of Paris; Nikolaus Schönberg, German Dominican and papal diplomat; two curial officials, Girolamo Ghinucci and Jacopo Simonetta; and Gasparo Contarini. Their selection was ratified in a long and stormy consistory,[1] testimony not only to the traditional reluctance of cardinals to add to their number but also to the repercussions that the political struggles between the Habsburgs and Valois were having at the highest levels of the church. The pope had to balance his appointees carefully so as not to appear partial. While opposition to Henry VIII played a role in the appointment of Fisher, du Bellay's new rank would reassure the king of France that Paul III was not leaning too far in the direction of the emperor in elevating Schönberg.[2] The two curialists and Contarini occupied a middle ground.[3]

1. Pastor, *Geschichte der Päpste* 5:102n.5, quotes from Biblioteca Apostolica Vaticana (hereafter cited as BAV), Ephemer. in Vat. Lat. 6978, fol. 137r, stating that the new cardinals were announced only after serious disagreement and altercation in the consistory.

2. The pope did not announce the appointment of the pro-imperial protonotary Marino Caracciolo until ten days later, keeping his name *in petto*. This appointment was intended to allay the misgivings of Charles V regarding the appointment of du Bellay; see Pastor, *Geschichte der Päpste* 5:102n.6.

3. Pastor, *Geschichte der Päpste* 5:102, calls Contarini pro-imperial on the strength of a letter by Cardinal Ercole Gonzaga, a partisan of Charles V, which characterized

The elevation of these men to the cardinalate received extravagant praise from contemporaries; scholars still describe it as a turning point in the history of the church, the beginning of serious reform in Rome.[4] In actuality, and leaving Fisher aside, other than Contarini only Schönberg had shown concern for church reform. And Contarini was known just to a limited number of people, since only one of his treatises had been published.[5] Still, his friends included some of the most important proponents of reform, and they saw in his appointment a sign that God was coming to the aid of the church at a critical moment.[6] The pope's choice of these new cardinals formed a striking contrast to the first group of appointments made shortly after his accession, when his two grandsons Alessandro Farnese and Guido Ascanio Sforza di Santafiora entered the sacred college at the ages of fifteen and sixteen, respectively. Benefices were heaped on them, and it appeared for a time that Paul III would continue the extravagant nepotism of Renaissance popes.[7] His second group of cardinals was therefore a most welcome surprise.

Contarini as "no less a servant of His [Imperial] Majesty" than Caracciolo and Schönberg were. About the latter Contarini had already reported on 8 March 1530 to the Venetian Senate: "è imperialissimo, e ha sempre tenuto questa fazione" (Albèri, *Relazioni*, 2d ser., 3:268). Nevertheless, in the light of Contarini's cautious attitude to Charles V, it would be more correct to consider him neutral, but realistic about the emperor's power.

4. See, for example, the dispatch of the papal nuncio in Venice, Girolamo Aleandro, 24 May 1535, in Gaeta (ed.), *Nunziature di Venezia* 1:314 (letter 145). Pastor considers the nomination a proof of Paul III's seriousness about reform; see *Geschichte der Päpste* 5:101, 103. See also Hubert Jedin, *Geschichte des Konzils von Trient* (Freiburg i.B.: Herder, 1951–75), 1:336 (hereafter cited as Jedin, *Trient*).

5. *De immortalitate animae*, Book I, appeared anonymously together with Pietro Pomponazzi's *Apologia* in 1518 in Bologna, and under Contarini's name in Venice in 1525.

6. Pole expressed this sentiment in a letter to Contarini, *Epistolarum Reginaldi Poli S.R.E. Cardinalis et aliorum ad ipsum collectio*, ed. A. M. Querini (Brescia, 1744–57), 1:450 (hereafter cited as *Ep. Poli*). See also the letter of Cosmo Gheri, bishop of Fano, to Contarini, in *Reg.*, 93 (no. 307); and that of Marcantonio Flaminio, who reported that "cognoscendo et affermando ognuno ch'el suo cardinalato non è proceduto da homini, ma da Dio, meritamente si crede che sua Maiestà voglia usarla per instrumento di qualche effetto novo et segnalato," in Marcantonio Flaminio, *Lettere*, ed. Alessandro Pastore (Rome: Edizioni dell'Ateneo & Bizzarri, 1978), 27. Further testimony is in *GC*, 321–23; and *Reg.*, 75–76 (nos. 255–256). Judgments of Paul III differ. Pastor, *Geschichte der Päpste* 5:17, stresses that his interest in his diocese of Parma and his becoming a priest in 1519 point to a concern with reform; he interprets Paul III's actions in a uniformly favorable light. Jedin, *Trient* 1:355, considers Paul III not as the first pope of Catholic reform but as its "precursor [*Wegbereiter*]," leaving open the vexed question of whether it is possible to reconcile the many contradictory aspects of his way of thinking.

7. Pastor, *Geschichte der Päpste* 5:100–101n.1. See also the bitter letter of Jan van Campen, later a member of Contarini's household, in *GC*, 317n.2.

The choice of Contarini is not easily explained, for it raises the larger question of the pope's intentions in regard to change in the church. Paul III, himself appointed cardinal by Alexander VI, had previously seemed a proverbial Renaissance prelate with little concern for church reform. Once elected pope, however, he proved sensitive to the new religious atmosphere with its demands for purification of the church. Intelligent and shrewd as well as deeply political, he began immediately to discuss the need for church reform and the calling of a council, unlike his weak predecessor. His appointments of May 1535 gave heart to those who hoped for Roman action at last. Indeed, the inclusion of Contarini among his cardinals was a deliberate, practical move toward building a bridge to the small but vocal and prestigious group of critical, reform-minded intellectuals in Rome and Italy.[8]

The possibility of elevation to the cardinalate could not have been completely unexpected for Contarini. His friend Giberti must have told him that Lodovico da Canossa, bishop of Baius, had earlier proposed him to Clement VII for the college of cardinals.[9] While on his embassy to the Medici pope, moreover, Contarini had become acquainted with the then Cardinal Alessandro Farnese, now pope, who was favorably impressed with the envoy. And Antonio Surian, Venetian ambassador to Paul III, reported to Doge Andrea Gritti, with whom Contarini was in continual contact, a conversation in which the pope inquired about certain of Contarini's views after telling the ambassador he was considering Contarini's nomination.[10] Nevertheless, the news of the appointment produced confusion rather than joy in Contarini's mind,[11] for it reopened the deeper question of how best to serve God in this life. After several days of uncertainty and meditation he concluded that his new dignity was God's calling and that he must accept it in order not to act against the divine will or offend his relatives and

8. Richard Douglas, *Jacopo Sadoleto, 1477–1547: Humanist and Reformer* (Cambridge, Mass.: Harvard University Press, 1959), 99–100, sees Contarini as "the symbol, if not the inspiration, of those Pauline reformers who by accident or design had remained free from curial venality, bureaucracy, and conservative bias." Jedin, *Trient* 1:336, thinks that Contarini's elevation to the cardinalate created "a secure support and a firm center" for the reform movement in Rome.

9. Beccadelli, "Vita," 21.

10. *Reg.*, 371–72 (Anhang no. 1). The text should be corrected by VBC, Cod. Cicogna 1540, fols. 115–117. The date of the letter is 20 May, not March.

11. Contarini to Cardinal Ercole Gonzaga, 29 May 1535, in Walter Friedensburg, "Der Briefwechsel Gasparo Contarini's mit Ercole Gonzaga," *Quellen und Forschungen aus italienischen Archiven und Bibliotheken* 2 (1899): 164 (letter 1).

friends. His brother-in-law and close friend Matteo Dandolo presented convincing arguments in favor of prayerful acceptance.[12]

A few days' hesitation in accepting the red hat may seem merely good form. Very few, after all, ever rejected the honor in the end. Contarini, however, was making real sacrifices by accepting. He was fifty-one years old at the time of his appointment. Becoming a cardinal meant giving up the high place he had reached in the government of Venice and embarking on a radically different career and way of life. He seems to have made the decision with the same earnestness that underlay his letter about the cardinalate to Querini long before.[13] The Benedictine Gregorio Cortese, abbot of San Giorgio Maggiore in Venice and one of his old friends, discussed this momentous step with him.[14]

Contarini received his first tonsure and minor orders from Gianpietro Carafa[15] and, unlike most cardinals, became a priest. In June 1537 Cardinal Ercole Gonzaga congratulated him on the celebration of his first mass.[16] Yet joined to his seriousness about the clerical vocation was a certain detachment about the cardinalate that enabled him to say to the pope during a disagreement: "I do not consider that the [red] hat is the greatest honor that has [ever] been bestowed on me!"[17] This, clearly, was the Venetian patrician speaking.

With the reception of that red hat at a consistory held in Perugia on 15 September 1535, Contarini entered the college of cardinals and became part of the society of Rome and the papal court.[18] While its highest offices were spiritual, it was also a mirror of the secular world with its social gradations. Cardinals, as princes of the church, were often politically powerful men, especially if they had the right connec-

---

12. Fragnito, *Memoria individuale*, 178.

13. Jedin, "Contarini und Camaldoli," 44–45.

14. Edmondo Solmi, "La fuga di Bernardino Ochino secondo i documenti dell'Archivio Gonzaga di Mantova," *Bullettino senese di storia patria* 15 (1908): 50.

15. Beccadelli, "Vita," 22.

16. Friedensburg, "Briefwechsel," 169 (letter 6).

17. Beccadelli, "Vita," 47. Both Della Casa, 15, and Quirini, 161, repeat this remark in their lives of Contarini.

18. ASVat, Arch. Consist., Acta Misc. 18 (1517–48), fols. 259v–260r. On 24 September 1535, still in Perugia, the ceremony of *aperitio oris* took place (fol. 260r), which conferred on Contarini the right to speak in consistory, to give advice, to participate in papal elections, and to receive a share of the collective income of the college of cardinals. For the ceremony and the form used by the pope, see Guillaume Mollat, "Contributions à l'histoire du Sacré Collège de Clément V à Eugène IV," *Revue d'histoire ecclésiastique* 46 (1951): 44.

tions. Among them were members of such princely families as the Gonzaga, Grimaldi, and Lorraine, of papal clans like the Cibo, of wealthy patrician and banker families like the Florentines Salviati, Ridolfi, and Pucci, the Venetians Grimani and Pisani, and other Italian and European aristocratic lines.

That the style of life of cardinals should—indeed must—reflect their social rank was taken for granted by the most complete "mirror of cardinals," Paolo Cortese's *De cardinalatu,* which drew an analogy between them and Roman patricians. Cortese described the ideal cardinal as wellborn and rich, living in a splendid palace with a household of 120 to 140 persons.[19] He thought that outward manifestation of wealth was important because it caused men to admire the possessor of such wealth, impressed them with his social eminence, and increased their respect for him. In point of fact the actual number of persons in cardinals' households less than a decade before Contarini's appointment was around 154.[20] The *familiae* of rich and noble cardinals were like miniature courts, with members of many social classes: noble relatives and dependents, scholars, artists, secretaries, friends, chaplains, adjutants, pages, guards, musicians, administrative officials, servants, cooks, grooms, footmen,[21] and even occasional disreputable characters.[22]

19. Paolo Cortese, *De cardinalatu, libri tres* (Rome, 1510), lvi^v–lvii^r. For other proposals concerning the size of cardinals' households, see Hubert Jedin, "Analekten zur Reformtätigkeit der Päpste Julius III. und Pauls IV.," *Römische Quartalschrift* 43 (1935): 111; Kathleen Weil-Garris and John F. D'Amico, *The Renaissance Cardinal's Ideal Palace: A Chapter from Cortese's "De Cardinalatu"* (Rome: Edizioni dell'Elefante, American Academy in Rome, 1980).

20. D. Gnoli, "Un censimento di Roma sotto Clemente VII," *Archivio della R. Società romana di storia patria* 17 (1894): 387, gives figures for 1526. Some households were considerably larger, like that of Cardinal Farnese, the later Pope Paul III, with 306 persons (p. 471) or that of Cardinal Cesarini with 275 (p. 481). There are no comparable figures for the 1530s that might make it possible to determine the effect of the sack of Rome on the style of life of cardinals.

21. These categories are found in a list of the household of another Cardinal Alessandro Farnese, Pope Paul III's grandson, which comprised 277 persons in 1544: BAV, Barb. lat. 5366, fols. 266–267. For the "families" of cardinals, see Gigliola Fragnito, "'Parenti' e 'familiari' nelle corti cardinalizie del Rinascimento," in *"Famiglia" del principe e famiglia aristocratica,* ed. Cesare Mozzarelli (Rome: Bulzoni, 1988), 565–87, with bibliography; and Pierre Hurtubise, "Familiarité et fidélité à Rome au XVIe siècle: les 'familles' des cardinaux Giovanni, Bernardo et Antonio Maria Salviati," in *Hommage à Roland Mousnier: clientèles et fidélité en Europe à l'époque moderne* (Paris: Presses Universitaires Franáaises, 1981), 335–50.

22. Paul Maria Baumgarten, *Von den Kardinälen des sechzehnten Jahrhunderts* (Krumbach: F. Aker, 1927), 36–38.

These households should not be dismissed simply as excesses peculiar to Renaissance cardinals. They belonged to a time when status in society carried definite duties with it, foremost that of furthering the social and economic standing of one's relatives and dependents. The aristocratic ethos accepted in the papal court meant that princely station was signalized by magnanimity and liberality.[23] Patronage of artists, architects, scholars, or writers was an important aspect of the *magnificentia* of rich cardinals, as was the duty of hospitality to important guests[24] and the employment of numerous retainers.

After the very rich cardinals came a middle group, wealthy enough but not on a scale that would permit them to maintain the large households necessary for assuming a princely or representative function in Roman society. They usually did not have their own houses but lived in rented quarters with smaller *familiae* than their wealthy counterparts. A good number of this group, such as the curial cardinals, had administrative or diplomatic responsibilities that did not require them to maintain magnificent households. The financial resources of members of this group varied widely,[25] for although benefices were their main source of wealth, the income derived therefrom could be substantial or relatively small.[26] Lower still on the economic scale were the so-called poor cardinals, who had none of the lucrative benefices.[27] They received shares of the collective income of the college of cardinals, and both Pope Paul III and afterward Julius III gave pensions to

23. The studies of Wolfgang Reinhard on these topics are fundamental: "Nepotismus: der Funktionswandel einer papstgeschichtlichen Konstanten," *Zeitschrift für Kirchengeschichte* 86 (1975): 145–85; "Kardinalseinkünfte und Kirchenreform," *Römische Quartalschrift* 77 (1982): 157–94; "Reformpapsttum zwischen Renaissance und Barock," in *Reformatio ecclesiae: Beiträge zu kirchlichen Reformbemühungen von der Alten Kirche bis zur Neuzeit. Festgabe für Erwin Iserloh,* ed. Remigius Bäumer (Paderborn: Schöningh, 1980), 779–96. See also his *Papstfinanz und Nepotismus unter Paul V. (1605–1621)* (Stuttgart: Hiersemann, 1974), esp. 1:157–60, for valuable observations.

24. Pierre Hurtubise, "La table d'un cardinal de la renaissance: aspects de la cuisine et de l'hospitalité à Rome au milieu du XVIᵉ siècle," *Mélanges de l'Ecole Française de Rome, moyen âge–temps modernes* 92 (1980): 249–82. The author reconstructs precise expenses for groceries (266–70) on the basis of account books of Cardinal Bernardo Salviati, whose *familia* in 1563–65 numbered 110 persons (258).

25. David S. Chambers, "The Economic Predicament of Renaissance Cardinals," *Studies in Medieval and Renaissance History* 3 (1966): 295. Reinhard, "Kardinalseinkünfte," 185, stresses that the family wealth on which some cardinals could draw is the chief unknown quantity in any attempt to determine incomes with exactness.

26. Barbara McClung Hallman, *Italian Cardinals, Reform, and the Church as Property* (Berkeley and Los Angeles: University of California Press, 1985), chap. 2.

27. A document of 1521 defined cardinals as poor if their annual income failed to reach 5,000 ducats; see Chambers, "Economic Predicament," 304.

those whose income did not reach what was considered a necessary minimum.[28]

Among the poor cardinals was Contarini. After two expensive embassies he was reluctant to draw more on family wealth, which he had described as "middling" already in 1529, stating that he was ashamed to be a further financial burden to his brothers.[29] As a cardinal, however, he had little choice but to turn to them for his needs.[30] It is not possible to determine how far their support extended. Contarini's most important source of income was a pension of two hundred ducats a month granted him shortly after his arrival in Rome and drawn from the office of the *dataria*. A second pension was assigned him in 1539.[31] In addition he was to receive eight hundred scudi a year from the bishopric of Pamplona, presented to him probably on the occasion of the emperor's visit to Rome in April 1536.[32] That October the pope nominated him to the bishopric of Belluno in Venetian territory, but the Senate did not accept the nomination until the following May, and even then only after strenuous efforts by the nuncio Girolamo Verallo.[33] Belluno, one of the poorest Venetian sees, brought Contarini

28. Reinhard, "Kardinalseinkünfte," 185. For the main sources of cardinals' incomes, see p. 184. Under Paul III eleven cardinals received pensions, while the number of recipients rose to twenty-two under Julius III.

29. *Reg.*, 45–46 (no. 126) and 53 (no. 165).

30. VBC, Cod. Cicogna 1540, fol. 113, contains a copy of a letter from the Venetian Senate to its ambassador in Rome, dated 26 August 1542, mentioning that Contarini's family had to spend money for his needs when he became a cardinal.

31. Contarini's name as a recipient of 200 ducats monthly first appears in the account books of the *dataria*, the "libri mastri," on 15 November 1535 (BAV, Vat. lat. 10600, fol. 74r). The records of payments continue regularly through May 1538. Then comes a break of four months when Contarini was absent from Rome, first at the meeting of Paul III and Charles V in Nice, then in Venice and Belluno. In October 1538 the payments resume (fol. 143v), and continue through September 1540 (Vat. lat. 10601, fol. 77r). In 1539 he was assigned a pension drawn from the legation of Bologna (*Reg.*, 121 [no. 440]). Both were paid for nine months, assuming that the second actually began in December 1539, when it was granted.

32. *GC*, 325. That the pension was not paid regularly can be seen from Contarini's letters of 10 December 1539 (ASVat, A.A., Arm. I–XVIII, 6461, fols. 55, 57r–v [*Reg.*, 120 (no. 436)]) and of late December or early January 1540 (ibid., fol. 63r [*Reg.*, 120 (no. 437, erroneously numbered 436)]). Contarini's secretary Girolamo Negri thought the pension was paltry, and wrote on 28 January 1537 that he was ashamed for Charles V at his having granted such a small sum (*Lettere di principi*, vol. 3 [Venice, 1570], 161v).

33. Contarini was granted Belluno on 23 October 1536 (ASVat, Arch. Consist., Acta Misc. 18, fol. 271r–v). But the Venetian Senate resisted the pope's appointment of a bishop in its territory, even though one of their own patricians was the nominee. Only after prolonged negotiations involving Venice's request for a levy on the clergy and the mediation of the nuntio Verallo was an agreement finally reached. On 24 May 1537

a little over a thousand ducats annually.[34] To these sums should be added whatever revenue his titular churches brought in,[35] which must have been modest, and his share of the *distribuzione del cappello*, or the corporate income of the college of cardinals, the precise amount of which in his case cannot be known.[36] On paper his income was increased greatly with his appointment as administrator of the see of Salisbury in 1539,[37] but the course of events in England prevented him from actually assuming that post. Contarini's income is unlikely to have reached more than half the twelve thousand florins that Cortese in his treatise deems necessary for a cardinal. He continued to be strapped for funds, especially in the late 1530s when poor harvests forced food prices up, but complaints about his financial position are rare in his correspondence.[38] It is difficult to say how sincere was the preference he expressed in 1535 for a relatively small pension over a lucrative benefice. In any case, he never had the opportunity to choose, for no rich benefice ever came his way.[39] He seems not to have been greatly concerned with money matters, if we can accept his secretary Girolamo Negri's description of him as a man who "is healthy in body and soul on account of his even-tempered nature as well as his acquired virtues, so that neither the death of his beloved brother nor the poverty in which he finds himself troubles him in the least or distracts

---

Contarini was accepted as bishop of Belluno; see ASV, Senato, Delib. Secreta, Reg. 58, fol. 18; and Gaeta (ed.), *Nunziature di Venezia*, vol. 2: *9 gennaio 1536–9 giugno 1542*, 95, 96, 98, 106, 117.

34. The Senate in 1542 referred to Belluno as "di poca valuta" (VBC, Cod. Cicogna 1540, fol. 114). In 1537–39 its income was 1,800 ducats a year; see Gaeta (ed.), *Nunziature di Venezia* 2:345.

35. For Contarini's titular churches, see Fragnito, "Contarini, Gasparo," in *DBI* 28 (1983): 181.

36. Chambers, "Economic Predicament," 297; ASVat, Fondo Concistoriale, Acta Camerarii, vol. 4, fol. 31v; vol. 5, fols. 24v, 34r, 46r, 53v, 60r. The *Cedularum et rotulorum libri* of the Archive of the College of Cardinals, which would show how much each cardinal received from the common income of the college, are missing for the period 1522–65; see ASVat, Indice 1121.

37. ASVat, Arch. Consist., Acta Misc., 18, fol. 316v.

38. Contarini wrote of the "strecta fortuna nella quale io mi ritrovo" (ASVat, A.A., Arm. I–XVIII, 6461, fol. 57r) and that he found himself "per la poca provisione, che io ho al mio vivere, in grande necessità" (*Reg.*, 120 [no. 437]). Pole, whose household was comparable to Contarini's, stated that it was not possible to get along on 500 ducats a month, which was probably more than the latter's regular monthly income; see *Ep. Poli* 2:28. For various reckonings of the minimum income for cardinals, see Jedin, "Analekten zur Reformtätigkeit," 108–11.

39. Report of Lorenzo Bragadin to the Senate, Rome, 2 Nov. 1535, in A. De Leva, "La concordia religiosa di Ratisbona e il Cardinale Gasparo Contarini," *Archivio veneto*, 1st ser., 4 (1872): 33.

him from his studies."[40] This poverty was of course relative, since Contarini's household was being compared implicitly with those of rich cardinals. He was, after all, established in the Vatican palace, where the pope had given him rooms, while his *familia* of forty persons was housed in nearby rented quarters large enough to include stables for about twenty horses. His household lived simply, yet Contarini did not abandon all the tastes of a nobleman, such as riding for pleasure in Rome during seasons of good weather.[41]

The first year in his new office seems to have been a rather quiet period with leisure for study, especially of Plato and Aristotle. He read unspecified "Christian books" as well, writing:

By the grace of God, I am well, living my customary life with friends, and when I have time, with some Christian books. I am making an effort to attain some [degree of] knowledge of Christian teaching and life, [but] the more I read about the latter the further from it I seem to be, living almost as if asleep and frozen still. I have not yet found a way of waking and rousing myself, unless it be through my hope in God's goodness, which makes ready the way to strengthen, awaken, and inflame man when he is keenly aware of his weakness and the infirmity he cannot overcome or heal by his own efforts.[42]

Twenty-five years earlier Contarini had written in strikingly similar terms to his friends Giustiniani and Querini, repeatedly mentioning his stony, hardened, and icy heart which he hoped to inflame through reading and study of the Bible.[43] The echoes of those distant letters can probably be best explained by Contarini's temperament. He was an emotional man who kept experiencing periods of spiritual sluggishness and dryness despite his unshakable belief that man is justified by faith. He struggled against these states through recourse to books as well as through action, in the conviction that "he who wishes to have a

---

40. To Marcantonio Michiel, 6 Dec. 1535, in *Lettere di principi* 3:149v.

41. *Lettere di principi* 3:149v; and Pastor, *Geschichte der Päpste* 5:833, no. 27. In 1535 Contarini's household comprised forty dependents, or "bocche"; see Girolamo Negri, *Epistolarum orationumque liber* (Padua, 1579), fol. 148v.

42. To Benedetto Accolti, Cardinal of Ravenna, 1 Jan. 1536, in Archivio di Stato, Florence (hereafter cited as ASF), Carteggio Accolti, Filza 12, inserto 13, fol. 154r: "Io, per la gratia de dio son sano et vivo la vita mia consueta cum li amici, et quando mi avancia il tempo, cum qualche libro christiano, sforzandomi de attingere a qualche cognitione della doctrina et vita christiana, da quale quanto piu ne lego, tanto piu mi pare essere lontano, et vivere quasi adormentato et agelato, ne ritrovo perho via di svegliarmi et accendermi sin hora, se non per la sperancia che ho in la benignita divina la quale alhora prepara il modo di fortificare, svegliare et accendere l'homo, quando esso è ben capace della sua debolezza et infirmita, la quale da per lui non puo superare et sanare." The text in *Reg.*, 263 (Inedita, no. 11), is inaccurate and incomplete.

43. See Jedin, "Contarini und Camaldoli," 25; also pp. 11, 12, 14, 16.

contented and peaceful mind must engage in activity which is fitting and necessary to it."[44] But despite this practical attitude he was subject to periods of melancholy. One such period, in the summer of 1536, coincided with a bout of physical illness; his "sadness of soul" was known to his friends,[45] who tried to cheer him with down-to-earth advice, or by the arguably less effective means of a treatise, "De animi tristitia," which Reginald Pole intended to write for him but did not get around to doing because of the intense heat of the season.[46]

While the full roster of Contarini's household cannot be reconstructed precisely, the names of several of the men whom he summoned to join him in Rome are known. His first secretary was Girolamo Negri, who later became his vicar in the diocese of Belluno. More prominent was Ludovico Beccadelli, member of an important Bolognese family and later papal nuncio to Venice and archbishop of Ragusa. Beccadelli first joined Contarini in November 1535, eventually becoming his secretary, friend, and biographer. Filippo Gheri, the younger brother of Cosmo Gheri, bishop of Fano, was also a member of Contarini's household, as was the Modenese Filippo Valentini. By the end of 1536 Contarini had prevailed on the Dutch Hebraist Jan van Kampen to come to Rome and enter his *familia* as well. Another foreigner in the household was the French scholar Pierre Danès, later bishop of Lavaur. Alvise Priuli, a close friend of Pole, and Galeazzo Florimonte, later bishop of Aquino, were with Contarini for a time. As a group these men were scholarly, open-minded, critical of abuses in the church, and interested in Protestant theology. Predictably, several later came under suspicion of heresy. One of them, Filippo Valentini, became a leading figure in Modenese heterodox circles, and eventually chose exile in Switzerland over submission to the Roman Inquisition.[47]

---

44. To Accolti, 14 May 1536, in *Reg.*, 264 (Inedita, no. 13); complete text in ASF, Carteggio Accolti, Filza 12, inserto 13, fols. 156r–157v.

45. Pole to Contarini, 24 June 1536, in *Reg.*, 88 (no. 289).

46. Pole to Alvise Priuli, 23 July 1536, in *Ep. Poli* 1:461.

47. On Beccadelli, see Giuseppe Alberigo, "Beccadelli, Ludovico," in *DBI* 7: 407–13; Gigliola Fragnito, "Per lo studio dell'epistolografia volgare del Cinquecento: le lettere di Ludovico Beccadelli," *Bibliothèque d'humanisme et renaissance* 43 (1981): 61–87. For Filippo Gheri, see Massimo Firpo and Dario Marcatto, *Il processo inquisitoriale del Cardinal Giovanni Morone* (Rome: Istituto Storico Italiano per l'Età Moderna e Contemporanea, 1981–89), 2(1):552n.23; for Filippo Valentini, ibid., 1:331–34; and M. Firpo, "Gli Spirituali, l'Accademia di Modena e il formulario di fede del 1542: controllo del dissenso religioso e nicodemismo," *Rivista di storia e letteratura religiosa* 20 (1984): 87. For Jan van Kampen, see Elisabeth Feist Hirsch, *Damião de Gois: The Life and Thought of a Portuguese Humanist, 1502–1574* (The Hague: Martinus Nijhoff,

Contarini and his household were exceptional in the Rome of 1535, when Pier Paolo Vergerio, papal nunzio to King Ferdinand, thus described other cardinals: "These great lords are so occupied with their pleasures and ambitions that they know nothing which is happening in distant Germany."[48] Even if this judgment by the critical Vergerio has to be taken with the proverbial grain of salt, the fact remains that Contarini, with his deep concern for church reform, stood alone among cardinals until the appointment of Sadoleto, Pole, and Carafa in December 1536. Support and encouragement first came from his friends in Venice, Verona, and his own *familia* rather than from other cardinals. But most important was the support of the pope himself, who drew Contarini into the preparations for a general council that was to meet in Mantua in May 1537.

The political background of the decision to hold this meeting and the complexities involved in convoking a council have been discussed in masterly fashion by Hubert Jedin.[49] Paul III, unlike his predecessor, understood that further delay in this matter would harm the papacy and the Catholic church, and so he decided to act. In the spring of 1536 he formed a commission to draw up the bull summoning the council, to which he appointed Contarini.

It is curious that the pope, who had known Contarini as the Venetian ambassador to Clement VII and as a skillful negotiator in Bologna, did not avail himself of the cardinal's diplomatic expertise during the preparatory stages of the council. Instead Contarini was assigned to various curial committees for the next four years. Keeping him in Rome was probably more useful for the positive image of the papacy than sending him on missions to European rulers would have been, since he was the visible rallying point for those who felt the urgency of

1967), 98; and H. de Vocht, *History of the Foundation and Rise of the Collegium Trilingue Lovaniense, 1517–1550* (Louvain: Bibliothèque de l'Université, 1951–19), 1:503–5, 2:120–22, and 3: passim. For Danès, see Mireille Forget, "Les relations et les amitiés de Pierre Danès (1497–1577)," *Bibliothèque d'humanisme et renaissance* 3 (1936): 365–83; 4 (1937): 59–77. For Florimonte, see Alberigo, *Vescovi italiani*, 209. For Priuli, see Pio Paschini, *Un amico del Cardinale Polo: Alvise Priuli* (Rome: Pontificio Seminario Romano Maggiore, 1921); and Firpo and Marcatto, *Processo inquisitoriale* 1:253–54.

48. Vergerio to King Ferdinand, 27 Jan. 1535, in *Nuntiaturberichte aus Deutschland nebst ergänzenden Aktenstücken*, 1st ser. (Rome: Königliches Preussisches Historisches Institut, 1892–1912), 1:327 (hereafter cited as *NB*). For Vergerio, see Anne Jacobson Schutte, *Pier Paolo Vergerio: The Making of an Italian Reformer* (Geneva: Droz, 1977).

49. On the projected council of Mantua, see Jedin, *Trient* 1:232–86.

church reform. Paul III was shrewd enough to understand the importance of not alienating the intellectual, liberal-minded ecclesiastics and
laymen who regarded Contarini as their spokesman.

Contarini's first significant task was to preside over a commission
convoked by the pope in July 1536 and charged with making recommendations for reform measures in preparation for the general council.
Such a commission had precedents from the first year of Paul III's
pontificate. Already in November 1534 the pope had declared that
reform of the curia and cardinals must precede a council.[50] Within a
week a commission for the "reform of mores" was established, followed by a second for the examination of all curial offices and the revision of their practices. Both bodies were to recommend initiatives to
the pope for his action.[51] But the seriousness of the enterprise can be
judged by the pope's admonition to members of the two commissions,
none of whom had any record of concern with reform, to take into
account "the nature of the present times" in their work.[52] In effect, this
meant simply that once more a list of remedies for some abuses would
be compiled, dutifully read in a consistory, and heard of no more.

Still, Paul III in 1535 and 1536 did issue several bulls aimed at
removing corruption and abuses in the church,[53] and thus at least kept
hope for reform alive. In August 1535 the bull "Sublimis Deus" was
published, creating yet another commission, this time for the reform of
the curia and clergy in Rome. As a step toward the council, abuses
were to be eradicated and opposition punished, and there was even
mention of measures for enforcing reform decrees.[54] However, the
resulting edict of 11 February 1536 was remarkable only for its length.
It dealt with the colors of ecclesiastical vestments, the necessity of tonsure, the desirability of having a *familia* that led an orderly life, the
injunction to priests to read the office daily, to celebrate mass properly,
to avoid places of ill repute, and similar matters.[55] The Venetian ambassador to Rome gave this insignificant edict its right name when

---

50. Pastor, *Geschichte der Päpste* 5:97.

51. Stephan Ehses, "Kirchliche Reformarbeiten unter Papst Paul III. vor dem
Trienter Konzil," *Römische Quartalschrift* 15 (1901): 154.

52. In the consistory of 3 March 1535: "Sanct^mus D.N. renuntiavit D^nis R^mis ... ut
temporis conditioni consuleretur" (*CT* 4:451). The cardinals on the commissions were
Piccolomini, Sanseverino, Cesi, Campeggio, Grimani, and Cesarini.

53. Ehses, "Kirchliche Reformarbeiten," 154–55.

54. *CT* 4:451. This bull should not be confused with a more famous one of 4 June
1537 having the same incipit, which incorporates the Amerindians into the human race.

55. Not incorporated into the consistorial acts; printed by Pastor, *Geschichte der
Päpste* 5:823–27, from a copy in St. Petersburg.

he called it "la bolla della reformatione delli habbiti delli cherici," adding resignedly, "at other times also similar reformations have been made, which have had no effect whatever." Discussion about regulating "matters of the *poenitentiaria*, the chancery, the *dataria*, and other offices,"[56] mentioned by him, resulted in nothing.

The prelates chosen for the commission over which Contarini presided were of a very different stamp from members of earlier commissions. Originally the pope had a group in mind that must have differed considerably from the final one, for it was to include Spaniards and Frenchmen,[57] whereas the actual commission was composed only of Italians with the single exception of Pole. Paul III accepted Contarini's judgment concerning who was suitable for membership, and the latter did not hesitate to recommend some of the most outspoken advocates of reform and friends on whose support he could rely.[58] In the summer of 1536 briefs were issued summoning eight men to Rome to assist the pope "with their advice, piety, and learning" in the preparations for the council.[59] They were Gianpietro Carafa; Gianmatteo Giberti, former *datario* to Clement VII and now reforming bishop of Verona; Contarini's friends Gregorio Cortese and Reginald Pole; his confessor Tommaso Badia, who as a Dominican also held the post of *magister sacri palatii*, or the pope's theologian; Federico Fregoso, archbishop of Salerno and bishop of Gubbio; Jacopo Sadoleto, bishop of Carpentras in southern France and former member of the curia under the two Medici popes; and Girolamo Aleandro, best known as a papal diplomat.[60] The last is the only surprising choice, due

56. Lorenzo Bragadino to the Senate, Rome, 12 Feb. 1536, in *CT* 4:453; see also Ehses, "Kirchliche Reformarbeiten," 157–58.

57. Contarini to Pole, Rome, 12 July 1536, in *Reg.*, 89 (no. 291).

58. " ... [Il papa] propose che si facesse una riforma delle cose più importanti, et volle che 'l Cardinale Contarino li ricordasse quelli, ch' a tal opera li parevano buoni, acciochè presto se ne venisse al fine" (Beccadelli, "Vita," 24). Cf. also the report of the Mantuan agent quoted by Carlo Capasso, *Paolo III* (Messina: Principato, 1923–24), 1:654n.4; and Pastor, *Geschichte der Päpste* 5:110n.3.

59. Briefs to Pole and Sadoleto in *CT* 4:26–27; to Carafa, in Friedensburg, "Briefwechsel," 221, and Carafa's answer, 222; to Pole in *Ep. Poli* 1:466; to Cortese in Gregorio Cortese, *Gregorii Cortesii omnia quae huc usque colligi potuerunt sive ab eo scripta, sive ad illum spectantia* (Padua, 1774), 1:52. That Contarini particularly wanted Cortese on the commission may be seen from *Reg.*, 89 (no. 292).

60. For Carafa, see Alberto Aubert, *Paolo IV Carafa nel giudizio della età della Controriforma* (Città di Castello: Stamperia Tiferno Grafica, 1990). For Giberti, see Prosperi, *Tra evangelismo e controriforma*. Peter Partner ascribes a larger role to Giberti than is usual, and thinks that "the chief minister of Clement VII was in effect Gian Matteo Giberti," *The Pope's Men: The Papal Civil Service in the Renaissance* (Oxford: Clarendon Press, 1990), 44. For Pole, see Dermot Fenlon, *Heresy and Obedience in*

probably to the pope's initiative because Aleandro had the reputation of being familiar with German affairs. He had given little evidence of zeal for church reform, though on occasion he had supported reform measures that he deemed expedient.[61]

The initial meeting of the commission took place toward the end of November 1536,[62] with Sadoleto delivering the opening oration. The usually mild prelate violently attacked corruption in the church, squarely blaming it on earlier popes, and calling on Paul III, who was not present, to break with the pernicious ways of his predecessors. Sadoleto painted a dismal picture of the ills besetting the church, most of which he attributed to the cupidity of the clergy. Mincing no words, he spoke of the mistrust and even hatred of the clergy on the part of the people, of disorder everywhere, and of the woes threatening disunited Christendom. He predicted worse things to come unless Paul III proceeded to take his calling as savior of the church seriously. Speaking to his colleagues "with the passion of a Hebrew prophet,"[63] Sadoleto set the tone for their deliberations. The seriousness and urgency of

---

Tridentine Italy: Cardinal Pole and the Counter Reformation (Cambridge: Cambridge University Press, 1972); J. P. Marmion, "Cardinal Pole in Recent Studies," *Recusant History* 13 (1975–76): 56–61; and Paolo Simoncelli, *Il caso Reginald Pole: eresia e santità nelle polemiche religiose del Cinquecento* (Rome: Edizioni di Storia e Letteratura, 1977). For Cortese, see Gigliola Fragnito, "Il Cardinale Gregorio Cortese e la crisi religiosa del Cinquecento," *Benedictina* 30 (1983): 129–71, 417–59; 31 (1984): 79–134; the more recent monograph by Francesco C. Cesareo, *Humanism and Catholic Reform: The Life and Work of Gregorio Cortese (1483–1548)* (New York and Bern: Peter Lang, 1990), is inadequate. For Badia, see Giuseppe Alberigo, "Badia, Tommaso," in *DBI* 5:74–76. For Sadoleto, see Douglas, *Sadoleto*. Little work on Fregoso exists; for a sketch of his life, see Luigi Grillo, *Elogi di Liguri illustri*, 2d ed. (Genoa, 1846), 1:390–98; also M. Abbondanza, "Federico Fregoso nella storia della diocesi di Salerno e la visita pastorale del 1510–11," *Quaderni contemporanei* (Salerno) 4 (1971): 7–19. For Aleandro, see Giuseppe Alberigo, "Aleandro, Girolamo," in *DBI* 2:128–35.

61. Pastor, *Geschichte der Päpste* 5:111, credits Contarini with the inclusion of Aleandro, a view accepted by Douglas, *Sadoleto*, 100. But Jedin, *Trient* 1:583n.44, rightly does not include Aleandro in Contarini's circle; nor does Franco Gaeta, *Un nunzio pontificio a Venezia nel Cinquecento (Girolamo Aleandro)* (Venice and Rome: Istituto per la Collaborazione Culturale, 1960), 115. Aleandro's life had not been exemplary; see Paul Kalkoff, "Zur Charakteristik Aleandros," *Zeitschrift für Kirchengeschichte* 43 (1924): 212–13, though Kalkoff's final judgment (219) is too negative.

62. Vinzenz Schweitzer, "Beiträge zur Geschichte Pauls III.," *Römische Quartalschrift* 22 (1908): 134–35, summarizes arguments for an earlier opening date and makes a good case against them. He thinks that the meetings began between 24 November and 2 December, most likely between 24 and 30 November. Pastor, *Geschichte der Päpste* 5:117n.4, remains unconvinced and thinks that the meetings began in the first half of November.

63. Douglas, *Sadoleto*, 101. The text of the speech is in *CT* 4:108–19.

their task as presented by Sadoleto was further underlined by his almost apocalyptic picture of the evils awaiting the church should it remain unreformed.

A greater contrast between the spirit in which these nine prelates began their work and the perfunctoriness of earlier so-called reform commissions would be hard to imagine. But it is also necessary to remember that Sadoleto could not have spoken as he did had there not been signals from the pope to Contarini and his group encouraging them to believe that they would be heard. The eulogies of Paul III's virtue and wisdom in Sadoleto's speech may strike a modern reader as too fulsome. Yet Sadoleto well understood the pope's determining role in any future change in the church; he therefore tried by all means possible to make an ally of Paul III, appealing to him as the man chosen by God to bring about the crucial, longed-for reform.

In a consistory on 9 March 1537 the commission's report, its *Consilium de emendanda ecclesia,* or "Plan for Reforming the Church," was presented to the pope, then read and explained by Contarini.[64] This was followed by Sadoleto's separate report, which has not been preserved but probably elaborated further on points made in the committee document.[65] There was no discussion at that time, and the immediate reaction of Paul III is not known. Copies of the *Consilium* were made available to the cardinals, who were given time to consult with their advisors.

The chief obstacle to grasping the intent of Contarini and his collaborators lies in the lack of documentation of the preparatory work that led up to their final report. An oath of secrecy had been imposed on them, but even after it was lifted no details of the meetings were disclosed, or at least none have survived. The author or authors of the *Consilium* remain anonymous;[66] that there was more than one

64. "Consilium delectorum cardinalium et aliorum praelatorum de emendanda ecclesia S.D.N. Paulo III iubente conscriptum et exhibitum," text in *CT* 12:134–45. English translation in Gleason, *Reform Thought,* 85–100. For the date of presentation, see Walter Friedensburg, "Zwei Aktenstücke zur Geschichte der kirchlichen Reformbestrebungen an der römischen Kurie (1536–1538)," *Quellen und Forschungen aus italienischen Archiven und Bibliotheken* 7 (1904): 260.

65. Friedensburg, "Zwei Aktenstücke," 255; and Douglas, *Sadoleto,* 107. Despite his apparent dissent or emendations, Sadoleto signed the *Consilium.*

66. The question of authorship has been debated, but not resolved. Pastor, *Geschichte der Päpste* 5:121n.1, discusses the attempts of biographers, especially Carafa, to assign to their several subjects the writing of the memorial; Capasso, *Paolo III* 1:656n.2, agrees that it is not possible to attribute the memorial to a definite author. See also Jedin, *Trient* 1:341; and *CT* 12:132–33.

responsible author seems likely because the document bears the marks of a committee report, with the characteristic ideas of one member or another appearing at different points. For example, there is a similarity between Carafa's memorial of 1532 to Pope Clement VII[67] and sections of the *Consilium*, and between the latter document and the reform proposal written long before by Contarini's friends Guistiniani and Querini, the *Libellus ad Leonem X*,[68] which Contarini knew well and with which men from the Venetian milieu like Carafa, Cortese, and Pole were also familiar.[69] Like the reports of previous commissions, the *Consilium* drew up a list of specific abuses that had become widespread throughout the church. These abuses, however, had now worked themselves so intimately and pervasively into the church's structure that it is difficult to see how Paul III could have freed himself from the fiscal web his predecessors had woven.

Fees had become customary for many transactions, including plurality of ecclesiastical benefices, reservations, compositions, and arrangements of various sorts which came perilously close to horse-trading, especially in the granting of churches and exceptionally rich abbeys to the "temporary" supervision of well-connected clerics and laymen. There was similarly busy traffic in dispensations from vows and obligations, and a host of indulgences. All had their ultimate origin in the papacy's need for ever more money, especially from Sixtus IV on, the sale of church offices being a particularly important source of income for the Renaissance popes. Indeed, the papal government acted like its secular counterparts in devising means to mobilize further income by various kinds of advances.[70] The inherited institutional structure of

67. The text is in *CT* 12:67–77; English translation in Gleason, *Reform Thought*, 57–80. See especially the recommendations regarding supervision and reorganization of conventual orders, the tightening of standards for admission to the priesthood, and the examination of candidates.

68. Text in Mittarelli and Costadoni (eds.), *Annales Camaldulenses* 9:612–719. Especially striking is the similarity with sections of part 5, "De Christianorum omnium, qui Romano obediunt pontifici, reformatione," which toward the end (cols. 701–3) discusses the reform of religious orders. Nelson H. Minnich, "Concepts of Reform Proposed at the Fifth Lateran Council," *Archivum historiae pontificiae* 7 (1969): 222–27, discusses the *Libellus*. See also Fragnito, "Cultura umanistica," 128–29, for possible links between the *Libellus* and the *Consilium*.

69. Carafa knew Paolo Giustiniani personally; see R. de Maulde La Clavière, *S. Gaetano da Thiene e la riforma cattolica italiana (1480–1527)* (Rome: Desclée, 1911), 12.

70. For a good general summary, see the following articles by Wolfgang Reinhard, "Ämterhandel in Rom zwischen 1534 und 1621," in *Ämterhandel im Spätmittelalter und im 16. Jahrhundert*, ed. Ilja Mieck (Berlin: Colloquium Verlag, 1984), esp. 46–47; "Finanza pontificia e stato della chiesa nel XVI e XVII secolo," in *Finanze e ragion di*

early modern states hampered the needed regular and predictable flow of resources to the administrative center, so that new ways had to be found to increase and regularize income.

Whatever the ethical and moral dimensions of Roman fiscal practices, historians now see them as part of the trend on the part of popes and curia to organize their finances and administration rationally. But Contarini and his committee saw matters in an entirely different light and judged by different criteria. They looked back to an idealized past of the church when fiscal problems were unknown and therefore regarded contemporary financial practices simply as abuses to be eradicated. Nor were they alone in this opinion, for reform proposals from various quarters regularly attacked papal fiscalism and demanded that the sale of church offices be curbed if not abolished.[71] For reformers the sale of offices was a scandal, but for investors it was a profitable and safe placement of their money that also conferred status.

The authors of the *Consilium* mention no specific point in the church's history when financial abuses in their sense of the term did not exist. For all practical purposes, however, there was no venality of offices before the Great Schism. During the Avignon period it had not been possible to buy a position that would make its holder a member of the papal bureaucracy.[72] But the pattern of expenditure changed sharply between 1378 and 1417, when large-scale borrowing by popes and antipopes made necessary new sources of income for the servicing and repayment of debts. Among these sources were the sale of offices and the exaction of payment for spiritual graces.[73] Moreover, from the late fifteenth century on the popes became Italian princes on a grand scale, and their courts, armies, navies, administration, building activity, patronage, nepotism, and dynastic policy required large sums

---

stato in Italia e in Germania nella prima età moderna, ed. Aldo De Maddalena and Hermann Kellenbenz (Bologna: Il Mulino, 1984), 353–87; and "Finanza pontificia, sistema beneficiale e finanza statale nell'età confessionale," in *Fisco religione stato nell'età confessionale*, ed. Hermann Kellenbenz and Paolo Prodi (Bologna: Il Mulino, 1989), 459–504. Still useful is Clemens Bauer, "Die Epochen der Papstfinanz: ein Versuch," *Historische Zeitschrift* 138 (1927): esp. 476–89 for the period from Martin V to Pius IV.

71. Or even that curial offices be granted according to merit; see John F. D'Amico, "Papal History and Curial Reform in the Renaissance: Raffaele Maffei's *Breuis Historia* of Julius II and Leo X," *Archivum historiae pontificiae* 18 (1980): 182.

72. Walther von Hofmann, *Forschungen zur Geschichte der kurialen Behörden vom Schisma bis zur Reformation* (Rome: Loescher, 1914), 1:163.

73. Peter Partner, "Papal Financial Policy in the Renaissance and Counter-Reformation," *Past and Present*, no. 88 (1980): 20–21; this article contains an excellent bibliography.

of money.[74] Beginning with Sixtus IV most offices in the papal chancery, *camera*, and *poenitentiaria* became venal, as did entire "colleges" or organized subgroups like the apostolic scriptors.[75] In addition, revenues were derived from increasingly liberal dispensations from impediments to marriage or from monastic vows and other binding obligations.[76]

The number of venal offices increased from 625 under Sixtus IV to 2,232 under Leo X, at which approximate level they remained under Paul III.[77] This pope also established papal knighthoods, among them those of St. George and St. Paul, which carried only ceremonial obligations but conferred resounding titles on their holders.[78] Clement VII in 1526 instituted a funded debt, the Monte della Fede, which produced capital but then required service of the debt. With all their sources of income, traditional and innovative, the popes still had to borrow heavily to cover their current obligations. Paul III was no exception; he borrowed at high interest rates and had to channel revenues from the papal state to the repayment and servicing of his debt.[79] Papal finances also involved the large Italian banking houses, so that wider and wider circles were directly interested in protecting the existing fiscal system and preserving the status quo. The question was where reform could begin in a system like this. Contarini's commission might in the end prove to be like one in 1497, which one of its members likened to a rider without spurs,[80] while another had said even more plainly, "The [hot] iron, not the salve, must be applied to the festering sores!"[81] knowing full well that this would not happen.

The crux of the matter was that Contarini and his colleagues were confronting not merely isolable abuses, but an entrenched economic

74. Ibid., tables 6 and 7, pp. 50, 51.

75. Hofmann, *Forschungen* 1:172–73; and Reinhard, "Ämterhandel," 49.

76. See the list in Emil Göller, *Die päpstliche Pönitentiarie von ihrem Ursprung bis zu ihrer Umgestaltung unter Pius V.* (Rome: Loescher, 1907–11), 2:43–69, for the kinds of dispensations given.

77. Hofmann, *Forschungen* 1:173, gives the first figure; the second is from Reinhard, "Ämterhandel," table on p. 52, where other sources are also indicated. Partner, *Pope's Men*, 38, considers the figure quoted for Leo X too high, arguing that it multiplies the real number of officeholders because of their pluralism.

78. See Felice Litva, S.J., "L'attività della Dataria durante il periodo tridentino," *Archivum historiae pontificiae* 5 (1967): 140–43, for the creation of *cavalieri* as a means of raising money.

79. Partner, "Papal Financial Policy," 25.

80. Léonce Célier, "L'idée de réforme à la cour pontificale du Concile de Bâle au Concile de Latran," *Revue des questions historiques* 86 (1909): 433.

81. Ibid., 435.

and social system. Any reform within that system would have threat-ened existing arrangements that provided for individuals, their families, and dependents, with wide repercussions for Roman as well as Italian ecclesiastical and secular society. The *Consilium* did not address these problems directly or submit a plan of practical steps toward reform. Yet the concentration of its authors on central theoretical issues gave the document a structure and content that set it apart from such predeces-sors as the *Libellus* and mark an advance over reform proposals that were essentially lists of grievances or abuses.

Nowhere is this clearer than in the question concerning the reason for existing evils in the church, posed at the beginning of the *Consi-lium*. For Giustiniani and Querini the answer had been that the greed and ambition of secular princes, and the ignorance, superstition, and disobedience of the clergy which spread to the people, were the causes of the woes afflicting Christianity.[82] Their memorial repeatedly applied the familiar metaphor of a sick body both to the church and to Chris-tendom at large, and demanded the action of the pope as the physician who alone could cure their ills.[83] For all its outspoken denunciation of specific abuses, however, the *Libellus* in no way questioned the existing system of papal government either in theory or in practice.

By contrast, the opening section of the *Consilium*, in seeking an explanation for corruption in the church, raised the central issue of the nature of papal authority and the bounds within which it could legiti-mately be exercised. Here the similarity with Contarini's *De potestate pontificis quod divinitus sit tradita* and with his speeches to Pope Clement VII is striking. Papal authority is accepted as divinely insti-tuted. However, the *Consilium* goes on to state that the popes have surrounded themselves with false counselors who assure them that their will is law and that they are absolute lords (*domini*) over the church and its goods, incapable of falling into simony because they sell what is their own, and therefore free to do as they please with the material goods of the church and its spiritual graces. This teaching is pinpointed as the root of all evils: according to the *Consilium*, the difficulties and ills now besetting the church have sprung from this idea as from a Trojan horse.[84] As the *Consilium*'s logical structure unfolds, all the abuses mentioned subsequently are seen as having their origin in the exaggerated claims made by curial jurists about the nature of papal power.

---

82. Mittarelli and Costadoni (eds.), *Annales Camaldulenses* 9:670–71.
83. Ibid., 670, 671, 675, 707.   84. *CT* 12:134–35.

The list of specific abuses is a list of symptoms of disease in the church. The prelates on the commission, like many advocates of reform before them, use the traditional metaphor of the sick body crying out for a cure. Their recommendations deal first of all with the administration of benefices and the reform of disorders arising from current practice, then point out the perniciousness of granting spiritual graces, such as dispensations and indulgences, for money. They urge that these practices be stopped in obedience to Christ's clear command: "Freely have you received, freely give" (Matt. 10:8).[85] This precept, and not elaborate legal theories, should regulate the granting of benefices and graces.

The *Consilium* then addresses the problem of discipline and order within the hierarchy. Besides echoing several of Carafa's recommendations of 1532, it proclaims the need to reform the entire clergy from the highest levels down to that of the simple cleric. It states that cardinals should reside in Rome, taking part in the government of the church and receiving equal incomes, and should not accept additional benefices, especially bishoprics, which are incompatible with their residence in Rome. Bishops should reside in their dioceses so as to be able to supervise them and to give good example to the clergy, who in turn must fulfill their own pastoral functions. The thorny problem of individuals and ecclesiastical corporations exempt from episcopal jurisdiction must be resolved, since such exemptions contribute to institutional disorder. The memorial closes with recommendations for improving the government and morals of Rome, and for removing public scandals.

The *Consilium* was neither a complete program for action nor "a major landmark…in the history of the church."[86] It failed, for example, to consider what measures should be taken against those who refused to follow its precepts. Even more important, it entirely left out of account two problems that underlay many of the specific issues it touched upon: the relations among the hierarchical levels of authority within the church, and the respective roles of pope and princes in matters of benefices and ecclesiastical appointments. Its significance does not lie primarily in its well-known criticism of abuses, but rather in its challenge to the prevailing system of papal government.

In essence, the memorial called for a different conception of the papacy and hence a break with the way business was then conducted by

85. Ibid., 140.   86. Pastor, *Geschichte der Päpste* 5:123.

curial offices and tribunals in Rome.[87] Contarini had argued in 1529 that a pope without a papal state was conceivable. The *Consilium* went even further. It did not discuss the pope as ruler of a state but appealed to him as head of the universal church, raising the possibility of a spiritual papacy purged of extreme papalist theories and freed of the dubious financial transactions in which it had become enmeshed. By the nature of the charge given by Christ to St. Peter and his successors, the pope was thought of as shepherd and father, rather than as a lord like secular princes. Restricting pontifical plenitude of power to the spiritual realm, the authors of the *Consilium* in effect condemned those canon lawyers standing in the long tradition both of medieval thinkers who argued that the pope wielded both swords and of famous jurists like Giles of Rome, Baldo de Ubaldis, or Augustinus Triumphus.[88] If the pope accepted the major thrust of the commission's report, he would have had to curtail the scope of his power, restructure the curia, and conduct a major housecleaning operation in Rome.

The *Consilium* brought a new element to the pontificate of Paul III in the emergence of a group of strict—by the standards of the time, even radical—advocates of reform in Rome, with Contarini as one of its chief spokesmen. Already in 1536 the poet Vittoria Colonna wrote him rejoicing that he had sustained the bark of Peter so well by his labors, and concluding: "It is secure from shipwreck, and Your Excellency holds the tiller."[89] This image of Contarini as the steersman of the ship corresponded to how his supporters perceived his role. Contarini was later to gain further reform-minded allies in the college of cardinals, but in 1537 the significant reformers were the authors of the *Consilium*, who championed the conception of a spiritual papacy that would initiate curial reform and bring about the restoration of discipline throughout the church.

None of Contarini's letters between July 1536 and February 1537

87. Wolfgang Reinhard, in calling the *Consilium* "ein systemkritisches Dokument" ("Reformpapsttum," 788), is in my opinion the only recent scholar to assess its significance accurately.

88. For a helpful summary of the entire issue of papal power in temporal affairs, see G. Gléz, "Pouvoir du pape dans l'ordre temporel," in *Dictionnaire de théologie catholique* 12(2), cols. 2670–2772, esp. cols. 2713–51. The *Summa de potestate ecclesiastica* of Augustinus Triumphus (d. 1328), which contains an uncompromising defense of the positions of Boniface VIII, was one of the earliest printed books to be published in Rome (1469).

89. Ermanno Ferrero and Giuseppe Müller, eds., *Carteggio delle lettere di Vittoria Colonna*, 2d ed. (Turin, 1892), 127 (letter 76).

are known to exist. His one dated piece from this period is a short treatise on free will in the form of a letter to Vittoria Colonna.[90] While the
essay testifies to their friendship, it offers no direct clues to Contarini's
ideas on reform. Contarini duly summarizes philosophical, mainly Aristotelian, distinctions between unfree and free will in the first part of
the treatise, then proceeds to a brief discussion of theological issues, or
"Catholic truth" as he phrases it. His biographer asserts that the theology of justification, touched upon very briefly in the treatise, is
unequivocally Catholic,[91] without explaining what this meant in the
pre-Tridentine period. The letter shows Contarini's familiarity with the
issues of the controversy on free will which divided Catholics and
Protestants, and some knowledge of Protestant thought. His ideas are
expressed without much energy, in a dry pedantic way, as if he had
written an academic exercise; it concludes with this declaration: "All
that I have said or written here I always submit to the judgment of
those who are better informed."[92] At a time when Contarini was grap-
pling with abuses in the church and criticism of existing conditions, he
found the all-sufficient remedy to lie in "Catholic teaching, to which
we are almost led by the natural light [of reason],"[93] and discussed free
will without a trace of contentiousness or originality. He was anxious
to preserve the image of man totally dependent on God, whose mercy
alone could incline the will toward himself, but in such a manner as to
stop short of Luther's formulations and leave room for man's own
decisions. One can only wonder what Vittoria Colonna thought of this
perfunctory letter, which virtually ignored Protestant theology.

While the commission was meeting Contarini continued to work on
a treatise begun the preceding summer that summarized the achieve-
ments of the most important councils and synods in the history of
the church. It was intended as background for the pope in preparing
for the coming assembly. The *Conciliorum magis illustrium summa*,[94]
despite occasional inaccuracy and lack of clarity, makes a valiant attempt to present the main issues facing the early councils, their most
notable decrees especially in regard to heresies, and the role of papal
authority. Contarini enlisted the aid of Cortese and other friends, who
searched through Venetian libraries for works on the councils and collections of their decrees, while Contarini himself had access to the

90. "Del libero arbitrio," dated 13 Nov. 1536, in *Quattro lettere*, 57–76. The Latin
version is in *Opera*, 597–604.

91. *GC*, 456.   92. *Quattro lettere*, 76.   93. Ibid., 75.

94. *Opera*, 546–63.

Vatican library.[95] His treatise, completed in 1537, reveals more about the author's thought in its omissions than in what it actually says. Less than one page altogether is devoted to the councils of Constance, Basel, Florence, and the Fifth Lateran! Avoiding any mention of the great controversies confronting the fifteenth-century councils, Contarini barely hints in half a sentence at the existence of conciliarism.[96] Instead of dwelling on disputes, he directs the reader's attention to the reconciliation with Greeks and Armenians in Florence, perhaps as a model of how to approach the Protestants. He affirms that it is up to the pope as "head . . . from whom governance and jurisdiction flow into the universal church, and on whom they depend,"[97] to call the bishops to the council. Again, the pope is pictured as physician to the sick church, who alone has the power to heal it.

Neither this short piece nor the letter to Vittoria Colonna deals directly with the questions before the commission Contarini was chairing. Yet they do evince certain attitudes consonant with those of the *Consilium*. The *Conciliorum magis illustrium summa*, like the *Consilium*, stresses the need for order in the church, which could only be attained by the strict upholding of the hierarchy and by the affirmation of the pope's power, legitimately exercised. Contarini in his personal tract shared the commission's view of the central, crucial role of the pope in the process of reform, likened to the healing of a sick body. Both works assume the possibility of the exercise of papal will with far-reaching results, as if that will were quite independent of economic and social conditions. Neither engages in polemics with Protestants; both documents stress instead the need for charity. The letter to Vittoria Colonna also reveals an open-minded, thoughtful Contarini, willing to add his ideas to one of the great debates of the Reformation. Those ideas are derivative, to be sure, but they are presented by their author as outgrowths of his personal religious development. Taken together, the treatise on councils and the letter on free will demonstrate his settled outlook and sense of mission. He hoped to guide Paul III toward his own understanding of the lessons offered by earlier councils, and Vittoria Colonna toward his ambiguous views on free will.

Among the proposals of the *Consilium de emendanda ecclesia* which

95. *Reg.*, 87 (no. 288) and 91 (no. 299).
96. "Post Constantiense concilium, ut servaretur Decretum de congregatione conciliorum, indictum fuit concilium, quod fuit Basileae coactum" (*Opera*, 563). Contarini does not mention the decree *Frequens* by its title.
97. *Opera*, 547.

provoked disagreement in the college of cardinals was one stating that the pope could not derive material benefit from the exercise of his spiritual power. Soon after the presentation of the memorial Contarini addressed a short letter to Paul III, explaining his views on that point in greater detail than could be done in the *Consilium*.[98] He argued that free bestowal is of the essence of spiritual graces, since they belong ultimately to God. Men, even bishops and popes, are only his stewards, not empowered to sell their master's gifts. At the time of writing this letter Contarini had not taken a firm position regarding compositions, but was beginning to make distinctions between the legitimacy of money payments for penalties imposed by ecclesiastical authorities and payments for spiritual graces. The brief letter does not go into detail on these matters, but its last paragraph urges the pope not to be concerned if his income should drop by twenty or thirty thousand gold ducats as a result of his reform measures. Contarini paints the picture of a pope second only to St. Peter, honored by the entire grateful church as another god for turning the tide of abuse, and merely hints that the pope could easily make up "in many ways," unspecified, any financial loss he suffered. The idea of a general outpouring of approval for the pope's actions that would translate into willingness to support him financially was now taking shape in Contarini's mind; it would be set forth more fully later on.

The reception of the *Consilium* by both Catholics and Protestants showed the difficulties that faced reform emanating from Rome, and dispelled any idea that the pope could cure the church simply by deciding to do so. The college of cardinals was badly divided.[99] An inert conservative majority, mainly concerned with preserving the status quo, had no intention of supporting Contarini and his associates, who

---

98. *De usu potestatis clavium*, in *CT* 12:151–53. The editor dates the piece to April 1537 (but adds a question mark). Dittrich, *GC*, 374, dates it to the day after the consistory in which the *Consilium de emendanda ecclesia* was read, identifying the consistory with the "conventus R^morum cardinalium" that met "hesterna die," mentioned in Contarini's letter, *CT* 12:152. Jedin, *Trient* 1:584–85n.56, thinks it was written in October 1538. I accept 1537 as its date. It is most likely to have been written in the two months after 9 March 1537, when the *Consilium* was presented. The most important argument for the spring 1537 date to my mind is Contarini's own statement that he is not familiar with how compositions work ("Nescio quidnam fiat in compositionibus"), *CT* 12:153. After he began working on the reform of the *dataria* in April 1537 he could not have made that statement (unless his words should be read, "I am not an expert in the matter of compositions, but ..."; the former translation fits the context better).

99. Douglas, *Sadoleto*, 110, describes the situation succinctly.

formed too small a group to be effective alone. The opinion of the conservatives, moreover, was voiced by a small group of articulate and intelligent curialists who had the great advantage of fighting for what most cardinals and curial officials wanted anyway: no radical change. Paul III asked the whole college to review the *Consilium* and then listened to the objections of those who stood to lose most if its recommendations were put into effect. Their predictable opposition, however, was not so effective as that offered by more subtle opponents such as the curial prelate Bartolomeo Guidiccione and probably also Cardinal Nikolaus Schönberg.

According to Paolo Sarpi, Schönberg delivered in consistory a long speech in which he sought to convince the pope that the time was not yet right for initiating sweeping reforms. He is reported to have argued that the sorts of changes urged by the *Consilium* would put additional ammunition into the hands of the Lutherans by virtually conceding that their charges of corruption in the church were well founded.[100] Because the speech is not extant, it is not possible to assess it more fully. Nevertheless, Sarpi's statement seems plausible, for Schönberg, as a German, would have been sensitive to how the memorial would strike Lutherans. Equally in character is the reply that Sarpi reports Carafa as making, that good must not be omitted out of fear that evil would result from it.[101]

In the response of Guidiccione we are on more solid documentary ground. Guidiccione was no merely reactionary prelate but an experienced lawyer who raised some hard-hitting points in his mordant attack on the reformers.[102] He had been for nineteen years the vicar-general of Cardinal Farnese in the diocese of Parma before retiring in 1528 to his country villa near Lucca. When Farnese became Pope Paul III he summoned Guidiccione in vain to return and work on the *Consilium*. But in 1539, when he was seventy, Guidiccione accepted an

100. Paolo Sarpi, *Istoria del Concilio Tridentino* (Bari: Laterza, 1935), 1:134. Stephan Ehses, "Zu den kirchlichen Reformarbeiten unter Paul III.: der deutsche Kardinal Nikolaus von Schönberg," *Historisches Jahrbuch der Görresgesellschaft* 29 (1908): 601–3, defends Schönberg against charges that he opposed reform of the church and for that reason opposed the *Consilium*. Schönberg was influential with Popes Clement VII and Paul III; see Albèri, *Relazioni*, 2d ser., 3:268 (Contarini's *relazione* of 8 March 1530) and 317 (*relazione* of Antonio Suriano, 1535).

101. Sarpi, *Istoria* 1:135.

102. "S.D.N. Paulo III Batholomaeus Guidiccionus de ecclesia et emendatione ministrorum eorumque abusuum per generale concilium facienda," in *CT* 12:226–56. This memorandum is part of a longer unpublished work entitled *De ecclesia*.

appointment as vicar of Rome, became a cardinal, and participated actively in church government until his death ten years later.[103] He knew the new pope well enough to be quite blunt in the congratulatory letter he sent him on his accession. He urged him to try first to bring about peace among princes, and only then to turn his efforts to reforming abuses in the church, the body of Christ, which he saw as diseased from the soles of its feet to the crown of its head.[104] Guidiccione had established his reputation as a prelate seriously interested in reform[105] who would not oppose initiatives in that direction without good reason.

Now Guidiccione turned sharply against the central idea of the *Consilium*, which attributed all problems in the church to the doctrine taught by papal counselors that the pope's will was law. Guidiccione as a young man in the households of Cardinal Galeotto della Rovere, nephew of Julius II, and of Alessandro Farnese, had had a close-up view of the most martial if not the most famous Renaissance pope, and he understood what a profound attack on the prevailing theory of papal authority the *Consilium de emendanda ecclesia* had launched. In defense of papal *plenitudo potestatis* he affirmed that true Catholic doctrine taught the supremacy of the pope over the entire church. He charged that the authors of the *Consilium* had misunderstood Christ's injunction, "Freely have you received, freely give": "That . . . was not said about benefices, which did not exist at that time . . . , but about the power of binding and loosing, of casting out demons, of powers, miracles, and sacraments," he argued.[106] Regarding the desire to purify the church in accordance with some nebulous ideal that was worse than utopian, actually harmful, Guidiccione stated firmly that nothing in the church's organization required to be changed. He therefore thought the *Consilium* unnecessary and answered it skillfully point by point, citing canon law at every step. His main contention was that reform of

103. For a sketch of his life, see Vinzenz Schweitzer, "Kardinal Bartolomeo Guidiccione (1469–1549)," *Römische Quartalschrift* 20 (1906): 27–53, 142–61, 189–204. His writings for the most part are still unpublished. For a description of the manuscripts, see Hubert Jedin, "Concilio e riforma nel pensiero del Cardinale Bartolommeo Guidiccione, *Rivista di storia della chiesa in Italia* 2 (1948): 34–35.

104. BAV, Barb. lat. 1173, fol. 152r.

105. That he was thought of as a reformer can be seen from the letter by his nephew Giovanni Guidiccione, bishop of Fossombrone, who warned his uncle not to come to Rome thinking he could change everything. The letter is a fascinating series of counsels on how to survive and succeed in the curia; see Giovanni Guidiccione, *Le lettere*, ed. Maria Teresa Graziosi (Rome: Bonacci, 1979), 2:14–19.

106. *CT* 12:231.

abuses could be accomplished only within established tradition, not through a sudden break with it. To him the *Consilium*, rather than proposing the reformation of the church and the restoration of its order, advocated its destruction.[107]

Guidiccione's views were diametrically opposed to those of Contarini and the rest of the reform commission. As a canon lawyer he was concerned in his way with the welfare of church and papacy, yet he showed a complete lack of sympathy for the *Consilium*. What gave his views particular weight were his proven devotion to Paul III, the consistency of his position, and the absence of personal motives in his tract. He saw the key to solving the church's problems as lying in the strict observance of existing laws and norms that were already on the books but not enforced. Predictably, he showed no glimmer of understanding for the ideas advanced by the Protestants. As far as he was concerned, they were merely reviving ideas of already condemned heretics,[108] and their spokesmen should be cited before a council and brought to justice.[109] There was no point in giving their criticism a hearing. Gradual removal of gross abuses in the church would be enough to answer the clamor of critics and presumably to quiet the authors of the *Consilium* as well.

The unequivocal expression of Guidiccione's position gives a revealing insight into the mentality of men who opposed almost everything Contarini and his supporters wanted to accomplish. Throughout his career as cardinal Contarini had to contend with numerous critics and adversaries like Guidiccione. He must have expected this. In any event, his Venetian government career had thoroughly prepared him for the intricacies of curial politics; he was no naive outsider in continual danger of being outmaneuvered by canny insiders. The major difference for him between Venice and Rome was the support networks on which he could count. In Venice he was a completely accepted member of the establishment, sharing its loyalties and part of a strong group of patricians who held decision-making posts of great influence. In Rome, in contrast, he was a member of a distinct minority that was critical of the prevailing system. Moreover, there was structurally a great difference

---

107. Ibid., 233. Jedin, "Concilio e riforma," 56, thinks that Guidiccione saw the radical principles of the *Consilium* as leading to revolution, not reformation.

108. *CT* 12:233–41. Guidiccione lists twenty specific Lutheran errors without having read a single work by Luther, relying instead on the writings of Luther's adversaries. But he did know Melanchthon's *Loci communes*, *CT* 12:234.

109. Ibid., 243.

between the positions of those he served, the Venetian doge on the one hand and the Roman pontiff on the other. In Venice, oligarchic government functioned to a great extent regardless of the doge's views, while in Rome everything depended on the pope's support. In Venice, Contarini had been a close associate of Andrea Gritti. At the papal court he was never to achieve special closeness to Paul III, who kept his own counsel and admitted few men other than members of his own family to his inner circle.

The effectiveness of Contarini and his commission was also hampered by the Protestant reaction to the *Consilium*. If Cardinal Schönberg in fact predicted another debacle like the backfiring of Adrian VI's confession in 1524, he was proved correct. In 1538 the *Consilium* appeared in three or possibly four Italian editions, three German editions, and one edition in the Netherlands.[110] Schönberg may well have sent the confidential text to Germany for reasons that are not altogether clear.[111] There it was eagerly read, and Luther himself provided the German translation of the memorial published in 1538 with an introduction and extremely caustic marginal comments.[112] On the title page was a woodcut showing three cardinals trying to sweep the church with foxtails, effectively symbolizing Luther's estimate of the authors of the memorial. He found them hypocrites whose only object was to help the pope in misleading Christianity further. Whatever their veneer, the reformers on the commission remained for him scoundrels and liars.[113]

Better known, and worthier of attention, is the more measured evaluation of the *Consilium* by Johannes Sturm in his preface to the translation published in Strassburg in 1538. He welcomed the memorial as marking a change for the better in papal policy and thought that the proposed correction of abuses should be applauded by all Christians. However, since the whole church was diseased, he said, it was not enough to remove the external symptoms of the malady without get-

110. For bibliography, see Ibid., 131–32. The publication and diffusion of the *Consilium* met with disapproval, as reported by the Mantuan agent in Rome, 3 June 1538: "Here there is universal and strong disapproval that [the *Consilium*] was allowed to be printed, because if it is not carried out the priests will seem to have confessed their sins and made them known everywhere, without wanting to correct their errors" (Solmi, "Fuga," 32). On the same page is mentioned a Milanese edition of the *Consilium*, thus far not found.

111. Ehses, "Zu den kirchlichen Reformarbeiten," 600.

112. Martin Luther, *The Career of the Reformer*, vol. 34 of *Luther's Works: American Edition* (Philadelphia: Muhlenberg Press, 1960), 231–67.

113. Ibid., 290.

ting at its cause.[114] Sturm applauded the *Consilium*'s criticism of exaggerated claims for papal power[115] but accused its authors of passing over in silence the greatest abuse in the church, which was the neglect of the gospel. Charging that the authors did not give an honest assessment of the situation for fear of offending the pope, he treated them to some bitter invective.[116] In the last analysis he doubted the readiness of Catholics to break with the past, and he expressed his apprehension that what was billed as reform would turn out to be only cosmetic change.

With the comments of Protestants ringing in the ears of irenic Catholics and the cardinals divided among themselves, Paul III was guided by the majority opinion that the recommendations of the *Consilium* not be put into effect. The pope thus prevented Contarini from assuming leadership of the movement for reform at a critical juncture when it seemed possible that the attitude and practice of church officials at the highest levels might change, and that the removal of abuses might begin to address the difficult questions raised by Protestants. The often-praised prudence of Paul III in this case amounted to stonewalling, and the *Consilium* produced no practical results. The critical, open-minded majority of the commission's members were too far ahead of what was acceptable to the general run of curialists and cardinals who were Roman organization men.

The Theory of Reform:
The Commissions of 1536–40

In a consistory on 20 April 1537 the pope announced that the opening of the council would have to be delayed until November.[117] The recommendations of the *Consilium*, drawn up in preparation for the council, thus lost their urgency. Still, Paul III determined to proceed with what he called reform of curial offices, thus showing

114. Walter Friedensburg, "Das Consilium de emendanda ecclesia, Kardinal Sadolet und Johannes Sturm von Strassburg," *Archiv für Reformationsgeschichte* 33 (1936): 17.
115. Ibid., 30.
116. Sadoleto answered Sturm, as did the German theologian Johannes Cochlaeus; see his *Aequitatis discussio super consilio delectorum cardinalium (1538)*, ed. Hilarius Walter, O.S.B., Corpus Catholicorum 17 (Münster i.W.: Aschendorff, 1931). For bibliography, see Remigius Bäumer, "Johannes Cochlaeus und die Reform der Kirche," in Bäumer (ed.), *Reformatio Ecclesiae. Festgabe Iserloh*, 333–54.
117. For the background, see Jedin, *Trient* 1:264ff.

some goodwill and satisfying Contarini and his group at least in part. He appointed a commission of four cardinals for reform of the *dataria*, balancing Contarini and Carafa with the conservative curialists Simonetta and Ghinucci.[118] On 12 May, Contarini wrote an optimistic letter to Pole, informing him of the new commission and adding, "Almost all cardinals favor reform; the appearance of the consistory has begun to change. Things which are proposed have started to be no longer expedited so routinely. [Now] canons are quoted, and what should or should not be done is carefully weighed, so that I cherish great hope (I do not say I conceive a great hope, for I have never despaired) that our affairs will proceed better every day."[119] Although the pope's political tactics gave neither side preponderance on the commission, Contarini hoped to sway the minds of those experienced curial cardinals who were not mere obstructionists and gain their support in effecting change in the *dataria*.

By the sixteenth century the *dataria* had evolved into a key curial office.[120] While there are differences of opinion concerning its origins, there are none concerning its growth in importance from the time of Sixtus IV onward. By the pontificate of Paul III it collected fees and taxes for large categories of compositions (originally agreed-upon settlements of disputed claims by means of some financial arrangement, though by the sixteenth century the term had come to be used of almost all fees paid to the *dataria*), dispensations (the granting of exemptions from norms and regulations of canon law in return for fees), and resignations (in effect, transfer taxes) connected with benefices. The head of the *dataria* (the *datario*) was also in charge of selling venal curial offices. The *dataria* had its own bank of deposit, and its income was managed separately from that controlled by the papal

---

118. Paul III's enigmatic stance, his indecision, and his compromises are puzzling, even to Hubert Jedin, who concluded that Paul III "cannot yet be considered the first pope of the Catholic Reformation, but rather its precursor," leaving the meaning of "precursor" in this context open; see Erwin Iserloh, Josef Glazik, and Hubert Jedin, eds., *Handbuch der Kirchengeschichte* (Freiburg i.B.: Herder, 1963–79), 4:477.

119. *Reg.*, 98 (no. 325).

120. See Nicola Storti, *La storia e il diritto della Dataria Apostolica dalle origini ai nostri giorni* (Naples: Athena Mediterranea, 1969); and Litva, "Attività della Dataria," esp. 85–112. Still useful is Léonce Celier, *Les dataires du XVIe siècle et les origines de la Daterie apostolique* (Paris: Fontemoing, 1910), which on pp. 8–9 illustrates the business practices of the *dataria* by following an imaginary petition through the required steps before it was definitely responded to. For a brief orientation on the place of individual offices in the structure of the curia, see Lajos Pásztor, "Histoire de la curie romaine, problème d'histoire de l'église," *Revue d'histoire ecclésiastique* 64 (1969): 353–66.

depository general.[121] The *datario* was responsible to the pope alone, who allotted the *dataria*'s revenues. During the thirty years beginning with the reign of Paul III, the office's annual median revenue was 141,000 gold scudi.[122]

At issue before the commission of 1537 were the theoretical, legal, and practical aspects of the *dataria*'s operations, most importantly the justification for payments exacted for spiritual graces and the fees fixed for various categories of compositions. Unfortunately, the surviving documentation does not illuminate the workings of the commission clearly, and vexing problems of chronology remain,[123] since none of the tracts and memorials that issued from it are dated. Contarini's participation in this commission produced several short writings that are most valuable in revealing both the strengths and the weaknesses of his position and way of thinking.

For one of their first meetings the four cardinals received a description of the *dataria*'s categories of business, ranging from major matters concerning benefices to relatively minor ones.[124] Contarini, chosen as secretary, was asked to summarize what presumably were the initial discussions of the commission and to add his own reflections. He did this in a document of the late spring or early summer of 1537, a combination of minutes and his own comments, which shows clearly that he was unfamiliar with canon law and innocent of legal terminology.[125] He and his colleagues had before them intricate legal issues arising from *dataria* practices with long precedents. Contarini's way of dealing with these was to cut the Gordian knot by repeating what he had

121. See the charts of curial financial organization in Partner, "Papal Financial Policy," 19; and Reinhard, "Ämterhandel," 60. Still valuable is BAV, Vat. lat. 13461, "Della Dataria Apostolica," of the later seventeenth or early eighteenth century, especially ff. 18r–53r, listing the most frequent categories of business in the *dataria*. However, since it postdates the curial reforms of Pope Sixtus V it cannot be used as a precise description of practices in 1537.

122. Litva, "L'attività della Dataria," 157. Paul III's total annual income was about 375,000 gold scudi: Partner, 54. The figures in Pastor, *Geschichte der Päpste*, 5: 124 should be corrected.

123. Jedin, *Trient* 1: 584–85, n. 56, has suggested the most detailed chronology thus far, which however stills leaves considerable uncertainty. I differ from it in several respects, noted below.

124. Contarini refers to this description or list from the *dataria* as *scheda scripta*: Friedensburg, "Zwei Aktenstücke zur Geschichte der kirchlichen Reformbestrebungen an der römischen Kurie (1536–1538)," *Quellen und Forschungen* 7: 263. So far it has not been found, but it can be reconstructed in outline from Contarini's notes.

125. Friedensburg, "Zwei Aktenstücke," 263–67. Contarini's secretary Beccadelli in describing Contarini's studies and reading makes no mention of law: "Vita," 40–44.

written before: that the pope (and, by extension, the officers who reported to him) could not sell spiritual graces. But even this short document exposes his difficulty in keeping spiritual matters separate from temporal, and in deciding whether in a given case the pope would be acting in his capacity as pope or prince.[126] Contarini's lack of legal training was a serious obstacle that in several cases prevented him from expressing his opinion clearly and led him to evade the need for a definite statement by using such phrases as "Your lordships must decide," "I am uncertain," and "This matter causes me great difficulty."

An illustration of his amateurishness is seen in his attempt to deal with the problem of avaricious confessors: "It would be scandalous for a confessor to hear confession, grant absolution, and then oblige the penitent, as a part of the penance, to give him money. Beware of any appearance of evil, says the Apostle Paul. [However,] the confessor might tell how poor he is, leaving the decision up to the penitent."[127] Here an impractical side of Contarini becomes evident, as if he never seriously considered the situation about which he was writing or just where the fine line lay between openly directing a penitent to pay and merely putting pressure on him to do so. A similarly unrealistic attitude is found in the beginning of the document, where Contarini speaks of the weighty charge laid on the four members of the commission to "give Christian and faithful counsel to [the pope], on which in my opinion seems to depend the betterment and reform of the entire church and the whole Christian people."[128] He expresses a narrow view that equates Rome with the church, as though repeating the old adage, "Purga Romam, purgatur mundus!" Yet these two passages are not so much evidence of Contarini's naïveté as of his deep-seated belief, seemingly impervious to diplomatic experience, that human beings were rational and would surely respond properly to a situation once its true import was understood. He consistently advocated honesty in human relations and openness that should pervade all of life, from confessor and penitent in the confessional to papal government in all its intricacies. Men should be willing to admit the existence of abuses, set about correcting them, and give a good example to the entire Chris-

---

126. For example, in the section on protonotaries (in Friedensburg, "Zwei Akten-stücke," 265), and in the quite confused final section (267), concerning the incomes of temporary appointees on the diocesan level.

127. Ibid., 267.

128. Ibid., 263. The idea that reform must begin in Rome and spread from there was a commonplace; see, for example, the letter of Cardinal Benedetto Accolti to Contarini, 20 Oct. 1538, in *Reg.*, 106 (no. 369).

tian world. Then everywhere the church would change for the better, spurred on by Rome.

Contarini's optimism about human reasonableness is expressed repeatedly in writings belonging to this period. He believed that a growing number of cardinals was ready to support reform, and that the pope's "honorable and noble" mind would prove steadfast. Bishops, too, were beginning to show themselves, he thought, as men "who carry a bright light before us; so that I think we need not doubt that God's grace will overflow in the place where once transgression abounded."[129] A year later, Contarini praised the German theologian Johannes Cochlaeus for his gentleness and restraint in dealing with the Protestants, and encouraged him to refrain from attacking them: "Let us show that the false things they preach and have brought to their assemblies contradict our fathers and the teaching of holy scripture. [Let us do this] not with bitter words or insults, but with great benevolence, friendly words, and such gentle and mild comportment as befits a Christian."[130] Here again we see Contarini's deep belief that people will respond to the force of good example and to serious, nonpolemical appeals to reason. While this outlook no doubt made his personality attractive, it also introduced a utopian element into his ideas on reform, and prevented him from making an acute assessment of the situation the church confronted in the Protestant challenge. In his desire to believe in the victory of good over evil, order over confusion, and reason over irrationality, Contarini sometimes minimized serious problems. The Mantuan agent sensed some of this when he reported to Cardinal Gonzaga that Contarini was "considered a man devoted to study rather than to affairs. When reform or such matters are discussed he seems to take them seriously. It is thought that he sincerely believes the talk of implementing [reform measures], notwithstanding the fact that despite the many discussions in the past no [specific] provisions have been made. This stems from his goodness."[131]

But this goodness or outward kindness did not come naturally to Contarini according to his secretary, who mentions that his patron overcame his natural irascibility by sheer willpower.[132] His gentleness was due not to blandness but to conscious self-fashioning, rooted in

129. To Isidore Clarius, 23 July 1537, in *Reg.*, 278 (Inedita, no. 22) (cf. Romans 3:20 for the allusion). The text should be corrected by ASVat, A.A., Arm. I–XVIII, 6461, fols. 32r–33r.

130. *Reg.*, 297 (Inedita, no. 30). For the date, 8 November 1538, see *GC*, 272n.4.

131. Nino Sernini to Ercole Gonzaga, Rome, 26 Feb. 1539, in Solmi, "Fuga," 83.

132. Beccadelli, "Vita," 48.

his view of man as able to control his inclinations by his reason. There was determination in Contarini's position on the curial reform commissions as well; he operated not just with good intentions, but with a definite strategy, one that becomes evident in his memorials and occasional pieces.

In a brief address to the members of the reform commission during one of their early meetings,[133] Contarini made his position clear in a lapidary sentence: "Simony is the willingness to buy or sell a spiritual thing or something connected with it." Referring to both Gratian and St. Thomas, he emphasized that any exchange of a spiritual benefit for a temporal one was simony, period.[134] The principle admitted of no exceptions, even if the end envisioned in the transaction was good. Spiritual graces must be given freely; principles of natural reason, the Scriptures, (unnamed) famous doctors, and the teaching of the fathers all agree, he concluded, that it is not permissible to withhold spiritual graces until the petitioner has made a payment.[135] Contarini's simple, radical position precluded the possibility of distinctions, exceptions, or mitigating circumstances. This uncompromising stand was his platform to which he returned over and over again, making it the basic premise for all he wrote on the subject of curial reform.

His moralistic absolutism and refusal to engage in legal argumentation conferred on Contarini an aura of purity and incorruptibility that undoubtedly appealed to some persons, including Carafa; but it also led to the splitting of the commission into two factions that shared no common intellectual habits and could not work harmoniously together. Ghinucci and Simonetta understood clearly the financial implications of doing away with all compositions and, despite Contarini's impassioned pleas, could not accept his view. They sought the help of another experienced curial official and lawyer, Tommaso Campeggio,[136] who drew up a short summary of the arguments against Contarini's position.[137] Despite its brevity it shows the cautious, basically conservative, but thoroughly informed mind of its author, who de-

---

133. *CT* 12:153–55. The meeting probably followed the one to which Contarini's minutes in Friedensburg, "Zwei Aktenstücke," refer.

134. *Summa theol.*, I^{a}II^{ae}, qu. 100, art. 1.   135. *CT* 12:155.

136. On the career of Tommaso Campeggio, bishop of Feltre and brother-in-law of the better-known cardinal Lorenzo, see Hubert Jedin, "Campeggi, Tommaso," in *DBI* 17:472–74. Especially useful is Jedin, *Tommaso Campeggio (1483–1564): tridentinische Reform und kuriale Tradition* (Münster i.W.: Aschendorff, 1958).

137. *CT* 12:155–57. It is addressed to an unnamed cardinal, probably one of the commission members.

ployed arguments from canon law expertly and effectively. By emphasizing twice that he could tolerate and excuse compositions without necessarily approving of them, he prudently avoided being labeled a mere defender of the status quo and thus losing effectiveness with the moderate cardinals and the pope. The prevalent tone in Campeggio's memorandum is far different from that of Contarini's pieces: in Campeggio we see a trained administrator open to limited change but confident of the basic justifiability of existing practices.

The reformers Contarini and Carafa also looked outside the commission for support, turning to two men with whom they had worked on the *Consilium de emendanda ecclesia*, Tommaso Badia and Girolamo Aleandro. Their choice made good sense: the former was Paul III's personal advisor in theological matters and thus a channel directly to the pope, while the latter was an ally valuable for his political acumen, even if his commitment to reform was less than enthusiastic. The four prelates drew up a separate memorandum for the pope, "Consilium quattuor delectorum a Paulo III super reformatione S. R. Ecclesiae."[138] The document was signed by all four, but Contarini was its author,[139] as can be seen from the many similarities with his previous address to the commission, particularly in the philosophical arguments and examples used and in the impatience with legal points.

If the pope picked up this memorial expecting to find a careful discussion of specific issues touching on *dataria* practices, he must have been taken aback. No attention was given to the arguments of curial lawyers. Contarini reiterated that all compositions constituted simoniacal practices when exacted in return for permissions or dispensations in spiritual matters. He scorned with unusual vehemence the argument that the fees were in compensation for the expenses connected with drawing up the documents connected with a particular case, and not for the dispensation itself, which was given free.[140] He thought that such sophistry in itself constituted a scandal; it gave Lutherans cause to curse the Holy See, and would make it possible to commit the worst irregularities in the granting of favors and benefices throughout the church. Flagrant simony could always be called the payment for documents. The image of the sick church reappeared, and the pope was

138. Ibid., 208–15.
139. Stephan Ehses, "Ein Gutachten zur Reform des päpstlichen Gnadenwesens aus dem Jahre 1538," *Römische Quartalschrift* 14 (1900): 107. Ehses (108) dates the document between 24 September 1537 and 13 March 1538.
140. *CT* 12:210.

urged to put an end to its diseases without regard to practical considerations. The repetition of some of Contarini's characteristic ideas is
significant: if the pope acted fearlessly for reform, then the Lutherans
would be confounded and the entire Christian people would return to
its former veneration of the papacy. Contarini added a fresh and startling thought by calling on Paul III not to feel he had to defend everything his predecessors did: "It would be an enormous and endless
undertaking to defend everything that all former popes have done!"[141]
If Paul III cleansed the church, his pontificate would witness an outpouring of love, and the faithful would make voluntary contributions
to support their head.

The curious mixture of earnest and even passionate pleading with
nebulous generalities about finances that we saw in Contarini's appeals
to Clement VII appears again in the "Consilium quattuor delectorum." It was not difficult for the conservative members of the commission to answer Contarini and his allies effectively, especially after they
added another formidable adversary of reform to their ranks as an advisor. Dionigi Loreri, general of the Servite order and later cardinal, replied to the memorial of the four prelates in a tract addressed to
Paul III. This reply showed considerable tact, an understanding of the
pope's character, and an appreciation of the psychological problems
that acceptance of the "Consilium quattuor delectorum" would involve.[142] Loreri freely admitted that much could be improved in the
practice of curial institutions, but offered no fundamental criticism. He
favored the removal of abuses connected with compositions but not
the compositions themselves. His case was built on the distinction between the *pretium*, or fee for a favor granted, and the *stipendium*, or
offering that the faithful were expected to make for support of the
clergy. While he agreed that the former was reprehensible, he emphasized that the latter had been sanctioned by many doctors of the
church, including Pope Gregory the Great himself, all of whom based
their opinion on Christ's words, "The laborer is worthy of his hire."[143]
Loreri's presentation of his case was effective because it was clear,

141. Ibid., 214.
142. "Fratris Dionysii ord. Servorum postea cardinalis S. Marcelli ad Paulum III
Optimum Pontificem Maximum compositionum defensio," in ibid., 215–26. For a summary of Loreri's main arguments, see "Ragioni di fra Dionigi dell'ordine de' servi, che fù
poi il Card. S^to Marcello a Papa Paulo 3° per difesa delle compositioni," BAV, Barb. lat.
5362, fols. 188r–189r. The original document was written no earlier than the latter half
of October 1537, since Loreri mentions that Paul III has been pope for three full years.
143. Luke 10:7, quoted and explained in *CT* 12:221.

learned, and rhetorically skillful. He was at pains to establish a link between his position and the tradition of the church from the fathers down to more recent theologians and canonists like Scotus, Aquinas, and Bonaventure. His graphic picture of how Protestants would react to the abolition of compositions was carefully calculated to contradict Contarini's and win the pope over. He argued that the Lutherans would exploit the admission of errors and corruption in the Catholic church, because such an admission would prove them right. Paul III must have winced as he read that if the Contarini group's recommendations were accepted Lutherans would point at him as tolerating abuses and committing simony for forty-two years as a cardinal and three more years as pope. Loreri besought him not to allow his predecessors to be charged with heresy and simony and thus destroy the authority of the Holy See.[144]

Loreri's tract, as impassioned in its way as Contarini's appeals were, could not fail to impress the pope, especially as it expressed views similar to his own. The pope must have been confirmed in his feeling that Loreri was right by the additional support of Campeggio. At a point in the controversy that cannot be dated with precision, Campeggio wrote a succinct memorial setting forth once again the arguments for the legitimacy of compositions.[145] Some years later he wrote yet another memorial for the pope that has been called "a classical summary of the reflections about curial reform on the part of a curial prelate open to reform but thinking along conservative lines."[146] Although the later report is not directly connected with the debates about the *dataria*, it makes clear Campeggio's steady conviction that reform as envisioned by the authors of the *Consilium de emendanda ecclesia* or the "Consilium quattuor delectorum" would be impracticably radical. Campeggio's solution was that the reform decrees promulgated in the eighth and ninth sessions of the Fifth Lateran Council, which had remained a dead letter, be revived.[147] He recommended making modifications to the existing system, respecting the rights that had been conferred in accordance with then-prevailing practice but introducing for the future a series of gradual adjustments that would avoid too sharp a break with the past. In the short as well as the long run, this was the approach that

144. Ibid., 224–25.   145. Ibid., 157–58.

146. Hubert Jedin, "Eine bisher unbekannte Denkschrift Tommaso Campeggios über die Reform der römischen Kurie," in *Festgabe Joseph Lortz*, ed. Erwin Iserloh and Peter Manns, vol. 1 (Baden-Baden: Bruno Grimm, 1958), 409.

147. Ibid., 413–14.

Rome actually took to reform,[148] for Campeggio's moderate, basically conservative measures could muster the support of the majority of cardinals and curialists, as Contarini's could not.

After the "Consilium quattuor delectorum" Contarini found himself in a strange position. Once the defender of papal power in the Venetian Senate, he now appeared to conservatives to be attacking it, or at least urging its retrenchment. Contarini was much too practiced in politics not to realize that he and his handful of supporters could be effective only if they received decisive help from the pope. As the debates over reform of the *dataria* dragged on into 1538 without definite result he appealed one last time to Paul III for support. This most personal and moving of his tracts is a *cri de coeur*, stripped of all rhetorical flourishes and legal niceties.

Contarini's "Letter to Pope Paul III Concerning the Pope's Power in the Area of Compositions" in all likelihood belongs to the summer or fall of 1538.[149] It deserves a closer analysis than it has received; indeed, it is not just another tract, but a most revealing piece of evidence for Contarini's state of mind at the time. Like many of his writings the tract begins with a philosophical discussion of the issue to be considered, in this case the limits of papal power. Contarini draws on Aristotle and Aquinas to demonstrate once more the irrationality and moral wrong of the thesis that the will of the pope is law. The *Consilium de emendanda ecclesia* had warned the pope of false counselors whose exaggerated view of papal authority had brought the papacy into disrepute. Although Contarini now reiterates his favorite idea that such false counselors deserve blame for their wrong theories, he builds his theory on something far more substantial than a mere attack on canon lawyers, by analyzing the nature of papal power and in so doing drawing an exalted image of it. He argues that a close correspondence exists between papal and the princely power, in fact between all forms

148. Campeggio continued to think about the issues of papal power in relation to benefices, as can be seen from his later writings, collected in *Opus Thomae Campegii Bononiensis, Episcopi Feltrensis, de auctoritate et potestate Romani Pontificis*...(Venice, 1555). "An Papa labem simoniae incurrere possit," fols. 162r–169r, examines the limits of the pope's power to grant benefices and stresses that he is their steward, not their lord. See also Jedin, "Analekten zur Reformtätigkeit," 135–36. The second part of this article has been reprinted under its original subtitle, "Kann der Papst Simonie begehen?" in the author's *Kirche des Glaubens* 2:264–84.

149. "De potestate pontificis in compositionibus epistola," in Jodocus Le Plat, *Monumentorum ad historiam Concilii Tridentini illustrandam spectantium amplissima collectio* (Louvain, 1781–87), 2:608–15.

of power exercised in an ordered society: such power is by its nature necessarily rational. Because no power on earth is superior to the pope's, his must be the most rationally exercised.[150] To argue, however, as some lawyers have done, that the pope's will is absolute is idolatrous, for it ascribes to the pope qualities that are God's alone.

Contarini's explanation of just why papal power is and must be rational follows, and the demonstration is striking in its deeply personal tone. Human beings have freedom of choice, and they can make bad choices or good. Only divine grace, given us because of our faith in the merits of Christ's blood, can ensure that we make right choices. Contarini here restates his view, so crucial in his own religious development, of man's utter dependence on God's grace. Divine grace guides the will to true freedom, and precludes arbitrariness. The vast power given to the pope by God, if exercised in accordance with its nature, can never degenerate into the sort of abuses that do harm to the people of Christ. The lawyers who have hitherto encouraged the popes to regard their own will as absolute have shown their ignorance of what papal power is by their false teaching: "That position is so very false, so repugnant to common sense, so contrary to Christian doctrine, as to deprive the whole Christian people of [good] government in such a way that nothing more pernicious could be found."[151]

Contarini's own basically Aristotelian views on human nature constitute one element in this discussion. A second, as we have seen, comprises his ideas of the relation between man and God. The third is his sense of due order in society and politics, rooted in his Venetian background and experience. With high approval he paraphrases Aristotle to the effect that making only one man prince is tantamount to giving the power to rule to a man and a beast, since in the human soul are also animal passions and inclinations. Laws, not the will of the ruler, make for good government. The pope is bound to follow the dictates of natural reason, divine precepts, and the mandate of charity. Subjection of Christians to arbitrary papal government would be contrary to the law of Christ, which frees man. The pope is not free to grant dispensations as he pleases, but only in accordance with existing laws and with due regard to all the circumstances of the petitioner. The justification of

150. " ... Nulli potest esse dubium, quin auctoritas et potestas haec pontificis sit rationalis, seu rationis potentia, a Deo optimo, beatissimo Petro ejusque successoribus collata. . . . Haec potestas est omnium maxima in terris, qua etiam inter homines nulla superior" (ibid., 610).

151. Ibid., 613.

arbitrary papal power has given Lutherans understandable cause to write about the Babylonian captivity.[152]

Contarini concludes his letter with this plea to Paul III:

Holy Father, you have received from Christ the highest power for governing the Christian people: [but] that [power] is a power founded in reason. Your Holiness should make every attempt to exercise that great power together with the freedom of the will to the greatest extent possible in order that, thanks to divine grace and your own effort, you may stand firmly by the rule of reason, as I have discussed above, and not turn toward the powerlessness of the will by which it chooses evil, or to the servitude by which it chooses sin. This is the liberty, this is the power of the will, which when joined to the pontifical authority committed to you by Christ will make you truly most powerful and free, and the source of life for the whole of Christendom. When you rule and govern thus you will manifest on earth as it were a heavenly example of how to live.[153]

This piece was no mere outpouring of utopian sentiments. It was an attempt to transfer to the government of the church some of the best aspects of what Contarini prized above all in the government of Venice: rationality, order, and the rule of law that made it impossible for one man to exercise arbitrary or tyrannical power. Contarini wished to reform Rome in the image of an idealized Venice, whose constitution he considered to be based on reason, equity, and concern for the common good. The question of compositions provided the occasion for the expression of his beliefs, since he was concerned here with general ideas rather than specific reform measures. This little tract remains indispensable for understanding the fusion of personal, Christian, and Venetian values that stamped his thought. If the tract lacks a well-defined systematic basis in either philosophy or theology, it nevertheless breathes a moral and ethical radicalism that centuries later makes it still accessible and attractive in an age more used to emotional appeals than to the patterns of thought characteristic of Contarini's time.

In a letter to Pole of November 1538, Contarini describes the pope's excursion to Ostia during a spell of Indian summer weather.[154] En route the pope, who had read Contarini's tract on compositions, called him to his side to discuss the question privately. Contarini admitted to Pole that he had despaired of any real action on reform, but

---

152. Ibid., 614.   153. Ibid., 615.

154. Ostia, 11 Nov. 1538, in *Ep. Poli* 2:141. Contarini describes the excursion and the pleasant weather in attractive detail. A short extract from the letter is in *Reg.*, 107–8 (no. 373).

now he "again became full of hope that God would bring about some good result and that the gates of hell would not prevail against the spirit of the Lord." On this occasion too, however, Contarini failed to fix the pope's purpose and spur him on to deeds instead of words— even though, as he reports, Paul III discussed many matters "in a Christian manner" with him. A week later Contarini and Pole were visiting Vittoria Colonna. When she asked why reform measures were not being implemented "they shrugged their shoulders, meaning to answer her (she has a quick mind) by their silence rather than by telling her openly the reason."[155] In the *dataria*, for all the desultory talk of reform, nothing changed, nor were there any definite plans for change.

In the spring of 1539, Paul III enlarged the original reform commission of Contarini, Carafa, Ghinucci, and Simonetta by doubling its membership. The four new appointees were Tommaso Campeggio and Cardinals Cupis, Cesarini, and Ridolfi, all four of them unsympathetic to sweeping change. It is easy to imagine what Contarini thought as he listened to Paul III remind the commission "how he had always desired reform, and now desired it more than ever, but wished that the compositions of the *dataria* be settled first, without any regard to [difficulties in the way]."[156] Although the pope's words were not to be taken seriously, Contarini continued to act as if he believed in the possibility of effective reform by continuing to insist on his strict interpretation of compositions that precluded any payment at all for the conferral of spiritual graces. At this point one of his most important supporters parted company with him. Gianpietro Carafa could no longer agree with Contarini's uncompromising position, "adducing many arguments in the opposite sense," according to the Mantuan agent Sernini, who obviously had excellent connections among the cardinals and knew details of the commission's discussions. The enlarged commission could come to no agreement, and eventually reform of the *dataria* fizzled out without any final decision.

The enlarged reform commission was also charged by the pope to reform the administrative tribunals—the *rota*, the chancery, and the

---

155. Report of the Mantuan agent De Plotis, Rome, 18 Nov. 1538, to Cardinal Ercole Gonzaga; quoted in Aldo Stella, "La lettera del Cardinale Contarini sulla predestinazione," *Rivista di storia della chiesa in Italia* 15 (1961): 416n.22. He corrects the text given in Solmi, "Fuga," 33.

156. Report of the Mantuan agent Nino Sernini to Cardinal Ercole Gonzaga, Rome, 19 Mar. 1539, in Pastor, *Geschichte der Päpste* 5:132n.3, correcting the text in Solmi, "Fuga," 35.

poenitentiaria, in addition to the *dataria*—with two members of the commission assigned to each office. Contarini and Carafa were to investigate the workings of the *poenitentiaria*, one of the oldest curial offices and the central agency for granting absolutions and dispensations of all kinds throughout Christendom.[157] When Protestant reformers attacked corruption at the Roman court, they most frequently had in mind the abuses of the *poenitentiaria* in the commutation of vows, the sanctioning of gross irregularities in discipline, and the resulting confusion and breakdown of order on the local level—all for a fee. But Protestants were not alone in attacking this office. Catholics, too, were highly critical of it, and many saw it as destroying the church. Among them Carafa stands out for the bluntness with which already in 1532 he charged the Venetian Franciscan Fra Bonaventura to transmit his message to Pope Clement VII: "Beg His Holiness for the honor of God, the welfare of Christendom, and most of all for his own well-being and honor, to muzzle those mad dogs of the *poenitentiaria*, so that their profit should not cost afflicted Christendom and the soul of His Holiness so dearly."[158] Now, seven years later, Carafa was called to Rome to take part together with Contarini in an effort to remedy what they both considered a scandal.

Little precise information exists for the work of the reform commission during the year after it was enlarged in the spring of 1539.[159] Jedin is right in saying that the new appointees brought about a change.[160] They were conservative men, and their proposals were not likely to threaten the status quo.[161] Contarini now had no illusions about the situation in which he found himself. He wrote no more memorials to the pope analyzing the basic problems, for they were apparently in-

157. For the history of the *poenitentiaria*, see Göller, *Päpstliche Pönitentiarie*. See also Gene A. Brucker, "Religious Sensibilities in Early Modern Europe: Examples from the Records of the Holy Penitentiary," *Historical Reflections/Réflexions historiques* 15 (1988): 13–25.

158. Gianpietro Carafa, "De Lutheranorum haeresi reprimenda et ecclesia reformanda ad Clementem VII," in *CT* 12:70. English translation in Gleason, *Reform Thought*, 57–80.

159. Pastor, *Geschichte der Päpste* 5:133, attributes the absence of information to a policy of keeping the deliberations of the reform commission secret as much as possible in order to obviate attacks by Lutherans.

160. Jedin, *Trient* 1:347: "Es begann das zweite Stadium der Reformtätigkeit Pauls III.: eine allgemeine Kurialreform auf konservativer Grundlage."

161. Hofmann, *Forschungen* 1:307, thinks that they understood reform in the medieval sense, as a return to existing norms, "together with the utmost regard for current practices."

soluble for the time being, and in any case he had already said what he had to say about them. To judge by the few references to curial reform in his letters or in the reports of ambassadors and agents in Rome, the pope did not press the commission to expedite its work. He was preoccupied with questions of the council, of war and peace. If meetings of the commission were held, they did not produce concrete results. Contarini had some satisfaction in the inclusion of his friend Federico Fregoso and the reform-minded Marcello Cervini (the future Pope Marcellus II) among the new cardinals named in December 1539,[162] but none in the progress of curial reform.

Not until early 1540 was there some sign of change. Papal legates and nuncios to Germany and France in that year reported mounting impatience with the dilatory ways of Rome and urged Paul III to action.[163] In March reports describing the current practices of the Roman tribunals were submitted to the pope, prompting the Mantuan agent to write: "There is no more talk about the *dataria*. Seriously speaking, everything will be reformed slightly, without touching the root of the matter."[164] In April, however, the pope seemed to take renewed interest in reform, enjoining the commission to accelerate and complete its work.[165]

Whatever efforts Contarini and Carafa made to comply with the pope's wishes were hampered by the highly resourceful and experienced Antonio Pucci. A member of a Florentine family long connected with the curia, Pucci had succeeded his uncle in the office of grand penitentiary and was determined to defend his turf. Made suspicious by the talk of reform, he had asked and received from Paul III already in 1538 a confirmation of the privileges conferred on the grand penitentiary by Sixtus IV.[166] How Paul III could grant Pucci's request and then urge Contarini and Carafa to proceed with reform of the *poenitentiaria* must remain one of the unanswered questions about that pope. Under the existing circumstances, Contarini and Carafa could

162. Fregoso to Contarini, Gubbio, 23 Dec. 1539, in *Reg.*, 120 (no. 438); and Contarini to Cervini, Rome, 27 Dec. 1539, *Reg.*, 120–21 (no. 440).

163. Ludwig Cardauns, *Zur Geschichte der kirchlichen Unions- und Reformbestrebungen von 1538 bis 1542* (Rome: Loescher, 1910), 59.

164. Nino Sernini to Cardinal Ercole Gonzaga, Rome, 13 Mar. 1540, Archivio di Stato, Mantua (hereafter cited as ASM), *Carteggio Gonzaga*, Esteri, 1540, fol. 410 (Cardauns, *Zur Geschichte*, 58, quotes the last sentence.) I wish to thank Professor Aldo Stella for obtaining this document for me.

165. *CT* 4:454, consistory of 21 April 1540.

166. Göller, *Päpstliche Pönitentiarie* 2(2):93–94, 82–85.

do little. Even the politic Aleandro, usually careful not to give offense, could not contain his anger when the subject of the *poenitentiaria* was brought up in consistory. He begged the pope not to require him to speak about it, for otherwise he would say things that would darken even the sun; he attacked Pucci so furiously as to leave the latter stunned.[167] Contarini and Carafa concentrated on Pucci. Their sessions were stormy at times; Contarini described them as combats,[168] while Pucci was enraged by what he saw as Contarini's stubbornness. He told the Mantuan agent: "Write to your lord [Cardinal Ercole Gonzaga] that he has never known a more passionate man or a worse judge than Contarini, who, disregarding everyone, wants his opinion to prevail over all others. He maintains that his conscience tells him to do this; however, I hope to God that reason will triumph."[169]

Pucci succeeded so well in defending his interests that many cardinals agreed with him. Contarini alone continued to attack him, prompting Pucci to ask that the pope decide between them.[170] Still, the grand penitentiary was under enough pressure to make him issue a series of reform decrees in the course of four years. The decrees are rather technical, however, bearing on protocol and minor matters (such as marriages during Lent) and leaving the principal issues untouched.[171] Paul III did not openly take sides in the dispute between Pucci and Contarini; but suddenly and unexpectedly a brief note appears in the consistorial acts: "In Rome on Friday, 6 August 1540, there was a secret consistory in which the reform of the sacred *poenitentiaria* was settled and concluded."[172] This reform amounted to nothing, though, for abuses in the *poenitentiaria* were not effectively dealt with until Pius IV's constitution *In sublimi* of 1562, followed by the transformation and reorganization of the whole office under Pius V in 1569.[173] Equally insignificant was the appointment in August

167. Pietro Ghinucci to Cardinal Ercole Gonzaga, Rome, 28 Apr. 1540, ASM, *Carteggio Gonzaga*, Esteri, 1540, fol. 84v.

168. To Cardinal Ercole Gonzaga, Rome, 10 Apr. 1540, in Edmondo Solmi, "Lettere inedite del cardinale Gasparo Contarini nel carteggio del cardinale Ercole Gonzaga," *Nuovo Archivio Veneto* 7 (1904): 263.

169. Bernardino De Plotis to Cardinal Ercole Gonzaga, Rome, 14 July 1540, in Edmondo Solmi, "Gasparo Contarini alla Dieta di Ratisbona secondo i documenti inediti dell'Archivio Gonzaga di Mantova," *Nuovo Archivio Veneto* 13 (1907): 12.

170. Contarini is described as attacking Pucci vigorously ("a spada tratta"); see ibid., 11.

171. Pucci's decrees are printed in Göller, *Päpstliche Pönitentiarie* 2(2):43–69.

172. *CT* 4:454.

173. The curia was restructured only in 1588 under Sixtus V; see Niccolò Del Re, *La curia romana*, 3d ed. (Rome: Edizioni di Storia e Letteratura, 1970).

1540 of Contarini, Carafa, and Loreri to a new commission for putting into effect Pucci's reform decrees and supervising their execution.[174] The plain fact was that for all the efforts of Contarini and the handful of like-minded men curial reform had not advanced, and there were no significant changes.

It would be tempting to assign the whole blame for the failure of reform in Rome between 1536 and 1540 to Paul III, but such a conclusion would be far too simple. The pope was maneuvering in an extremely complex political situation, as the first volume of Jedin's *History of the Council of Trent* amply demonstrates. While Paul III sought to be peacemaker between the emperor and the king of France, he had also to face Protestant strength and increasing militancy. After the *Consilium de emendanda ecclesia* backfired in Germany, the pope was understandably reluctant to heap more ashes on his own head in public; Guidiccione's representations had made their impact on him. By comparison with war, peace, the approaching council, and the Protestant challenge, curial reform was of only secondary interest to the pope. Contarini's perspective was different. He continued to insist on his ideas, though at times he was unfortunate in the moment he chose to do so, as in 1538 while Paul III was preoccupied by wider issues.

Another factor contributing to Contarini's failure to move the pope was the economic situation. In 1540 prices rose steeply. Contarini himself felt the inadequacy of his income and had to remind the bishop of Pamplona that a pension he was to receive from the income of that bishopric was overdue.[175] At this point nothing could have been less welcome to curial officials than a plan like Contarini's that would decrease curial revenues, since they, too, were pressed for money. Determined opposition to reform came from associations of minor curial officials such as scribes, secretaries, and abbreviators, and they drew up memorials explaining their various positions regarding proposed changes that would affect them.[176] Paul III was too politic to disregard their opinions, especially since men he trusted, like Tommaso Campeggio, urged him to respect the rights of curial officials.[177] Indeed, the pope seemed to need little urging, for on seven occasions between 1535 and 1540 he confirmed their privileges, which for most

174. *CT* 4:454. The commission was again enlarged, this time to twelve members.
175. Cardauns, *Zur Geschichte*, 62.
176. For examples of these objections, see *CT* 4:471–79.
177. For Campeggio's views on this subject, see Jedin, "Eine unbekannte Denkschrift," 409–10.

officials included the right to dispose of their offices as their property, even through their wills.[178]

The pope's actions of course had the effect of almost completely negating the effectiveness of the reform commission's work. But then again, Paul III had no realistic alternatives. There was no possibility of abolishing venal offices, since to do so would require that they all be bought back from their holders. Contemporaries were well aware of this fact. The astute Cardinal Gonzaga, for example, in writing to Contarini of his desire to see the *poenitentiaria* reformed, raised two uncomfortable questions:

> What benefit will Christianity derive from the correction of abuses in the *poenitentiaria* if the same documents that it currently executes are executed by some other office at the [papal] court? It does not seem to me that anything would be accomplished in that case except to take the profit away from Santiquattro [Pucci, whose titular church was Santi Quattro Coronati] and give it to someone else. The second thing I want to know is what will be done with the officials of the *poenitentiaria* who bought their offices in good faith from those entitled to sell them, in order to get a certain percentage [as return on their investment]. How will it be possible not to injure them?[179]

Cardinal Gonzaga expressed here what many even of those sympathetic to reform must have thought, especially since more conservative cardinals insisted that officials who had bought their offices must be reimbursed before changes could be initiated.[180]

Contarini was unable to give answers to Gonzaga's questions or come up with practical alternatives. But then, his concern with reform was of a theoretical order; finding new sources of papal revenue was not an issue. His firm conviction was that details of papal finances would be taken care of in the wake of serious actual reform of curial offices, and that change would have to begin with the pope himself. Only he could break with the financial policies of his predecessors by refusing to agree with canon lawyers who maintained his freedom to decide in financial matters.

It was a strangely paradoxical situation in which Contarini called on

178. See Hofmann, *Forschungen* 2:68, for these confirmations. He mentions (1: 315) the possibility that Paul III dealt with the curia in this way in order to break the resistance to reform as such, but this explanation seems improbable since the confirmations did not lessen opposition to reform in the least. Jedin, *Trient* 1:338, mentions the toughness of curial officials in defending their rights and privileges.

179. Friedensburg, "Briefwechsel," 204–5.

180. Pietro Ghinucci to Ercole Gonzaga, Rome, 5 May 1540, ASM, *Carteggio Gonzaga*, Esteri, 1540, fol. 87r.

Paul III to assert his independence of the curia and his authority over it by denouncing extreme papalism and the exaggeration of his power. Behind all the debates in which Contarini had engaged, the proposals and memorials he had written, lay something of great significance for the church: a radical concept of reform. Contarini and his partisans saw clearly that it was no longer possible to define reform, as for example Guidiccione or Campeggio had done, as a return to the observance of existing decrees and laws. Open to the new spirit of their own age, Contarini and sympathizers with his view understood the gravity of Protestant attacks on existing ecclesiastical authority and wanted to redefine it with respect not only to the past but also to the future. Contarini's constant message to the pope during the years he was a member of various reform commissions had an elegant simplicity and austerity. He urged Paul III to cut the Gordian knot of technicalities, verbiage, custom, and abuse, which had come to obscure the true nature of his power. That power was spiritual and paternal. There was no need to feel trapped in the web former popes had spun, or to excuse their aberrations. Look to the future, Holy Father, Contarini urged Paul III again and again, and make use of your authority in full charity for the good of all men!

Contarini did not live to see meaningful reform in Rome. The results of his work were ultimately disappointing, attempts to attribute importance to the reform commissions notwithstanding.[181] He did not succeed in swaying the pope, who throughout his reign remained the great compromiser, unwilling to throw in his lot with any one group. His court remained entangled in nepotism and dubious political and financial deals. Girolamo Seripando, general of the Augustinians, summed up his reform activities epigrammatically: "Dixit et non fecit"—he talked but did nothing.[182] Even the conservative Ghinucci warned the pope of the danger he ran by talking about reform without following up his words by deeds.[183]

Contarini, despite the setbacks he experienced in Rome, was objective in appraising the success of reform at the papal court. King Ferdinand of Austria complained to him in 1541 that the pope had

181. Pastor, *Geschichte der Päpste* 5:150–52; and Ehses, "Kirchliche Reformarbeiten," 167. Both overestimate the importance of curial reform under Paul III, especially Pastor, who compares the Farnese pope with Adrian VI in stating that both "aimed at the same lofty objectives"—an excessively favorable judgment of Paul III by any standard.

182. *CT* 2:449; and Jedin, *Trient* 1:588n.92.

183. Solmi, "Fuga," 37.

promised reform many times without any result. Contarini gave a wise answer:

First of all I said His most wise Majesty knows that it is not possible to do everything at once, and that it is necessary to go forward according to the nature of the issues. The reform [of the curia] had not reached perfection, but I pointed out to him that many things were reformed, reminding him of episcopal residence,[184] which he praised highly. I mentioned that many highly worthy men had been promoted to the rank of cardinal, and he agreed with the truth of that. I concluded [by saying] that His Majesty could see for himself, if he examined the ways of the [Roman] court, how different they are from the practices that existed in times past under other popes.[185]

Here we see another side of Contarini, that of the realist familiar with the situation in Rome who seeks to defend Paul III by putting his few positive actions in a long-term perspective and arguing for their significance.

Nevertheless, the Habsburg brothers were not impressed with the progress of curial reform, and their attitude was reinforced by Granvelle, who in a report some months later to Charles V said bluntly that Paul III's aim was to retain all the spiritual and temporal powers of the papacy and to forget reform as soon as it was no longer talked of.[186] Contarini's defense of the pope's reform activities was, however, a sensible and, as it proved, correct assessment of the situation in Rome. His judgment still stands: the one notable achievement of Paul III in furthering church reform before the Council of Trent was that he drew outstanding men to Rome and appointed enough of them cardinals so as to begin changing the Sacred College for the better. He invited reform-minded prelates to speak their mind, giving them a forum for their views and treating them with respect. In the end, though, he failed to support them or to create an environment in Rome in which they could put their ideas into practice. The concrete proposals made by Contarini and his friends during their work on the reform commissions were important only insofar as they survived in the thought of others who came after them.

184. Contarini is referring to attempts by Paul III to require bishops to reside in their dioceses; see *CT* 4:454 and n. 5; and Cortese to Contarini, San Benedetto, 29 Dec. 1540, in *Reg.*, 138 (no. 523).

185. Ludwig von Pastor, "Die Correspondenz des Cardinals Contarini während seiner deutschen Legation (1541)," *Historisches Jahrbuch der Görresgesellschaft* 1 (1880): 487.

186. Friedensburg, "Das Consilium de emendanda ecclesia," 4. The report was of 28 November 1541.

The Practical Cardinal

The best-known aspect of Contarini's curial career before his mission to Germany in 1541 is his work on the reform commissions, and their failure has led to a distorted image of him as an outsider battling entrenched interests in Rome. While there is some truth to this view, it should be stressed that Contarini was no impractical dreamer among seasoned curial hands, or the proverbial Venetian sheep among Roman wolves. He took an uncompromising stand on the nature of papal power, but he did not break with those of his colleagues who thought otherwise. His diplomatic training stood him in good stead, and on the whole he managed to retain the goodwill of men with whom he disagreed. Pucci's sharp words about Contarini's manner are an exception; in other quarters there was general praise for his kind ways. The pope and his ever more important grandson, Cardinal Alessandro Farnese, were not alienated by Contarini's occasional criticism, as when he openly disapproved of a pageant organized during the carnival of 1539 by Paul III to please Margaret of Austria, the wife of his grandson Ottaviano.[187] Toward both men Contarini consistently maintained a respectful attitude whatever his private reservations may have been, and they reciprocated by displaying their esteem for his person.

Contarini participated actively in the day-to-day business of the college of cardinals, involving himself in numerous practical problems. His career had a large and perfectly ordinary component of routine activity, and there is no reason to think that he considered himself or was regarded by others as an outsider. Paul III put him on committees other than those dealing with reform, for example one "for matters pertaining to the council" made up of nine cardinals.[188] Contarini wrote about it to Cardinal Gonzaga: "We have met together many times. [Lorenzo] Campeggio is in charge of German problems [*gravami*], and I of theological matters [*materie della fede*]. Therefore I have formed a separate [sub]committee of theologians and we often meet together. If everyone has good will there won't be many issues."[189] Nothing is known about these meetings (they are not

---

187. Report of the French ambassador Grignan, Rome, 19 Feb. 1539, in Guillaume Ribier, *Lettres et memoires d'estat, des roys, princes, ambassadeurs, et autres ministres, sous les regnes de François premier, Henry II et François II* (Paris, 1666), 384.

188. On 7 January 1537; see *CT* 4:142.

189. Rome, 8 Feb. 1538, in Friedensburg, "Briefwechsel," 188 (letter 20).

mentioned in the very few surviving letters of Contarini from 1538) or about the theologians he consulted. But the fact that the pope gave him discretion to chair such a subcommittee and drew him closely into the preparations for the council is indicative of the confidence Paul III felt in him.

Contarini's other offices in the curia included the important position of treasurer, or *camerarius*, of the college of cardinals for the year 1540, in which post he succeeded a notable curial insider, Cardinal Simonetta.[190] He had the assistance of two clerks of this college in the discharge of his responsibilities. One of his main functions was to oversee the division of the collective income of the cardinals; but although the dates on which this was done are recorded, the sums involved are not mentioned.[191] He was succeeded as *camerarius* by Carafa, elected for 1541.[192] That both these prominent reformers held this high elective position argues strongly against their being considered outsiders by their colleagues.

Further proof of Contarini's good standing with Paul III was his inclusion in the papal train at the meeting in Nice between Francis I and Charles V in May and June 1538. Again, extant documents do not indicate the extent of Contarini's involvement in the diplomatic negotiations for a ten-year truce between the Habsburg and Valois rulers; yet he fully supported any effort by Paul III to bring about peace and considered the pope as potentially the most effective peacemaker among European princes, as we have seen. Contarini was regarded highly at both the French and imperial courts. Francis I spoke with him at length, and the king's sister, Margaret of Angoulême, literally overwhelmed him with her affectionate greeting and kisses;[193] meanwhile, Charles V asked him to explain his position regarding war against the Turks to the Venetian government, thus to act as a trusted intermediary.[194] Paul III empowered him to negotiate with the Signoria regarding the perennially troublesome question of taxation of church property.[195] All these instances show that Contarini was an important and respected member of the papal court; the idea that he was on its fringes is simply not tenable.

190. ASVat, Fondo Concistoriale, Acta Camerarii, vol. IV, fol. 24r.
191. Ibid, fol. 31v.
192. Ibid., vol. V, fol. 22r.
193. Beccadelli, "Vita," 29.
194. Ibid.; Cicogna, *Delle inscrizioni veneziane* 2:231.
195. The nuncio Verallo to Cardinal A. Farnese, Venice, 9 Aug. 1538, in Gaeta (ed.), *Nunziature di Venezia* 2:183.

Among Contarini's practical concerns during his years on the curia was the administration of the diocese of Belluno. There is no way of reconciling his position as absentee bishop with his earlier pronouncements on episcopal residence and his unequivocal condemnation of pastors who abandoned their flocks, including the sharp words on the subject in the *Consilium de emendanda ecclesia* written while he himself was an absentee bishop. Did he remember what he had written twenty years earlier about absentee bishops?

They really feel they are adequately fulfilling their duties if they hand over the government of their city to a procurator while they receive the income. They swell the train of some great figure in the Roman curia, and concern themselves with matters of statecraft and war, but as to the people over whom they rule they do not so much as send a messenger to find out whether they are making progress or going backward in their practice of the Christian religion, and they completely neglect the poor of their flock. Is this what it means to be a bishop? Is this the imitation of Christ's disciples and the observance of gospel precepts?[196]

The author of these words was bishop of Belluno for over five years, during which time he paid a single visit to his diocese in the summer of 1538. Evidently he accepted the bishopric for financial reasons: it increased his revenue by over a thousand ducats a year and after his death passed to his nephew Giulio, illegitimate son of his brother Ferigo, thus remaining in the family.[197] We see Contarini behaving here remarkably like those whom he had castigated, but with one important difference. He chose serious and able vicars for Belluno, among whom Girolamo Negri stands out, and to that extent showed concern for the spiritual welfare of his flock. But the fact remains that his actions contradicted his words, a discrepancy that did not go unnoticed by his contemporaries. Even his adulatory biographer Dittrich could do little more than note that Contarini "did not suspect, as he wrote this [the passage about absentee bishops quoted above], that he too would be among the bishops to whom it was not granted to reside in the midst of their flock. Of course, his work on the curia and later during his legation to Germany served the interests of the whole church to such

196. *Opera*, 412–13. See also Prosperi, *Tra evangelismo e controriforma*, 303, for Giberti's preoccupation with residence as shown in his testament.

197. ASVat, Fondo Concistoriale, Acta Misc., vol. VIII, fol. 318v. Nilo Tiezza, "I vescovi di Belluno Giulio e Gaspare Contarini e il Concilio di Trento," *Dolomiti* 2, no. 6 (1979): 7–10, exaggerates both Contarini's role as bishop and his influence, and offers no new information.

an extent that he could justifiably have a tranquil conscience."[198] Dittrich refused to see that for Contarini financial considerations outweighed scruples in this case; he concentrated on the advice and guidance Contarini gave Negri, and the clergy and people of Belluno, rather than on his absenteeism.

What emerges from Contarini's letters to Belluno is another illustration of his temperament and outlook. He highly prizes peace and concord among the citizens, and he is most anxious to restore order in what must have been a particularly dissolute cathedral chapter. At the same time, he realistically realizes the limits of his power to check abuses. A continuing source of disturbance lay in the scandalous goings-on of a convent of nuns just outside the town. Contarini's two earlier experiences with disorderly convents, Corpus Domini in Venice and S. Maria Maddalena in Verona,[199] had shown him how difficult it was for civil or ecclesiastical authorities to deal with recalcitrant nuns who were supported by their families. Now he was faced by a nunnery exempt from his jurisdiction. All he could do was issue an edict against those who frequented the convent without his or Negri's permission and declare them excommunicate.[200] This measure failed to have the desired effect, however, and the matter dragged on, creating unrest in the town that drew a reproof from Contarini and finally his threat to call on the Venetian government for assistance.[201]

There is no doubt that Contarini was solicitous for his diocese and concerned for the clergy and people.[202] But the fact remains that he never had pastoral experience there except for his single visit of two months. His letters, thus, are an extension of *De officio episcopi* rather than the fruit of direct involvement. They convey his self-image of a paternal spiritual guide, but this, however admirable, gives no basis for

198. *GC*, 414.
199. In February 1537 Pole was sent as papal legate to France, and Giberti accompanied him. During the latter's absence Contarini was entrusted with the government of the diocese of Verona; see Prosperi, *Tra evangelismo e controriforma*, 170–71. For Contarini's indignation at the behavior of the nuns of S. Maria Maddalena, see *Reg.*, 266–67 (Inedita, nos. 32, 33). The text should be corrected by ASVat, A.A., Arm. I–XVIII, 6461, fols. 51r–52v. Contarini called on the doge of Venice to punish male relatives of the nuns who offered armed resistance to the bishop's agents seeking to restore order in the convent.
200. *Reg.*, 298–99 (Inedita, nos. 32, 33). Again the text should be corrected from ASVat, A.A., Arm. I–XVIII, 6461, fols. 69r–v, 68r–v.
201. ASVat, A.A., Arm. I–XVIII, 6461, fol. 92v; and *Reg.*, 302 (Inedita, no. 38).
202. See *GC*, 411–22; and *Reg.*, 268–70 (Inedita, nos. 18–19), 297–304 (Inedita, nos. 31–40), and 305–9 (Inedita, no. 42).

judging how effective he would have been in a small diocese with complex social and economic problems.[203] His letters to Belluno, although incomplete, form a great contrast to his correspondence as papal legate in Bologna in 1542, where he dealt with very down-to-earth matters.[204] The former are mini-sermons, while the latter are succinct business letters.

In accepting a bishopric Contarini was merely inconsistent, given his own previous statements on the subject of absentee bishops. But another, more serious example of his accommodation to existing practices at the curia is not so easily explained and presents a challenge to the modern imagination. Beginning in November 1535 and continuing throughout almost the entire time he was working on the reform commissions, trying in vain to change the practices of the *dataria* and the *poenitentiaria* and vigorously attacking prevailing ideas concerning compositions, he himself was receiving a monthly pension of 260 scudi from the income of the *dataria*. The pension was increased to 500 scudi in April 1541, when he was papal legate in Germany. His close associate in reform efforts in Rome, Gianpietro Carafa, also received a pension of 100 scudi a month from the *dataria* beginning with June 1537, which was increased to 200 scudi in November; the same holds for Reginald Pole, who had joined the *dataria* pensioners for the first time in December 1536 with 100 scudi a month.[205]

The hard facts from the account books help to illuminate the narrow parameters within which the commissions for reform of the curia could be effective. Figures make it possible to understand better Paul III's vacillation and his ultimate neutralizing of the commissions. He cannot be interpreted as turning his back on reform at the curia for political reasons alone, reasons that included a profound desire not to split the college of cardinals into sharply opposed factions and not to play into the hand of Protestants. By a fortunate chance the registers, or *libri mastri*, of the *dataria* are preserved for the entire reign of Paul III,

203. Ferruccio Vendramini, *Tensioni politiche nella società bellunese della prima metà del '500* (Belluno: Tarantola, 1974).

204. Alfredo Casadei, "Lettere del Cardinale Gaspero Contarini durante la sua legazione di Bologna (1542)," *Archivio storico italiano* 118 (1960): 77–130, 220–85.

205. For Contarini, see BAV, Vat. lat. 10600, fols. 74r, 77v, 79v, 81v, 83r, 85r, 87r, 89v, 91v, 93r, 94v, 96r, 99r, 100v, 102v, 104r, 106r, 108r, 110r, 111v, 114r, 115v, 116v, 119r, 121v, 124r, 126r, 129r, 131r, 133v, 135r, 143v, 116v (at this point the foliation begins again with 116, which follows 145), 119v, 123r, 126v, 128v, 132r, 134r, 137v, 140r, 142v, 145r; Vat. lat. 10601, fols. 46r, 49r, 55r, 59r, 61v, 64r, 68r, 70v, 73v, 77r. For the first payment to Pole, see Vat. lat. 10600, fol. 100r; to Carafa, fol. 109v.

permitting a summary of income and expenditures from that key office.[206] They permit insights into papal finances such as Contarini and his supporters never had, since the books were meant only for the *datario* and the pope.

The registers show first of all that if fees for compositions had been abolished, as Contarini proposed, the pope would have lost almost half of the *dataria* revenues,[207] and the door would probably have been opened for an attack on the other half, derived from the sale of offices. This income was the basis for the pope's running expenses, of which monthly pensions to members of his immediate family formed a large part. For the years 1540–41, for example, pensions to members of his family amounted to 81,438 gold scudi, or more than one-quarter of the total income of the *dataria*, whereas sums for charity came to a meager 6 percent of the total. In addition, Paul III gave his family extra sums for unusual expenses or costly presents. Thus for January 1540, for example, we find these entries: to the master of the household of Ottaviano Farnese, the pope's grandson, 1,500 scudi; to his wife, Margaret of Austria, 500 plus 700 more for the purchase of a pearl.[208] Among the entries for January 31 is this: "On the last day of the month, 600 gold scudi to his Lordship Ottaviano Farnese, prefect of Rome, to spend for his pleasure during this carnival."[209] By contrast, Michelangelo, then working on the Sistine Chapel, is listed for an occasional 100 scudi. Another cluster of entries in March for clothing, extraordinary expenses, and the households of Ottaviano and Margaret comes to a total of 1,647 scudi.[210] Almost every month large, even exorbitant sums are listed, as in January 1541, when Margaret received 4,000 scudi, or July, when 4,600 scudi went to Ottaviano.[211] To these amounts were added others from different sources. Thus two account

206. Seven volumes are preserved, covering the period 1 March 1531–7 February 1550, and 1 March 1554–31 March 1555. While not unknown, they have never been analyzed in detail. The best recent study, by Litva, "Attività finanziaria," makes extensive use of them for statistical purposes without, however, offering the systematic examination of payment records that would be of particular interest to historians. Hallman, *Italian Cardinals*, also uses the *libri mastri* extensively as part of her evidence, though not as the focus of her inquiry.

207. From 1534 to 1564 the annual average of *dataria* revenues was 141,500 gold scudi. The annual median derived from compositions was 63,000 scudi, while that from the sale of offices was 78,300 scudi.

208. BAV, Vat. lat. 10601, fol. 52r.   209. Ibid., fol. 53v.

210. Ibid., fols. 57v, 58r, 59r.

211. Ibid., fol. 104v. Hallman, *Italian Cardinals*, 151, has calculated that the subsidies to Ottaviano and Margaret from the *dataria* came to 23,246 scudi in 1539, 25,747 scudi in 1540, and 34,833 scudi in 1541.

books of the secret treasury during this period list twenty-three persons bearing the surname Farnese among the recipients of monetary gifts.[212] Only a thorough prosopographical study, yet to be done, would reveal the extent of patronage to the pope's relatives, in-laws, and dependents of various sorts.

Paul III was the center of an extensive network of dependents whose income and social station derived from him. Indeed, nepotism was a key reason for the pope's inability to accept the proposals of reform-minded cardinals, for to do so would have threatened the complex structure that in the eyes of Italian society of the time involved absolute obligations. Nepotism and patronage formed part of the ideas, norms, and patterns of behavior involved in familial *pietas*, the safeguarding and advancement of family wealth, honor, and prestige expected especially of powerful family members.[213] For the papal clan nepotism was the crucial vehicle for building fortunes and ascending in the social scale. The *libri mastri* of the *dataria* give us evidence of the process by which the wealth of the Farnese was accumulated—to be supplemented, of course, by other and more important records, such as lists of the benefices conferred on the family of the reigning pope. When Contarini called on Paul III to reform the curia without worrying about loss of income, he had no precise conception of what such a loss would have meant for the Farnese and how inconceivable it was for the pope to accept his radical proposals.

Barbara Hallman has argued that sixteenth-century Italian cardinals before the Council of Trent were enmeshed in the problems of accumulating, maintaining, and passing on to their families wealth derived from the church and that therefore any reform touching their vested interests was bound to fail. Reform efforts are thus thought to have been limited to areas that did not threaten property, such as matters of doctrine, education, or the suppression of heresy. These observations are helpful in elucidating an important aspect of the Roman situation

212. Léon Dorez, *La cour du Pape Paul III d'après les registres de la Trésorerie secrète* (Paris: E. Leroux, 1932).

213. For the best analysis of nepotism as a sociocultural phenomenon, see the studies of Wolfgang Reinhard: "Ämterlaufbahn und Familienstatus: der Aufstieg des Hauses Borghese," *Quellen und Forschungen aus italienischen Archiven und Bibliotheken* 54 (1974): 328–427; "Nepotismus"; and "PAPA PIUS: Prolegomena zu einer Sozialgeschichte des Papsttums," in *Von Konstanz nach Trient: Beiträge zur Geschichte der Kirche von den Reformkonzilien bis zum Tridentinum. Festgabe für August Franzen*, ed. Remigius Bäumer (Munich: Schöningh, 1972), 262–99. Although it deals with a later period, there are many valuable general observations in the same writer's *Papstfinanz und Nepotismus*.

and offer one answer as to why no sweeping, comprehensive Catholic reform occurred during the pontificate of Paul III. But it is necessary to go still further. The Italian cardinals do not bear the main responsibility for the failure of reform. They, along with the popes, the entire curia, indeed anyone of social and economic consequence in Rome, from these men's dependents down to the simplest clerks of the offices and tribunals, were part of a specific society that had evolved over the centuries, taking its final shape under the Renaissance popes. Only a revolution could have changed that society suddenly and drastically, an upheaval akin to the restructuring of institutions and patterns of property holding in the areas or states that became Protestant. In the Catholic church of the 1530s, that sort of change was unthinkable. The only other alternative was that which was actually realized: gradual change from within the existing system, far-reaching and sweeping in its effects but masked by the rhetoric of continuity with tradition.

During his years at the papal court Contarini and his supporters should be seen against the actual circumstances of the Roman ecclesiastical society to which they belonged, rather than set apart in a category labeled "reformers." Historians have judged Contarini by his writings and his efforts for reform of the curia, which certainly formed a sharp contrast to the inertia and obstructionism of most cardinals at the time. But his tracts on institutional reform were entirely theoretical, consistently exploring the principles according to which popes ought to act and culling arguments to support his views from philosophy and theology. If we examine what Contarini actually did as cardinal, not only what he said, it becomes much more difficult to distinguish him from the others. Granted that he and his friends were working toward an ideal and that as advocates of reform they were admirable men. But they were also practical and understood that, given the system, radical changes were not very likely. Pending the hoped-for but far distant reform, they still had to live, and they showed no qualms about receiving income from the sources that were available, sources their contemporaries did not consider unusual, let alone unacceptable. Contarini and Carafa, with no substantial family wealth on which to draw, depended on what the pope granted them. While on the theoretical level they worked for reform of the *dataria*, in practice they were its pensioners. Neither man should be accused of hypocrisy, nor should Pole, who behaved similarly. They simply did not think in our categories but accepted the standards of their world, separating quite neatly what existed in reality from what should have existed but was confined to theory. Contarini's technical pluralism after he was appointed administrator of the see of Canterbury is further proof that what he condemned in his writings could nevertheless be part of his actual practice. He was not Mr. Smith going to Washington, but a man with a good grasp of how government and fiscal affairs were conducted in actuality, and he benefited from the system to which he belonged without what most Italian contemporaries would have regarded as too many scruples. Fundamental change in church government had to come from the top, from the pope himself, and not from reform commissions that were empowered to do no more than make recommendations. Meanwhile, reform commissioners had to live too.

In a very clear way the ineffective commissions and the unsuccessful reform of the *dataria* expose some nuts and bolts of the concrete situation at Rome, practical matters that should be given greater weight than they have been by historians attempting to elucidate the nature and limits of reform within the Catholic church. We are faced by pieces of a puzzle that demands a clearer explanation than has yet been given of both the thought and ideas of advocates of Catholic reform. Together, the pieces offer clues to the much larger question of why the church and the popes moved so slowly in matters of reform, and why that reform was so cautious and gradual when it finally did begin.

CHAPTER FOUR

Illusion and Reality: Regensburg, 1541

The Choice of a Legate

The best-known and most fully documented episode of Contarini's life is that of his mission as papal legate to the religious colloquy of Catholics and Protestants at Regensburg in 1541, a role that has assured his inclusion in histories of the Reformation period and perpetuated his fame. His biographer Franz Dittrich, in fact, considered Regensburg to be the culmination of his subject's career and so devoted minute attention to it. Contarini has received almost uniformly favorable treatment as a champion of religious concord in a singularly contentious age and as a man of goodwill who refused to abandon the hope of unity among Christians. While no modern scholar has gone quite so far as to assert that "the work of concord . . . attempted at Regensburg . . . is one of the most decisive moments in the course of modern history,"[1] the image of the idealistic legate bent on healing the scandalous division in the church is still virtually an icon. He has elicited much sympathy as a proponent of toleration and as a leading figure in the "party of the middle" during the confessional struggles of the sixteenth century.[2]

1. De Leva, "Concordia religiosa," 5.
2. Friedrich Heer, *Die dritte Kraft: der europäische Humanismus zwischen den Fronten des konfessionellen Zeitalters* (Frankfurt: S. Fischer, 1959), offers one of the most explicit arguments for the strength of the "third force" of humanists who occupied a middle ground between doctrinaire Catholics and Protestants.

In reality, Contarini's legation is at most an instructive episode in the history of the German Reformation and of Charles V's reign. While it assumes a more central place when seen from the perspective of the papacy, the mission of Contarini did not significantly affect the diplomatic chess game between pope and emperor, or change the prevailing Roman attitude toward German Protestants. It did, however, serve as a catalyst for Contarini's ideas about the relation of Catholics and Protestants, and of individual Christians to religious authority. Another issue is whether the Roman "vote of no confidence in his conduct of affairs in Regensburg meant the defeat of his party in Italy, and with it the loss of any hope of Catholic ecumenical initiative for decades, if not centuries to come," as has been maintained.[3] The examination of Contarini's part in the meeting at Regensburg should enable us to understand its importance for him personally, its effects on his supporters and sympathizers, and finally its influence on Rome's attitude toward the Protestants.

In the background to the colloquy of Regensburg was the dangerous buildup of tension between Catholics and Protestants in Germany after the Diet of Augsburg in 1530 and the continuing Turkish threat to Habsburg lands. Charles V, supported by Granvelle and Ferdinand of Austria, was hoping to end or at least mitigate the religious dissension in Germany in preparation for a campaign against the Turks that required the support of the Protestants. Thus he became the chief advocate of colloquies between theologians of the two confessions in 1539 and 1540. The idea was not new. In 1534 and 1539 colloquies were held in Leipzig,[4] and in April of the latter year the German princes and estates agreed in the *Frankfurter Anstand*[5] that a meeting without Roman participation should be held in the summer in Nuremberg. While that did not take place, another was called at Speyer in June 1540, transferred to nearby Hagenau because of an outbreak of the plague, then adjourned to Worms for the fall.[6] When the meeting

---

3. Peter Matheson, *Cardinal Contarini at Regensburg* (Oxford: Clarendon Press, 1972), 153. Ludwig von Pastor, *Die kirchlichen Reunionsbestrebungen während der Regierung Karls V.* (Freiburg i.B., 1879), 270, also writes about the "sudden fall" of Contarini's "party of the middle" (*Partei der Mitte*) after Regensburg.

4. For discussions of the colloquies of the decade preceding Regensburg, see Marion Hollerbach, *Das Religionsgespräch als Mittel der konfessionellen und politischen Auseinandersetzung im Deutschland des 16. Jahrhunderts* (Frankfurt: Lang, 1982), 108–54; and Wilhelm H. Neuser, *Die Vorbereitung der Religionsgespräche von Worms und Regensburg 1540/41* (Neukirchen-Vluyn: Neukirchener Verlag, 1974), 9–24. Both contain references to the older literature.

5. The text is in Neuser, *Vorbereitung*, 75–85.

6. For a fuller discussion, see Jedin, *Trient* 1:301–2.

finally opened on 25 November, Melanchthon and Bucer as heads of the Protestant delegation faced the controversialists Eck and Gropper leading the Catholics.[7] Almost at the last moment Tommaso Campeggio, bishop of Feltre, was sent by Pope Paul III as his representative, but he was given no real power to maneuver. An observer rather than an active participant, he was charged with ensuring that the meeting at Worms did not usurp the competence of a general council. Several theologians accompanied him as advisors, foremost among them the Italian Dominican Tommaso Badia and his Dutch confrere Albert Pighius.[8] He was quite overshadowed, however, by Giovanni Morone, nuncio to King Ferdinand, whose experience in German affairs was greater and whose diplomatic ability surpassed Campeggio's. The tension between the two men emerges from their correspondence[9] as well as from the letters of the officious Pier Paolo Vergerio, self-appointed expert on the religious situation in Germany.[10]

After sharp differences of opinion arose concerning matters of procedure, and after several fruitless meetings were held in January 1541, the emperor adjourned the colloquy to Regensburg, where an imperial diet was to convene. But the official meetings at Worms were not the whole story. Secret talks between theologians of both sides resulted in a curious document, the so-called Regensburg Book, which was to serve as the basis for discussion at the upcoming colloquy. Its formulation of articles of faith avoided controversy as much as possible. The imperial secretary and chief counselor of Charles V, Granvelle, was solidly behind it and declared it to be the work of Flemish theologians, now deceased, but such a mystifying explanation of its authorship in the end satisfied nobody. For once Melanchthon and Eck were of one mind: the former disliked the book because of its vagueness, while the latter was conspicuously violent in his denunciation of it.[11]

Actually, the Regensburg Book was the result of secret conferences between Catholic and Protestant theologians.[12] Composed by Gropper, then secretary to the archbishop of Cologne, with additions and

7. Ibid., 374–77.

8. For a complete list of participants, see *NB* 6:100–102.

9. See, for example, Campeggio's letter to Farnese, Worms, 15 Dec. 1540, in ibid., 69; or very clearly in Morone's to Cervini, 10 Jan. 1540, ibid., 121.

10. For Vergerio's role in Worms, see Schutte, *Pier Paolo Vergerio*, 139–52.

11. "…Haveva fatto l'Ecchio le furie contro quel libro vituperandolo infinitamente" (Contarini to Farnese, Regensburg, 28 Apr. 1541, in Pastor, "Correspondenz," 369.

12. Hastings Eells, "The Origin of the Regensburg Book," *Princeton Theological Review* 26 (1928): 358. More recent is Cornelis Augustijn, "De gesprekken tussen Bucer en Gropper tijdens het godsdienstgesprek te Worms in December 1540," *Nederlands archief voor kerkgeschiedenis*, n.s., 47 (1965–66): 208–230.

emendations by Bucer,[13] it contained twenty-three articles in two parts. The first section dealt with points of doctrine such as creation, free will, the causes of sin, original sin, and justification, while in the second questions of sacraments, church organization, and authority were discussed. The work has a tentative and hesitant tone; one is struck by its effort to remain within the ever-diminishing area of shared beliefs.[14]

Charles V was determined to do everything in his power to ensure that the diet and colloquy at Regensburg would be more fruitful than their predecessors. Exasperated by the indifference of the Catholic princes to the Turkish menace and hampered by mistrust on the part of Protestant rulers who feared an emperor strengthened by a possible victory over the Turks, he was unable to come alone to the aid of his brother, Ferdinand. He therefore intended to lay before the diet the magnitude of the Turkish danger and ask for help. But first he wanted religious concord as a result of which the situation within Germany could be stabilized and the division of the country into two armed camps averted.[15] His aims and priorities in 1540 were clear.

Pope Paul III on principle opposed religious colloquies in Germany. He feared, with good reason, that a national diet presided over by the emperor which might ratify agreements between German theologians would leave little room for guidance from Rome and raise the specter of a national church. As an all-German solution became conceivable, the pope stated repeatedly that only a general council of the church convoked by himself was competent to deal with the doctrinal issues raised by Luther.[16] The papal nuncio Giovanni Morone, who was present in Hagenau and Worms, was of one mind with the pope on this matter and let it be known that he was not in favor of colloquies. In his dispatches he stressed that for the emperor political questions were paramount and that he thought Charles V would use a religious accord

13. Cornelis Augustijn, "Die Religionsgespräche der vierziger Jahre," in *Die Religionsgespräche der Reformationszeit*, ed. Gerhard Müller (Gütersloh: Mohn, 1980), 46; and Eells, "Origin," 371.

14. The text of the Regensburg Book is in Georg Pfeilschifter, ed., *Acta Reformationis Catholicae Ecclesiam Germaniae concernentia saeculi XVI*, vol. 6 (Regensburg: F. Pustet, 1974), 21–88. This supersedes the version in Philip Melanchthon, *Opera*, vol. 4 of *Corpus Reformatorum*, ed. Karl Gottlieb Bretschneider (Halle, 1837), 190–238.

15. For a succinct summary of Charles V's religious policies in Germany, see Heinrich Lutz, *Reformation und Gegenreformation*, 2d ed. (Munich and Vienna: R. Oldenbourg, 1982), 146–49 and his bibliography; Jedin, *Trient* 1, bk. 2, chaps. 3–5 and bibliography; and Matheson, *Contarini at Regensburg*, chaps. 1–3.

16. For the pope's position, see Jedin, *Trient* 1, bk. 2, chaps. 6–7.

only to further his own purposes,[17] which might be detrimental to the Catholic church.

It was against this background that Contarini was chosen as envoy. He has been singled out as a "commanding figure," the "public champion of Evangelism in Italy,"[18] who was paradigmatic of a whole generation. These statements imply the existence of a movement, with Contarini as one of its leaders. The movement in question is Italian Evangelism, that vexingly elusive phenomenon of sixteenth-century religious history in the peninsula. At present there is no consensus concerning its definition, and the debate about its nature reflects divergent trends in Italian, European, and American scholarship of the last two generations.[19] What in 1953 was a name for "the last Catholic reform movement before the Council of Trent and the first ecumenical movement after the schism of the Reformation"[20] has by now become so complex that it is possible to wonder, as one historian has done, whether Evangelism might not be a mere historiographical construct.[21] The usefulness of the term and its meaning need to be rethought if it is to be rescued from purely nominalistic involutions. To what extent was it a distinct movement with a religious and political program?

The evidence for Evangelism as a movement depends primarily on the writings of a small number of well-known figures, on their correspondence, and on statements made in inquisitorial proceedings. Conclusions have been drawn on the basis of selected passages from their letters, and their personal religious stance has been explained by citing their supposed membership in a movement. The attribution of ideas held by some individuals to their friends or correspondents raises serious methodological problems.[22] Without resorting to fanciful interpretations of sources, we can start with the fact that a general religious

17. Morone's dispatches have been published by Franz Dittrich, "Die Nuntiaturberichte Giovanni Morone's vom Reichstage zu Regensburg 1541," *Historisches Jahrbuch der Görresgesellschaft* 4 (1883): 395–472, 618–73; and in *NB*, vols. 5–6.

18. Philip McNair, *Peter Martyr in Italy: An Anatomy of Apostasy* (Oxford: Clarendon Press, 1967), 12.

19. See Elisabeth G. Gleason, "On the Nature of Italian Evangelism: Scholarship, 1953–1978," *Sixteenth Century Journal* 9 (1978): 3–25.

20. Eva-Maria Jung, "On the Nature of Evangelism in Sixteenth-Century Italy," *Journal of the History of Ideas* 14 (1953): 512.

21. Susanna Peyronel Rambaldi, "Ancora sull'evangelismo italiano: categoria o invenzione storiografica?" *Società e storia* 5, no. 18 (1982): 935–67.

22. Andrea Del Col's acute observations on this point are useful; see Rita Belladonna and Andrea Del Col, "Per una sistemazione critica dell'evangelismo italiano e di un'opera recente," *Critica storica* 17 (1980): 272.

outlook was shared by a specific group, the *spirituali*,[23] who on closer examination turn out to be few in number and for the most part associated in one way or another with either Contarini or Pole, especially during the latter's residence in Viterbo as papal governor between 1541 and 1545.

This outlook included but was not restricted to "the positive reaction of certain spiritually-minded Catholics to the crucial doctrine of justification by faith"[24] as "discovered" by Luther or as formulated by others. While acceptance of justification by faith was characteristic of the *spirituali*, they differed concerning its implication. At one end of a continuum there were some who saw no basic conflict between this key theological belief and the teachings of the Catholic church, while on the other end we find men and a few women for whom irreconcilable differences with the old church were the inevitable result of adhering to *sola fide* as a central doctrine. Still, the term *Evangelism* to denote that which united them, their basic religious program, is useful and should be retained. It has become a convenient shorthand designation for a whole cluster of ideas and aspirations found in varying combinations in different people over most of the sixteenth century.[25] Foremost was the focus on ethical and moral reform of the individual Christian who encountered God's word in the Bible, specifically the Gospels and Pauline epistles, and responded with faith and trust in the divine mercy through which man had been given the incalculable benefit of Christ's death on the cross. Beyond that Evangelism was certainly

23. For the use of the term in contemporary sources, see Gigliola Fragnito, "Gli 'spirituali' e la fuga di Bernardino Ochino," *Rivista storica italiana* 84 (1972): 780–81 (reprinted in her *Gasparo Contarini*, 255–57); also Prosperi, *Tra evangelismo e controriforma*, 285–86, 314. The term is not easily defined; it referred to the juxtaposition of carnal and spiritual man, but could be used in an ideological and political sense as well. See also the letter of Marcantonio Flaminio to an unknown correspondent, 12 Sept. 1542, in Flaminio, *Lettere*, 130 : " . . . Signor mio, risvegliamoci horamai, et consideriamo che siamo christiani, cioe figlioli di Dio et non servi del mondo, creature spirituali et non carnali; conserviamo dunque il nostro decoro, et come legitimi figlioli di Dio et superiori alla vilta della carne, habbiamo uno animo grande et generoso che resista valorosamente a tutti gli impeti del mondo, della morte, del demonio et dello inferno." See also the thoughtful observations concerning the term *spirituali* by William V. Hudon, *Marcello Cervini and Ecclesiastical Government in Tridentine Italy* (De Kalb: Northern Illinois University Press, 1992), 161–74.

24. McNair, *Peter Martyr*, 8.

25. Schutte, "The *Lettere Volgari*," shows the persistence of Evangelism after 1542. John Martin, "Salvation and Society in Sixteenth-Century Venice: Popular Evangelism in a Renaissance City," *Journal of Modern History* 60 (1988): 205–33, shows that Evangelism was not restricted to the educated elite.

"dogmatically manifold,"[26] while emphasizing the practice of Christian virtues and the *imitatio Christi*. It had a common doctrinal nucleus from which its adherents then fanned out in various directions. One meaning of the term, then, refers to the core of beliefs held by the *spirituali*.

Evangelism also refers to a movement, if this term is used with care. Criticism of ecclesiastical institutions and proposals for church reform had been persistent themes of Italian religious thought during the first three decades of the sixteenth century.[27] Of the many plans and projects for the reform of abuses and church doctrines, only a small fraction surfaced at the Fifth Lateran Council. During the 1520s and 1530s we find individuals and groups in Rome, Venice, Verona, Mantua, and other places reading the Bible, the fathers, and also Protestant works and pondering the relation of sinful man to merciful God. But of a recognizable movement there is as yet no evidence. Only after Contarini was made cardinal in 1535, to be later joined by Sadoleto, Pole, Fregoso, Cortese, Badia, Morone, and even Bembo, was there a focus in Rome toward which reform-minded men and women could look with hope. In that sense it is true that "it is not possible to speak of Evangelism prior to the elevation of Contarini to the cardinalate and the appointment of the commission from which the *consilium de emendanda* originated."[28]

The cluster of prelates who had produced the *consilium* was visible proof that aspirations for reform were no longer confined to scattered individuals or a few study circles, but that reform had become an issue at the very center of the Catholic church. When some of the most vocal advocates of reform were appointed to the commission of 1536, Evangelism assumed a more definite physiognomy. It now could be described as the shared outlook and aims of a small but conspicuous brotherhood of intellectuals, many of whom held high positions in the church. Besides their stress on the necessity of individual reform—the Pauline *metanoia*—most saw an urgent need for institutional reform and revitalization. An exception would be those who followed Juan de

26. The phrase is Manfred Welti's: *Kleine Geschichte der italienischen Reformation* (Gütersloh: Mohn, 1985), 20.

27. Gleason, "On the Nature of Italian Evangelism," 21–22.

28. Massimo Firpo, "Juan de Valdés e l'evangelismo italiano: appunti e problemi di una ricerca in corso," *Studi storici* 26 (1985): 752 (reprinted with slight modifications in his *Tra alumbrados e "spirituali": studi su Juan de Valdés e il valdesianesimo nella crisi religiosa del '500 italiano* [Florence: Olschki, 1990], 127–53). Jedin, *Trient* 1:335, thinks that 1536 was an important date for the formation of a visible "firm center" of reform in Rome, although he defines Evangelism more broadly than does Firpo.

Valdés in having no special concern for the institutional church because they detached themselves from its external framework and ceremonies, which receded almost to the category of *adiaphora*.[29]

Dividing Evangelism as a movement into "right" and "left" wings,
meaning respectively the group interested primarily in institutional
reform and the philo-Protestants, correctly points to its diversity but
also introduces an inappropriate analogy with modern political parties.[30] Similarly, proposing the existence of a "politics of Evangelism"
suggests a cohesive group or party that planned its strategy with definite objectives.[31] The movement was in fact never cohesive or strong
enough to constitute a long-term successful pressure group in the
curia. What gave it prominence in Rome in the late 1530s was the caliber of its members, who undoubtedly were among the most attractive,
educated, and spiritual figures at the papal court and who had correspondents and friends in Italian cities ranging from Venice to Naples,
especially during the years of Valdés's residence there. It is possible to
speak of Evangelism as a "party of reform" for about half a dozen years
after 1536, if that term is not given a rigid definition but is applied to a
network of men and a few women held together by bonds of friendship, sympathy, mutual support, and, in some cases, notably those of
spirituali cardinals and bishops, collaboration in attempts to reform
the church.

In this brotherhood linked by ties of friendship and sympathy
Contarini had a prominent place. Aleandro, in a letter of 1539, called
him "one of the main supports of the Holy Church."[32] Even allowing
for some hyperbole, this sentiment was shared by others and was more
than flattery. Pole saw in Contarini's elevation to the cardinalate the
direct intervention of God finally coming to the rescue of his church;
as he put it to Contarini, "You did not rise to this position by chance
or through human favor, but because of the call of him whose bride is
the church and who knew best which men's service she needed. He
could not be ignorant of what you are able to shoulder."[33] Letters from

29. Firpo, "'Ioanne Valdesio è stato heretico pessimo': forme, esiti e metamorfosi
dell' 'heresia' valdesiana," in *Tra alumbrados*, esp. 43–84.

30. Welti, *Kleine Geschichte*, 16, 22.

31. Paolo Simoncelli, *Evangelismo italiano del Cinquecento: questione religiosa e
nicodemismo politico* (Rome: Istituto Storico Italiano per l'Età Moderna e Contemporanea, 1979), passim.

32. "...Una delle principali columne di santa chiesa," *Reg.*, 378 (Appendix, no. 8).

33. *Reg.*, 80 (no. 270); and *Ep. Poli* 1:428. A few months later, in April 1536, Pole
in a letter to Alvise Priuli compared Charles V with Theodosius, and Contarini with
St. Ambrose, for God had called Contarini like a new Ambrose to heal the church; see
Reg., 86 (no. 283); and *Ep. Poli* 1:451.

friends and acquaintances repeatedly expressed the hope that God would use Contarini for the purification and rebuilding of his church,[34] or even as an instrument in a grand plan.[35]

Untarred by deals or by jockeying for ecclesiastical position, power, and influence, Contarini in 1536 and the years that followed certainly was an encouragement to those who had almost despaired of reform in the church. In addition to his probity he brought to his high office a certain measure of detachment, and did not use his position as an excuse for immediate involvement in curial politics or the quest for benefices. Nino Sernini, agent of Cardinal Ercole Gonzaga in Rome and a keen observer of the papal court, reported to Mantua soon after Contarini's arrival the prevailing impression of the new cardinal as a man devoted to learning who was not interested in practical affairs[36]— a first impression that was proved wrong quite soon by Contarini's participation in the various reform commissions, as we have seen.

One year after his appointment he was definitely perceived as the champion of reform among the cardinals. Though he was not the leader of any group in the usual sense of the word, he emerged as the most influential spokesman for reform, which pitted him against the majority of his colleagues in the Sacred College. As he encountered resistance and hostility he became more outspoken and political, and of course more conspicuous. The eyes of sympathizers and enemies alike were on him. While Contarini did not exactly hold the tiller like a pilot steering the church, this view of him became an important part of his image, especially among the *spirituali*.[37]

Prelates who were concerned primarily with disciplinary reform of the church, but without advocating doctrinal changes, did not hold such a favorable view of Contarini. By 1541 these men included Marcello Cervini, tutor and advisor of Cardinal Alessandro Farnese, the pope's grandson, and also Carafa. The latter, having parted company with Contarini over the reform of the *dataria* and *poenitentiaria*, displayed no sympathy for Contarini's irenic attitude or his endeavors on behalf of religious concord in Germany, and subsequently failed to

34. See the letters in *Reg.*, 76–78 (nos. 255, 256, 258, 260, 266).

35. Marcantonio Flaminio to Contarini, in Flaminio, *Lettere*, 26–27 (letter 3): "Questo non resterò già di dire, che tutti gli homini da bene hanno fissi gli occhi della mente in quella [i.e. Your Excellency], perchè cognoscendo et affermando ognuno ch'el suo cardinalato non è proceduto da homini, ma da Dio, meritamente si crede che sua Maiestà voglia usarla per instrumento di qualche effetto novo et segnalato."

36. "[Contarini] è tenuto più homo da studii che da negotii" (quoted by Solmi, "Fuga," 82).

37. Ferrero and Müller (eds.), *Carteggio delle lettere di Vittoria Colonna*, 127 (letter 76).

support him in the college of cardinals. Much more serious, even sinister, was his early mistrust of *spirituali* like Pole, Morone, and the poet Marcantonio Flaminio, on whom he gathered incriminating evidence even before the reorganization of the Roman Inquisition in 1542.[38] It is possible that Contarini, Fregoso, Badia, and Cortese, had they lived longer, would all have been treated like Morone, who was imprisoned in 1557 by the inquisition. In Carafa's view, *spirituali* were suspect of heresy precisely because of their uncertainty in doctrinal matters that he considered to be above discussion and of their willingness to entertain novel ideas. To him, they seemed like a cancer in the body of the church.[39] Thus, already in the late 1530s one can discern an increasingly sharp difference in Rome between, on the one hand, a group that wanted institutional reform without any change in traditional Catholic teaching and, on the other, the *spirituali*, who looked to men like Contarini and Pole for inspiration in their search for a more vital, personal, and unconstricted Christianity, in addition to reform of the institutional church.[40]

Did old curial hands, including Pope Paul III, perceive the *spirituali* as a "party"? A century ago the Italian scholar Giuseppe De Leva made the intriguing suggestion that the pope, prompted by Carafa and Aleandro, chose Contarini as legate to Regensburg in a deliberate attempt to disgrace him and his sympathizers, knowing that the mission was bound to fail.[41] With Contarini discredited, the initiative for reform of the church could then be seized by the conservative narrow constructionists of institutional reform, and the plans of the *spirituali* shunted aside. More recently, the same hypothesis has been advanced at greater

38. Massimo Firpo and Dario Marcatto, "Il primo processo inquisitoriale contro il cardinal Giovanni Morone (1552–1553)," *Rivista storica italiana* 93 (1981): 85–86 and passim. Carafa made friends of Contarini uneasy, even fearful, already in the 1530s, as can be seen, for example, in a letter of Cortese to Contarini of 22 June 1536, which mentions that Carafa had found Flaminio possessing or reading books by heretics without permission to do so; see Alessandro Pastore, *Marcantonio Flaminio* (Milan: Franco Angeli, 1981), 94. Cortese requested Contarini to obtain for him a license from Paul III to read books by Protestants, and was especially worried about Carafa's reaction unless he had permission. See also Gigliola Fragnito, "Il Cardinale Gregorio Cortese," *Benedictina* 30 (1983): 429. For a suspicion that Cortese was tainted with heresy, see Firpo and Marcatto, *Processo* 1:86.

39. Firpo and Marcatto, "Primo processo," 138.

40. For the contrast between concepts of reform held by the two groups, see Alberto Aubert, "Alle origini della Controriforma: studi e problemi su Paolo IV," *Rivista di storia e letteratura religiosa* 22 (1986): 315–21, 327–38.

41. De Leva, *Storia documentata* 3:412. Capasso, *Paolo III* 2:144, takes issue with De Leva's view. Capasso regularly interprets the actions of Paul III favorably, and defends him against the imputation of double-dealing.

length by Paolo Simoncelli.[42] In his view Roman diplomacy expertly used Contarini and the *spirituali* to keep face with Charles V by sending a legate he requested who was known for his conciliatory stance, since the emperor's top priority was accord with the Protestants. All the while the pope and his closest advisors sabotaged Habsburg religious policy, having no intention of allowing serious negotiations between the two religious groups in Germany. In sum, according to Simoncelli, they did all they could to undermine the emperor and his brother abroad and to remove the *spirituali* from a position of prestige at home.[43] Contarini was used very cynically as protagonist of a religious policy that had no support at the Roman court, only to be "burned" and discarded when he proved no longer necessary for the diplomatic web spun by curial intransigents.[44] In this interpretation, Contarini and his sympathizers were perceived by intransigents at the papal court as a coherent group and a party advocating what to their opponents were unacceptable positions. That they were consciously thrown to the wolves in a premeditated move by those who saw diversity within the church as a danger if not outright heresy proved how crucial it was for conservatives to isolate and weaken them.[45]

This argument hinges on the supposed perception of the *spirituali* as a pressure group with a definite agenda, which was made ineffective through a Machiavellian strategy. But who could be considered their chief enemies in 1540, when Contarini was first appointed to his German legation, and in 1541, when he was finally sent? Carafa comes to mind immediately, but he was not yet an influential figure at the papal court. The second man mentioned by De Leva was Aleandro, who on close examination does not emerge as an intransigent curialist in 1540. While he may have been playing his own political game, he supported Contarini, at least in public. In a curious letter, Aleandro stated that as an expert on German affairs he was pressed strongly (*combattuto*) by the pope and many others for forty days to accept the legation himself. After reporting that he refused on account of his age and ill health (about which he provided some graphic details), he continued: "Today I broke four or five hefty lances on behalf of the appointment of the cardinal [Contarini] who is most suited for the enterprise [in question]. I did it gladly, not only because of his virtues, but also to do

42. Simoncelli, *Evangelismo italiano*, 227.
43. Ibid., 236–37.   44. Ibid., 239.
45. See Aubert, "Alle origini," 325–26, for Carafa's view of diversity and dissent.

honor to his fatherland, and on many [other] accounts."[46] A month earlier, however, Cardinal Farnese had written from the imperial court quite plainly that Aleandro would not be accepted there if he were sent.[47] One wonders whether the importuning that Aleandro describes corresponded to reality; Paul III trusted the opinions of his grandson and would hardly have insisted on a legate who was likely to be rejected by the emperor. In the same letter, Aleandro adds a puzzling note: "While [Contarini] was praised by all after being openly proposed by the pope, and the appointment was approved, yet in private, where deals are made, he was much attacked."[48] Aleandro stressed that he came to Contarini's defense and that he was instrumental in swaying Paul III to appoint the Venetian cardinal as legate.

How truthful he was is difficult to determine without some corroborating evidence, of which we find just a bit in a letter sent seven months later to Aleandro by Contarini's close friend and confessor Tommaso Badia, then in Germany: "Among the consoling news I received from Rome, the most special was that I heard that the holy and affectionate friendship between Your Reverence and Card[inal] Cont[arini] not only continues but is growing daily. [It is] most useful to the Sacred College and edifying to Holy Church."[49] Granted that this evidence is not conclusive, still, it militates against adding Aleandro to the opponents of Contarini in 1540, or to those who plotted to discredit him, unless Aleandro was entirely double-faced.

Carafa had no voice in the appointment of Contarini, and Aleandro was probably not among Contarini's enemies at that particular point. There remains Cardinal Marcello Cervini. His loyalty to the pope

46. Aleandro to Leone Maffei, Rome, 21 May 1540, in *NB* 5:258–59.

47. Farnese to Pope Paul III, Ghent, 26 Apr. 1540, in ibid., 201; see also 197.

48. Ibid., 259. The Italian text is not clear, and admits of different interpretations: " . . . et sappi V.S. [Maffei] che, sì come da poi la aperta propositione di N.S. [Paul III, to appoint Contarini] fu da tutti molto laudato egli et approbata questa commissione, così in secreto, ove si danno li syroppi preparatorii, hebbe molto contrasto." I thank Professor Rita Belladonna for help with this passage. That Contarini had enemies also appears from a sentence in the dispatch of Marco Bracci, the Florentine agent in Rome, of 31 May 1540: "May God grant that he [Contarini] achieves something good and does not make an accord with the Lutherans, since he is a blood-brother of Lucifer" (quoted by Pastor, *Geschichte der Päpste* 5:272n.5. I wish to thank Professor Paolo Simoncelli for verifying this quotation in ASF, and informing me that Bracci gives no further explanation of his meaning.

It is likely that the opponents of Contarini belonged to the pro-French group in the curia and the college of cardinals, and therefore worked against religious concord in Germany, which would have strengthened the Habsburgs.

49. Worms, 28 Dec. 1540, in *NB* 6:95; and *Reg.*, 139 (no. 525).

earned him the trust of the Farnese family. In 1539 he accompanied Cardinal Farnese to Flanders, and subsequently he was appointed legate to the imperial court, where he resided from May to October 1540. A man of great religious seriousness, he had the reputation of being a supporter of reform in Carafa's sense rather than Contarini's. His former pupil Cardinal Farnese is reported to have characterized him as "more of a Theatine than Chieti [Carafa]."[50] If that was the case, then his hesitations about a religious colloquy become comprehensible. He wanted to make sure that Contarini as legate would have no independence and that everything was remanded for decision to the pope and the college of cardinals, as he emphasized to the emperor.[51]

Cervini in several letters reiterated that the pope must proceed with extreme caution in dealing with the emperor and the Protestants.[52] There is nothing in his dispatches against Contarini personally, about whom he usually speaks in neutral tones. On several occasions he reports that Contarini is viewed favorably by Charles V and his advisors, for example on 10 August 1540: "If it seems [suitable] to His Holiness to send a legate to the colloquy, as it does to His Majesty, the Rev. Cardinal Contarini has already been designated [for the mission]. I see that he pleases everybody wonderfully well [*mirabilmente*]. It would be well to send him soon, and with him persons who are learned in theology, especially in exegesis, in canon law and councils [of the church]."[53] Cervini reports without disapproval Granvelle's statement that Charles V would like to see no fewer than three legates to the colloquy, and concludes: "with all [due] respect [I would like to] add that if in the meantime a real reform were undertaken, as I hope, we could expect greater results, since in truth we can defend anything better than our abuses."[54]

These are hardly the sentiments of a mere conservative who did not want to rock the boat. Cervini was no sycophant, and at times he wrote things that were blunt indeed. His wish for reform of the church at this point was secondary to his main concern, which was to uphold the honor of the papacy and give firm support to the political aims of

50. Quoted in *NB* 5:269n.1, from a letter of Leone Maffei to Cervini, Rome, 4 June 1540.
51. Cervini to Cardinal Farnese, Bruges, 25 June 1540, in ibid., 313. For Cervini's negative view of religious colloquies, see esp. his letter to Farnese, Brussels, 5–6 Sept. 1540, in ibid., 389.
52. Ibid., 315; also same to same, Bruges, 3–4 July 1540, ibid., 329.
53. Same to same, from Leiden, in ibid., 367.
54. Ibid.

Paul III. In a very real way Cervini was the mouthpiece of the pope and his grandson. He comes closer than anyone to "using" Contarini in the sense suggested by Simoncelli.[55] Convinced that the religious colloquies favored by the emperor would have no results, he wanted to ensure that a good front would be put on Catholic participation in what he considered an essentially hopeless enterprise. He obviously was not interested in Contarini's success as such, and had no sympathy for a conciliatory approach to Protestants. The dispatches he sent back to Rome show his realization that the initiative in German affairs lay with the emperor and that the papacy had to respond to the policies proposed by the Habsburg brothers. Thus he encouraged the appointment of Contarini for weighty reasons, not just as an attempt to discredit him. In his opinion, such an appointment was the best response to the emperor's explicit wishes for a reasonable legate whom he could trust. Although Cervini himself did not trust Contarini fully, he realized the Venetian cardinal's usefulness for the pope, and he was unconcerned about Contarini's likely loss of prestige in discussions with the Protestants, which would probably prove unsuccessful.[56] That he felt somewhat uneasy about Contarini, however, can be seen from his repeated urging of Cardinal Farnese to set strict limits within which the legate was to operate.[57]

An early mention of Contarini as possible legate was actually made by Cardinal Farnese, and its context is clear. In a long letter to the pope dealing with political issues he expressed his concern about the effects that meetings between Protestants and Catholics might have on the interests of the papacy. Anticipating the possibility of sending a legate, Farnese urged Paul III to dispatch Contarini to his bishopric of Belluno, or Pole to Verona, "or others like them to similar places, who ostensibly are going on business of their own. Thus, having them close

55. See esp. Simoncelli, *Evangelismo italiano*, 250–57.

56. In a letter to Farnese, Brussels, 12 Sept. 1540, Cervini is quite explicit about the likely failure of religious colloquies, at the same time counseling the pope to send Contarini if a colloquy were to be held, "so that it could never be said that Your Holiness was the cause of any trouble." He thinks that a way of preventing the colloquy and the diet would be through the marriage of Vittoria Farnese, the pope's granddaughter and a member of the French house of Lorraine, presumable because a Franco-papal rapprochement would deflect the attention of Charles V from Germany; see *NB* 5:399. Cervini does no more than a strong supporter of the pope would have done by advising Paul III to send a man most acceptable to the emperor if a colloquy proved unavoidable. He showed no special interest in Contarini as an individual, he simply happened to be convenient at that moment. In that sense he, like all successful diplomats, was anxious to make use of whatever would be helpful in achieving his objectives.

57. For example, in his letter from Utrecht, 14 Aug. 1540, in ibid., 369. See also Hudon, *Marcello Cervini*, 37–38.

to Germany, they would always be ready to go to the meeting in Speier [where the colloquy was to be held] when Your Holiness orders it."[58] To make sure that there would be no delay, they should be provided beforehand with instructions and be prepared to set out immediately. To Cardinal Farnese's mind the interests of Rome had to be safeguarded by keeping close watch on the course of events in Germany and by making sure that papal representatives were present. Since Morone and Cervini were not trusted by the emperor and his brother because of their negative views of religious colloquies, he suggested other, more acceptable candidates. Soon afterward the papal nuncio Poggio wrote that the first secretary Granvelle, speaking for the emperor, had let it be known that Charles V would be pleased if Contarini were sent.[59] By the end of April 1540, Contarini was repeatedly named by Cardinal Farnese as one of the most suitable potential legates from the perspective of the Habsburgs,[60] while Charles V was reported to consider Contarini as his friend and a man of integrity.[61] In addition, the Venetian cardinal was included among the handful of men at the Roman court acceptable to the Protestants.[62]

The appointment of Contarini quite clearly came about in response to the reports of papal envoys regarding the emperor's wishes.[63] The available evidence does not suggest the existence of a concerted plan

58. Letter of 17 April 1540, ibid., 180.

59. Poggio to Paul III, Ghent, 24–25 Apr. 1540, in ibid., 198.

60. Farnese to Paul III, Ghent, 26 Apr. 1540, in ibid., 201; and 26 and 27 Apr., ibid., 205.

61. Cervini to Farnese, Bruges, 25 June 1540, in ibid., 313. The emperor had singled out Contarini on a previous occasion, when they met in Bologna in 1530, treating him as a friend; see Albèri, *Relazioni*, 2d ser., 3:162.

62. Bernardo Sanzio to Farnese, Worms, 15 Dec. 1540, mentions several other possible candidates for the office of legate; see *NB* 6:67. A week later, on 23 December, the nuncio Tommaso Campeggio reports that the Protestants have confidence in Contarini, Sadoleto, Pole, and Fregoso; ibid., 90.

63. A. Farnese, in a letter to Poggio from Rome, 8 Jan. 1541 (BAV, Chigi L. III. 65, fols. 121v–122r), expresses this clearly: "Ma perchè, come per altre mie ho scritto a V.S., la fede che N. S^{re} ha nella prudentia et religione di S. M^{ta} et il desiderio grande che la tiene di satisfarle, è stata quella sola cagione, che ha mosso S. Sta di mandare al Colloquio con speranza che tanto piu S. M^{ta} debba esser pronta alla difesa della fede Chr^{na} et autorità della Sede Ap^{ca} quanto S. B^{ne} piu si sforzasse di contentarla.... La persona del legato sarà Monsr mio R^{mo} Contarino, il quale oltra allo havere quelle conditioni et di lettere et di prudentia che S. M^{ta} ha detto ricercarsi in questo caso è stato ancora approvato da lei come amico et confidente." On 28 January, Farnese wrote again to Poggio: "Mons mio R^{mo} Contareno questa mattina col nome di Dio è partito di Roma per il viaggio suo alla Dieta, alla quale N. S^{re} lo ha deputato Legato. Il che S. Sta ha fatto con quella intentione et animo che ho scritto per le altre a V.S., cio è piu per satisfare al desiderio et iuditio di S. M^{ta} Ces^{a} che per nessuna altra cagione" (ibid., fol. 137v). The first letter is summarized in *NB* 6:182–84, and the second on pp. 188–89.

to undercut the *spirituali* through Contarini's mission, or to discredit him and his friends. Contarini's prestige was certainly used in a calculated fashion, and arguably with callous disregard of his personal success or failure, to the advantage of the papacy. Cardinal Farnese, Cervini, Morone, even Aleandro realized that Contarini's reputation as a learned and good man interested in reform could serve the Catholic side well.[64] But they thought of him first and foremost as a diplomat in the service of the papacy, not as a proponent of his own views in a religious colloquy. His personality had earned him the emperor's good opinion, which was a decided advantage for Rome,[65] as was the fact that he had become familiar with the German situation already during his residence at the imperial court and continued to be informed about it in his correspondence with Catholic scholars, especially Cochlaeus and Eck.[66] All these reasons explain the choice of Contarini better than a hypothetical plot against him and his supporters.

The Chimera of Concord

Contarini did not approach his mission with starry-eyed idealism and optimism. He was, after all, a seasoned diplomat who knew how extremely difficult it was for third parties to navigate between the Scylla and Charibdis of the Habsburgs and the Valois and to face German Protestant princes and theologians. He announced his appointment as legate on 21 May 1540 to Cervini, Morone, and Sadoleto in almost identical letters, with however, small and telling differences. To the first he wrote that although the task he was undertaking surpassed the strength of his mind and body, he accepted it in obedience to the pope and in the hope of doing some good to the church.[67] In informing Morone, he strikes a more personal note: "Recognizing that this charge is beyond my strength, I place my confidence in God's goodness, which will have to come to my aid, otherwise I shall be lost."[68] To Sadoleto he adds that he accepted the lega-

---

64. The puzzling remark in the dispatch of Marco Bracci, the Florentine envoy in Rome, of 31 May 1540, shows that some curialists thought Contarini too "soft" on Lutheranism; see note 48 above.

65. Farnese is quite unequivocal on this point in his letter to the nuncio Poggio, Rome, 28 Jan. 1541; see *NB* 6:189.

66. See *GC*, 511–17, and the references there to the letters exchanged with them.

67. *Monumenti Beccadelli* 1(2):84.   68. Ibid., 81; and *Reg.*, 125 (no. 470).

tion so that he might try to the best of his ability to do something for the honor of God during the last part of his life.[69] These were no empty phrases, but the sentiments of a man who bore no illusions of the difficulties he would face yet who gladly undertook a task that no fellow cardinal envied him.[70]

Contarini did not imagine a colloquy as a means of quickly healing the breach of religious unity, as can be seen from a letter to Cervini that he drafted on behalf of Cardinal Farnese in the spring or summer of 1540. He stressed that the pope did not think a colloquy likely to be useful to the church unless the Catholic participants and the two Habsburg rulers promised to submit everything to the Holy See for approval before entering into any agreements with the Protestants.[71] Morone's dispatches had revealed to Contarini the extent of the problems he faced, as had letters from Tommaso Badia, who warned about the "obduracy" of the Protestants and expressed pessimism concerning the possibility of a genuine exchange of views with them.[72]

Contarini knew well that as legate he could not be an independent agent and that his sphere of action would be strictly circumscribed. To Eck, who congratulated him on his legation, he wrote: "You have no reason to congratulate me. My task is very difficult, and it goes far beyond my powers. Nevertheless, as I underook it gladly, trusting in God's help, so I hope that with God's guidance some good will come of it."[73] A few months previously, however, Contarini had written a more revealing letter to the same correspondent, emphasizing that "even in a desperate situation the Christian must not completely abandon hope, but hope against hope. . . . I believe that our task is to carry on the fight with benevolence and good deeds so that our adversaries will be ashamed, or at least should be ashamed because they are separating themselves from loving brothers."[74] Although more than a decade separated these words from the conclusion of his *Confutatio articulorum seu quaestionum Lutheranorum*, we see here the same idea

69. *Reg.*, 126 (no. 471); and *Monumenti Beccadelli* 1(2):81.

70. Report of the Ferrarese envoy to Rome, Ruggieri, 12 Jan. 1541, as quoted by Capasso, *Paolo III* 2:145n.2: "Viene notato che questo signore [Contarini] mostra di andare molto volontieri forse confidandosi per la bona mente che tiene di poter trovare qualche modo et forma a questa unione delle chiese . . . et non vi è alcun di questi Rev[mi] [cardinals] che ne gli habbia una invidia al mondo." Also Pastor, *Geschichte der Päpste* 5:840, no. 38.

71. *Reg.*, 313 (Inedita, no. 48).

72. To Contarini, Worms, 28 Dec. 1540, in *Reg.*, 138 (no. 524).

73. Regensburg, 10 Apr. 1541, in *Reg.*, 316 (Inedita, no. 54).

74. Rome, 6 Jan. 1541, in *Reg.*, 314–15 (Inedita, no. 51).

that if only the Catholics are sincere and loving, they will impress the Protestants. This attitude has been wrongly interpreted as showing Contarini's kindness as well as his wishful thinking and lack of a clear personal plan of action.[75] Actually, as we have seen, he consistently held the view that human beings were rational creatures responsive to reason, argument, and example. Unlike many of his contemporaries, he did not see enemies in those who had different opinions from the ones he held, but quite literally brothers who were within the bounds of the Christian family.

Although Contarini was appointed on 21 May 1540, his mission was delayed for eight months because of political and procedural issues,[76] and the colloquy of Hagenau opened in June 1540 without a papal legate present. Morone defended the interests of the papacy with mixed success, since the German Catholics were disunited and he was not given their firm support. His situation was difficult as well as unpleasant, and his pleas for Contarini's arrival increased in urgency. What with the Venetian cardinal's delay and the calling of the colloquy to Worms, Morone became very pessimistic, predicting that the whole of Germany would become Protestant unless the pope acted decisively.[77] He repeatedly transmitted requests from Granvelle for Contarini's presence.[78] On 8 January 1541, Farnese informed the nuncio Poggio of the pope's decision to send a legate to Regensburg: "That legate will be my lord Contarini, who in addition to possessing the qualities of learning and prudence which His Majesty considers desirable for [someone entrusted with] this mission also has the approval of [the emperor] as a friend and confidant."[79] Contarini was formally designated as legate two days later,[80] and on 28 January he left Rome for the arduous trip across the Apennines and Alps in winter; as

75. Matheson, *Contarini at Regensburg*, 50, maintains that "Contarini was perhaps clear enough about what he wanted to achieve. On the question of how it was to be achieved he was intolerably and inexcusably vague."

76. See Pastor, *Geschichte der Päpste* 5:273–74, 277–78; *GC*, 523–25; and *Reg.*, 134 (no. 507).

77. Morone to Farnese, Hagenau, 23 July 1540, in Franz Dittrich, *Nuntiaturberichte Giovanni Morones vom deutschen Königshofe, 1539–1540* (Paderborn, 1892), 177.

78. To Farnese, Worms, 10 Jan. 1541, in *NB* 6:119; or 18 Jan. 1541, ibid., 128.

79. Dittrich, "Nuntiaturberichte Morone's," 649. See also note 63 above.

80. ASVat, Arch. Consist., Acta Misc. 18 (1517–48), fol. 336v, records Contarini's appointment: "S.D.N. creavit in S.R.E. Legatum de latere Rm^um D. Gasparem Presb^rum Cardinalem Contarenum in partibus Germaniae, et ad ea potissimum loca, ad quae eum declinare contigerit, cum facultatibus prout in literis continebatur."

Farnese repeated, he was sent "most of all in response to the wishes and judgment of His Imperial Majesty rather than for any other reason."[81]

Contarini's written instruction, which reached him after his arrival in Trent, was drawn up by a committee composed of Cervini, Ghinucci, and Aleandro, then submitted to Farnese and the pope for the final wording. Aleandro considered himself an expert in German affairs and adopted a tone of condescension toward Contarini in the letter to Farnese that accompanied the draft of the instruction: "I am so bold as to say that, since through much experience in this matter I know German affairs very well, it has seemed [appropriate] to me to insert [into the instruction] certain specifics and suggestions for doing things which cannot be appreciated properly by those who are not as expert [as I], even though they excel in knowledge, intelligence, and good judgment."[82] In the name of the committee he urged Farnese to be sure to remind Contarini to "[read and] reread the instruction carefully and to do what he is ordered in it, and if he has any objections, to put them in writing."[83]

Contarini's instruction is of extraordinary importance for revealing how his mission appeared from the perspective of Paul III and his grandson.[84] Absolutely nothing in its tone or substance hints at an interest in promoting or even countenancing genuine discussion of theological issues with the Protestants. The legate is not sent with authority to conclude anything, contrary to what the Habsburgs had hoped. The reasons for this circumstance are spelled out. First, it remained to be seen to what extent the Protestants, "who have departed from the bosom of the church," were still in accord with Catholics on such key doctrines as papal primacy, the sacraments of the church, and others

81. See note 59 above. Contarini wrote from Bologna to Farnese about the bad roads, continuous snowfall, and the strain on men and horses; see ASVat, Arm. 62, vol. 36, fols. 5v–6r. See also the descriptions by Contarini's companions of the hardships en route in *Monumenti Beccadelli* 1(2):31n.44.

82. Aleandro to Farnese, Rome, 15 Feb. 1541, in *NB* 7:3.

83. Ibid., 4.

84. The instruction, dated 28 January 1541 and signed by Farnese, reached him on 24 February. The original is in ASVat, Arm. 64, vol. 21, fols. 5r–10r (hereafter cited as *Instr.*); it is printed in part in *CT* 12:192–93. The complete but frequently incorrect text (or one for which another version was the source) is in *Ep. Poli* 3:cclxxxvi–ccic, reprinted in *Monumenti Beccadelli* 1(2):112–22. Anton Pieper, *Zur Entstehungsgeschichte der ständigen Nuntiaturen* (Freiburg i.B., 1894), 171–72, offers a very incomplete list of corrections of the text in *Ep. Poli* on the basis of the above manuscript; one suspects that he relied on the hasty collation of an assistant. Thus the manuscript remains the only reliable version of the document.

confirmed by Scripture and tradition. "From the very moment that there is disagreement on these issues, any attempt at agreement on other controverted matters would be bound to fail,"[85] Contarini is told. Second, he cannot be sent as a plenipotentiary because the demands of the Protestants are not known. Finally, what can be guessed about these demands is such that not even the pope, if he were personally present in Regensburg, could grant them without consulting other nations lest he cause scandal or imperil souls.[86]

These arguments demonstrate that in 1541 the break in Christian unity was regarded as a given at the highest levels of the Catholic church. The pope and his closest advisors on religious matters in Germany, far from searching for accommodations and compromises or showing openness to Protestant concerns, drew firm lines of defense behind which Contarini was instructed to remain. If taken literally, his instruction would have precluded any dialogue between representatives of the two confessions unless the Protestants accepted the Catholic positions on some of the most controverted issues.

The same mentality can be seen in the repeated references to heresy and heretics in the instruction. Contarini is to work for the convocation of a general council, "which has always been the specific and usual remedy of the church against heresy and schism."[87] He must employ all his efforts to prevent a national council in Germany, where "the Lutherans could easily defend their heresies against the dogmas and glorious rituals of the Holy Catholic Church."[88] The solution to the religious discord in Germany is simple: if the Germans really desire peace, they should strive to preserve the faith in the spiritual realm and justice in the temporal as regards the property of the church, and should submit those articles on which there is disagreement to the judgment of the pope, who as the good shepherd would find a way of settling the differences.[89]

Paul III viewed the Protestants simply as heretics. If the role of peacemaker in Germany that he proposed for himself seems utterly unrealistic to us, we should nevertheless take it seriously as an indi-

85. *Instr.*, fols. 5v–6r: "Primum quia videndum in primis est, an protestantes, et ii qui ab ecclesiae gremio defecerunt, in principiis nobiscum conveniant, cuiusmodi est huius sanctae Sedis primatus tanquam a Deo et Salvatore nostro institutus, sacrosanctae ecclesiae sacramenta, et alia quaedam, quae tum sacrarum litterarum autoritate, tum universalis ecclesiae perpetua observatione hactenus comprobata fuerunt, et tibi nota esse bene scimus. Quibus statim initio omissis, omnis super aliis controversiis concordia frustra tentaretur."

86. Ibid., fol. 6r.   87. Ibid., fol. 7r; and *CT* 12:192.
88. *Instr.*, fol. 7v; and *CT* 12:193.   89. *Instr.*, fol. 6r.

cation of his way of thinking, and also of his limited imagination. For him there was a clearly defined hierarchy in the religious universe, at the top of which stood the pope—that is, himself. In this hierarchy there was no place for heretics. He might extend his kindness to those who erred; but of a serious discussion with them there was no question. The only relation envisioned by him was a strictly vertical one. He could stoop toward the Protestants because of the duties imposed by his pastoral office to find lost sheep. Any arrangement that positioned the two sides as equals in a discussion, however, was precluded by the very definition of what heretics were thought to be in the church: the sowers of error and untruth. Paul III's view was like that of Gianpietro Carafa, who almost a decade before had written to Pope Clement VII on this subject in a similar vein, maintaining that heretics must be treated as heretics, and that gentleness toward them only increased their obduracy.[90] Cutting the cord rather than building bridges to them would become the attitude of the Counter-Reformation church.

The pope and Cardinal Farnese, as well as the three drafters of the instruction, knew that Contarini thought otherwise and that he was no hard-liner. A hint of exasperation accompanies a telling passage of the instruction which betrays the worry that Contarini might be too accommodating to the Protestants. He is reminded of ideas he had previously expressed in conversation, that no concord could be achieved by sharp words or violent ways. What he was then told orally is now repeated in writing: Lutherans are extremely crafty, they have in the past twisted the words uttered by their opponents in good faith, and they will do so again. Contarini is enjoined quite emphatically to safeguard his dignity as papal legate first and foremost. Although he is of course an agent, he is also the pope's "deputy,"[91] and his personal views are to be subordinated to those of the sovereign whom he represents. He is permitted to deal with the heretics (as they are flatly called) in a conciliatory manner, but warned to be on the alert to anything that might harm the Holy See.[92]

Here we see a mistrust of Contarini's manner that reminds us of Cervini's letters from the imperial court to Farnese urging that Contarini be given explicit instructions for his mission from which he may not depart. The mind of the more conservative advisors of Paul III was

90. "De Lutheranorum haeresi reprimenda et ecclesia reformanda ad Clementem VII [4. octobris 1532]," in *CT* 12:68; English translation in Gleason, *Reform Thought*, 59.

91. William Roosen, "Early Modern Diplomatic Ceremonial: A Systems Approach," *Journal of Modern History* 52 (1980): 455, discusses the diplomat as "stand-in."

92. *Instr.*, fol. 9v.

made up: they had no difficulties in drawing the sort of lines between truth and error, Catholicism and Protestantism, or obedience and rebellion over which Contarini hesitated and agonized. Quite simply, his view of Catholicism was not theirs.

A negative outlook can also be seen in the orders to Contarini on how to deal with the emperor. The legate is not to support Charles V's quest for peace in Germany if that means making any concession to Protestants. Should the emperor be inclined toward a truce with them, or toward affirming the decisions made in Nuremberg in 1532, Contarini is instructed to remind him of his duties as protector of the church. Over and over the same idea is repeated: only a general council is the proper body for the resolution of religious differences; no national assembly has any standing in the eyes of the pope.[93] If any agreements contrary to the interests of the Holy See were to be made, Contarini is ordered to condemn and declare them void and to withdraw from the diet, without, however, leaving the imperial court before receiving further instructions.[94] Nobody seems to have cared to imagine how extremely uncomfortable Contarini's position would have been in such a case.

This instruction proves beyond any doubt that the colloquy at Regensburg was not viewed either as an event of major importance by the pope and his curial advisors or as a real chance for solving the differences with the Protestants. The pope had to respond to the emperor's wishes or be accused of sabotaging religious peace in Germany. So he responded, without any expectation of substantive results, by sending an expert diplomat, a good and learned man who, as he well knew, would make a favorable impression on all he met or dealt with. But Paul III and his grandson also made sure that the legate's wings were clipped and that he had no freedom of movement. In fact, his chief purpose was unequivocally spelled out. Contarini was instructed to take a notary and witnesses to all his political or religious discussions, so that a documentary record might exist which would prove to posterity that the pope had made every effort in the cause of the faith, omitting no opportunity of working for the convening of a general council.[95] In sum, Contarini was not to negotiate with the Protestants but instead was expected to speak for a pope who was anxious not

---

93. Ibid., fol. 7r; and *CT* 12:192.   94. *Instr.*, fol. 7v; and *CT* 12:193.

95. *Instr.*, fol. 8r: "Et omnibus his per te sic dicendis, agendis et faciendis, notarium et testes adhibebis, prius secreto commonefactos, ut ea, quae in huiusmodi casibus dices et facies, et tibi respondebuntur, diligenter attendant, et observent, et notarius ipse in

to appear before the world as dragging his feet on the matter of the council but who resolutely rejected any purely German solution of the Protestant-Catholic split as unacceptable and harmful to the welfare of the universal church.

The literature on the colloquy of Regensburg is vast.[96] The dramatic meeting captured the imagination of scholars especially in the nineteenth century and again in our own time, when ecumenical concerns have become important to almost all Christian denominations.[97] But opinions on whether Regensburg was the last chance for religious concord differ considerably, as do assessments of the possibility of any substantive agreement in 1541.[98] It is tempting to romanticize the situation and the participants, or to entertain "what if" scenarios. Even historians of the stature of Ranke and Pastor, for very different reasons,

---

notam sumat, unde unum vel plura confici possit instrumentum, vel instrumenta, per quae perpetuis temporibus cognoscatur nos causae fidei nullo unquam tempore, nullisque modis defuisse."

96. For a bibliography, see Karl Schottenloher, *Bibliographie zur deutschen Geschichte im Zeitalter der Glaubensspaltung*, 2d ed., vol. 3 (Stuttgart: Hiersemann, 1957), 22, nos. 28073–83. Paul Vetter, *Die Religionsverhandlungen auf dem Reichstage zu Regensburg 1541* (Jena, 1889), despite its age, is still an excellent survey. Also still useful is Pastor, *Die kirchlichen Reunionsbestrebungen*. Among more recent works Pierre Fraenkel's *Einigungsbestrebungen in der Reformationszeit* (Mainz: Institut für Europäische Geschichte, 1965) is most helpful for a brief overview. See also Robert Stupperich, *Der Humanismus und die Wiedervereinigung der Konfessionen* (Leipzig: M. Heinsius Nachfolger, 1936); Walter Friedensburg, *Kaiser Karl V. und Papst Paul III. (1534–1549)* (Leipzig: M. Heinsius Nachfolger, 1932); August Korte, *Die Konzilspolitik Karls V. in den Jahren 1538–1543* (Halle a.d.S.: E. Karras, 1905); Cardauns, *Zur Geschichte der kirchlichen Unions- und Reformbestrebungen*; Cornelis Augustijn, *De godsdienstgesprekken tussen rooms-katholieken en protestanten van 1538 tot 1541* (Haarlem: De Erven F. Bohn, 1967); Basil Hall, "The Colloquy Between Catholics and Protestants, 1539–41," *Studies in Church History* 7 (1971): 235–66; and Gerhard Müller, ed., *Die Religionsgespräche der Reformationszeit* (Gütersloh: Mohn, 1980). For a briefer survey, see Jedin, *Trient* 1:299–315.

97. See, e.g., "U.S. Lutheran-Roman Catholic Dialogue: Justification by Faith," *Origins: NC Documentary Service* 13, no. 17 (6 October 1983); and H. George Anderson, T. Austin Murphy, and Joseph A. Burgess, eds., *Justification by Faith*, Lutherans and Catholics in Dialogue 7 (Minneapolis: Augsburg Publishing House, 1985), 28–33, 200–217.

98. Hubert Jedin, "An welchen Gegensätzen sind die vortridentinischen Religionsgespräche zwischen Katholiken und Protestanten gescheitert?" *Theologie und Glaube* 48 (1958): 50–55; Joseph Lortz, "Wert und Grenzen der katholischen Kontroverstheologie in der ersten Hälfte des sechzehnten Jahrhunderts," in *Um Reform und Reformation*, ed. A. Franzen (Münster i.W.: Aschendorff, 1968), 9–32; Karl-Heinz zur Mühlen, "Die Einigung über den Rechtfertigungsartikel auf dem Regensburger Religionsgespräch von 1541—eine verpasste Chance?," *Zeitschrift für Theologie und Kirche* 76 (1979): 331–59; and Vinzenz Pfnür, "Die Einigung bei den Religionsgesprächen 1540/41: eine Täuschung?" in Müller (ed.), *Religionsgespräche*, 55–88.

were strangely optimistic, indulging in what can only be called wishful thinking when they discussed the instruction for Contarini.[99] They saw much greater possibilities of success than a careful reading of the document in fact warrants. It is important to remember that neither knew the original. Dittrich (who also did not) is somewhat more cautious in assessing the instruction, but in the end gives the pope the benefit of the doubt: "Whether Paul III was at all prepared to make concessions remains uncertain. Perhaps he wanted to leave it up to his legate to see how far he could get in his negotiations with the Protestants, but [the pope] reserved the final decision for himself."[100] This is a frankly apologetic interpretation of the clear directives Contarini was given, and says more about Dittrich's willingness to shed the most favorable light on the motives of the pope than about the instruction. For Rome, the question was not at all whether a genuine meeting of minds would occur during the colloquy, since Rome's understanding of concord was entirely one-sided: it meant the return of the Protestants to the one fold and its one shepherd, period. But even from the curial perspective there was a kind of last-chance atmosphere about Regensburg. At one point, the instruction compares the colloquy to a sheet-anchor; should it fail, the pope would no longer be gentle with the heretics, but was resolved to become more severe.[101]

Contarini and his small suite arrived just outside Regensburg on 11 March. No distinguished churchman accompanied the legate. While several high-ranking prelates had originally been proposed, and Contarini had his own candidates, the group with him in the end was made up mostly of younger men in sympathy with his views, who were to fulfill various secretarial duties.[102] On 12 March, the legate was

99. Leopold von Ranke, *Die römischen Päpste in den letzten vier Jahrhunderten,* 9th ed. (Leipzig, 1889), 1:105, writes that "in the vague nature of the papal words there lay the possibility of success"; and Pastor, *Geschichte der Päpste* 5:300, echoes this opinion: "This indefinite wording was chosen on purpose: it left the cardinal a certain space for maneuvering, and opened the possibility of success."

100. *GC,* 568.

101. *Instr.,* fol. 9r: "Nam quum constans omnium iudicium sit, si Caesarea Maiestas ab isto conventu seu Dieta Imperialis (ad quam bene gerendae rei omnis spes velut ad sacram (ut aiunt) ancoram, remissa fuerat) in iis, quae ad religionem pertinent, vel re infecta, vel male gesta discesserit, totam religionem in Germania pessum ituram, non abs re facturi videamur, si post humanitatem et mansuetudinem, quibus in hac causa usi sumus, tandem in hoc postremo articulo autoritatem nobis a Domino traditam aliquanto severius exerceamus."

102. He was accompanied by his secretary Lodovico Beccadelli; his vicar in Belluno, Girolamo Negri; and his friends Adamo Fumano, Trifone Benci, Vincenzo Parpaglia, and Filippo Gheri; see Gigliola Fragnito, *Gasparo Contarini: un magistrato veneziano al*

received with great ceremony, and "it seem[ed] that everyone was very glad that he had come," as Francesco Contarini, the Venetian ambassador to King Ferdinand, reported to the Senate.[103]

The dispatches of this distant relative of the legate are an important source for the diplomatic aspects of Contarini's mission. The ambassador saw the legate frequently, was acquainted with men in his suite, and reported a good deal of hearsay that helps us to recreate the atmosphere of the meeting. That the Catholic side in the colloquy was facing no easy task can be seen even in the left-handed compliment Francesco Contarini paid the Lutherans (or was he deliberately espousing the stance of a naive observer?) when he wrote:

His Holiness [the pope] is praised to the skies for having decided to send the Rev. Contarini here. As for myself, I believe and hold that which Holy Mother Church believes, and intend to die in this [belief]. Hearing the Rev. legate talk, I am extremely pleased, and it seems to me that there is no one who understands matters better than he does. However, when I then talk with Lutherans (since it is not possible to avoid being also with them), they present so many arguments with a flood of words that I must frankly confess to Your Excellencies that I do not know what to answer them, since that is not my profession.[104]

If even a Venetian detached from the German religious situation felt the strength of the Lutheran cause, it is not difficult to imagine the depth of support for it held by the convinced Protestants whom Contarini was about to meet.

---

servizio della cristianità (Florence: Olschki, 1988), 57. Contarini had invited his friend Gregorio Cortese and the poet Marcantonio Flaminio to accompany him, the first as theological advisor and the second as an outstanding Latinist. But Cortese excused himself on account of illness (see *Gregorii Cortesii omnia* 1:140), while Flaminio refused, ostensibly fearing for his life if he had to make such a journey in his poor state of health. His letters to Beccadelli and Contarini—in which he protests perhaps too strenuously— are in his *Lettere*, 96–100. Flaminio clearly did not want to go. Pastore, in ibid., 97n.1, gives a list of men originally proposed to go with Contarini. Eberhard Gothein, *Ignatius von Loyola und die Gegenreformation* (Halle, 1895), 287, maintains that Aleandro, "der alte Intrigant," suggested that the narrowly orthodox Pedro Ortiz, Charles V's ambassador to Rome, accompany Contarini as a sort of check.

103. Regensburg, 13 Mar. 1541, in VBM, MSS It., Cl. VII, 802 (=8219), fol. 173v (cited hereafter as F. Contarini, Dispatches). Excerpts or summaries of many of his dispatches are in *CSPV*, vol. 5, and some are excerpted in *Reg*. They deserve to be read in full for the lively quality of the reporting. Mackensen, "The Diplomatic Role of Gasparo Contarini at the Colloquy of Ratisbon of 1541," *Church History* 27 (1958): 322, errs in thinking that Francesco Contarini was the legate's brother.

104. F. Contarini, Dispatches, 26 Mar. 1541, fol. 176r; and, in a different translation, *CSPV* 5:94.

Contarini found the emperor in Regensburg waiting for German princes who were slow to come or to send their representatives. Contrary to his expectations, no theologians were present, and even in late March the fate of the colloquy was still uncertain.[105] Among Catholics, the dukes of Bavaria led the opposition to the colloquy, while on the Protestant side the powerful elector of Saxony and his supporters considered the meeting pointless. For all his experience as a diplomat Contarini was still taken aback at the extent of disagreement on the Catholic side. The difference in outlook between the Bavarians, the duke of Brunswick, and the prince-bishop and cardinal of Mainz, on the one hand, and Charles V and Granvelle, on the other, was vast. The first group wanted war against the Protestants, whereas the emperor and his chancellor, unwilling to offend the Lutherans, strove for negotiations, discussions, and compromises. Contarini was drawn into the thick of their maneuvering and had to decide quickly on a strategy that would not alienate him from either camp.[106] Realizing that the aims of these two Catholic groups were mutually exclusive, Contarini adopted a middle way between the bellicose Bavarians and the overly compliant Granvelle, and tried to pacify the dukes while preventing Granvelle from making concessions to the Lutherans. He expressed his dismay about the lack of unity among Catholics to Cardinal Farnese: "Consider and reflect, Your Reverence, with what sorts of minds we have to deal, and yet they are all Catholics! ... Negotiating with such heads is truly most difficult; I have great need of God's help, and hope that he will not fail me."[107]

An added hurdle lay in the French king's suspicious attitude toward Contarini.[108] Francis I opposed anything that might strengthen the emperor, especially a religious peace in Germany. He did his best to

---

105. Report of the Frankfurt ambassador Johann von Glauburg, 30 Mar. 1541, in Pastor, *Die kirchlichen Reunionsbestrebungen*, 231.

106. For his and Morone's plan of dealing with the Bavarians and Granvelle, see Morone to Cardinal Farnese, Regensburg, 17 Mar. 1541, in Victor Schultze, "Aktenstücke zur deutschen Reformationsgeschichte," *Zeitschrift für Kirchengeschichte* 3 (1878–79): 615–16. Dittrich, *GC*, 581, compares Contarini to the pilot of a ship steering carefully between two opposing dangers.

107. Dispatch of 16 March 1541, in Victor Schultze, "Dreizehn Depeschen Contarini's aus Regensburg an den Cardinal Farnese (1541)," *Zeitschrift für Kirchengeschichte* 3 (1878–79): 158. See also that of 30 March, 166.

108. Francis I made known his view that Contarini was so much under Habsburg influence that he could serve the papacy but poorly; see *GC*, 589–90; and Mackensen, "Diplomatic Role," 321–24, for French efforts to hamper the legate. Capasso, *Paolo III* 2:150n.3, shows that Francis I was spreading rumors about Contarini even before any news of the legate's action could have reached him.

hamper the plans of Charles V, instructing his envoys to counteract efforts to solve the German religious crisis, since a disunited neighbor to the east suited him well.[109] Apprehensive of concord, he cast aspersions on Contarini as a man too weak to stand up to the emperor and an inept emissary unable to defend properly the interests of the papacy. The legate, who was prepared for confronting the Protestants, thus realized even before the colloquy opened that some of his difficulties would come also from Catholics.

Contarini found himself in an extremely complex political situation.[110] His extensive correspondence offers detailed and often vividly written testimony of how he regarded the various interest groups assembled in Regensburg.[111] It is a rich and important source for understanding his thought and attitudes. He was guided by a steady stream of letters and instructions from Cardinal Farnese,[112] which reveal the concerns of the pope, his grandson, and their advisors as the meeting progressed, enabling us to follow step by step the exchanges between them and the legate.

109. Girolamo Dandino, Nuncio to France, to Contarini, Blois, 25 Mar. 1541, in *Monumenti Beccadelli* 1(2):128; and the same to Cardinal Farnese, Melun, 31 Dec. 1540, in *CT* 4:191–92, 193–94.

110. Paolo Prodi rightly stressed that some of the recent works dealing with the colloquy of Regensburg do not sufficiently develop the influence of politics on events and decisions made there; see Prodi, "I colloqui di Ratisbona: l'azione e le idee di Gaspare Contarini (tavola rotonda)," in Cavazzana Romanelli (ed.), *Gaspare Contarini e il suo tempo*, 208.

111. Ludwig von Pastor published Contarini's letters from Regensburg in "Die Correspondenz des Cardinals Contarini während seiner deutschen Legation," both in *Historisches Jahrbuch der Görresgesellschaft* and separately under the same title in Münster i.W. (n.d.). While still important, this collection has to be used with caution, since it is based upon imperfect copies in ASVat, Fondo Pio, 58 (old signature: Bibl. Pia, D-129). As Pastor later realized, the original register of Contarini's letters is in ASVat, Arm. 62, vol. 36. Dittrich used the same codex of the Fondo Pio (*Reg.*, 144n.1) and later saw the original register, which he cites under the old signature of Cod. 36 (Trid.). Victor Schultze found thirteen letters of Contarini's in the Neapolitan Archives; see his "Dreizehn Depeschen." Several letters were printed earlier: to Cardinal Farnese, 28 and 30 Apr. 1541, in *Ep. Poli* 3:ccliii–cclvi; and to various correspondents, in *Monumenti Beccadelli* 1, pt. 2. The latter group was reprinted by Theodor Brieger, "Zur Correspondenz Contarini's während seiner deutschen Legation: Mitteilungen aus Beccadelli's Monumenti," *Zeitschrift für Kirchengeschichte* 3 (1878–79): 492–523. Capasso, *Paolo III* 2:148n.1, briefly discusses Contarini's correspondence.

112. The originals, all signed by Farnese, are in ASVat, Arm. 64, vol. 20. Pastor found the codex after he had prepared Contarini's letters for publication, and therefore drew upon it only superficially. He intended to devote greater attention to it but did not bring the project to fruition; he used selections from the letters in his *History of the Popes* (see "Correspondenz," 334). Ludwig Cardauns used it for *NB*, vol. 7, excerpting letters of special interest for German affairs. Dittrich did not know the codex at the time he published *Reg.*

From the beginning of the correspondence it is obvious that Contarini had a different order of priorities for his mission than did Cardinal Farnese, speaking for Paul III. Nowhere can this be seen more clearly than in the matter of the pope's rebellious subject Ascanio Colonna. This affair, which has been given too little attention in the context of the Regensburg meeting,[113] casts no favorable light on the pope as spiritual leader, for the documents show him behaving in this case like a purely temporal prince preoccupied with the challenge of a defiant subject whose power in the papal state he wanted to break. At the very time negotiations between Catholics and Protestants were about to begin, Colonna's insubordination was of far more immediate concern to the Farnese family than events in far-off Germany, and it continued to preoccupy them. Even Dittrich, always ready to attribute the best motives to Paul III, admitted that "the letters of Cardinal Farnese to him [Contarini] during the first period of his mission to Regensburg contain more about the Colonna affair than about negotiations for concord."[114] These letters are not just footnotes to the meeting at Regensburg, but evidence of the relative weight given to events in the scheme of papal politics in 1541. From the perspective of Paul III and Cardinal Farnese, the Colonna affair was a major issue; from that of Contarini, however, it was but another difficulty to be dealt with in the pursuit of his chief objective.

Ascanio Colonna, member of the great Roman aristocratic family and holder of extensive possessions from the pope, was also one of the emperor's most devoted Italian partisans.[115] He had fought on the imperial side in the conflict between pope and emperor that culminated in the terrible sack of Rome in 1527. Trusted by Charles V, who rewarded him with income and office in the kingdom of Naples, Ascanio seemed to put the past behind him when Paul III was elected and proclaimed himself a loyal vassal of the pope, even acting as one of the bearers of the new pontiff's throne on the way to church. Paul III, too, wanted a fresh beginning in his relations with the powerful Colonna clan. On 3 November 1534, he issued a lengthy bull absolv-

113. Dittrich chronicled it summarily (*GC*, 592–97), while Matheson devoted less than a page to it (*Contarini at Regensburg*, 74–75) and did not use Farnese's letters. Mackensen, "Diplomatic Role," ignored the episode altogether. Pastor, in *Geschichte der Päpste*, vol. 5, incorporated it into a chapter on the papal states and the rise of the Farnese family, treating the whole episode from the vantage point of the pope challenged by a disobedient vassal, and made no reference to Farnese's letters.

114. *GC*, 593.

115. Franca Petrucci, "Colonna, Ascanio," in *DBI* 27:271–75, gives an up-to-date sketch of his colorful life, with bibliography.

ing Ascanio and his followers from the excommunication imposed by Pope Clement VII and from all censures, penalties, confiscations of goods, or anathemas.[116] This sweeping bull is impressive for the solemnity with which it stresses that the pope was not acting on a petition of Ascanio or anyone else but was proceeding freely, "de nostra mera liberalitate," in absolving Colonna from all condemnations and penalties—"[Te] absolvemus et totaliter liberamus ac penas ipsas tibi plenarie remittimus indulgemus et condonamus"—and in lifting the interdict on his territories. The kinds of crimes of which Ascanio was accused were enumerated: homicide, sacrilege, adultery, rape, arson, violence, treason, rebellion, and lèse-majesté—a lengthy catalogue that even in a violent age was unusual. Nevertheless, the pope confirmed Ascanio in possession of lands, towns, fortresses, and all rights that he held as vassal of the Holy See. Paul III at the beginning of his reign was clearly willing to go out of his way to restore order and peace in the lands of St. Peter, and to bind powerful nobles like Colonna to himself as their sovereign. The bull testifies how important these concerns were to him.

Despite this good start, frictions over taxation arose between the papal government and Ascanio as early as 1537; conflicts about other matters followed, until open defiance by the powerful noble made a serious clash likely.[117] The immediate cause for the outbreak of hostilities was Ascanio's refusal to allow an increase of the papal salt tax in his lands. A short time before, the town of Perugia had resisted this increase and precipitated the so-called Salt War, a bitter conflict that the Perugini lost in 1540, resulting in a diminution of their rights of self-government.[118] It is curious that Colonna persisted on the same path despite the events in Perugia. He may have placed exaggerated hopes in the support of Charles V, knowing him and the pope to be at odds and gambling that the emperor would side with his staunchest Roman partisan.[119] The disproportion of the means for waging war between the pope and his vassal was so great that Colonna's motives called for

116. The original is in Rome, Archivio Colonna, III BB.VII, no. 3. Its solemnity is underscored by the formal execution on parchment, the decorations, and the careful writing style. I would like to thank Donna Maria Giulia Gentile for obtaining permission for me to use this archive.

117. Summaries of events leading to war are in Pastor, *Geschichte der Päpste* 5: 237–39; and Capasso, *Paolo III* 2:184–90.

118. Rita Chiacchella, "Per una reinterpretazione della 'guerra del sale' e della costruzione della Rocca Paolina a Perugia," *Archivio storico italiano* 145 (1987): 3–60.

119. Colonna was reported to have boasted that he was waging this war in order to serve Charles V; see Dittrich, "Nuntiaturberichte Morone's," 619.

explanation. At the French court a plausible one was offered: it was assumed that Charles V had goaded Colonna into militancy for the purpose of creating difficulties for the pope, which in turn would make him grateful when help was offered and more amenable to imperial religious policy and political schemes.[120] But Paul III this time proved entirely unwilling to bend to the pro-imperial Colonna.

In a curt papal brief of 25 February 1541, Ascanio Colonna was given three days to appear in person before Paul III.[121] The instances of his defiance were listed, and he was threatened with confiscation of all lands, goods, privileges, and graces granted him previously, and with treatment as a rebel if he failed to obey the summons. When Ascanio ignored the writ armed conflict became inevitable, despite the efforts of his sister, the poet Vittoria Colonna,[122] to bring about some sort of compromise, and despite the attempts of the viceroy of Naples, Pedro de Toledo, and the imperial ambassador in Rome, the marquis de Aguillar, to find a solution.

"Here they talk of nothing else but the contention between the pope and Lord Ascanio Colonna. It seems very inappropriate in these times and during the current negotiations to receive such news. His Majesty, as I heard, wrote to the one party as well as to the other, and made every effort to have them put down their arms," reported Francesco Contarini to the Senate on 18 March.[123] The emperor was placed in the awkward position of having to dissociate himself publicly from the pope's disobedient vassal, whose loyalty to his own person he valued highly. But more unpleasant was the position of the legate who was charged with keeping Charles V informed of events in the Roman *campagna*. Time after time he was instructed by Cardinal Farnese to remind the emperor of his duties as protector of the church and defender of the Holy See, and he was sent detailed accounts of events so that the seriousness of Colonna's rebellion could be made manifest and the pope's severity justified.[124]

120. Giroloamo Dandino to Contarini, Blois, 25 Mar. 1541, in *Monumenti Beccadelli* 1(2):129.

121. The original is in Rome, Archivio Colonna, III BB.XVI, no. 77. Pastor, *Geschichte der Päpste* 5:239n.3, mentions its existence without giving details about its content.

122. She was in touch with the emperor about this matter. Charles V paid her the dubious compliment that she was "too wise for a woman"; see Contarini to Cardinal Farnese, Regensburg, 20 Mar. 1541, in Schultze, "Dreizehn Depeschen," 163.

123. F. Contarini, Dispatches, fol. 174v.

124. Farnese to Contarini, 28 Feb. 1541, ASVat, Arm. 64, vol. 20, dwells at great length on these themes. Farnese and the pope suspected that Colonna was acting with

In his first audience with the emperor, Contarini stated forcefully that he was appointed legate because of his overriding desire for Christian unity.[125] Although he would have preferred to dwell on religious issues, he had to bring up the matter of Ascanio Colonna, only to be informed that a courier from the latter had already arrived with news for the emperor. Contarini tried to move the discussion to the more general topic of vassals who disobeyed their lords, hoping thereby to engage the emperor's sympathy. But Charles V became Ascanio's advocate and asked Contarini to transmit his request for a papal pardon. Contarini, on his own authority, then replied that he believed that "His Holiness, because of his respect for His Majesty, and provided that his honor was satisfied, would show clemency [to Colonna]."[126] He evidently hoped that the quarrel would be settled so that he could devote himself to more important and central matters. However, neither party budged, despite some negotiations and attempts to avert war.[127]

Paul III was most concerned with Ascanio's attack on his authority as ruler of the papal state. He addressed the emperor as one prince would another, in the confidence that they both spoke the same language in defense of their prerogatives and that Charles V would sympathize with a fellow ruler who was protecting his state from disorder. But the irony of the situation could hardly have escaped the emperor: the pope, using the language of traditional medieval political discourse, was asking Charles V for help against Charles's own partisan.

The actions of Paul III in regard to Colonna were, however, not motivated only by the need to defend the papal state. The decision to

---

the emperor's knowledge. They thought his behavior "tanto esorbitante, che pochi sono quelli che si possino persuadere che il Sor Ascanio si fosse mosso a fare uno atto così strano senza qualche intentione più occulta" (fol. 28r). The same words are repeated in Farnese to Poggio, 29 Feb. 1541, BAV, Chigi L. III. 65, fol. 147r, which also gives a full account of the Colonna matter for transmission to the emperor.

125. Contarini to Farnese, Regensburg, 13 Mar. 1541, in Schultze, "Dreizehn Depeschen," 153.

126. Ibid., 154, and again, in almost the same words, 155.

127. Farnese to Contarini, 7 Mar. 1541, ASVat, Arm. 64, vol. 20, fol. 38r–v. This letter gives very full details about Colonna's evasion of the pope's order to appear before him. Cardinal Farnese was especially anxious that Charles V be fully informed about the "insolentia così notoria" of Ascanio; he sent reports also to the nuncios to the emperor Poggio, who was recalled to Rome, and Morone, who was replacing him. In addition, Farnese included evidence of Ascanio's deeds and a document signed by Pope Clement VII and Charles V in which each party obliged himself not to shield the other's rebellious or criminal subjects (fol. 39v).

proceed to actual war, which began on 14 March,[128] was a small part of a vastly more significant development, that is, the gradual reduction of the Roman nobility from the status of feudal lords to that of courtiers without independent political power.[129] Their autonomy on their lands was whittled away until they were indistinguishable from the new courtly nobles in everything but their memories of past greatness. Paul III's near obsession with Ascanio Colonna's rebellion transcended the mere pique of the old pontiff, and can be read as a conscious step in the gradual process of centralization and administrative modernization of the papal state, in which the Farnese pope played an important part.

It was predictable that German princes and nobles, upon learning of the conflict, would side with Colonna. The Protestants used the war as yet another proof of the pope's worldliness and, like many Catholic princes present in Regensburg, identified with a fellow noble rather than with a ruler trying to reduce his vassal's power. Charles V was criticized for defending the pope's interests against his own loyal supporter,[130] despite the emperor's ostensible evenhandedness. The accounts of the war brought by the special imperial emissary to Colonna, a Captain Maldonato, only heightened sympathy for Ascanio at the imperial court. "In truth, if the pope only knew how much harm he is doing to his side in the current negotiations, he would think twice before waging war in Italy as he does," was the pithy assessment of the Venetian ambassador, who thought that the pope's behavior would come home to roost when the question of papal power was considered in the colloquy. "[The pope] gives everyone cause to speak against him," was his conclusion.[131]

Lively, at times impassioned, letters and a multitude of documents

128. On 9 March the pope discussed preparations for war in consistory; see Farnese to Contarini, 11 Mar. 1541, ASVat, Arm. 64, vol. 20, fol. 55r. The pope's son, Pierluigi Farnese, left Rome with seven thousand troops on 14 March and on the following day attacked Marino, the first town of the Colonna; see same to same, 22 Mar. 1541, fol. 57r.

129. Paolo Prodi, *The Papal Prince* (Cambridge: Cambridge University Press, 1987), 48–49, 72–73, sees this process as a consistent part of papal politics from Nicholas V to Paul III, and suggests that "its final drama was played out in the political waning of the Colonna family with the capture of the fortress of Palliano in 1542 [actually in 1541]" (49). Capasso, *Paolo III* 2:186, thinks that Ascanio Colonna's rebellion appeared to Paul III as an attempt by a feudal noble to assert autonomy against his lord, and as such had to be stopped.

130. F. Contarini, Dispatches, 25 Apr. 1541, fol. 180r. Also *CSPV* 5:99–100; and Girolamo Negri to the Bishop of Corfu, Regensburg, 27 Apr. 1541, in Schultze, "Dreizehn Depeschen," 637.

131. F. Contarini, Dispatches, 16 May 1541, fol. 183r.

enable us to follow the war against Colonna almost day by day. Not only were Contarini and Morone supplied with full details of the affair, but the pope asked the emperor to listen to their explanation of events "as if we ourselves were speaking to you."[132] Whatever their own views on the matter, the two diplomats were ordered to be spokesmen and apologists for Farnese politics. Morone's defense of the pope's course of action was extremely skillful: he mustered strong arguments in its favor, and reported that the emperor had admitted Colonna's actions to be foolhardy and reckless.[133] With great finesse and diplomatic ability Morone fastened on the weak points of Colonna's case in order to nudge Charles V toward supporting Paul III. To what extent his well-organized dispatches with their clear summaries of what was said impressed the pope, or whether the latter realized that Contarini was handling both religious and political affairs to the point of being overburdened, is impossible to determine. Rather suddenly, though, in a letter of 28 April, there is mention that the conduct of the Colonna affair had been entrusted to Morone.[134]

Nonetheless, Contarini continued to receive information about the progress of the war, and was told that he and Morone should act together in keeping the emperor abreast of events.[135] Thus the Colonna matter continued to occupy Contarini, who was by no means as unburdened of it as he had hoped to be. For two and a half months, until the Colonna town of Palliano surrendered on 10 May, and its fortress on the twenty-sixth, the war was a central concern to the Farnese pope, his son, and his grandson. After the papal victory the fortifications of the former Colonna towns of Marino, Rocca di Papa, and Palliano were razed, and Ascanio had to go into Neapolitan exile with his family and adherents.[136] Paul III, refusing to grant pardon, proved that he was master in his own house; but his actions appeared far different in Germany than they did in Rome.

132. Brief from Paul III to Charles V, 1 Mar. 1541, ASVat, Arm. 64, vol. 20, fol. 45r.
133. To Farnese, 28 Apr. 1541, in Dittrich, "Nuntiaturberichte Morone's," 447–49. This letter is a good example of Morone's eloquence and skill.
134. Contarini to Farnese, ASVat, Arm. 20, vol. 36, fol. 76v, where Contarini thanks the pope "che mi habbi scaricato del negocio del Sor Ascanio et commessolo al Rev. Nuntio [Morone], il qual oltra le altre ragioni potendo più frequentare l'audientia di Cesare di quello che posso io, potrà etiam più facilmente expedirlo."
135. Cardinal Farnese to Contarini, 12 May 1541, ASVat, Arm. 64, vol. 20, fol. 77r.
136. Pastor, *Geschichte der Päpste* 5:241–42. The victory was to be celebrated in the whole papal state, and the pope was extremely pleased about it; see Cardinal Farnese to the Duke of Castro, Rome, 11 May 1541, ASVat, Carte Farnesiane, vol. 2, fol. 143. Valuable materials for the course of the war are Giovanni Guidiccione's detailed reports in his *Lettere* 2:222–79.

Contarini and Morone were well aware of the growing resentment caused by the pope's intransigence. The former constantly slid recommendations for pardon of the rebellious noble into his dispatches, whereas the latter could hardly have been more forceful in reporting the emperor's "bitterness of soul" on account of the sums of money Paul III had spent for the war, which "our Lord [the pope] as head of all Christians should have spent for the good of Christianity."[137] The emperor was annoyed that he had received no papal aid for the defense of Hungary against the Turks, as also were the German princes. Morone bluntly counseled that the pope should send money for Hungary and make peace with Colonna in order to counteract the scandal caused by his course of action. The letter closed with a fervent appeal to Paul III to do the right thing by God, man, and posterity.[138]

The two papal diplomats had not only to defend an unpopular cause, but also to deal with the marked sympathy for Ascanio Colonna among German princes. "It is impossible to put into words how much His Holiness is talked about by everyone because of the war he is waging in Italy," reported Francesco Contarini to the Venetian Senate.

It is generally thought that [the pope] does not care if he ruins the church if [only] he succeeds in aggrandizing his own family. I was recently told at a banquet of German princes by someone who is trustworthy that at the diet nothing else is discussed every day but this. The majority [of the princes] said that the Lord Ascanio should come here, and if the emperor does not want to help him, he will be assisted by others. [All this was said] with such coarse words, and such strong language was used against His Holiness, that I am ashamed to write it.[139]

The Venetian ambassador correctly caught the mood of many princes who were present at Regensburg. The Protestants gloated, and many Catholics felt alienated from the head of the church, whom they saw behaving first and foremost as an Italian secular ruler. Their ill will toward the pope affected their attitude toward what he proposed through his legate. If Contarini was personally well liked, he still represented a power toward which the hostility in Germany was increasing, not least because of the war against Colonna.

Contarini conscientiously kept Cardinal Farnese informed about religious issues in his dispatches, only to receive in return detailed reports about fighting, sieges, or surrenders. During the first period of

137. To Cardinal Farnese, 12 May 1541, in Dittrich, "Nuntiaturberichte Morone's," 462.

138. Ibid., 463.

139. F. Contarini, Dispatches, 29 May 1541, fol. 184r.

Contarini's mission political concerns were uppermost in Farnese's letters.[140] His father, Pierluigi, commander of the papal troops, could
not prevent his soldiers from looting, raping, and committing brutali-
ties against the civilian population in Colonna territory. Neither could
he deter armed bands from the kingdom of Naples from coming to
the support of Ascanio Colonna. Although the imperial ambassador to
Rome stated that this was happening in contravention of the emperor's
express orders, the pope was particularly upset by what he took to be
interference in the internal affairs of his state, and instructed Contarini
to protest to Charles V.

Contarini's situation was highly ironic. He had been fearless in his
outburst before Clement VII in 1529, when he argued that it would
be far better for Christianity and the church if the pope had no state.[141]
Now, as a cardinal of the Roman church, he had to justify the Colonna
war. It would be easy to think him vacillating or worse, a "trimmer"
who adjusted his sails to the prevailing wind. But a close reading of his
dispatches shows that he was consistent in his views.

His strong sense of order and hierarchy, so marked in his career in
the service of Venice, militated against his sympathy for Ascanio. Despite his friendship with and affection for Vittoria Colonna, Contarini
could not in conscience defend the actions of her brother. His cardinalate had not changed the political views he had expressed in the treatise on the Venetian state of how society is best governed. As the lawful
sovereign of a state, the pope in his eyes was justified in preserving
order. Contarini the Venetian aristocrat would not take the part of
someone who broke the compact between subject and ruler, of which
he was especially conscious after the troubled period of the War of the
League of Cambrai. Pietro Ghinucci, the Mantuan agent in Rome, accurately picked up the close and continuing identification of Contarini
with Venice when he reported shortly before the legate left for Germany: "This lord [Contarini], as Your Grace knows better than I do, is
considered wise, learned, and good, but he has the reputation of being
too attached to his *patria*, and is held as such [too Venetian]."[142]

140. Of the thirty-three letters in ASVat, Arm. 64, vol. 20, from Farnese to Contarini, eight include reports of the war against Colonna, while nine are written after the
end of the diet and are brief instructions concerning the legate's return to Italy. Of the
remaining sixteen, several deal with subjects other than the colloquy.

141. VBM, MS It., Cl. VII, 1043 (=7616), fols. 150v–151r; also *Reg.*, 43–44
(no. 126).

142. Ghinucci to Cardinal Ercole Gonzaga, Rome, 8 Jan. 1541, in Solmi, "Contarini alla Dieta di Ratisbona," 16. Beccadelli, "Vita," 56, mentions that Contarini
remained in close contact with Venetian ambassadors in Rome, who confided their affairs

Despite his defense of political hierarchy, however, Contarini's impatience with the deflection of the pope's attention from the colloquy in Germany to a local war in the papal state is detectable. In a full account of the discussion he and Morone had with the emperor after the taking of Palliano became known, Contarini skillfully inserts criticism of the pope by putting it in the mouth of Charles V, who he reports was suspicious that the Colonna feudal holdings would be declared vacant and transferred to the Farnese. Contarini writes that he reiterated his confidence in the pope by saying to the emperor, "I do not doubt that he [Paul III] will use all [possible] clemency [toward Ascanio Colonna], because he who is magnanimous habitually does this, that is, he shows clemency and kindness toward those who humble themselves."[143] The legate obviously wished that the pope would bring the war to an end by acting not like a secular prince but as the spiritual leader of Christianity, and by giving an example of Christian behavior. Yet Paul III turned a deaf ear to the emperor's appeals, and Colonna was never forgiven by the "papal prince," who made an example of his rebellious subject for the benefit of other nobles.[144]

The clearest indication that Contarini had not changed his views on the nature of papal power is in another report of a conversation with the emperor, in the course of which the legate remarked:

Your Majesty went to Tunis [in 1535] at enormous cost for the sake of the temporal state of Christians, exposing your own life, yet the temporal state is not the substance of [our] faith. The martyrs lived at a time when Christians had no temporal state, but then the faith was most efficacious, having as its body and essence the articles [of faith, including transubstantiation]. . . . The temporal state, in comparison to them, is like clothing, accidental to the body.[145]

These words are strikingly similar to those Contarini spoke to Clement VII when he stressed the spiritual nature of the papacy before the papal state came to exist. Now, though, as cardinal, he obeyed his lord notwithstanding his own views.

---

to him, "believing him to be no less of a [Venetian] gentleman [*zentilhuomo*] than a cardinal."

143. To Farnese, 23 May 1541, ASVat, Arm. 62, vol. 36, fol. 98v. An incorrect copy is in *Reg.*, 328–31.

144. The strongest defense of Paul III's dealing with Colonna is in the letter of Cardinal Farnese to Morone, Rome, 29 May 1541, *NB* 7:57–59. Farnese demanded that Charles V punish Colonna, and adopted a remarkably censorious tone regarding the emperor throughout his letter.

145. To Farnese, 15 May 1541, in Pastor, "Correspondenz," 389.

The Colonna affair called on Contarini's diplomatic skill for a purpose distinctly tangential to his mission, and embarrassed him by glaringly revealing the political aims of the Farnese family. He honored fully his obligations as legate to be the spokesman of Paul III, without, however, going along uncritically with what the pope wanted. For him personally, the Colonna war could hardly have occurred at a more inopportune time. Francesco Contarini summed up the situation at the end of the war: "Everyone has concluded that just as the emperor seeks in every possible way to make peace, to calm the [German] princes, and to support and defend the affairs of the pope, so His Holiness does everything to start a fire in Italy and to keep it going, [and to do] things that are not fitting for the vicar of Christ. And everyone speaks of these things publicly."[146]

The one good result for Contarini was the growth of his friendship with Morone. The precocious nuncio, who was only thirty-two but already a seasoned diplomat when Contarini joined him in Regensburg, had been decidedly hostile to the idea of religious colloquies.[147] Gradually, under the influence of the older man, Morone became more sensitive to the enormous complexities of the religious situation and modified his views. The story of the friendship between the two men still remains to be written.[148] Their close collaboration and continuous exchange of information, especially about the Colonna war, cemented a friendship that flourished and deepened as long as Contarini lived.

Thus, between his arrival in Regensburg on 11 March and the opening of the diet on 5 April, Contarini was fully initiated into the diplomatic intricacies[149] with which he would have to deal. "I see little good here in Germany, nor am I surprised that the people are in such confusion, given the conditions I see prevailing among their secular and ecclesiastical leaders and those of religious orders," he wrote to Farnese.[150] The counselors of the Bavarian dukes annoyed him with their suspicions. He tried to pacify them with assurances that he would not cede an iota of the truth to the Protestants, and by going out of his

146. F. Contarini, Dispatches, 23 May 1541, fol. 183v.

147. To Farnese, Regensburg, 5 Feb. 1541, in Dittrich, "Nuntiaturberichte Morone's," 435.

148. Heinrich Lutz, "Kardinal Morone: Reform, Konzil und europäische Staatenwelt," *Politik, Kultur und Religion im Werdeprozess der frühen Neuzeit*, ed. M. Csàky (Klagenfurt: Universitätsverlag Carinthia, 1983), 185–86.

149. Mackensen, "Diplomatic Role," 316–26; and Matheson, *Contarini at Regensburg*, chap. 6, give sketches of the diplomatic tangle into which Contarini entered.

150. Dispatch of 30 March 1541, in Schultze, "Dreizehn Depeschen," 166.

way to try to charm them.[151] Contarini's personality once again proved to be a major asset. The documents repeatedly mention the esteem in which he was held and his ability to win over men who initially were hostile to him.[152]

Contarini had to be on his guard with Granvelle, who was most anxious to impress his and the emperor's point of view on the legate. Their first long interview is of particular significance for understanding Contarini's mind. Granvelle warned him that unless a solution were found at the diet, the Catholic religion would be ruined, since the license introduced by the Protestants attracted people to their teaching everywhere, even in Italy. Granvelle pressed him hard to support fully the emperor's religious policy of appeasement, arguing that otherwise all would be lost. The two men engaged in a discussion that perhaps more than any other indicates Contarini's attitude before the colloquy even began. To Granvelle's remark that Lutherans agreed about Christ's presence in the sacrament of the Eucharist but denied the transubstantiation of the bread, a matter that should be referred for decision to a future council, Contarini replied: "This article is essential and most certain, and a [future] council cannot determine anything to the contrary"; the Fourth Lateran Council, after all, had decreed it. He firmly believed that there were essential articles of faith, every word of which must be accepted, since they were proclaimed by the teaching authority of the church. At the same time, disputes about words must be avoided because they were fraught with danger for the church, as could be seen in the disagreement over the word *filioque*, which had resulted in the schism between Greek and Roman Christianity.[153]

Contarini did not doubt the existence of clearly defined essential articles of faith, belief in which was necessary for salvation. He came to Regensburg firm in the conviction that central Christian doctrines were beyond discussion. Those he considered not essential were the

151. Ibid., 164–65.

152. Morone to Cardinal Farnese, 3 May 1541, in Dittrich, "Nuntiaturberichte Morone's," 454: "La sodisfattione, qual si ha del R^mo Legato, ogni hora cresce, et Monsr di Granvella et gli altri Ministri dicono, ch'Iddio per sua bontà l'ha creato a questo effetto, perchè si porta con grandissima mansuetudine, prudentia et dottrina, nella quale (pace d'ognuno) è reputato avanzare tutti gl'altri, quali sono in questo luoco, di maniera che gli adversarii istessi cominciano non solo ad amarlo, ma ancora a reverirlo con grande honore di N.S. et de quella Santa Sede Apostolica."

153. To Farnese, Regensburg, 18 Mar. 1541, in Schultze, "Dreizehn Depeschen," 159–60.

adiaphora; these could be debated, and on them reasonable men could well differ. While similar to that of Erasmus,[154] Contarini's distinction had a more profoundly subjective basis. At this stage, he did not yet realize the extent to which agreement on what constituted central articles of faith would in itself be a major problem. He assumed a broader area of consensus than existed in actuality, not because of some sort of naïveté or inexcusable vagueness,[155] but because he belonged to the last generation whose intellectual and theological formation had occurred before the Reformation. It was still possible for Contarini to think of Lutherans as protesters who could be brought back to the one church from which they had temporarily dissociated themselves. The means for accomplishing this task were understanding and discussion of Lutheran grievances with kindness and patience on the part of Catholics,[156] who, in turn, had to take reform of the church seriously.

An overwhelming mass of documents sheds detailed light on the events connected with the religious colloquy.[157] Thanks to these abundant sources, it is possible to follow Contarini's mind closely. But actually understanding the legate's thinking is another matter. The most recent monograph on Regensburg hardly offers the reader much help by asserting that the "denizen of the modern theological world . . . is confronted with the almost total incomprehensibility of Contarini's language and thought-patterns . . . the code [of which], it appears, has yet to be cracked."[158] The legate is seen by the author as an eclectic, with the clue to his theology lying "in the coexistence, in rather unstable equilibrium," of his "ecumenism, his Catholicism, and his Curialism."[159]

154. Erasmus's position is expressed in his *Inquisitio de fide*; I have used the translation by Craig Thompson (New Haven: Yale University Press, 1950). Here Erasmus repeatedly reminds both Protestants and Catholics that they are in agreement on the most important articles of the faith. Luther and post-Tridentine Catholic teaching rejected the distinction between *Fundamentalartikel* and those that can be doubted or denied *salva fide et salute*; see "Fundamentalartikel," *Lexikon für Theologie und Kirche*, vol. 4 (Freiburg i.B.: Herder, 1960), cols. 450–51.

155. This is the accusation of Matheson, *Contarini at Regensburg*, 50.

156. Jedin, *Trient* 1:154, points to the paradox that nothing promoted the split between the confessions as much as the illusion that it was not serious or that it did not exist.

157. Prodi thinks it unlikely that significant new documents about the colloquy and diet will emerge: "We can only change the angle from which we take the shots, and of course the interpretation of the testimonies themselves" ("I colloqui di Ratisbona," 207).

158. Matheson, *Contarini at Regensburg*, 173.

159. Ibid., 178.

A different interpretation of Contarini's mind will be offered here. We see in Regensburg not the confusion of a well-meaning man face to face with hard facts, or his arcane thought pattern, but a critical stage in his intellectual and religious development. Contarini was a prelate of the pre-Tridentine Catholic church, which was much more open and doctrinally indeterminate compared with the church of the Counter-Reformation. Yet even in the Catholic church of 1541 ever clearer lines were being drawn as a result of continuous confrontation with Protestantism. At Regensburg, Contarini had to make choices for which he had not been prepared. Individualistic and emotional in his own spiritual life, which had justification by faith as its cornerstone, he was at the same time traditional in his views of ecclesiastical institutions, the structure of authority in the church, and the theology of the sacraments. Now he was forced to rethink the relation between his personal religious stance, church doctrine, and ecclesiology. He did arrive at a conclusion. But in his letters from Regensburg we see how difficult, painful, even bitter the process of human and religious maturation of a Catholic reformer of that time could be.

The religious colloquy of Regensburg opened on 28 April, and the discussions ended on 22 May. The emperor chose the six participating theologians: for the Protestants, Philip Melanchthon, Martin Bucer, and Johannes Pistorius; for the Catholics, Johannes Gropper, Julius Pflug, and Johann Eck. Granvelle and Count Frederick of the Palatinate were to preside, while six witnesses were to be present at all discussions.[160] Except for Eck, championed by the Bavarian dukes, and Melanchthon, whose prestige among the Lutherans made his inclusion mandatory, the participants were men sympathetic to or even adherents of Erasmian humanism and genuinely interested in religious concord. Contarini as the representative of the pope was excluded from the talks, since they were not recognized as official in Rome. But Granvelle ordered the Catholic collocutors to consult Contarini every morning, with Badia and Morone also present, and to report to him again after the meetings. The basis for discussion at the colloquy was to be the Regensburg Book, equally disliked by Melanchthon and Eck. The former had called it "a hyena"—presumably because of the belief

---

160. Contarini to Cardinal Farnese, 28 Apr. 1541, in Pastor, "Correspondenz," 367–68. Augustijn, "Religionsgespräche der vierziger Jahre," 50, regards the colloquies of 1539–41 as "dominated by Erasmians," in the sense that these men sought to formulate the central religious doctrine of *sola fide* in such a way as to make it compatible with both Lutheran and Catholic understanding of Christianity.

that this animal can speak with a human voice and tempt people into sin[161]—whereas the latter rejected it so vehemently that the legate had to put pressure on him to soften his stand.[162] Contarini himself was not entirely comfortable with the text, to which he added more than twenty annotations; he realized that the document was an attempt to create a single, united German church, which in itself would be a danger to Rome.

We can well imagine the setting for the colloquy: the religious discussions were conducted at the same time that the disunited German princes and estates met in the diet, with Charles V and Granvelle desperately trying to forge some sort of agreement among the religious and political factions, to avert further conflict or even war, and to obtain aid against the Turks. All the while, intransigent Lutherans on the one side and their Catholic counterparts on the other were intent on sabotaging accord. That the theologians were not free agents in this tense atmosphere is obvious. The Protestants deferred to Melanchthon, who in turn deferred to the elector of Saxony and to Luther. Sick and under pressure from his prince, Melanchthon did not show his mild face this time. He attacked the Catholics as intending to cheat and harm the Protestants.[163] Bucer vainly tried to exert his influence over the other two men on his side, only to be met with suspicion by Melanchthon. Among the Catholics, Eck was the dominant figure, and he openly supported the political aims of the bellicose Bavarian dukes.

Contarini's vicar Negri described the legate on the eve of the colloquy as instructing his troops like a good captain, and added: "He believes everything, hopes for everything, and sustains everything. His Reverence would gladly remain here for a long time in order to recover this poor lost people, if that were possible."[164] But in his own letters Contarini does not seem quite so otherworldly. "If we cannot do anything good this time, that will be the end," he wrote to Cardinal Gonzaga.[165] Therefore, he set out to make things work. As a seasoned diplomat, he cultivated both friend and foe. Eck was soon under his influence. When Sturm and later Bucer came to see him, he was so

161. Bretschneider (ed.), *Corpus Reformatorum* 10, col. 576.

162. Contarini to Cardinal Farnese, 28 Apr. 1541, in Pastor, "Correspondenz," 369–70. According to Morone, Contarini succeeded even to the point of getting Eck to be gentle and change his mind on questions of philosophy and theology; see his letter to Cardinal Farnese, 28 Apr. 1541, in Dittrich, "Nuntiaturberichte Morone's," 449.

163. Vetter, *Religionsverhandlungen*, 73.

164. *Reg.*, 172 (no. 687).

165. Letter of 30 April 1541, *Reg.*, 175 (no. 696).

gentle and tactful that Bucer eventually judged him "much too learned and too pious for a cardinal, as well as too willing to reform the church."[166] Contarini wanted to impress these men with only one objective in view: to soften the "harshness" of the Protestants and to induce them to return to the "right way" of the Catholic church.[167]

Already on the first day both sides agreed on the four initial articles of the Regensburg Book dealing with the condition of man and human nature before the fall, free will, the cause of sin, and original sin.[168] The theologians then moved on to a discussion of the fifth article, on justification. Because the original wording pleased neither side, several alternative versions were drafted, only to be rejected one after the other.[169] On 2 May, after four days of deliberations, a formula was worked out on the basis of article 5 to which both Catholic and Protestant collocutors assented.[170]

At Regensburg the impossible seemed to have been achieved. Justification by faith was the *articulus stantis et cadentis* of the entire Protestant edifice, the doctrine by which it stood or with which it fell. If theologians agreed on that central article of faith, could there be a more auspicious beginning of the colloquy?

Article 5, "On man's justification,"[171] was a curious theological compromise offering a theory that came to be called, not entirely accurately, double justification. It begins with the acknowledgment that all justification comes through Christ. But then, two quite different views demanded recognition. Justification is thought to begin when the sinner cooperates with the Holy Spirit, who moves his mind to repentance and to belief in the remission of sins for those who believe in Christ. The response is thus an act of the intellect and the will (the verb used is *assentior*,[172] to give one's assent), which leads to trusting faith that one will be forgiven. Through this faith the Christian receives the Holy Spirit, remission of sins, imputation of Christ's justice, and innumerable other gifts.

"The doctrine that the sinner is justified by living and efficacious

166. Quoted in Augustijn, *Godsdienstgesprekken*, 78n.3.
167. Contarini to Cardinal Farnese, 3 May 1541, in Pastor, "Correspondenz," 373.
168. Pfeilschifter (ed.), *Acta Reformationis Catholicae*, 6:24–30.
169. Vetter, *Religionsverhandlungen*, 92–93.
170. Contarini sent the agreed-upon article to Cardinal Farnese on 3 May 1541; see Pastor, "Correspondenz," 372.
171. "De iustificatione hominis," in Pfeilschifter (ed.), *Acta Reformationis Catholicae*, 6:52–54. The first two drafts are on pp. 30–52.
172. Cf. the famous Ignatian formula "sentire cum ecclesia," by which is meant not only to accept the formulations but to appropriate them inwardly.

faith is true and sound, for through it we become pleasing to God and accepted because of Christ," the article continues. This initial, or indwelling justice (*iustitia inhaerens*) is communicated by Christ. The believing soul, however, does not rely on it, but only on Christ's justice given to us freely, "without which there absolutely is not and cannot be justification." We are justified by faith in Christ whose justice is imputed to us, making us righteous before God. The second or imputed righteousness is clearly the more important and higher, the immeasurable gift of God to man, which in no way depends on human efforts. As to the justified Christian's good works, God rewards them if they are the fruit of faith. Thus good works are accommodated and made meaningful within the framework of justification by faith alone. [173]

Both style and content make it obvious that article 5 was the work of a committee. The modern reader will search in vain for logical consistency, since the essence of the agreed-upon text was a compromise between two basically incompatible positions. In the progress toward the first, or indwelling, righteousness, intellect and will have a role; the sinner can choose to cooperate with the Holy Spirit or to reject his promptings. In the second there is no choice. It is one of the benefits of Christ, and nothing whatsoever that sinners do can make a difference; it depends totally on Christ as the giver of a free gift. This is hardly the theory of a double justification if that term is taken to mean the existence of two equal entities. "Two-stage justification" or "preliminary and complete justification" would be a clumsy but somewhat more accurate description of the theory put forth in article 5. *Iustitia inhaerens* and *iustitia imputata* are not equal in importance, for salvation really hinges on the second. The first concept was crucial to the Catholic collocutors, who were anxious to preserve the teaching that man cooperates with grace in the process of justification.[174] The second, by incorporating the assertion that "only by faith in Christ are we justified or reputed just, that is accepted, not because of our own dignity or works," reassured the Protestants.

The relative importance of the prevenient motion of the Holy Spirit and the response of the human intellect and will is left unclear. More to the point, the article leaves the connection between indwelling and imputed justice unexplained. Thus it is uncertain whether and how the

173. Pfeilschifter (ed.), *Acta Reformationis Catholicae*, 54.
174. Dittrich, *GC*, 656, translates portions of article 5 too freely, obscuring some of its illogicalities.

two are causally or chronologically related. It is not surprising that later theologians found the article to be either basically Lutheran, basically Catholic, or a more or less muddled third thing, and that there is no agreement concerning the extent of its dependence on the discussion of double justification in Gropper's *Enchiridion*.[175] There is no doubt, however, that the text of the article not only was determined by theological considerations but has a historical dimension as well. The unusual concatenation of especially irenic collocutors on both sides, together with the political urgency of accord that they felt, must not be forgotten in any examination of the words of the text. Historical circumstances go a long way toward explaining what is only too easily dismissed as a "mere compromise."[176] It must be stressed that despite all its problems, article 5 was a noble attempt by a handful of men not merely to stem but to reverse the breakup of the one Christian church into mutually hostile faiths.

On the day after accord was reached, Contarini wrote a report to Cardinal Farnese that reflected his joy: "Yesterday, praised be God, the Catholic and Protestant theologians came to a conclusion and concurred in the article on justification, faith, and works, in the concord and agreement which your Reverence will find enclosed. This [agreement] has been found to be Catholic and holy in my judgment and in that of Morone, Badia, Eck, Gropper, and Pflug."[177] Contarini sent copies of the text to several of his friends in Italy, including Pole and Cardinal Ercole Gonzaga, asking for their opinion. When the latter's theological advisor expressed reservations about the article, Contarini composed an apologia for it in the *Epistola de iustificatione* of 25 May 1541, which is an elaboration of his own views that helps greatly in elucidating his mind.

Contarini's main concern in this apologia was to show that article 5 was not only consonant with Catholic teaching, but actually

175. Walther von Loewenich, *Duplex iustitia: Luthers Stellung zu einer Unionsformel des 16. Jahrhunderts* (Wiesbaden: Franz Steiner, 1972), 37–38.

176. Prodi rightly insists that most discussions of the colloquy of Regensburg do not give adequate consideration to the political context in which it was held; see "I colloqui di Ratisbona," 208.

177. Letter of 3 May 1541, in Pastor, "Correspondenz," 372; and of May 1541 (ibid.): "Hieri, dio laudato, questi theologi et Cattolici et Protestanti si risolsero et convennero nell'articolo de iustificatione, fide et operibus nella concordia et conventione che V. Sig. Rev^ma vedra qui inclusa, la quale da me e dal Sig. Nuntio [Morone] e dal Padre Maestro [Badia] e dall'Ecchio, Groppero et Fluch è stata veduta come cattolica et santa per quel giuditio che noi havemo."

"cattolichissimo."[178] He may also have intended to defend the Catholic theology of salvation against Protestant charges of Pelagianism.[179] Contarini expresses here some of the most characteristic ideas of the *spirituali*, in the fervent hope that the church will recognize them as her own doctrine and thus open the way for a reconciliation with the Protestants.

The *Epistola* proposes the same solution to the problem of justification as article 5 by arguing that the sinner becomes just through his own inherent justice and the imputed justice of Christ, freely granted by God to man. Unlike article 5, however, Contarini's tract uses the term *duplex iustitia* several times. Thus, "we attain double justice, the first which inheres in us, through which we begin to be just and become partakers of divine nature, and have charity poured into our hearts. The second, not inherent but given to us with Christ, I call the justice of Christ together with all his merits."[180]

Although in the next sentence Contarini decides that "both are given us at the same time and we reach both through faith," they are clearly not equal. The efficient cause of the first is the Holy Spirit, who illuminates the intellect and moves the will to turn away from sin and toward God. Man therefore is free to cooperate with God. In his explanation of this process Contarini closely follows St. Thomas;[181] however, when his own experience of sin and forgiveness enters, he writes in another key which is far less systematic.

There is more than a touch of impatience in Contarini's sidestepping of technical theological discussion on the priority of one form of justice over the other: "Which of the two by its nature is first [is a question] that belongs to scholastic disputations rather than to the realm of faith about which we are here concerned."[182] He thinks that

178. To Cardinal Farnese, 9 June 1541, in ibid., 478. See also Mackensen, "Contarini's Theological Role," 49.

179. Jedin, *Trient* 1:309.

180. *CT* 12:318, lines 34–37. I use this edition of the tract in preference to that in Hünermann's edition of the *Gegenreformatorische Schriften* because it is based on additional manuscript versions, especially one belonging to Aleandro (*CT* 12:314). But see Simoncelli, *Evangelismo italiano*, 187n.241, for an argument affirming the existence of the original.

181. Rückert, *Theologische Entwicklung*, 82; and Loewenich, *Duplex iustitia*, 42.

182. *CT* 12:318, lines 38–39. Cardinal Seripando in his defense of the doctrine of double justification during the first session of the Council of Trent used a similar argument: "The doctrine of justification should be open, clear, and easy...so that those for whom Christ died might not be repelled from it by any difficulties. This teaching is not to be sought from the schools, in which thorny and quite difficult questions are treated,

everything depends on faith, not on the construction of a logically rigorous and intellectually satisfying theory. By holding that faith is an act of the will, Contarini differs from later Tridentine doctrine, which defined faith as an act of the intellect consisting in the belief that God's revelation and promises are true.[183] Like Luther, Contarini conceives of the essence of faith as trust and hope in God's mercy.[184] In fact, he uses the Lutheran terms *fiducia* and *assensus* in describing that faith.

Christ's imputed justice is crucial for sinners. "I, for my part, consider it a pious and Christian opinion that we are to depend—depend, I mean, as on a sure foundation that will certainly sustain us—upon the justice that Christ has conferred on us, and not on any holiness and grace that inheres in us."[185] This imputed justice is true and perfect, unlike our own imperfect inherent justice. In a short explanatory note to article 5 that he sent on 3 May to Cardinal Gonzaga and probably also to other friends in Italy,[186] Contarini discusses the text of article 5: "The first section is that which says that we should not rely on the justice which is inherent in us, through which we are made just and do what is good, but that we must rely on the justice of Christ which is imputed to us because of Christ and the merits of Christ. By this latter we are justified before God, that is considered and reputed just. I think that this conclusion is most true, Catholic, and conducive to piety."[187]

Good works play no part in our justification, which is due to faith alone.[188] But unless the Christian progresses in holiness, he can lose both kinds of justice. Good works constitute evidence of such because true faith is active in love, not because the Christian expects them to be meritorious in the sight of God. They necessarily follow the sinner's

---

which are indeed useful for exercising talents and acquiring the wisdom of this world but are not so well-suited to knowing the wisdom hidden in mystery and instructing the people of Christ into justice." The translation is by James F. McCue, "Double Justification at the Council of Trent: Piety and Theology in Sixteenth-Century Roman Catholicism," in *Piety, Politics, and Ethics: Reformation Studies in Honor of George Wolfgang Forell,* ed. Carter Lindberg (Kirksville, Mo.: Sixteenth Century Journal Publishers, 1984), 41.

183. H. J. Schroeder, O.P., trans. "Decree on Justification," chap. 6 in *Canons and Decrees of the Council of Trent* (St. Louis: Herder, 1941), 32–33, 311; and Angelus Walz, O.P., "La giustificazione tridentina," *Angelicum* 28 (1951): 129.

184. Contarini, *Gegenreformatorische Schriften,* 26.

185. *CT* 12:319, lines 29–31.

186. Theodor Brieger, "Contarini's Begleitschreiben zu der Formula Concordiae de iustificatione," *Zeitschrift für Kirchengeschichte* 5 (1882): 592.

187. "Gasparis Contareni scheda minor de iustificatione," in *CT* 12:313, lines 26–30.

188. Ibid., 27.

justification, but are in no way its cause. In that specific sense they are proof that man is justified. Contarini concludes his tract by asserting, "Those who say that we are justified through works are right; and those who say that we are not justified through works but through faith are also right."[189]

It is easy to see why there is no agreement among interpreters of Contarini's ideas in the *Epistola de iustificatione*, who fall into three groups: those who think it basically Catholic; those who consider it an expression of Lutheran teaching about justification; and those who see it as a compromise between Catholic and Protestant theology.[190] Most modern scholars belong to the last group maintaining that Contarini's *Epistola* was a theological hybrid,[191] the roots of which are variously sought in Gropper's *Enchiridion* of 1536,[192] the works of Pighius,[193] or late medieval Pauline and Augustinian currents in Italian religious thought.[194] In recent literature a sort of consensus has emerged to the effect that Contarini undoubtedly had goodwill and sympathy for Lutheran theology, but that he was too unsystematic, thus unable to give his opinions cogency and clarity or to organize them into a coherent theological argument.[195]

If his theology is measured against the standard set by the works of St. Thomas or Luther, that charge is true, for Contarini was not a trained theologian. Jedin was the first rightly to emphasize the link between Contarini's early religious experience and the expression of his ideas on justification at Regensburg.[196] To Contarini, thought and experience were inseparable, forming one whole that he sometimes

189. Ibid., 322, lines 14–15.
190. Hünermann lists the leading older scholars in each group in Contarini, *Gegenreformatorische Schriften*, xxi–xxii.
191. Ricca, in Prodi, "I colloqui di Ratisbona," 227–29.
192. Rückert, *Theologische Entwicklung*, 96–106, tries to account for both the similarities and differences in the theory of justification of the two men. Walter Lipgens, *Kardinal Johannes Gropper (1503–1559) und die Anfänge der katholischen Reform in Deutschland* (Münster i.W.: Aschendorff, 1951), 194, believes that Contarini's ideas are derived from Gropper.
193. *GC*, 661–69.
194. Ricca, in "I colloqui di Ratisbona," 229–31.
195. Rückert, *Theologische Entwicklung*, 108, asserts that Contarini lacked élan and the power of thinking systematically: "Was ihm fehlte, war Schwung und war systematische Kraft." This judgment is echoed in attenuated form by von Loewenich, *Duplex iustitia*, 47: "Als systematischer Theologe mag Contarini enttäuschen; als Mensch und Christ bleibt er uns ehrwürdig. Das religiöse Element war in ihm stärker als die theologische Gestaltungskraft."
196. Jedin, "Ein 'Turmerlebnis,'" 129–30. Mackensen, "Contarini's Theological Role," follows Jedin.

struggled to express in the technical language of theology he had learned as a student. Yet beyond words was his absolute conviction that we are justified by faith in Christ, about which he had written eloquently in 1523[197] and to which he clung unwaveringly thereafter. His experience, together with his knowledge of at least some of the writings by the northern reformers, made it impossible for him to remain content with a purely Thomistic explanation of the process of justification. He tried to break through the restrictive terminology of Scholasticism without having a new language in which to express himself. Thus his tract is at once traditional and objective in form and personal and subjective in content. He uses the familiar terms weighed down with accretions of meaning developed over the centuries. Nevertheless, he sometimes is able to invest those terms with his own spirituality and the living, ardent piety that he poured into the proverbial old wineskins where they could not be contained.

When subjected to analysis Contarini's treatise is bound to strike the reader as unclear.[198] One reason is his inability to reconcile Thomistic and Lutheran theology.[199] But another reason surfaces as well: Contarini's tendency to escape from verbal controversy into a religious feeling that to him is stronger than scholastic logic because based on the authenticity of his emotions.[200] Already in his famous letter to Giustiniani of 24 April 1511 he had written in fervent tones about Christ as the head of those who want to unite themselves with him as his members.[201] Later, the Pauline language of "putting on Christ," "dying with Christ," and "rising with Christ" becomes Contarini's. Especially clear expressions of his emotional bent are found in a letter to Pighius that repeatedly mentions our being "grafted into Christ," and that ends with this affirmation: "I flee all contentions more than

197. To Giustiniani, in Jedin, "Contarini und Camaldoli," 67 (letter 30).

198. Loewenich, *Duplex iustitia*, 46.

199. Zur Mühlen, "Einigung," 350, discusses the tension between them which Contarini does not solve. Rückert, *Theologische Entwicklung*, 105, thinks that Contarini unsuccessfully tried to "give expression to ideas that were at home in Lutheranism and that were among its most important strengths, within [the structure of] Catholic dogma, which was shaped starting with entirely different foundations." Otto Hermann Pesch, *Die Theologie der Rechtfertigung bei Martin Luther und Thomas von Aquin* (Mainz: Matthias-Grünewald Verlag, 1967), argues for a basic agreement between the two positions. But reflecting on these issues four centuries later, in an atmosphere of ecumensim, is an entirely different matter from having to deal with them in the thick of things, as Contarini did.

200. Rückert, *Theologische Entwicklung*, 88–90, first noticed Contarini's "Ansätze einer Christusmystik," citing some very brief passages in support.

201. Jedin, "Contarini und Camaldoli," 14 (letter 2).

hell, especially those with friends."[202] Contarini did not have the habits of mind or the ready language of the controversialist. He was at his best when discussing his ideas and feelings with like-minded men who did not require philosophical and theological precision in order to be persuaded. When pitted against the likes of Eck or Melanchthon in debate, he simply could not hold his own.

The *Epistola de iustificatione* should not, however, be read as if it proved Contarini's shortcomings as a systematic theologian. He shared the ideas of eminent Catholic theologians like Pighius and Gropper, who sought answers to the question of justification not so much in scholastic formulations but in the thought of St. Augustine. Gropper's *Enchiridion*, published in 1538, was enthusiastically received in Italy by men with considerable theological training, including Pole, Giberti, and Cortese.[203] The general of the Augustinians, Cardinal Seripando, defended double justification at the Council of Trent, and had the support of several theologians.[204] It would be a mistake to think that only the theologically inexpert were proponents of double justification.

Contarini's treatise should be read primarily as an important document in the history of pre-Tridentine Catholicism.[205] With his concept of inherent justice Contarini argued for man's freedom of consent to divine grace, while his explanation of imputed justice affirmed the centrality of Christ's sacrifice for the believing Christian. He sensed the unresolved tension between the formality of theological discourse and the reality of Christian experience, and opened Catholic theology to the possibility of a less technical as well as more personal understanding of the teaching about justification.[206] That teaching would be accessible to

202. *Reg.*, 350 (Inedita, no. 88).

203. Jedin, *Trient* 1:298. Also Cortese's letter to Contarini, San Benedetto, 4 July 1540, in Cortese, *Gregorii Cortesii omnia* 1:132.

204. Besides McCue, "Double Justification," see also Stephan Ehses, "Johannes Groppers Rechtfertigungslehre auf dem Konzil von Trient," *Römische Quartalschrift* 20 (1906): 187; and P. Paz, "La doctrine de la double justice au Concile de Trente," *Ephemerides theologicae Lovanienses* 30 (1954): 5–53.

205. In my judgment, McCue, "Double Justification," 39, offers the most sensible interpretation of this doctrine: "The doctrine of double justification is not so much an alternative theological proposal as it is a complaint about the way that theology as it had been practiced within the Latin church for four centuries was unable in principle to express some of the most obvious truths about the Christian life and experience."

206. Calvin, who was at Regensburg together with the Strassburg delegation, and who was hostile to the colloquy from the beginning, wrote to Farel after the agreement on article 5: "You will marvel when you read the copy [of the article on justification]... that our adversaries have conceded so much. For they have committed themselves to the essentials of what is our true teaching. Nothing is to be found in it which does not stand

laymen, and only incidentally also very close to Protestant ideas simply because it was valid for all believers. Agreement on this doctrine he considered a major step toward the restoration of the seamless tunic of Christ, the unity of all Christians.

The day of 3 May 1541 was the highpoint of the Regensburg colloquy, a moment in which better relations between Catholics and Protestants seemed for a short while not merely conceivable but genuinely possible. A generation earlier, Luther's ninety-five theses had opened the ever-widening rift between the confessions. Now Contarini had high hopes that the colloquy would succeed in building a bridge between the two Christian camps, which for the first time since 1517 were drawing closer together rather than farther apart.

The End of a Dream

An ominous indication of what lay ahead came from the reactions of Melanchthon and Eck to article 5. The former called it "laboriously patched together" and accused the Catholics of having tried to use subterfuge to deceive the Protestants.[207] Eck, for his part, did not want to sign it until Granvelle urgently pressed him to do so.[208] Despite misgivings, however, the talks continued while answers to reports sent to Rome and Wittenberg were awaited.

The debate proceeded to article 6, on the church and its authority in interpreting the Scriptures. From Contarini's account it appears that the collocutors circled around the topic like the proverbial cats around the hot porridge. The issue before them was whether councils can err. "In order not to delay the rest [of the articles] or to exasperate their [the Protestants'] minds further at this point, [article 6] remained unresolved and its discussion was deferred until the other matters are concluded," Contarini wrote to Cardinal Farnese.[209] The colloquy

---

in our writings. I know that you would prefer a more explicit exposition and in this you are at one with myself. But if you consider with what sort of men we have to deal, you will acknowledge that a great deal has been achieved" (in Matheson, *Contarini at Regensburg*, 109).

207. Melanchthon's report to the Elector of Saxony, in *Corpus Reformatorum* 4:421.

208. *GC*, 622. Morone reported on 3 May to Cardinal Farnese that Melanchthon and Eck were difficult; see Dittrich, "Nuntiaturberichte Morone's," 453–54.

209. Dispatch of 4 May 1541, in Pastor, "Correspondenz," 375.

touched on the next seven articles before beginning deliberations on the fourteenth, dealing with the sacrament of the Eucharist.

Soon serious disagreements surfaced. The very men whom Contarini had hoped to "induce to follow the right road" with divine help "and with reason and kindness"[210] now resolutely rejected his insistence that the word *transubstantiation* be added to any discussion of the sacrament of the altar. Nineteen Protestant theologians held a meeting on 8 May; Calvin, who was among them, summarized their conclusion: "It was the opinion of all that transubstantiation was a fictitious thing, that reservation [of the host] was superstitious and its adoration idolatrous, or at least dangerous, since it is done without the word of God."[211] Contarini drew a line between subjects that should and should not be discussed: "Our aim was to preserve truth and to agree in truth, which in this article was very clear, having been declared in the words of Christ and St. Paul, explained by all the ancient and modern doctors of the church, Greek as well as Latin, . . . and defined by a most famous council under Innocent III [the Fourth Lateran]."[212] There was nothing more to add as far as he was concerned; the doctrine of transubstantiation was there for all to see. "We shall stand firm in the truth and see what God wishes to do" is the resigned ending of his report.

But Contarini's second thoughts are shown in another letter of the same date. He confessed that on further reflection it appeared that

this whole issue of the authority of councils is closely connected with the question of papal power in which there are strong disagreements among Catholic doctors. The entire University of Paris holds that a council is above the pope, while others hold the opposite view, namely that the pope is above the council,

210. Dispatch of 3 May 1541, in ibid., 373.

211. Joachim Mehlhausen, "Die Abendmahlsformel des Regensburger Buches," *Studien zur Geschichte und Theologie der Reformation: Festschrift für Ernst Bizer*, ed. Luise Abramowski and J. F. Gerhard Goeters (Neukirchen-Vluyn: Neukirchener Verlag, 1969), 193. For the discussions among Protestant theologians, see pp. 192–95. See also Pierre Fraenkel, "Les Protestants et le problème de la transubstantiation au Colloque de Ratisbonne: documents et arguments du 5 au 10 mai 1541," *Oecumenica* 3 (1968): 70–115.

212. To Cardinal Farnese, 9 May 1541, in Pastor, "Correspondenz," 377. I agree with Jedin, "An welchen Gegensätzen," 54, in thinking that for Contarini the main issue was not the the definition of the Eucharist or the wording of the decree as promulgated by the Fourth Lateran Council, but the principle of the church's *magisterium*: "Es handelt sich für ihn also nicht in erster Linie um den materiellen Inhalt der Lehre, sondern um das Formalprinzip, das kirchliche Lehramt." For the definition of the Fourth Lateran Council, see H. Denzinger, *Enchiridion symbolorum*, 33d ed. (Freiburg i.B.: Herder, 1965), no. 802.

which opinion in my judgment is more in conformance with the text of the gospel; nevertheless there is great controversy here.[213]

Fearing that by an examination of these issues "we will enter into chaos from which only God knows how we can extricate ourselves," Contarini wanted the collocutors to proceed by confining themselves to general statements concerning this matter as well as that of papal authority. He offered "this good and true formula without any prejudice, which avoids all difficulty: . . . that Christ instituted the hierarchy of the church by putting bishops in their dioceses, [as well as] archbishops, patriarchs, and primates, and above all of them, to preserve church unity, he constituted the Roman pontiff, giving him universal jurisdiction over the entire church, as can be clearly read in the gospel." The texts he adduced were Matthew 16:19, John 21:17, and Luke 22:32, without realizing how far apart Catholic and Protestant theologians were in their exegesis of these passages, which to him admitted of only one interpretation.

Contarini adopted the strategy of a practiced diplomat: he tried to postpone consideration of difficult topics by offering blandly formulated general statements on which both sides could agree for the time being. Clearly, he was hoping that agreement on a large enough number of articles might create a certain momentum that would enable the collocutors to tackle even the thorniest outstanding issues with goodwill toward each other. His chief contribution at this point lay not in some sort of fatuous optimism, but in the example he gave to the Catholic side by his willingness to see fellow Christians rather than enemies in the Lutherans.[214]

The strategy of postponement did not work. Ironically, it was Contarini himself who moved against it in the course of discussions with Gropper and Pflug on 13 May. Perturbed by the omission of the word *transubstantiation* in the revision of article 14 by the two Catholic theologians, Contarini insisted that it be included. Moreover, his attitude toward Protestants began to change in an almost startling fashion.

I read the writing of the Protestants [their draft of article 14] by which it is manifest that they want to adhere to their erroneous idea that the substance of the bread remains in the Eucharist after consecration. So I told [Gropper and Pflug] that I clearly realized that we differed from them [the Protestants] concerning the meaning [of the Eucharist] while difficulties are made about

---

213. To Cardinal Farnese, in Pastor, "Correspondenz," 380.
214. Pfnür, "Einigung," 75, rightly calls attention to this important element.

the words. I will never consent to what is an agreement only in appearance, or make the sense of the church ambiguous.[215]

Contarini reiterated these words to Granvelle, who begged him not to disrupt the colloquy by his insistence on the term *transubstantiation*. But the legate stood his ground, telling Granvelle: "Now that I saw that the difference between us concerned the meaning and not the words, I will never depart one iota from Catholic truth, or place it in doubt behind a screen of words." In no case should the word *transubstantiation* be omitted, because if that were to happen, "we would do great harm to the truth and to ourselves. His Lordship [Granvelle] tried very hard to calm me by telling me of his hard work and the danger [in which the colloquy was]. I answered him that I sympathized with him, because he truly was making an all-out effort, but one cannot injure the truth."[216]

As a result of Contarini's insistence, the word *transubstantiation* was added to the Catholic draft. Granvelle continued to mediate, and managed to get a statement from the Protestants that they were willing to postpone the discussion of transubstantiation until the end of the colloquy. But Contarini had come to see the futility of the strategy that he himself had recommended only a short time before. Postponing difficult issues could not mask the fact that the two sides had fundamentally different points of departure in their theology of the Eucharist. "I see the Protestants very obstinate and pertinacious, and have no hope, unless God performs a miracle, that concord among us will be achieved," he wrote to Cardinal Farnese. "I trust in God, and shall remain firm in the truth and proceed with God's help in such a way that the world will never be able to accuse the Apostolic See of disturbing concord and peace, [but will see it as] the preserver of Christian dogmas."[217]

Contarini's stance hardened further when, on 14 May, the theologians began to discuss the sacrament of penance. Here the Protestants did not agree with the Catholics about the necessity of confessing mortal sins, even though they declared that confession was useful. At this point Contarini did not wait for more specific information; he began to suspect the Protestants of actively seeking words that could be interpreted in ambiguous ways. Fearing that the emperor was not well

215. To Cardinal Farnese, 13 May 1541, in Pastor, "Correspondenz," 385, corrected by ASVat, Arm. 62, vol. 36, fol. 89v.

216. ASVat, Arm. 62, vol. 36, fol. 90r; Pastor, "Correspondenz," 385.

217. ASVat, Arm. 62, vol. 36, fol. 90v; Pastor, "Corresondenz," 386.

informed and therefore might support "false concord," he requested an audience at which he arrived with a written memorial that underscored his oral presentation to Charles V. The report of this audience shows not only the profound and rapid changes in Contarini's view of the Protestants, but also the beginning of the emperor's changing attitude toward the papal legate.

Belief in three articles of faith was necessary for Christians, Contarini argued: the Trinity, the incarnation of the Divine Word, and the Eucharist. They were fundamental, and any agreement presupposed their acceptance by all parties. Contarini urged the emperor to use his authority over Protestant theologians and princes to make them declare their adherence to these fundamental articles. Here he thought like a Venetian and conceived of imperial power in Germany as similar to that of the government of Venice, which freely issued commands or prohibitions to its citizens. Charles V did not accept Contarini's advice, as the latter reports:

His Majesty heard me attentively, then answered that I did well to fulfill my duties because he himself was not a theologian. Therefore he had requested the pope to send someone here whom he could trust, as His Holiness then did. He added that Monsignor Granvelle had reported to him that the difference [between the theologians] lay in one word concerning the Eucharist, namely transubstantiation, and that the Protestants were willing to institute confession among their population because experience had shown them how useful and necessary it was for the maintenance of obedience and the prevention of many scandals. It seemed best to him to proceed and get from them the most that was possible, and then at the end to treat the articles where there were differences. The necessary provisions must be made, since breaking up the negotiations was easy and could always be done. And he went on at some length about such a break.[218]

Charles V was obviously annoyed by Contarini's insistence and probably agreed with Granvelle's view, as reported by Morone, that "transubstantiation was a difficult matter that pertained only to the learned and did not touch the people, for whom it was enough to believe that the body of Christ was in the sacrament and that it should be adored, remaining there until it was received."[219] But there was a veiled reproach in the emperor's words as well: he had trusted Contarini, and the legate was beginning to let him down. Yet for Contarini, there

218. Contarini to Cardinal Farnese, 15 May 1541, ASVat, Arm. 62, vol. 36, fol. 92v; Pastor, "Correspondenz," 388–89.

219. Morone to Cardinal Farnese, 29 May 1541, in Dittrich, "Nuntiaturberichte Morone's," 471.

could be no change in the doctrinal foundation on which the structure of the church rested. He insisted on the word *transubstantiation* because he considered the question about the nature of the Eucharist to have been settled centuries before by a council with the authority to do so. He literally could not imagine how the Protestants could slight tradition, or how they could justify picking and choosing among conciliar decrees.

Contarini's suspicions of the Protestants were reinforced by the intransigence of Melanchthon,[220] who was anxious to please both Luther and the elector of Saxony by not appearing to be "soft" on Catholicism. Even Granvelle became impatient with Melanchthon and the arguments he used to bolster the theological stance of the Protestants.[221] The meetings of the collocutors continued until 22 May, but it was obvious to both sides that they were not moving toward agreement on the articles considered following the discussion of the Eucharist. On 31 May the Regensburg Book and separate articles drawn up by the Protestants were presented to the emperor, and the colloquy was formally over.

Contarini remained in Regensburg in the awkward position of a lame-duck legate until the end of the diet and the departure of the emperor for Italy on 29 July. The colloquy had concluded before the replies to the agreed-upon articles arrived from Wittenberg and Rome. Interestingly, Luther did not reject article 5 as such, but worried that it created wrong impressions and left the door open to further confusion.[222] He thought that the necessary first step should have been a confession of guilt by the Catholics followed by the repudiation of the "abominations [Greuel]" concerning justification which their theologians had taught for centuries.[223] In brief, he mistrusted their motives and saw them as deceivers bent on interpreting justification in a sense contrary to the truth of the gospel; he ultimately rejected the whole Regensburg Book as merely a new patch on an old cloak. Elector Johann Friedrich of Saxony was just as blunt. He wrote to Melanchthon

220. Augustijn, *Godsdienstgesprekken*, 93–95, with full bibliographical references.

221. Contarini to Cardinal Farnese, 16 May 1541, ASVat. Arm. 62, vol. 36, fols. 93v–94r: "Monsr di Granvela per quanto mi ha detto disse al Melantone: Io non sono theologo, ma le vostre ragioni et authorità mi pajono tanto frivole, che non mi movono un capello."

222. Martin Luther, *Werke, Briefwechsel*, vol. 9 (Weimar: Hermann Böhlaus Nachfolger, 1941), 410 (no. 3617) and 436–45 (no. 3629).

223. Pfnür, "Einigung," 67. For a summary of Luther's reaction to the colloquy, see pp. 64–68.

that "those who want accord, should seek accord with God and his word. . . . Let those who want to deal with patchwork be damned."[224] Calvin, however, though little more than an observer in Regensburg, considered that the article contained the "essence of true doctrine."[225]

On 29 May, two crucial documents were written. The first was Contarini's most personal letter yet to Cardinal Farnese; the other was Farnese's reply to the legate's report of 3 May concerning the agreement on article 5. Contarini's letter with suggestions about the course of action the papacy should take in Germany is the most revealing of all his dispatches. Here he spoke not ex officio, but as an anguished Christian. Farnese's letter was official and peremptory. When read successively, these two letters reveal the gulf that separated Contarini, the advocate of church reform, from Farnese and his curial advisors, practical bureaucrats whose priorities were the preservation of papal supremacy and victory over the Protestants.

Contarini expressed his deeply felt convictions in a passionate plea as the pope's good servant whose duty it is to give counsel. The Lutheran heresy, he warned, has taken root in the minds not only of Protestants, but of all the German people. Even if concord were to be achieved in this diet, only the foundations would have been laid of a structure that had yet to be built, namely a real reformation in Germany: "Just as it is impossible to live in a house which consists only of its foundation, so nothing will have been achieved if a serious reformation is not erected [on this foundation]."[226] Because Protestantism was something new, and because people avidly hanker after novelty, the new confession was spreading rapidly, especially because it had removed a series of obligations such as confession, fasting, attendance at mass, or abstinence from meat. In order to counteract Protestantism in Germany, three things were necessary. First, no territory that was presently Catholic should be allowed to join the Protestant League of Schmalkalden. Rather, the Catholic League must be strengthened. Second, the German bishops must be exemplary in their own lives and, like the Protestants, must instruct their people by using good preachers

224. Quoted in Augustijn, *Godsdienstgesprekken*, 115.

225. *Ioannis Calvini opera quae supersunt omnia*, vol. 11 (Braunschweig, 1872), 215 (no. 308). See also Wilhelm H. Neuser, "Calvins Beitrag zu den Religionsgesprächen von Hagenau, Worms und Regensburg (1540/41)," in Abramowski and Goeters (eds.), *Studien zur Geschichte und Theologie der Reformation*, 235.

226. ASVat, Arm. 62, vol. 36, fols. 102v–103r. The first part of this letter is printed in *Reg.*, 333–334 (Inedita, no. 71), from an incorrect copy, while the second and longer, with many inaccuracies, is in Pastor, "Correspondenz," 474–76.

and teachers.[227] "If only, God willing, certain Italians whom I know were familiar with the German language, I believe that they could bear much fruit!" he added.[228]

Contarini suddenly reached back in memory to his student years in Padua, echoing his teacher Pomponazzi: "Today we are alive, and tomorrow dead. The life of man, let alone of the Christian, consists in doing one's duty... as if we did not expect any reward or punishment in the next life. Speaking like philosophers, we must perform our task and not fail to do our duty, as natural reason tells us and as every philosopher would say, basing this idea on principles of natural reason."[229] How much more Christians should do! Like an Old Testament prophet, Contarini castigated the shortcomings of the Catholic prelates by citing Deuteronomy on the subject of the ungrateful, fattened, and bloated people that had forgotten God.[230] The letter ends with his third recommendation: the pope should grant Germans the right to receive communion under both species. This would be a most useful concession bearing on a rite to which the German people attributed great importance, and for which there were precedents not only among the Greeks but in western Europe as well.

The letter from Rome arrived in Regensburg on 8 June. It was drafted by Cervini and signed by Cardinal Farnese.[231] Despite its

227. Contarini already reported that the archbishop of Mainz had praised the excellent Protestant schools in Germany: "Imperoche non essendo scuole appresso Cattolici, et all'incontro essendone buone et copiose appresso Protestanti, tutta la gioventù di Germania s'instituisce nelle scuole loro, et cosi dalli primi anni bevono il veleno" (to Cardinal Farnese, 4 June 1541, in Pastor, "Correspondenz," 336).

228. ASVat, Arm. 62, vol. 36, fol. 103r. Cardauns (*NB* 7:xxiv) thinks that Contarini has the Jesuits in mind here, while Pastor ("Correspondenz," 475n.2) opts for members of the Oratory of Divine Love. The first hypothesis is unlikely; the second is based on the erroneous idea that Contarini was a member of the Oratory. Contarini was most likely thinking of outstanding preachers like Ochino whom he knew. On the ignorance of German among Italian prelates, see Barbara M. Hallman, "Practical Aspects of Roman Diplomacy in Germany, 1517–1541," *Journal of Medieval and Renaissance Studies* 10 (1980): 193–206.

229. ASVat, Arm. 62, vol. 36, fol. 102v.

230. As he frequently does, Contarini cites from memory. Here he refers to the Song of Moses, specifically Deut. 32:15, 18.

231. William V. Hudon, "Papal, Episcopal, and Secular Authority in the Work of Marcello Cervini," *Cristianesimo nella storia* 9 (1988): 498n.15, calls this document "a long reproof/instruction drafted by Cervini on behalf of Alessandro Farnese" and mentions that it "was actually signed by Niccolo Ardinghello on Farnese's behalf." Matheson, *Contarini at Regensburg*, 151, cites it as "Ardinghelli/Contarini." Both use the text in *Ep. Poli* 3:ccxxxi–ccxl (not ccxxx, as erroneously printed), which is headed "Niccolò Ardinghello a nome del Cardinal Farnese al Card. Contarini Legato in Germania." From this it might appear that the task of answering Contarini was left to a

conventional epistolary style and polite phrases, it contained a stinging rebuke of the legate's ideas and actions.[232] Contarini was told that the article on justification was not read in consistory, since the pope wanted only a few persons to see it. The legate was accused of failing to exercise proper care to keep proceedings at the colloquy secret. Paul III neither approved nor rejected article 5, as if it did not warrant further discussion. "I am notifying you," Farnese continued, "that all those who saw it are of the opinion that even supposing that its sense were Catholic, the words could have been clearer. Therefore [they think] that in this important article ambiguity and mere semblance of concord were not avoided, which Your Reverence so prudently rejected and abhorred in the two succeeding articles on the Eucharist and confession."[233] Contarini was enjoined not to approve any article whatsoever, and warned against allowing himself to be carried away in the hope of achieving concord. Everything had to be expressed so clearly in the Catholic sense that even the malice of the adversaries would not be able to misinterpret it. Like a schoolboy, Contarini was instructed not to use ambiguous or novel words that could put clear matters in doubt, and above all not to concede anything to the Protestants.

Still sharper criticism followed. Contarini was taken to task for his dispatch of 9 May in which he had expressed his views of councils and stated that the hierarchy of the church had been instituted directly by Christ. He was reprimanded for both, and told that neither Paul III nor anyone else agreed with him; only the pope had the authority to convoke councils,[234] and he alone as successor of St. Peter was given full power by God.[235] The legate was informed that at the French court he was considered too obsequious to the emperor, and too cold in defense of the truth. Next, he was admonished to supervise his own household more closely, for its members were leaking information to Rome even before his official dispatches could be read in consistory.[236] Contarini, the experienced diplomat and cardinal, was criticized and treated to elementary instructions regarding diplomatic practice.

---

mere secretary. Actually, the original in ASVat, Arm. 64, vol. 20, fols. 83r–90v, makes no mention of Ardinghelli, Farnese's secretary, but is written in the first person and signed by Farnese like all the other letters.

232. Vetter, *Religionsverhandlungen*, 164, rightly writes of the "beleidigende Verächtlichkeit" of this letter.

233. ASVat, Arm. 64, vol. 20, fol. 83v. The text printed in *Ep. Poli* diverges markedly from the manuscript, which I cite. *NB* 7:20 offers only a very few corrections of the printed text.

234. ASVat, Arm. 64, vol. 20, fol. 85v.

235. Ibid., fol. 86v.   236. Ibid., fol. 89r–v.

What had happened? If we examine the reactions of Luther and Cardinal Farnese closely, we notice some remarkable similarities. In both Wittenberg and Rome the main issue was not the accord itself, which had been reached regarding justification, but fear that the other side would misuse the words of article 5, interpreting them in the "wrong" sense. The image of the naive Contarini who could not deal with theological complexity simply is not borne out by the documents. He, along with the collocutors, had believed that the two sides could actually agree on one of the central Christian doctrines. Neither he nor the other theologians merely deceived themselves because of their supposed Erasmian bent into minimizing differences between Catholics and Lutherans, as has been argued,[237] nor were they misled by fuzzy thinking and ill-founded optimism. Something tragic had occurred before the colloquy even opened that would have profound repercussions for the history of Christianity: polemics between the two confessions had reached a point where their leaders were no longer capable of giving the other side the benefit of the doubt.[238] Passions and emotions shaped Catholic attitudes toward "heretics" as much as Protestant ones toward "servants of the Antichrist." After over twenty years of political and ideological conflict, Protestants and Catholics saw each other as enemies, not fellow Christians, and treated each other accordingly. Even apart from theological differences, a psychological wall had been erected between the two confessions. By 1541 it could no longer be breached or removed by six theologians, no matter how learned and full of goodwill, much less by one single papal legate. Neither side could envision making a fresh start at this point. Besides, the aims of the two sides had diverged completely. While Rome now wanted a council convoked by the pope as the best defensive measure against the onslaught of Protestant criticism, the Protestants were still hoping for a reform throughout all of Germany that would build a single Protestant church. The Protestants had succeeded in seizing the initiative, and Rome was deeply concerned.

237. Stupperich, *Humanismus und Wiedervereinigung*, passim.

238. Pfnür, "Einigung," esp. 68 and 75, stresses the importance that the "Verfeindung" of the other side had for both Catholics and Protestants. Augustijn, *Godsdienstgesprekken*, 102, points to the mutual mistrust of the two sides as an important element in the religious colloquies. Peter Vogelsänger, "Ökumenismus im 16. Jahrhundert: zur Geschichte des Religionsgesprächs von Regensburg 1541," in *Unterwegs zur Einheit: Festschrift für Heinrich Stirnimann*, ed. Johannes Brantschen and Pietro Selvatico (Freiburg, Switz., and Freiburg i.B.: Herder, 1980), 647, also discusses the deep-seated mistrust each side had for the other in 1541, and rejects the idea that the theologians hoping for union were naive.

On 8 June, when Cardinal Farnese's letter of 29 May arrived, Contarini was no longer thinking as he had been on 3 May, when he wrote his report about the agreement on article 5. The intervening month had forced him to make important choices and to formulate the reasons for his decisions. The debate about transubstantiation had pushed him into espousing a quite rigid definition of tradition, which he subsequently defended against all comers. But it would be a mistake to consider him as "retreating into curialism" and crumpling before the arrogance of Cardinal Farnese's letters. Rather, he evolved a coherent personal stance the elements of which formed a pattern that would become impossible after Trent.

In his crisp answer to Farnese's strictures, entirely different in tone from his emotional dispatch of 29 May, Contarini first of all reaffirmed a position he would hold and defend until the end of his life: that the agreed-upon article on justification correctly expressed Catholic teaching. Even if the article seemed somewhat obscure, Contarini insisted that its sense was "cattolichissimo" and that not a word in it was ambiguous.[239] Though willing to change words that in Rome might be interpreted in any but a strictly Catholic sense, he unhesitatingly stood by article 5. The accusation against members of his household he dismissed in a sentence or two, proceeding to the more important matter of papal supremacy. Morone and he had not insisted on its discussion once the discord among the collocutors became obvious; however, Contarini intended to follow instructions and try to include a statement about it in the final document.[240] Farnese's reproaches did not have "an almost traumatic effect" on Contarini, nor did he be-

239. To Cardinal Farnese, June 9, ASVat, Arm. 62, vol. 36, fol. 111r: "Quanto all'articulo de iustificatione, fide et operibus, potria essere che a qualch'uno havesse parso un poco oscuro, ma il senso è cattolichissimo, ne vi è clausola overo parola ambigua, cioè che si possa tirare in senso erroneo."

240. Ibid., fol. 112r: "Al Sig. Nuntio [Morone] pareva che non dovendossi fare accordo, minor contraditione che si havesse in quest'articolo de primatu fusse meglio et io sarei stato dell'istesso parere, quando non fussi stato altrimenti avertito, ma a me basta l'obedire." This sentence must be read in conjunction with the preceding folio, 111v, where Contarini clearly states that he did not have specific instructions concerning the discussion of papal supremacy that he could have given to the Catholic collocutors before the Regensburg Book was presented to Charles V. He tried to add a passage to the margin of the text, but Granvelle rejected this because it would seem like a falsification. Nevertheless, Contarini was to include an affirmation of papal supremacy in his presentation to the emperor and in the revision of the text on which several Catholic theologians were working. Hence I translate the quoted sentence as follows: "To the nuncio it seemed that, since there was to be no accord, the less disagreement there was on the article about papal primacy the better. I would have been of the same opinion if I had not been admonished otherwise, but for me it suffices to obey."

come merely "the submissive tool of papal diplomacy," as Matheson thinks.[241]

This can best be seen in his acerbic reply to the French accusation relayed by Farnese that he was cold in defense of the truth. Treating the matter quite deliberately as an afterthought, as if it did not merit more than a passing reference, Contarini expressed his wish that he were indeed cold enough to stop the great conflagration that reached from northern Europe all the way to Italy: "Believe me, Your Reverence, there is no need to add heat, but to bring such cooling as can be brought!"[242] In a clear dig at fanatical Catholics, whether in Rome or Germany, Contarini assured Farnese that those who opposed the Lutherans but were themselves ignorant about the articles on grace, free will, original sin, and faith and justification actually fortified the reputation of the Lutherans and thereby caused their errors to spread further.[243] It is characteristic of Contarini that he continued to voice his personal opinions while acknowledging and accepting the duty of obedience he owed as papal legate.

In this attitude we see the second element of Contarini's stance: his acceptance of the church's authority, whether papal, episcopal, conciliar, or sacerdotal.[244] He agreed with the Thomist conception of the church as the mystical body of Christ, but he also defended the necessity of Roman legal, constitutional, and administrative structures. With all its faults as an organization, the church for him was the means Christ had established to safeguard his message through the magisterium and to dispense grace to the Christian people through the sacraments. The tie that bound the individual member of the church to its hierarchy was obedience. For Contarini, the church was the visible, institutional *ecclesia sacramentorum*, not the *ecclesia abscondita* known only to God.

Contarini's ecclesiology was traditional. Nowhere in his writings is there evidence of disaffection from late medieval conceptions of the nature of the church.[245] He had interiorized the respect for institutions

241. Matheson, *Contarini at Regensburg*, 153. Vetter, *Religionsverhandlungen*, 201, thinks that Contarini gradually became "a tool of others, without a will of his own" (*ein willenloses Werkzeug anderer*).

242. ASVat, Arm. 62, vol. 36, fol. 112v. He wrote on 12 June to the nuncio in France on the same subject in milder terms; see *Monumenti Beccadelli* 1(2):178.

243. ASVat, Arm. 62, vol. 36, fol. 111v.

244. Klaus Ganzer, "Zum Kirchenverständnis Gasparo Contarinis," *Würzburger Diözesangeschichtsblätter* 35–36 (1974): esp. 249–57.

245. The considerable differences among late medieval conceptions of the church are shown by Friedrich Merzbacher, "Wandlungen des Kirchenbegriffs im Spätmit-

that his upbringing as a Venetian gentleman had instilled in him, and he firmly believed that institutions made human life civilized in the secular sphere while giving it direction and guidance in the religious. His commitment to upholding order in both spheres, together with his understanding of the role of a papal legate as quite literally that of an intermediary, led to Contarini's sometimes misunderstood phrase "to me it suffices to obey," meaning that he was willing to subordinate his own views to the decisions of the pope, once they were made. But while these decisions were being debated, the legate felt quite free to inform Paul III through Cardinal Farnese of his own opinions. For this reason his vivid letters still make good reading after almost half a millennium, and remain more accessible evidence of his thought than his formal and for the most part dry treatises.

That Contarini was not regarded as unconditionally submissive to Rome can be seen in Cardinal Farnese's dispatch of 14 June. On its surface, this is a straightforward set of instructions accompanying a letter of credit for fifty thousand scudi to be used for the Catholic League in Germany. But extraordinary care went into its composition, as shown by two drafts annotated by Cardinal Cervini that preceded the final version sent to the legate.[246] Contarini is given detailed orders on how to explain the pope's mind to Charles V. The emperor and the German Catholic princes must be convinced that Paul III was willing to spend as much money as the league and the defense of true religion required, and even to lay down his own life if necessary. While he did not want to be either the initiator or a counselor of armed conflict, he went on record as fully supporting the actions of Charles V that benefited Catholicism.[247]

---

telalter," *Zeitschrift der Savigny-Stiftung für Rechtsgeschichte* 39 (1953): 274–361. See also Jedin, "Die Entwicklung des Kirchenbegriffs im 16. Jahrhundert," in *Kirche des Glaubens* 2:7–16.

246. Two drafts (not three, as stated in *Reg.*, 199n.1) and the fair copy are in ASF, Carte Cerviniane, filza 3, nos. 25–27, fols. 48r–65v. Theodor Brieger, "Nic. Ardinghelli im Namen des Papstes an Contarini, Rom, 15. Juni 1541: die beiden ersten Entwürfe dieser Depesche, vom 10. Juni," *Zeitschrift für Kirchengeschichte* 5 (1882): 595–604, compared the first and second drafts. The fair copy agrees with the version printed in *Ep. Poli* 3:ccxl (misnumbered ccxxx)–ccxlix, except for minor details and two matters of substance: the absence of the last three paragraphs, and the dating, which is "xiiii" in the manuscript but "XV" in the published text. This text is corrected in *NB* 7:20–22 on the basis of yet another draft found in Archivio di Stato, Naples, Carte Farnesiane, 700C. The copy actually sent to Contarini on 15 June and dated the previous day (ASVat, Arm. 64, vol. 20, fols. 96r–105r) is a copy of the fair copy now in Florence, mentioned above. An excerpt from the Vatican copy is printed in *CT* 4:194–96 (no. 150). I cite according to the printed version in *Ep. Poli*, as corrected from the Vatican copy.

247. *Ep. Poli* 3:ccxliii.

There is no hint that Cardinal Farnese and his advisors even for a moment seriously discussed the merits of "the damned opinions" of the Protestants. Contarini was warned that there could be no toleration of the articles not agreed upon in the colloquy, because faith is indivisible and cannot be accepted piecemeal. Because concord was not achieved, toleration was not allowed, and war was difficult and dangerous, only one course of action remained: the convocation of a general council.[248] Paul III instructed his legate to counteract demands for a German council in German lands that would deal with the issues Luther had raised. A valid council could only be universal and summoned by the pope. From this point on, Contarini had no more room to maneuver or negotiate. His orders were unequivocal, and as a practiced organization man he understood that fact clearly.

When compared with the drama of the colloquy and its culmination in the agreement on article 5, the two following months seem anticlimactic, especially the weeks after 21 June, when this last instruction arrived and effectively tied Contarini's hands. Even so, his letters from this period remain lively and important. The most interesting aspects of his correspondence during June and July 1541 are his steadfastness in defending his ideas about justification and his changing view of the religious and political situation in Germany.

Ludwig Cardauns, editor of the *Nuntiaturberichte* covering the period of the Diet of Regensburg, thinks that after the end of the colloquy Contarini had a complete change of heart of the sort that "disappointments cause in people of such disposition,"[249] such that he not only despaired of Germany but also threw in the towel by drawing closer to the most outspoken enemies of religious concord, the dukes of Bavaria. In this interpretation, Contarini's personality explains the change from the irenic legate to the stern spokesman for papal political aims. For Matheson, Contarini abandoned the idea of reunion in the sense of a "return of the Protestants to the true Faith. Now . . . the keyword is consolidation, reform seen as a weapon *against* the Protestants." Because of his curialism, he went over to the Counter-Reformation, speaking the "language of Aleandro and Carafa in Rome, of Loyola's new movement, of St. Theresa in Spain."[250]

In actuality, Contarini fully understood that his conciliatory approach

248. Ibid., ccxlv.

249. *NB* 7:XXII: "Der Ausgang hat in Contarini einen Gesinnungswechsel erzeugt, wie ihn Enttäuschungen bei Menschen von solcher Veranlagung hervorzurufen pflegen."

250. Matheson, *Contarini at Regensburg*, 164.

to Protestants had not worked. Neither his personality nor his "curial-ism" explain the new tone in his letters, but the realism of a practiced diplomat does. After it became clear that concord could not be achieved, his first objective was to defend the papacy from accusations of having sabotaged the colloquy. The second was to encourage a defensive Catholic League. Since the dukes of Bavaria were its leaders, he obviously had to discuss the matter with them. Finally, he hoped to influence the emperor so as to prevent the acceptance of Granvelle's project of toleration. The latter proposed that the sixteen articles dis-cussed by the collocutors should be accepted by both sides, and the others tolerated for the time being.[251] Charles V was sufficiently an-noyed by the lack of any solution to the German religious situation to seriously consider granting the Protestants provisional freedom to practice their religion,[252] something the legate was instructed to pre-vent by insisting on the necessity of convoking a general council that would examine the issues raised by the Protestant reformers.

The pursuit of these three objectives was the major theme of his correspondence. The minor, but recurring and insistent, theme was something else: his continued defense of the formula on justification. If his tone concerning the Protestants became sharp, and if at times he even condemned their views, he never wavered in his certainty that the agreement on justification was in accordance with Catholic teaching.

Gradually his friends' reactions to the formula he had championed began to reach him. One of the first to write was Pole. While express-ing his joy that concord had been achieved, he used rather noncom-mittal language that veiled his own views: "What I think about this you already know, and it is not necessary to say more about it."[253] When read attentively, Pole's letter reveals his discomfort with the Regens-burg formula, despite fulsome but very general praise. The reason for this ambiguous stance was twofold: Pole thought the formula not incontrovertibly scriptural and worried about being too closely associ-ated with it.[254] Contarini had counted on him and was let down when

---

251. Augustijn, *Godsdienstgesprekken*, 113–14.

252. Contarini to Cardinal Farnese, Regensburg, 15 June 1541, ASVat, Arm. 64, vol. 36, fol. 115v, which corrects Pastor, "Corresondenz," 483.

253. Capranica, 17 May 1541, *Ep. Poli* 3:25. A month later Pole continued his cau-tious tone and expressed the wish that Contarini had faced a more aggressive adversary so that he would have been constrained to develop his ideas more fully, silencing those who opposed him. Pole in a tactful way in effect said that he, too, was not convinced of the scriptural basis of Contarini's arguments (ibid., 27).

254. Fenlon, *Heresy and Obedience*, 56, 61.

Pole remained in Capranica, his summer residence, as the college of cardinals was about to discuss the agreement on justification.[255] Pole had used poor health as a face-saving excuse for his absence. Instead of going himself, Pole sent his friend Alvise Priuli to Rome to sound out curial opinion about the concord reached in Regensburg.

Priuli contacted the most influential papal advisors, about whose judgment Pole was naturally anxious. The first was Carafa, who objected to the term *inherent justice* that had been used, considering it novel and likely to be deliberately misused by the heretics. The absence of the term *merit* troubled him as well. Priuli tried to the best of his ability to explain what he took to be Contarini's meaning, but the most he achieved was Carafa's admission that "good and Catholic sense" could be given to everything that had been agreed upon. Carafa warned, however, that the Protestants were certain to interpret the article on justification in a manner contrary to that of the Catholics.[256] Cervini thought the same. Aleandro was radically skeptical about the whole matter, believing that even if accord were reached on all points, Germany would not be pacified merely because theologians had reached an agreement.[257] Sadoleto, who was generally in sympathy with Contarini's ideas, eventually wrote from his residence in Carpentras to reject article 5 as too Lutheran and a distortion of Catholic doctrine.[258] Only two prelates at the papal court took the legate's part: Bembo, who came to the aid of his countryman with more goodwill than theological acumen,[259] and Fregoso, who defended Contarini strongly in consistory.[260] But his voice was not decisive; he soon left

255. To Bembo, Regensburg, 28 June 1541, *Reg.*, 341 (Inedita, no.78): "Desidereria che il R.mo Polo fusse in Roma a questi tempi et a questi manegi, in vero non poteva essere absente a tempo piu incomodo. Io lo haveria excitato a ritornare, si non havessi habuto rispecto al periculo della sanita sua."

256. Priuli to Beccadelli, Rome, 20 May 1541, in Carlo Dionisotti, "Monumenti Beccadelli," in *Miscellanea Pio Paschini*, ed. A. Casamassa (Rome: Facultas Theologica Pontificii Athenaei Lateranensis, 1949), 2:266.

257. Ibid., 268.

258. Douglas, *Sadoleto*, 158–60; and Simoncelli, *Evangelismo italiano*, 109–11.

259. Paolo Simoncelli, "Pietro Bembo e l'evangelismo italiano," *Critica storica* 15 (1978): 19–25; and idem, *Evangelismo italiano*, 112–13. Gigliola Fragnito, "Evangelismo e intransigenti nei difficili equilibri del pontificato farnesiano," *Rivista di storia e letteratura religiosa* 25 (1989): 46, argues that Bembo believed in justification by faith alone and was in full sympathy with Contarini.

260. Bembo to Contarini, Rome, 27 May 1541, in *Monumenti Beccadelli* 1(2):169; and 13 July 1541, ibid., 183. Nino Sernini to Cardinal Ercole Gonzaga, Rome, 1 July 1541: "esso [Fregoso] nel concistorio ha sempre favorite le cose fatte dal Contarino in la dieta di Ratisbona" (ASM, Carteggio Gonzaga, Esteri 1541). Possibly Fregoso had a

Rome for his diocese of Gubbio, where he died on 22 July. As a result, Bembo remained the lone champion of Contarini's views on justification at the papal court.

By mid-July, though, these views really no longer mattered except as expressions of his individual belief. Although justification had not proved to be the basic issue at the colloquy after all, for Contarini personally it remained crucial, as can be seen by his repeated defense of article 5 even after Farnese's insulting letter of 29 May had reached him on 8 June. Although he participated in a new committee that the emperor appointed to go over the Regensburg Book once more and examine it from the Catholic perspective,[261] Contarini had no second thoughts about the formula on justification. The most he admitted was that there was room for clarification and amplification of some passages of the Regensburg Book. In an unusual display of irritation with "learned men" in Rome who objected to the absence of the term *merit* in article 5, he attempted to explain to Cardinal Farnese the reasons for its omission. His theologically rather amateurish explanation hinges on the idea that if the word *merit* were introduced, the greatness of God's free gift of eternal life would be diminished. "Our sense and their [the Protestants'] sense is the same, but it did not seem to us necessary to force on them the term merit, so we left it out,"[262] he wrote in the vain hope of silencing his critics.

In fact, he knew that they were becoming more insistent. Already on 27 May Bembo had informed him that his views on justification had been the cause of some disagreement among the cardinals, but that he should not worry about that. "You know the character of the senate [the college of cardinals] and the way people are: there are as many opinions as there are individuals. The one among them who was most in your debt was least willing to pay."[263] Bembo did not want to

---

low opinion of his fellow cardinals. Ochino, admittedly not a reliable source, years later reported Fregoso's statement that on the day before the matter was discussed in consistory, at least thirty of the fifty cardinals did not know what justification was, and the majority of the remaining twenty would regard anyone who defended the Regensburg formula as a heretic; see *Reg.*, 187 (no. 730).

261. Contarini to Cardinal Farnese, Regensburg, 14 June 1541, ASVat, Arm. 62, vol. 36, fols. 113r–114r; and in part in Pastor, "Correspondenz," 481–82.

262. Contarini to Cardinal Farnese, Regensburg, 22 June 1541, in *NB* 7: 13. This letter is missing from ASVat, Arm. 64, vol. 36.

263. *Monumenti Beccadelli* 1(2):169: "Nosti enim vel morem Senatus, vel naturam hominum: Quot enim capita, tot sententiae. Qui omnium tibi plus debebat, ille minus tribuit."

make an issue of the fact that an important cardinal on whose help Contarini had relied (in all likelihood either Aleandro, Cervini, or Carafa) had turned against him. A week later he mentioned in passing that malicious comments were being made in Rome about Contarini but tried to downplay their importance.[264] Shortly afterward Bembo comforted the legate by writing from Rome that he personally agreed with the article on justification but that "the matter has not been understood well by some people here."[265]

Some curialists whom Contarini does not mention by name wrote to him and to members of his household that he and Badia were being blamed for exalting faith over works. Others wrote that even though true, the agreed-upon article 5 was nevertheless scandalous: if people did not consider good works meritorious, they would not perform them. "I was most amazed at this and cannot believe that there is any learned and serious man at the papal court who holds such views, but think it certain that they belong to persons who are not as well informed as they should be. If I thought otherwise, I would humbly and charitably show it in writing, so that it could be well considered what a great error this is"[266] was Contarini's exasperated reply.

He defended his ideas not only against those who should have known better, but also against his most conspicuous critics such as Cardinals Laurerio and Aleandro. The first had tangled in consistory with Fregoso, to Contarini's obvious annoyance, who wondered whether the article on justification deserved all the attention Laurerio was lavishing on it. Contarini repeated the accusations that he and Badia, along with the emperor, had been too accommodating to the Protestants. The new tone in his letters shows that he was deeply wounded: "Now I am beginning to be a good Christian suffering in the troubles and dangers in which I have placed myself for the sake of religion, and I am certain that this foolish calumny will [ultimately] result in my good, so that I am cheerful about it," he wrote to Laurerio.[267]

264. Bembo to Contarini, June 4 1541, in ibid., 172: "Nostro Signor Dio che può il tutto, doni felice sucesso a V.S. R^ma di quelle cose, che ella così prudentemente tratta anchora che quì non le manchino delle invidie."

265. Letter of 11 June 1541, in ibid., 177.

266. To Cardinal Farnese, 10 July 1541, ASVat, Arm. 64, vol. 36, fol. 132r–v, correcting Pastor, "Correspondenz," 494.

267. Regensburg, 22 July 1541, in *Monumenti Beccadelli* 1(2):185; and *Reg.*, 218 (no. 820). Dittrich wrongly identifies the recipient as Cervini.

A fuller defense of Contarini's actions is found in a carefully worded letter to an unnamed but clearly influential cardinal whom he suspected of originating the rumor in Rome that he, together with Badia and the emperor, had signed Lutheran articles. He reproached the cardinal in question for having discussed the term *merit* in consistory "as if it were an essential article of faith, like that on the Trinity, or something similar."[268] Like the fighter on the front lines, he now speaks to those carping at him from the safety of Rome. Resigning himself to being misunderstood by people without direct experience of discussions with Lutherans, he explains that it was impossible to force them to use the terminology of scholastic philosophy. All the Catholic theologians had rightly agreed to omit the word *merit* in the interest of reaching agreement.

Then follows one of the most crucial passages in Contarini's correspondence of these last two months in Regensburg. Here he reveals that, far from retreating into intransigent curialism, as Matheson would have it, he still holds the same convictions he held at the beginning of his mission.

For myself... I am renouncing any reason I might have for thinking that God owes me anything, and the good things that he gives me I wish to acknowledge as coming from his loving kindness, mercy, and generosity rather than from anything he owes me or any obligation he has toward me. Moreover, what happens to love of neighbor at this important point? Let me assure Your Reverence that I am not interested in entering into a meaningless battle of words. Through such battles the Christian church is being radically damaged, and there is no one who feels compassion for her. Instead, the highest praise goes to him who knows how to invent some new cause of strife. God grant that we don't all too soon have cause to regret this; for my own eyes see clearly what those people there do not see. I may have said more than I ought to have, but the love of Christ forces me to do it, and Your Reverence will pardon me for it.[269]

---

268. To Cardinal N. N., 22 July 1541, in *Monumenti Beccadelli* 1(2):186. Morandi thinks that the cardinal is Aleandro, but this is not clear.

269. Ibid., 188: "Io per me... rinuncio a quanta ragione potessi havere, che Dio mi fosse debitore, et tutto quello che mi darà di bene, voglio riconoscerlo dalla sua benignità, misericordia, et liberalità, et non da debito suo, et obbligo suo alcuno. In oltre dov'è la carità del prossimo in così importante occasione? V.S. R.ma si assicuri, che languemus circa inutilem pugnam verborum, et in questo mezzo per le nostre contentioni si ruina funditus la Cristianità, nè vi è chi gli abbia compassione, anzi quello è più laudato, il quale sa meglio ritrovare qualche modo, et qualche nuova causa di dissidio. Dio voglia, che non ce ne pentiamo presto; ben il veggio io coi miei occhi quello,

A similarly critical tone is found in Contarini's letter to his brother-in-law Matteo Dandolo, Venetian ambassador to the French court. Considering himself no longer bound to keep matters secret, Contarini summarized his view of the colloquy and emphasized that he personally found nothing heretical in the Regensburg Book despite Eck's objections to it. Still, he did not want to approve it, because the Protestants accepted the book only in part and might interpret the rest in a sense contrary to truth. "Now concord is entirely out of the question...I now see clearly that the greatest good fortune which I had in the course of this legation was that no concord was achieved, because I would certainly have been stoned by various groups, and some would even have become heretics in order to make me appear to be one," was his exasperated conclusion. But far from feeling downcast, Contarini ended on a defiant note: "Be of good cheer, [for] more are with us than with them."[270]

The dispatches from Cardinal Farnese that followed his letter of 15 June gave Contarini no guidance in religious questions and avoided discussion of the main issues for the ostensible reason that it would be far easier to deal with religious matters orally after the legate's return to Italy. But Farnese clearly stonewalled by not responding to Contarini's reports about the debates on justification: "it seems to His Holiness, because of the way things are going, the less said and written about [justification], the better."[271] Instead, the legate's final instruction was to work toward Habsburg support for the convocation of a general council, and against the emperor's granting of any form of toleration to the Protestants.

As a result of this charge, the relations of legate and emperor grew cool. Granvelle had made no bones about his disappointment with the pope, Morone, and Contarini, accusing them of having done nothing to reform the Catholic clergy and bishops of Germany. The secretary was extremely distressed and bluntly declared that the Holy See was

---

che lì non si vede. Son trascorso più di quello che doveva, la carità di Cristo mi costringe, però V.S. R.ma mi perdoni."

270. Regensburg, July 1541, in ibid., 203: "Hora la concordia è in tutto disperata... Ben veggo che oramai la maggiore ventura, che io habbia avuto in questa Legatione, è stata, che non si sia fatta la concordia, perchè certamente io saria stato da diverse bande lapidato, et qualch'uno si haveria fatto eretico per farmi parere eretico....State di buona voglia, *plures sunt nobiscum quam cum illis.*"

271. Cardinal Farnese to Contarini, Rome, 7 July 1541, ASVat, Arm. 64, vol. 20, fols. 118r–120r; and *NB* 7:22–24.

tolerating appalling scandals.[272] At the insistence of Granvelle, speaking for the emperor, on 7 July Contarini addressed the German bishops present in Regensburg concerning the necessity of reform.[273] He admonished them to be true shepherds of their flock and to set examples of modesty, sobriety, and avoidance of ostentation in their households. They were told to counteract Protestant doctrines by choosing learned and honest preachers capable of instructing the people by word as well as example. However, these preachers do not bear much resemblance to the later Counter-Reformation militant defenders of Catholicism. Despite his recent experiences, Contarini repeated one of his favorite ideas by urging that they be neither contentious nor animated by hatred toward their adversaries, but capable of loving them and desiring their salvation. He stressed the importance of instructing youth, an area in which he thought Catholics lagged behind Protestants, and enjoined Catholics to found schools, especially for nobles, in order to counteract the successes of the Protestants. Here Contarini echoed what the archbishop of Mainz had told him a month earlier—that Protestant schools were good and numerous, whereas Catholics had none.[274]

As with so much else he did in Regensburg, Contarini has been both praised and blamed for this last act. Jedin considered his address to the German bishops "replete with the ideas of Catholic reform," while in Augustijn's opinion Contarini's allocution was "nothing more than a funeral speech."[275] Contarini's address was in fact so perfunctory that one must agree with Augustijn. The legate knew full well that he could make no difference at this point, but he did his duty in accordance with the emperor's wishes.

The Diet of Regensburg closed on 29 July amid disagreement over the wording of Charles V's final declaration.[276] Contarini's last letters from this legation were written by a man who knew that he had lost a

272. Morone to Cardinal Farnese, 21 June 1541, in Dittrich, "Nuntiaturberichte Morone's," 622.

273. Pfeilschifter (ed.), *Acta Reformationis Catholicae* 4(2):5–7.

274. Contarini to Cardinal Farnese, 4 June 1541, in *Reg.*, 336 (Inedita, no. 73), corrected by ASVat, Arm. 62, vol. 36, fol. 108v.

275. Jedin, *Trient* 1:313; Cornelis Augustijn, "The Quest of Reformation: The Diet of Regensburg as a Turning-Point," paper presented at the the conference "The Reformation in Germany and Europe: Interpretations and Issues," Washington, D.C., 25 September 1990. I would like to thank Professor Augustijn for giving me a copy of his paper.

276. *GC*, 767–70.

battle yet had not despaired. He continued to defend the article on justification and to condemn Protestant rejection of defined doctrines. There was, moreover, no bitterness in his reflections about the failure of the colloquy. Rather, such bitterness as he expressed was directed at people in the court of Rome who not only knew all too little about the German situation and about Lutheran as well as Catholic theology, but also lacked charity. His dream of religious concord was utterly shattered. Now he had to defend himself for having been its champion.

CHAPTER FIVE

After the Storm

The Return to Italy

In early August Charles V left Germany for Italy, from where he proceeded to an expedition against the corsairs of North Africa. Contarini, too, began his return journey, planning to stop in his diocese of Belluno before continuing to Rome. When he arrived in Trent, a dispatch from Cardinal Farnese reached him with orders to accompany Charles V first to Milan and then to Lucca, where emperor and pope were to meet. Paul III was anxious to discuss events in Germany with the legate as soon as possible, and to receive a full report of the colloquy and diet.[1] Thus Contarini had to subordinate his wish to visit Belluno to the duties of his diplomatic mission and resign himself to yet another journey.

The emperor was welcomed to Milan on 22 August with pomp and festivities, which Contarini described in a dispatch of the next day to Farnese.[2] But the legate's mind was on other and more personal matters. In a blunt paragraph he mentioned that he had heard about being

---

1. Farnese to Contarini, 9 Aug. 1541, ASVat, Arm. 64, vol. 20, fols. 133r–134r. Contarini's previous orders had been that wherever the pope might be he was to come to him immediately, for the pope wished to be informed about "many things that cannot be written conveniently" (*molte cose, che male si possono scrivere*) (same to same, 3 Aug., fol. 131r).

2. Milan, 23 Aug. 1541, ASVat, Arm. 62, vol. 36, fols. 145v–146r; printed in *Reg.*, 346–47 (Inedita, no. 84); and excerpted in Pastor, "Correspondenz," 500–501.

called a Lutheran in Rome, and asked that the pope suspend judgment until their meeting. His calumniators did not know Lutheran doctrine, he continued, and were also ignorant of what St. Augustine and St. Thomas taught. Luther himself thought that the accord on justification was contrary to his own doctrine: "Thus the Roman theologians are very wrong in condemning so hastily something they probably do not properly understand, and in burdening their fellow man to such an extent," was his conclusion.[3]

Beccadelli reported that on his passage through Brescia the legate was asked by a friend about the "outrageous articles" to which he had agreed with the Lutherans. When Contarini protested, he learned that the source of this report was a letter of "a great cardinal," at the mention of whose name Contarini became extremely perturbed. According to his secretary's account, Contarini on that occasion not only denied that he had signed "outrageous articles" in Regensburg, but also declared that "without the authority of the church, he would not accept any doubtful articles or even the Gospel of St. John."[4] Beccadelli quite obviously was defending his patron by depicting him as a "hero of the church and the faith," a type that would be developed more fully in the literature of the Counter-Reformation.[5]

But even if the statement here attributed to Contarini is apocryphal, it expresses his real attitude. He had made the deliberate choice to subordinate himself in Regensburg to the *magisterium* of the church, narrowly and traditionally defined. Obedience to the pope was a matter of conviction as well as of honor to him. Always a team player, a diplomat who had risen through the *cursus honorum* of a Venetian patrician and filled with credit some of the highest offices in the Republic, Contarini internalized the virtue of obedience to an exceptional degree. A scant three weeks before his death he repeated solemnly, "I have always and inviolably kept my word and what I promised, and shall always do so, for I consider that keeping one's word and promises is the principal quality that belongs to a gentleman."[6] The particular combination of ideas about the necessity of hierarchical order in the church and his own duty of obedience as a gentleman, so characteristic of Contarini, continued to lend him the inner strength that derived from a secure

3. *Reg.*, 347 (Inedita, no. 84).   4. Beccadelli, "Vita," 36–37.
5. Fragnito, *Memoria individuale*, 121.
6. To the Duke of Ferrara, 3 Aug. 1542, in Casadei, "Lettere," 274: "La fede mia et quello che prometto sempre ho inviolabilmente osservato et sono per osservare, reputando che il servare la fede et le promesse sij la precipua parte che deve essere in un gentilhomo."

self-image. At times, however, it also circumscribed his field of vision, as we have already seen.

On 7 September the pope held a consistory at Lucca "because of the arrival of the Rev. Card. legate Contarini, who has returned from the Diet of Regensburg." This entry in the consistorial acts adds merely that "religious matters were discussed."[7] The pope's attitude toward his legate remained favorable; Contarini is said to have "entirely satisfied those to whom he had to give an accounting of his actions."[8] Pole assured Contarini on 1 September that he was spoken of "in most honorable terms" by Paul III and by others in the papal presence.[9] Beccadelli reports that the pope supported Contarini, exhorting him "not to care about the vain gossip of ill-disposed people."[10] Nevertheless, such gossip persisted for months after he had returned to Rome,[11] making the continued defense of his actions in Regensburg necessary.[12]

Although little of Contarini's correspondence from the remainder of 1541 has survived, what letters we do have contain indications of his somber but calm mood during this period. The emperor's defeat in North Africa aggravated the "wound," which he tried to heal by assiduously reading the Scriptures when time permitted.[13] To Pole he wrote about his "low state," his discouragement and wish to be united perfectly with Christ, yet also about his inner peace.[14] Despite, or maybe because of, his disappointments, Contarini became increasingly detached from the controversies that surrounded him, declaring unequivocally, "God, whom I want to serve above all, knows my mind and heart!"[15]

7. *Reg.*, 224–25 (no. 854).

8. Paolo Sadoleto to Ludovico Beccadelli, Carpentras, 22 Oct. 1541, quoted in Fragnito, "Evangelismo e intransigenti," 25.

9. To Contarini, Capranica, 1 Sept. 1541, *Ep. Poli* 3:31.

10. Beccadelli, "Vita," 39.

11. Sadoleto to Contarini, Carpentras, 6 Dec. 1541, in *Monumenti Beccadelli* 1(2):209.

12. Contarini received a copy of the recess of the Diet of Regensburg and was perturbed about inaccuracies he found in it, especially the assertion that he had promised that a council would be held in Germany; see his letter to the Archbishop of Mainz, Lucca, 19 Sept. 1541, in *Reg.*, 349 (Inedita, no. 86); and ASVat, A.A., Arm. I–XVIII, 6461, fols. 93r–95r.

13. Cristoforo Madruzzi to Contarini, Trent, 22 Dec. 1541, in *Monumenti Beccadelli* 1(2):210.

14. Pole paraphrases a letter of Contarini to him that has not survived: Viterbo, 23 Dec. 1541, in *Ep. Poli* 3:44–45.

15. To Farnese, Milan, 23 Aug. 1541, in *Reg.*, 347 (Inedita, no. 84).

That Contarini had suffered a personal defeat as a result of his mission to Regensburg is obvious. The same cannot be said of his role in the curia during the fall of 1541. It is easy to jump to conclusions about the political defeat and isolation of Contarini and the triumph of the intransigent wing among curialists. But was this the true state of affairs?

At the papal court Contarini was not ostracized or isolated from affairs but drawn into them—with precautions, so to speak. Immediately after the meeting at Lucca he was instructed by Farnese to precede the pope to Rome, there to join with Aleandro in working up a list of suggestions for Paul III in preparation for the announced council. In addition, the two cardinals were asked to draft "a formula to be used in preaching everywhere, in Germany as well as in Italy and elsewhere, in view of the fact that as regards preaching we are now far removed from the original sound practice."[16] Farnese trusted the conservative Aleandro more than the outspoken Contarini who had recently irked him, as his responses to the legate's dispatches occasionally intimate. Still, he and the pope wisely decided to use Contarini's experience for the benefit of papal politics. Aleandro was already suffering from a stomach ailment and remained frequently confined to his bed (he was to die on 1 February 1542). This fact may explain Contarini's sole authorship of the *Instructio pro praedicatoribus* (Instruction for preachers), completed by 21 October.[17]

This tract of a mere eight pages has received little notice from scholars. Yet it is of the first importance for understanding Contarini's thought after Regensburg. When juxtaposed with Contarini's first treatise on preaching, the *Modus concionandi*, it helps to answer at least partially the vexed question why the *spirituali*, and Contarini as

16. Farnese to Contarini, Bologna, 5 October 1541, in *Reg.*, 385 (Anhang no. 12); and ASVat, Arm. 64, vol. 20, fol. 143v.

17. This *Instructio pro praedicatoribus* is mentioned at the end of the "De concilii celebratione sententia Contareni cardinalis," in *CT* 4:208–9, which the editor dates around 15 October 1541. Pole acknowledged the receipt of the former in a letter to Contarini from Viterbo of that date; *Ep. Poli* 3(2):40, calling it "li scritti soi [Contarini's] della forma di predicare al popolo Christiano." Querini, the editor of Pole's letters, wrongly ascribed this treatise to Pole, who also began writing a tract on preaching that was not completed. Contarini's piece is printed as "Litterae Pontificiae de modo concionandi, MDXLII," in *Ep. Poli* 3(1):75–82. Contarini's autograph draft is in ASVat, A.A., Arm. I–XVIII, 6461, fols. 114r–118v, and a fair copy on fols. 110r–113r. I cite the printed version corrected by the last-mentioned manuscript, entitled "Instructio pro praedicatoribus."

their most visible member, lost the impetus they had possessed until the spring of 1541, and why the leadership of the church passed to more conservative men. The significance of this little work requires that we examine its unusually complex context, which begins with a controversy about preaching in Siena in 1537.

When Hubert Jedin, the later historian of the Council of Trent, in the 1920s was gathering materials in the Neapolitan archives for his biography of the Augustinian Girolamo Seripando, he came across a collection of letters dealing with the impact of Protestant ideas on the audiences of preachers in Siena. In a series of Sienese public Lenten sermons in 1537, the Augustinian friar Agostino Museo of Treviso treated such topics as justification, the nature of grace, and redemption. Attacked as a Lutheran heretic by the Capuchin Giovanni da Fano, Museo was imprisoned.[18] A year later he was solemnly exonerated by his two judges, Girolamo Aleandro and Tommaso Badia.[19]

This episode provided the occasion for an epistolary exchange among *spirituali* which included discussions about the nature of preaching. Museo had argued that it was the duty of preachers to stress the Augustinian doctrine of predestination in order to counteract the "Pelagian self-confidence" which he thought widespread among ordinary people. Answering his opponents, he cited the church fathers as the sources of his theology, and decidedly rejected the label of Lutheran, given him by his critics, by exclaiming: "Why do [my enemies] call me a heretic? Was Augustine perhaps a disciple of Luther? If I have erred, I have done so with Augustine, with Paul, with Christ and the saints!"[20]

A Sienese nobleman, Lattanzio Tolomei, reported the matter to Contarini, who at this point enjoyed high visibility and prestige in the curia as the chairman of the reform commission that drew up the *Consilium de emendanda ecclesia*. He was also the bishop of Belluno—an absentee bishop, to be sure, but one who was concerned about the welfare of his flock. The problem of what and how to preach to the people immediately caught his interest as a practical and pastoral, as well as a theoretical, issue.

18. Valerio Marchetti, *Gruppi ereticali senesi del Cinquecento* (Florence: La Nuova Italia, 1975), 18–24.

19. Hubert Jedin, "Ein Streit um den Augustinismus vor dem Tridentinum (1537–1543)," *Römische Quartalschrift* 35 (1927): 354–57.

20. Ibid., 358–59.

In a long letter to Tolomei, Contarini took up the topics debated in Siena, most notably predestination.[21] He considered Tolomei as someone on his own intellectual level with whom there was no need for hedging or constraint. Writing rapidly and citing his authorities from memory, he was impatient to find a middle way between two warring camps. First there were "those who in their pride and ignorance want to persecute Lutherans and be superior to them. They call themselves Catholics but in reality are Pelagians rather than Catholics."[22] The second group, "having read some Augustine, and wishing to show that they know what others do not, go about putting foolish ideas into the heads of the people, preaching things which the people are not able to understand and which they themselves do not understand. They pervert the good way of preaching, which they should adopt, into infinite abuse and utter madness."[23] Contarini sought a middle ground between these two positions, a "medietas" that was more diplomatic than theological. He explained to Tolomei his own view, essentially derived from St. Thomas, that God's foreknowledge should not be confounded with predestination,[24] especially predestination to damnation, and tried to mitigate St. Augustine's harshness. When his arguments became feeble, he sought recourse in a version of St. Paul's exclamation "O the depth of the wisdom of God,"[25] and retreated to advocate contemplation rather than explication of a mystery. God, the eternal present, bestows his grace on man in baptism. Man can only thank God for the *beneficium* he receives, and in return put all his trust in Christ.[26]

Woven throughout this very personal and theologically unsystematic letter is the theme of the right way to preach to the people. Warning that the devil was using the pride and ignorance of preachers

21. The text is in Stella, "Lettera del Cardinale Contarini sulla predestinazione," 421–41. It was written before 19 January 1538, when Contarini mentioned it in a letter to Cardinal Ercole Gonzaga (420). Stella showed that the Italian version preceded the Latin translation and corrected Hünermann, in Contarini, *Gegenreformatorische Schriften*, xxvii.

22. Stella, "Lettera," 422.   23. Ibid., 428.

24. Ibid., 434. Contarini explained his views further in a letter to Tullio Crispoldi, written shortly after the letter to Tolomei; see *GC*, 866–71. Again, the emphasis is on the impossibility of God's predestining anyone to damnation. For bibliography on Crispoldi, see Firpo and Marcatto, *Processo* 1:343–44n.214.

25. Romans 11: 33. Contarini cites this verse from memory in two successive paragraphs, each time differently; see Stella, "Lettera," 431.

26. For an interpretation different from mine of this letter and its place in Contarini's thought as well as in that of other *spirituali*, see Simoncelli, *Evangelismo italiano*, chap. 2, esp. 69–91.

and the common people as his instruments in the battle against truth, Contarini wished to see preachers draw back from tackling the sorts of questions he himself discussed so freely with Tolomei. They should join the Seraphim in calling "Holy, holy, holy" and St. Paul in admiring divine greatness, rather than speaking about "such high and profound matters" as predestination before the people.[27] Paradoxical questions should not be vented, especially those that might give scandal.

We see here a double standard and an aristocratic point of view. Contarini and the *spirituali* felt themselves free to discuss the issues raised by northern reformers because they had the necessary education. A more problematic note appears, however, in a letter of Contarini to the theologian Tullio Crispoldi, where we read that his own knowledge of these issues derived also from direct religious experience, which was "clearer than the sun."[28] Because, unlike Contarini, the people lacked education that would enable them to bring order to experience, preachers must not go beyond clear catechetical parameters in their sermons. They should deflect, channel, and neutralize the emotions aroused by popular misunderstanding of issues like justification, free will, and predestination.[29]

Not all *spirituali* accepted this categorization of some questions as beyond discussion from the pulpit, or were prepared to deny the common people the right to discuss current theological issues. They were being talked about widely anyway, "in the piazze, in the taverns, even in women's laundries," as one bishop was to write with dismay.[30] The most famous of the *spirituali* bishops at the time, Giberti, addressed this problem repeatedly in instructions for the clergy of his diocese of Verona in the 1530s. He encouraged an innovative and, to Rome, frequently suspect style of preaching, enjoining his clergy to give the people an "explanatio Evangelii" and teach what was contained in the Gospels without picking and choosing.[31] Preaching was not to be primarily a weapon against heresy, but a method of instructing the

27. Stella, "Lettera," 436.   28. *GC,* 866.

29. Predestination was listed among the "difficilia fidei" already in a brief of Pope Clement VII in 1532 which ordered that "the difficult questions of Catholic faith are not to be discussed before ignorant people; it is evident that predestination is among the most difficult matters of the Christian religion, and therefore not a proper subject on which to preach to the people, the majority of whom are ignorant and uneducated." Bartolomeo Fontana, "Documenti vaticani inediti contro l'eresia luterana in Italia," *Archivio della R. Società romana di storia patria* 15 (1892): 132.

30. Prosperi, *Tra evangelismo e controriforma,* 241.

31. Adriano Prosperi, "Di alcuni testi per il clero nell'Italia del primo Cinquecento," *Critica storica* 7 (1968): 157.

people. Thus in 1537, the year of the debates in Siena, Tullio Crispoldi preached in Verona on the Gospels, and Reginaldo de Nerli on the Pauline epistles. The latter, Giberti's collaborator, also compiled a summary of model sermons for the use of preachers in which he linked the explanation of gospel texts with specific theological problems that agitated the people, including faith versus works and justification.[32] In a letter to Giberti, Cardinal Ercole Gonzaga remarked somewhat sarcastically that as a result of Nerli's sermons the common people went about preaching on predestination and screaming with crucifixes in their hands: "Christ, Christ!"[33]

At first glance, Giberti seems to have diverged deliberately from the aristocratic line, being willing to bring the full New Testament to the people. However, this was to be done with very specific controls. Giberti's insistence on episcopal residence is well known; he considered it crucial not only as a step toward church reform, but also as a sine qua non for the establishment of the bond between bishop, clergy, and people. The bishop must instruct and supervise preachers, who ideally were loyal and trusted members of his household and of the diocesan clergy. They, in turn, were not to treat the common people as incapable of understanding the "difficilia fidei," but to offer them guidance in an orderly manner and within a tightly controlled setting, mindful of their own instructions by the bishop. If the laity were protected from the "Scylla and Charybdis" of widespread error, it would then submit freely to the authority of its spiritual leaders.

These concerns can also be found in the writings of Isidoro Chiari, a Benedictine monk belonging to the Cassinese Congregation and a close friend of many leading *spirituali*. In a treatise of 1537, which he sent to Contarini for comment, he took up many of the questions the cardinal had discussed in his letter to Tolomei.[34] Chiari elucidated a difference between, on the one hand, scholars and the educated who could and should examine themes like free will, faith and works, justification, and predestination and, on the other hand, the "unlearned masses," *imperita multitudo*, who were incapable of understanding such issues. The latter perverted the doctrine of justification by faith, and their errors endangered all of society, leading to turmoil and

---

32. Prosperi, *Tra evangelismo e controriforma*, 244.

33. Quoted in Firpo and Marcatto, *Processo* 2(1):298n.5.

34. Isidoro Chiari, *Ad eos qui a communi ecclesiae sententia discessere, adhortatio ad concordiam* (Milan, 1540). For a discussion of its main theological ideas, see Barry Collett, *Italian Benedictine Scholars and the Reformation* (Oxford: Clarendon Press, 1985), 102–12.

license. Ideas such as the priesthood of all believers, if spread among the people, would destroy order and hierarchy. One might conceivably even hear such arguments as "If the priesthood were extended to the female sex, and that were done with the approval of men, then there would be no reason why women could not exercise any ecclesiastical functions whatever."[35] Chiari is explicit at the end of his treatise that discussion of difficult doctrines and biblical texts supporting them should be restricted to monasteries and intellectual circles, where it belonged, and removed from city squares and the common multitude.[36]

Similar issues occupied other *spirituali* whom Contarini knew well, including Cortese. In the same spring of 1537, a Benedictine preacher gave a series of lectures on the Gospels and epistles to students at Padua. This Marco da Cremona, much admired by Pole and his circle, lectured to a large audience gathered in the monastery of Santa Giustina on the sensitive subjects of free will, predestination, and justification. He was promptly attacked by Dionigi Zanettini, suffragan bishop of Vicenza. When Contarini heard about the controversy, he intervened to prevent measures from being taken against Don Marco. He defended the Benedictine as "a man of most holy life and sound belief," whose enemies,

because Luther said various things about the grace of God and free will, . . . now oppose anyone who preaches and teaches about the grandeur of grace and human infirmity. Believing that they are contradicting Luther, they contradict Saints Augustine, Ambrose, Bernard, Jerome, and Thomas—in brief, moved by commendable zeal . . . they do not realize that they deviate from Catholic truth, move toward the Pelagian heresy, and cause disturbances among the people.[37]

Cortese was worried about the uneducated, "li poveri idioti," whose beliefs and certainties were being shaken. Like Chiari, he wanted to see

35. Quoted in Peyronel Rambaldi, "Ancora sull'evangelismo italiano," 955.

36. Ten years later, after he became bishop of Foligno, Chiari changed his views somewhat, sounding more like Giberti. He envisioned the task of the bishop as imitation of Christ and the spreading of His word with the aid of loyal and docile preachers who would think of their "lectio" and "explicatio" of the Scriptures as equal in importance to their administration of the sacraments; see Boris Ulianich, "Scrittura e azione pastorale nelle prime omelie episcopali di Isidoro Chiari," in *Reformata reformanda: Festgabe für Hubert Jedin zum 17. Juni 1965*, ed. Erwin Iserloh and Konrad Repgen (Münster i.W.: Aschendorff, 1965), 1:632–33.

37. Contarini to an unknown addressee, Rome, 12 June 1537, in *Reg.*, 270 (Inedita, no. 20); and ASVat, A.A., Arm. I–XVIII, 6461, fols. 54r–55r. Fragnito, "Il Cardinale Cortese," 439n.228, identifies the recipient of the letter as the vicar of the patriarch of Venice.

discussions of thorny questions restricted to small groups of intellectuals, preferably in a monastic setting, and to exclude common people from the debates.[38] Contarini, however, approved of Don Marco's addressing students, since they belonged to a different category from the common people. Students had education, therefore could profit from erudite instruction. He thus broadened the group before whom the "difficilia fidei" could be discussed, believing university students capable of deriving great spiritual benefit from preachers like Don Marco, and minimized the dangers of disaffection or confusion.

This was the immediate background to Contarini's brief tract on preaching for the clergy of his own diocese of Belluno. Unlike Giberti, he was an absentee bishop who could not instruct and supervise the preachers in person. The issues that had emerged in the debates of 1537 left him sufficiently perturbed to write the *Modus concionandi* during the following year.[39] In it he adopted the perspective of a bishop deeply concerned with the spiritual welfare of his entire and for the most part unlettered flock, which, unlike the Paduan students, was not able to comprehend theological disputes. How were preachers to help their people avoid falling into the heresy and confusion that plagued other Italian cities?

One answer was to revive the prescription of St. Francis that preachers should speak about virtues and vices, punishment and glory.[40] Contarini thus counsels the preacher addressing simple people: "If you wish to stir your listeners effectively to penance, you must bring them to come to understand rightly for themselves both the excellence of virtues (even if they have to be treated one by one) and the ugliness of vices, together with the rewards which virtues bring and the punishments which are visited upon sinners by God's just judgment."[41] But

38. Fragnito, "Il Cardinale Cortese," 442.

39. On 16 January 1539 Cardinal Ercole Gonzaga acknowledged its receipt in a letter to Contarini; see Friedensburg, "Briefwechsel," 194. Franz Dittrich, "Nachträge zur Biographie Gasparo Contarinis," *Historisches Jahrbuch der Görresgesellschaft* 8 (1887): 273, argues for 1540. For the dating of this tract by Simoncelli (*Evangelismo italiano*, 117–20), see Fragnito, "Il Cardinale Cortese," 441n.234.

40. Frederick J. McGinness, "Of 'Vices and Virtues, Punishment and Reward': Authentic Preaching, Reform, and a Counter-Reformation Riddle," paper read at the Sixteenth-Century Studies Conference, St. Louis, October, 1990. I wish to thank Professor McGinness for a copy of his paper. He cites (13n.5) as the source of the Franciscan formula the Second Rule of St. Francis, in *Seraphicae legislationis textus originalis* (Quaracchi, 1897), 44.

41. *Reg.*, 307 (Inedita, no. 42). The text is on pp. 305–9 and should be corrected by the autograph manuscript in ASVat, A.A., Arm. I–XVIII, fols. 161r–170v. A later hand added the incorrect date 1540. To Prof. McGinness's question of how Contarini

that venerable formula was not sufficient to deal with the more difficult issues raised by the Protestant Reformation, the echoes of which resounded in the cities and even small towns of northern Italy.

The second and, for Contarini, much more important task was to search for an answer to the old problem of whether the gospel in its fullness could be preached to the people. He knew full well that Luther affirmed the ability of the baptized Christian to grasp the word of God. In the process of deciding where he himself stood, Contarini performed some curious mental acrobatics. Castigating preachers who used the pulpit to exhibit their learning, he enjoined them to imitate Christ in his humility. Pride was the root of all evil and disturbance, he declared: "Put away pride, put away display, then peace and concord will be everywhere! Therefore let our preacher put on the love of God and of the people, telling them those things which they are able to understand, and which lead to their edification."[42] Although preachers must touch on justification in their discussion of sin, contrition, and confession, Contarini tried to limit their scope by warning that a detailed discussion of justification was not their task, but that of the doctors who taught theology in the universities.[43]

Now follows a strange passage. Preachers, Contarini writes, must not detract from good works in any way or tell the people that man is justified without them. Even though this is true, if understood rightly, nonetheless the people cannot grasp it correctly. If this message were preached, they would become slack in doing good works. Nor will the prudent preacher preach that our will is weak and incapable of desiring the good unless moved by God. While this, too, is true, the ignorant people will only be induced to spiritual torpor upon hearing it, drawing the conclusion that man must passively wait for God to prod him.[44] Similarly, predestination should rarely be discussed before the people,

---

knew this formula, I would answer that it was probably a result of his work on the commission appointed by Paul III in 1536 to examine the Capuchin order; see Father Cuthbert, O.S.F.C., *The Capuchins: A Contribution to the History of the Counter-Reformation* (New York and Toronto: Longmans, Green, 1929), 1:99; and Cargnoni, Costanzo, ed., *I frati Cappucini: documenti e testimonianze del primo secolo* (Perugia: Edizioni Frate Indovino, 1988–), 1:1185n.6. Contarini certainly was familiar with the Capuchin Constitution of 1536, which states that preachers should discuss vices and virtues, punishment and glory: "E secundo che 'l nostro padre serafico ne la Regula ci admonisce *annuncient vitia et virtutes, poenam et gloriam cum brevitate sermonis*" (ibid., 418). He was also informed about the preaching of the first Capuchins through a long letter addressed to him by Vittoria Colonna (ibid., 2:214–27).

42. *Reg.*, 306 (Inedita, no. 42).   43. Ibid., 307.   44. Ibid., 308.

and then only with great caution, since they would jump to wrong conclusions from this difficult teaching as well: either they would fall into despair or become overconfident. "From all this it can be seen clearly that we must definitely avoid discussing these deep questions before the ignorant people. Let the pious and prudent preacher therefore descend to the [level of] knowledge and capacity of the people, and treat of divine things in such a way as to be understood by the people and be able to instruct the sheep of Christ in charity. If he observes this principle of charity, he will certainly never go wrong," is his final advice.[45]

Contarini sidestepped the tough issues by establishing a two-tier model of the Christian community, drawing a sharp horizontal line between the mass of believers and the educated elite of the church, much like the line that in another context separated patricians from the rest of the population in Venice. The ordinary people he considered incapable of dealing with ideas that, while true, would be likely to lead them to wrong conclusions because of their ignorance. Better not to discuss these dangerous concepts, he warned the preachers of Belluno. Contarini the bishop treated his people quite literally like sheep to be taken care of and shielded from unsettling doctrines.

An attempt has been made to establish a parallel between the *Modus concionandi* and Cardinal Cervini's instructions concerning preaching,[46] and to argue that the two men "in facing a problem that was part and parcel of the confrontation between Catholicism and heresy in sixteenth-century Italy . . . developed very similar responses."[47] Yet it is the differences, not the similarities, between the two sets of instructions that are striking and significant. Cervini espoused an outlook that clearly contradicted Contarini's two-tier model by directing preachers not to shy away from the complex doctrines brought to the fore by the Reformation, but rather to counteract them in such a way as to "preach and follow the doctrines which were declared in the Council of Trent."[48] Two points are material here: first, Cervini wrote a decade or so after Contarini in the enormously changed atmosphere of the Counter-Reformation; second, the repressive apparatus of the reorganized Roman Inquisition was in place, and the Tridentine decree on justification had been promulgated. Justification by faith alone, the key doc-

---

45. Ibid., 309.

46. William V. Hudon, "Two Instructions for Preachers from the Tridentine Reformation," *Sixteenth Century Journal* 20 (1989): 457–70.

47. Ibid., 468.   48. Ibid., 465.

trine of Protestantism, was condemned. It simply will not do to retreat to a formulation of fifty years ago that "it might be more correct to say that [Contarini's text] reflects the theological uncertainty existing in the Catholic world at that time."[49]

Contarini accepted justification by faith and thought it compatible with Catholic teaching; Cervini, in contrast, considered that tenet heretical. For Contarini, there was nothing to fear from theological discussions among the educated, whom he thought to be men of reason whose ideas could differ; for Cervini, conciliar decrees had put an end to speculation about some of the most debated issues of the age. Contarini was a paternalistic bishop who believed that he knew what was best for his flock[50] and a Venetian aristocrat who had no doubt that the elite of society and the common people existed on different planes with different religious understanding; Cervini already thought like the leaders of the Counter-Reformation, for whom the division of religion into the faith of the learned and that of the common people was inadmissible. Finally, Contarini was still at home in the church of the Renaissance, whereas Cervini at the time he wrote his tract already belonged to the much more militant Catholicism of the Counter-Reformation.

In a letter to two friends also dating from 1537–38, Contarini discussed his views further. Again, the subject was preaching to the people about predestination. After explaining that he personally could not adhere to the strict Augustinian doctrine because it seemed to detract from God's mercy, he added:

As bishop, I want to preach to my people thus: "I tell you, my people, that there is no unconquerable defect in reprobates that is the cause of their damnation. . . . God does not fail them, but they fail God." If you should tell me that I preach badly, I would disagree with you. If you tell me that I preach well, and that you would say the same, then I would ask you whether your preaching and mine agrees with the doctrine you approve in your heart of hearts. If you answer no, but that you preach thus in order not to scandalize the people, I would part company with you, because we must not preach falsehood or that which goes against the sentiment of our heart.[51]

49. Ibid., 466. The term *theologische Unklarheit* was first used by Joseph Lortz, *Die Reformation in Deutschland* (Freiburg: Herder, 1940), vol. 1, pt. 1, chap. 5. A year later, in the preface to the second edition, he called this idea his "Grundthese," but emphasized that he had used it in reference to Germany, not Italy or Spain.

50. Unlike Hudon, I agree with John Martin, "Salvation and Society," 209n.7: "Contarini's views were paternalistic, and he feared that the doctrine of salvation by faith alone would lead the people into error, encourage them to abandon good works, and possibly result in revolution, as it had in Germany."

51. Jedin, "Streit um den Augustinismus," 368.

This passage has been interpreted as evidence that Contarini affirmed "the unity of the intellectual content of religion; no distinction or difference in truth was admissible between the people and the educated."[52] Taken by itself, it seems reasonable to construe the passage this way. But in fact such an interpretation is not satisfactory, since the passage belongs to the wider context sketched above. Contarini was arguing here against preaching what one does not believe oneself. In the *Modus concionandi,* he endorsed the withholding of certain truths even though one believed them—quite a different matter. The last-cited passage warns against hypocrisy, not the passing over of controversial issues in silence. Going against the "sentiments of the heart" for Contarini was wrong, but silence under certain circumstances was the prudent, even preferable, course for preachers.

By October 1541, then, Contarini had written about preaching on several occasions. Yet the *Instructio pro praedicatoribus* was not just a summary of the main points found in the *Modus concionandi* or in passages of his letters that dealt with the topic. While some key phrases of the first tract reappear in the second, a comparison of the two texts reveals very marked differences. Internal evidence suggests that Contarini discussed the *Instructio* with Aleandro, whose voice can be discerned in it even though his name does not appear. The significant fact, though, is that Contarini was its author, as his autograph text shows. We must believe that he expressed his own ideas—or at least those he agreed with at this time—otherwise he himself would be guilty of "preaching that which goes against the sentiment of our heart."

In the *Modus concionandi* Contarini had given preachers "a precis [*summa*] to be used as a guide in preaching the Christian gospel."[53] Quoting Romans 3:20 that "the law gives us the full consciousness of sin," Contarini enjoined his preachers first to expound the commandments so that the listeners might learn to recognize and detest sin. Then the congregation should be told that they cannot turn away from sin by their own efforts, but only through the freely given grace of God.

We cannot obtain that grace except through faith in the blood of Christ: we receive this grace through faith, and with it all good things come to us: the for-

---

52. Adriano Prosperi, "Intellettuali e chiesa all'inizio dell'età moderna," in *Storia d'Italia, Annali* 4: *Intellettuali e potere,* ed. Corrado Vivanti (Turin: Einaudi, 1981), 188. I agree with Roberto Rusconi, "Predicatori e predicazione," in ibid., 988–89, that Contarini is among those advocating a double truth in preaching.

53. *Reg.,* 306.

giveness of sin, charity, goodness, and all other virtues by means of which we rise from sin, which no longer has power over us unless we yield to it. For this reason we must assiduously pray to God from whom arise right desires, right counsels, and just works, that his mercy may stand ready to guide and perfect our actions. From him are all our good things. Let this suffice as a precis of the scope of preaching and teaching.[54]

There is no word in this *summa*, as Contarini calls it, of absolution given to the faithful by priests. He deeply and consistently believed that we are justified and saved by faith in the merits of Christ on the cross, and enjoined the preachers of Belluno to stress the immensity of God's freely given saving grace. A Lutheran could have written the above passage; for all his criticism of Lutheran theology, Contarini clearly agreed with its central doctrine.

The *Instructio pro praedicatoribus* is very different in tone. Written at the behest of Paul III,[55] it states that the pope considers it opportune to establish rules for all preachers "without, for the time being [i.e., until the meeting of the forthcoming council], in any way repudiating official dogmas."[56] A few lines later we read almost the same words—that preachers must not contradict established doctrines. First of all they should exhort their audience to do penance, "without which it is impossible to hope for the remission of sins through our Lord Jesus and through faith in his blood . . . nobody can begin a new life unless he repents of his old, or draw close to God through Christ and faith in him, unless he first dies to sin with Christ." The people should be taught that Christ is their only mediator, and that only through faith in his passion and resurrection is there forgiveness of sins.[57] Twice more on the next page the phrase *per fidem in sanguine eius* is repeated, the second time added by Contarini in the margin of his autograph draft immediately following the statement that we obtain

54. "Non tamen accessum habemus ad dictam gratiam nisi per fidem in sanguine Christi; per fidem impetramus hanc gratiam, cum qua proveniunt nobis omnia bona, peccatorum remissio, caritas, bonitas, omnes aliae virtutes, quibus resurgimus a peccato, neque peccatum amplius nobis dominabitur, nisi ei cesserimus. Quamobrem orandus etiam est assidue deus, a quo sunt recta desideria, recta consilia, et iusta opera, ut eius misericordia et praeveniat nostras actiones ac dirigat et perficiat, inde etenim sunt omnia bona nostra" (*Reg.*, 307).

55. Dittrich states that it was published in 1542 under the title "Literae pontificiae de modo concionandi" (*GC*, 793) but gives no reference. In *Reg.*, 225–26 (no. 859), he states, again without a reference, that it was published as a papal brief. This is repeated in *CT* 4:209–10n.5, citing *Reg.* above as the source. I have not been able to find such a brief.

56. *Ep. Poli* 3(1):76.   57. Ibid., 77.

remission of our sins "through the sacrament of penance and the power of the priest to absolve."[58] Nothing like this sentence, which links sacramental confession and faith in the merits of Christ, can be found in the *Modus concionandi*. Although there is no direct evidence of Aleandro's input, the text clearly is a hybrid of two conceptions of the process of justification, Contarini's and a much more traditional one that emphasizes the role of the priest.

The latter is even more evident in a long marginal insert on the following page of the autograph draft to the effect that the people should be taught that baptism and penance are two different sacraments, in which the merits of Christ's passion are applied differently. After a theological explanation that stresses the role of the priest in the sacrament of penance, the text continues:

> All mysteries that the Catholic church and the orthodox religion hold with most certain faith concerning our Lord Christ can be taught to the people. Any sinner can obtain great consolation and trust from them, provided he is grafted into Christ[59] through faith and love. At this point it would be pertinent to teach the people about what the orthodox church believes concerning faith, hope, and charity, and what is useful for the Christian to know, abstaining, however, from more difficult investigations and accommodating oneself to the capacity of the people.[60]

Here can be seen the uneasy combination of emphasis on the importance of institutional Catholicism, on the one hand, and the language of individual *Christusmystik* of being "grafted into Christ," on the other, so congenial to Contarini's thinking. It is tempting to think that we have before us the result of discussions between him and Aleandro, and that we are hearing the voices of both men.

Besides the strong emphasis on the institutional church and its function in the spiritual life of the believer, there is another change in this tract relative to the earlier one. Gone is the "ignorant multitude" to

58. ASVat, A.A., Arm. I–XVIII, 6461, fol. 116r.

59. Contarini's terms *inseri Christo* and *fides in sanguine Christi* might have been derived from St. Bernard; see Rückert, *Theologische Entwicklung*, 79–80. However, Contarini uses them in the specific context of the Reformation period, knowing the significance given them by Protestant theologians.

60. "Omnia etiam mysteria, quae Ecclesia Catholica, et Orthodoxa fides de Christo Domino nostro credit certissima fide, poterit populus doceri, ex quibus magnam consolationem et fiduciam quivis peccator capere [so in both MS versions: the printed version has percipere] potest, dummodo sit insertus Christo per fidem et caritatem. Ad hunc locum pertinebit docere populum, abstinendo tamen a difficilioribus perscrutationibus, et capacitati populi sese accomodando, de fide, spe, et caritate, quae sentit Orthodoxa Ecclesia, et quae Christianum hominem nosse operae pretium est" (*Ep. Poli* 3[1]:79).

which the *Modus concionandi* repeatedly referred, replaced simply by "the people" without an adjective, except in one place where we read "uncultivated people" (*rudis populus*). The division of believers into two levels has been much mitigated. There is one faith for all, guarded and taught by the orthodox church, in which the people must be carefully instructed by trustworthy and educated preachers.

The unresolved tensions throughout this little tract are much more striking than in Contarini's first treatise on preaching. Now the preacher is instructed never to preach about good works without also talking about the merits of Christ, "on which all our works depend," and never to discuss the faith in Christ without treating penance and good works in the same sermon.[61] As experience teaches (a reference to Germany), truth will be perverted to justify weakness of the flesh. The good preacher emerges as a sort of tightrope walker, always conscious that the assembled people can draw wrong conclusions from his words and therefore continually on the *qui vive*, as it were. A funambulist when discussing current—and, obviously, burning—theological issues, the preacher finally has firm ground under his feet when he teaches the people "those things which the Catholic and orthodox church has always been preaching to this day" concerning the five last things (heaven, hell, purgatory, resurrection of the dead, and last judgment).[62] He should not omit instructing the people about the veneration of saints, the observance of fasts and of ceremonies and rites of the church, and finally, he should incorporate St. Augustine's dictum that to hope for remission of sins outside a united church is a sin against the Holy Spirit.[63]

If this tract in fact expresses what Contarini thought in September 1541, as is argued here, then it offers strong evidence that he accepted the logical consequences of his choice made in Regensburg to obey absolutely the *magisterium* of the church, including its teaching about the necessity of ceremonies and rituals. In this respect the last part of the *Instructio* demonstrates a move to a much more conservative position than the one he held in 1538, when he said nothing about the utility of sacred rituals or forms of worship. Then he was one of the

61. Ibid., 80.
62. It is possible that this recommendation should be read as reflecting an Ignatian accent. Contarini might have gone through the *Spiritual Exercises* under the guidance of Loyola a year or two before he wrote this. There is no conclusive evidence that he did, despite the assertions of Angel Suquìa, "Las reglas para sentir," 381; and *GC*, 407.
63. *Ep. Poli* 3(1):82.

spirituali against whose emphasis on salvation by faith alone Agostino Steuco had written in *Pro religione christiana adversus Lutheranos*.[64] Steuco, appointed prefect of the Vatican Library in 1538, and certainly known to Contarini, was insistent that the Lutheran view of justification destroyed piety, without which men would "return to their original beastly nature."[65] He thought that Luther's rejection of Catholic rituals and ceremonies undermined social and ecclesiastical order, and endangered the very bonds of civilized society. Steuco "always associates the need for religious rituals, sacred surroundings and pious activities with the *vulgares*—meaning the ordinary Christian—while he repeatedly states that only a few men—the wise—are capable of maintaining their piety and worshiping God without the benefit of exterior religion."[66]

What had once been the conservative position on the necessity of rituals, fully and carefully articulated by Steuco, became much more comprehensible to Contarini after his return from Germany. Shocked by the disorder there, he came to agree with the view that external constraints were necessary to counteract the human tendency to lawlessness. Like Steuco, he believed that only a few possessed the kind of deep religious yearning that moved them to seek union with God, the supreme good, without the need for ceremonies.[67] The vast majority of men had to be shepherded and supported through life with the aid of instruction, sacraments, and ritual. This explains Contarini's full agreement with the recommendation for preachers at the end of the *Instructio*. He was not going "against the sentiments of [his] heart"; rather, he now accepted the full implications of the position he had espoused by submitting himself to the teaching authority of the church.

When Pole in Viterbo received Contarini's *Instructio pro praedicatoribus* he hedged in answering, just as he had done with the *Epistola de iustificatione*. He resolutely refused to respond in writing and to take a stand, for he was not able to agree with the tract and obviously did not want to offend Contarini. He found an elegant way out by recalling Plato, "who, when it became necessary to communicate with another about things divine, preferred to do so by means of a living letter." Pole was going to follow Plato's example and use Beccadelli as his "living letter" to Contarini, ostensibly because he feared to bore

64. Published in Bologna in May 1530. I owe this reference and information about Steuco's views to Dr. Ronald Delph, whom I should like to thank for allowing me to read his unpublished paper on Steuco and quote from it: "From Venetian Visitor to Curial Humanist: The Development of Agostino Steuco's Counter-Reformation Thought," read at the Sixteenth-Century Studies Conference, St. Louis, October 1990.

65. Ibid., 3.   66. Ibid., 8.   67. Ibid., 10.

Contarini with his own writings.[68] This labored explanation of his silence on the subject of the *Instructio* reveals the growing differences between the two men. To Pole, Contarini had turned his back on the *spirituali* and sought the shelter of rigid orthodoxy in the heat of battle over central doctrines.[69] Pole almost baited Contarini by describing the circle of his friends in Viterbo who enjoyed the "holy and useful company" of Pietro Carnesecchi (burned for heresy in 1567) and Marcantonio Flaminio (later suspected of heresy), who was giving Pole and most of his *familia* a taste "of that food which does not perish."[70] That "food" certainly was not a reading from the lives of saints, as Contarini knew full well. The increasingly radical theological positions espoused by Pole and his circle, the "ecclesia Viterbiensis," made them the leaders of the Catholic intellectual avant-garde in Italy by the end of 1541. But their history during the following years is another subject.

Contarini's *Instructio* reveals his own mind after Regensburg; it also suggests why the *spirituali* were no longer a major force in the Catholic church as the lines separating it from Protestantism became ever more clearly drawn. The doctrine of justification by faith alone had momentous implications for the entire structure of the church and the hierarchy, embracing also ritual, ceremonies, theology, and the position of the laity. Justification by faith, as Protestants understood it, simply could not be integrated into sixteenth-century Catholicism without quite literally destroying it. Some *spirituali*, including Contarini, had tried to bridge the chasm between two ways of conceiving Christianity. In the one, the church was the mediatrix between man and God and dispensed the means of salvation. In the other, man stood before God with only his faith in the cross and the merits of Christ to offer him hope of salvation.

Contarini's solution, when faced with the problem of teaching the people the enormous complexities of doctrines like justification, free will, and predestination, was to counsel a retreat into silence. His way of addressing these issues was to urge a stop to "vain disputes" and to stress the necessity of charity, mildness, and good example; he made no attempt to grapple head-on with the hard theological and moral questions involved. Of course, Contarini cannot be faulted for not offering a solution to problems with which the church had struggled

68. To Contarini, Viterbo, 26 Oct. 1541, in *Ep. Poli* 3(2):41.
69. For a detailed and polemical discussion of the growing tension between Contarini and moderate Evangelism, on the one hand, and Pole and radical *spirituali*, on the other, see Simoncelli, *Evangelismo italiano*, chap. 2.
70. To Contarini, Viterbo, 9 Dec. 1541, in *Ep. Poli* 3(2):42.

intermittently almost from its beginnings. What he can be faulted for is his inability, perhaps also his unwillingness, to understand that the Catholicism of his time and justification *sola fide* could not be harmonized.

A passage from an unexpected quarter throws sharp, cold light on our subject. Antonio Gramsci, the influential twentieth-century theoretician of the Italian political left, observed:

The strength of religions, and of the Catholic church in particular, has lain, and still lies, in the fact that they feel very strongly the need for the doctrinal unity of the whole mass of the faithful and strive to ensure that the higher intellectual stratum does not get separated from the lower. The Roman church has always been the most vigorous in the struggle to prevent the "official" formation of two religions, one for the "intellectuals" and the other for the "simple souls." This struggle has not been without serious disadvantages for the Church itself, but these disadvantages . . . only serve to emphasize the organisational capacity of the clergy in the cultural sphere and the abstractly rational and just relationship which the Church has been able to establish in its own sphere between the intellectuals and the simple. The Jesuits have undoubtedly been the major architects of this equilibrium.[71]

In this instance, Gramsci saw correctly. What the *spirituali*, for all their goodwill and personal excellence, could not do, the Jesuits later could. They and the other leaders of the Counter-Reformation church defined clear norms and emphasized the reality of a single faith for all, with the clergy as its guardian. The Protestants set themselves the objective of opening to all Christians access to the full word of God. But the *spirituali* made distinctions between the faith for the mass of believers and that of the educated elite. Their hesitations and ambiguities do credit to their anxiety and subtlety, but precluded their leadership in a contest for the souls of the mass of the people, the *imperita multitudo* whom they cherished but also disdained. The winners were those who articulated the belief that there was one church for all, with the same doctrines for the high and the low.

In Another World: Bologna, 1542

On 27 January 1542, Paul III appointed Contarini legate to Bologna. On 25 March the new legate made his solemn

---

71. *Selections from the Prison Notebooks of Antonio Gramsci*, ed. and trans. Quintin Hoare and Geoffrey Nowell Smith (New York: International Publishers, 1971), 328–29.

entrance into the city,[72] where he was to reside until his death five months later. In contrast to the dearth of Contarini's correspondence from the preceding fall, a wealth of his letters from the Bolognese period has been preserved,[73] enabling us to follow his activities almost day by day.

Bologna, with over fifty thousand inhabitants, was second only to Rome in importance among the cities of the papal state. At the head of its government was the cardinal-legate whose "primary duties were justice and information."[74] In addition to being the chief judicial officer with power over life and death, he was the link between the central and local governments, responsible for gathering and transmitting back to Rome information about all aspects of city life. Bologna's civic institutions included various appointive and elective councils, with the highest prestige attached to a hereditary senate of forty nobles, the Reggimento, which in theory governed together with the legate.[75] In actuality, the power to govern Bologna was not evenly balanced: the senate was the dominant force in local affairs, with the legate as a supervisory rather than commanding official.[76]

Two conflicting views have been advanced about Contarini's appointment to Bologna—that he was chosen for "the most important and at the same time most honorable legation of the entire papal state"[77] because the pope wanted to make manifest his continuing trust in him, or that he was sent into exile[78] in a provincial city. While neither

72. *Reg.*, 231 (no. 885).

73. A total of 225 letters written by Contarini between 25 March and 17 August 1542 have been published by Alfredo Casadei, "Lettere del Cardinale Gaspero Contarini durante la sua legazione di Bologna."

74. I am grateful to Prof. Laurie Nussdorfer for allowing me to read and quote her unpublished paper "Civic Institutions and Papal Control in Sixteenth-Century Rome and Bologna," presented to the Sixteenth-Century Studies Conference, St. Louis, October 1986. The quotation is from p. 3.

75. Mario Fanti, "Le classi sociali e il governo di Bologna all'inizio del secolo XVII in un'opera inedita di Camillo Baldi," *Strenna storica bolognese* 11 (1961): 157. I thank Prof. Nussdorfer for this reference.

76. Paolo Colliva, "Bologna dal XIV al XVIII secolo: 'governo misto' o signoria senatoria?" in *Storia della Emilia Romagna*, ed. Aldo Berselli (Bologna: University Press of Bologna, 1977), 2:13.

77. *GC*, 798. Dittrich here echoes Beccadelli's "Vita": the pope "creò il Cardinale Legato di Bologna, ch'è la più honorata Legatione, che la Chiesa habbia nel Stato suo" (*Monumenti Beccadelli* 1[2]:39). Pastor, "Correspondenz," 352–53, also accepts Beccadelli's view, calling the legation to Bologna "the most honorable and important that the pope could bestow" (diese Legation war die ehrenvollste und bedeutendste, welche der Papst zu vergeben hatte).

78. For example, by Simoncelli, *Evangelismo italiano*, 45, 115, and passim. Giorgio Cracco in his review of the "Lettere" considered Contarini's legation to Bologna as "an

view, taken by itself, is satisfactory, the two are not mutually exclusive. Politically, the initiative in Rome had passed to the more intransigent cardinals. After his return from Germany, Contarini had no power base and no strong constituency at the papal court. His vision of church reform did not coincide with that of the men who did have power in the curia and who were trying to close ranks in the crisis besetting the church by fighting heresy through legal and institutional means, including the inquisition and eventually the index. Though personally admired, he was no longer able to function as a planner of Roman strategy because of his own lack of success. Appointing him to Bologna was a shrewd tactical move by Paul III, who thereby avoided the semblance of dropping Contarini. As legate, the latter would have a conspicuous and honorable[79] but circumscribed part in papal government, at a safe distance from the milieu in which he had become increasingly ineffective.

Contarini had barely reached Bologna before he was plunged into the midst of affairs. He had to deal immediately with cases of violence, involving vendetta, homicide,[80] and the murder of two Florentine students in a brawl.[81] Local quarrels, disputes among families, assaults, and lawsuits claimed his time.[82] As the mouthpiece of the pope, he had to announce to the Bolognese senate a rise in the extremely unpopular and resented salt tax, and to negotiate with the senators and other magistrates who tried to get it reduced or paid in a lump sum.[83] Although the legate's task was to transmit the pope's decisions in this dispute, we get a glimpse of his sympathies in a letter to Guido Ascanio Sforza di Santa Fiora, grandson of Paul III and papal chamberlain, to whom he mentioned the poverty of the peasants on the nobility's estates and the rise in taxes, adding: "I would not like us to oppress them too much."[84]

administrative office not of prime importance, [which] signified an intense humiliation [for Contarini] and the victory of the conservative faction of the curia" (in *Bollettino dell'Istituto di storia della società e dello stato veneziano* 3 (1961): 307.

79. Pole to Contarini, Viterbo, 29 Jan. 1542, expressed his delight at the unexpected appointment: "Sia laudata la bontà divina, la quale così expressamente nelli honori di V.S. Reverendiss. vole monstrare, che tutti vengono dalla mano soa, essendoli conferiti a un tale tempo, quando o non era causa di aspettare tanto, o pocha speranza, come ho notato neli altri honori de V.S. Reverendiss. praesertim Ecclesiastici, & in questo adesso non so quando le persone potevano havere manco causa di expectare per le resone, che sa V.S. Reverendissima" (*Ep. Poli* 3[2]:49). Paolo Sadoleto called the Bolognese legation "honorable"; see Fragnito, "Evangelismo e intransigenti," 27n.23.

80. Casadei, "Lettere," 85 (no. 5).   81. Ibid., 91 (no. 12).

82. Ibid., 256–57 (no. 167); and *Ep. Poli* 3:ccl–ccli.

83. Casadei, "Lettere," 101 (no. 33) and 106–7 (no. 45).

84. "Non vorrei che troppo noi gli oppressimo . . . " (ibid., 252 [no. 156]).

Even though the subject of almost all his letters is official business, Contarini's private thoughts and personal concerns find expression in many. His inner peace is evident; despite the recent disappointments, he does not write as an embittered or hostile man, but as one who has accepted the will of God in his own life. This quality shows itself at the very beginning of his legation in a letter to Alfonso Avalos, marquis del Vasto, the Spanish governor of Lombardy, a missive that illuminates Contarini's attitude of this period:

I sincerely thank God in his goodness, the fount from which all good things come, for having deigned to enlighten the mind of Your Excellency with his light and for infusing his Holy Spirit in your breast, having regard not only of your private good (which I have at heart virtually as much as I do my own), but even more of the good of innumerable others who will share and enjoy the gifts and talents given you from above. These are the true interior reformations which only God can bring about, and not merely the exterior reformations which men can effect. Blessed be God, and Jesus Christ be thanked without end.[85]

The note struck here and repeated in other letters is one of resignation to the course of events, which may not be comprehensible to men, or controllable by their efforts, but which have an inner meaning known only to God.

His belief in a divine plan for the church and the world gave Contarini tranquillity. Rather than fretting about the past, he now devoted himself to fulfilling his duties to the best of his ability. "I am overwhelmed by affairs, and from morning to night am always [giving] audiences and [involved in] business matters,"[86] he wrote to the legate of the eastern part of the papal state, Rodolfo Pio di Carpi. Three weeks later, he struck a wistful chord: "Here I am [engaged] in continuous business affairs and [lead] a life very different from that in Rome, but provided that it is done well, which I try to do as much as I am able, all is for the praise of God."[87] The mention of his presumably

85. "... Molto ringratio la bontà divina, fonte donde ha origine ogni bene, che si havesse degnata de illuminare la mente di V.ill.ma S. del lume suo, et infundere nel suo petto il suo santo Spirito, non solamente considerando il bene suo privato, il quale però mi è a cuore poco meno del mio proprio, ma più il bene de infiniti altri, li quali sono per essere participi et di godere di questo dono et talento dato a lei di sopra. Queste sono le vere riformatione interiore, quale solo Dio puole fare, et non solamente exteriore, quale possono fare li homeni. Sia benedetto Iddio, et senza fine ringratio Iesu Christo" (29 Mar. 1542, ibid., 87 [no. 9]).

86. "Io sono pienissimo di facende, et dalla mattina alla sera me ne sto sempre in audienze et negocj ..." (2 Apr. 1542, ibid., 94 [no. 19]).

87. "Io sono qui in continui negoci, vita molto diversa da quella di Roma ..." (to Carpi, 20 Apr. 1542, ibid., 110 [no. 50]).

more leisurely life in Rome was the expression of a passing mood. More typically, Contarini reported: "Praised be God, I am well, and do not lack business affairs here, of which I gladly take care, and which do not oppress me at all."[88] Again, he wrote to Carpi: "Through the grace of God, I am well, engaged in continuous and not unpleasant work, for which I have the great help of the vice-legate [Benedetto Conversini, bishop of Iesi]."[89] And to Sadoleto, with whom there was no need for reticence, he remarked: "As usual, I attend to government affairs, devoting myself entirely to the active life, in which I have no other aim than to do my duty for the honor of God and of our lord [the pope] who has honored me with this charge. If I am up to it, let the Divine Majesty be thanked for that; if I fail, may He pardon my fault. Rest assured, Your Reverence, that there is no lack of goodwill, thanks be to God."[90] These are not the expressions of a beaten-down person, but of a serene and above all resigned man whose deep trust in God is as evident as is his sense of duty to his earthly lord and to the church. A careful reading of Contarini's letters from Bologna makes sweeping generalizations about his exile, alienation, or bitterness impossible.[91]

The *vita activa*, the life of action about which Contarini wrote, included matters familiar to him from the time of his career in the government of Venice. As a young man, he had dealt with problems of flood control in the Po basin. Now he faced disputes between subjects of Ferrara and Bologna over attempts of the latter to divert and channel the river Reno, causing floods and damage in Ferrarese territory.[92] Despite his diplomatic experience, Contarini was not able to negotiate a settlement on this matter with the duke of Ferrara; it remained a nagging issue for his successors.

A recurring topic in many of his letters is Contarini's worry about

88. "Io, lodato Dio, sto bene, et qui non mi mancano facende le quali esequisco volentierj nè mi gravano punto . . ." (addressee missing, ibid., 237 [no. 125]).

89. "Io per la gratia di Dio sto bene all'usato in continue et non dispiacevoli occupationi, nelle quali ho un gran solevamento della persona di mons. Vicelegato . . ." (ibid., 253 [no. 158]).

90. "Io all'usato attendo alli negoci di questo governo, tutto volto a questa vita attiva, nella quale altro obietto non ho che satisfare all'honor di Dio et di N.S. che mi ha honorato di questo carico, nel quale, se bastarò, sia da ringratiarne sua divina Maestà, et mancando, da perdonare alla mia imperfettione. V.S. r.ma stia pur sicura che buon volere, ringratiato Dio, non manca" (5 July 1542, ibid., 256 [no. 165]).

91. Contarini's secretary, Ludovico Beccadelli, was of a different mind about his stay in Bologna, disliking the pressure and the kind of business there, and even referring to it as "this hell"; see Fragnito, "Gli 'spirituali,'" in *Gasparo Contarini*, 298n.139.

92. Casadei, "Lettere," 116 (no. 62), 122–23 (no. 75), 127 (no. 84), 222 (no. 96), and 246 (no. 143).

another looming Habsburg-Valois conflict. Paul III decided to remain neutral and prohibited the recruitment of soldiers for either side in the papal state. The enforcement of this prohibition was not easy for the legate, since it required prompt, reliable information from all parts of the Bolognese territory as well as manpower that he did not have. Contarini's request for an increase in the number of Swiss soldiers in Bologna was not granted, despite his argument that they were necessary for the maintenance of order.[93] His fear of war is evident, especially since he knew that the French were trying to use Mirandola as a power base in northern Italy.[94] He regarded peace everywhere, whether among families in Bologna or in Italy and Europe generally, as an immensely desirable good. In the last letter of this collection, written when his final illness had already begun its course,[95] he expressed his willingness to go on yet another mission to Spain in the cause of peace.[96] His worry and pessimism about Germany notwithstanding,[97] Contarini was trusting that God would help "poor Christendom" and that some good might result from his own efforts.[98] To that end, he repeated what he had said when he embarked on his journey to Regensburg—that something which seems impossible to men is possible to God.[99] This attitude of quiet surrender to God's unfathomable ways is very striking in Contarini's last letters.

Yet there was no passivity in the exercise of his office. His diocese of Belluno continued to occupy his thoughts, as did the long-postponed visit to his flock, which in the end was never to take place.[100] As vice-protector of several religious communities, including the Benedictines

93. Ibid., 244 (no. 139).

94. Ibid., 123–24 (no. 76), 125 (no. 80).

95. On 17 August 1542 he wrote to Cardinal Farnese that he was indisposed since the day before; see ibid., 284 (no. 223).

96. Ibid., 285 (no. 225).

97. His personal disappointment aside, Contarini was pessimistic about the course of German events: "Prego Iddio che non lasci rovinare quella provincia di Germania, come par che sia per fare, che con quella il resto della Christianità staria pur troppo male" (ibid., 275 [no. 205]). He saw clearly how critical the situation in Germany was: "dalle cose di quelle parti [Germany] pende tutta la salute della Christianità" (281 [no. 218]).

98. Ibid., 284 (no. 224).

99. The tone of Contarini's letter to Cardinal Farnese of 11 August is striking. He expresses thanks for the love the pope has shown him by appointing him once again to the emperor, "an undertaking which I know to be only a little less difficult than the extremely difficult one to the Lutherans in Germany," adding: "as for the hardship of the journey, I do not regard it as much, having dedicated my remaining years to the service first of God, then of His Holiness. To me it suffices to obey promptly" (ibid., 282 [no. 219]).

100. Ibid., 248 (no. 146), 251 (no. 153), 257 (no. 167), 260 (no. 176), and 275 (no. 205).

of the Cassinese Congregation and the Franciscans, Contarini wrote many letters of counsel and direction. They reveal some of his characteristic attitudes, as, for example, this to the friars of the monastery of St. Anthony in Padua, whose discord about an election he tried to end: "We do not want to command you, [since] we desire that your reformation be entirely voluntary and proceed from you, as we see that you, too, desire, and we wish even more than you do that it be more than voluntary, because nobody can be good if he is not good from his own will."[101] Contarini did not in the least change his mind that persuasion was distinctly preferable to coercion, with good example as the most effective means for moving men's hearts: "We see clearly that the life we members of the clergy lead has given great scandal to the Christian people, and from it have arisen the many tumults and troubles we now face. Our duty is to realize this and return to a life that will edify the people by our example, and to remedy the scandal that has already been caused," he wrote to the Franciscans in Venice.[102] Even plainer is his assertion that the wrath of God was provoked to a great extent by the life of bad secular and regular clergy,[103] and that their decadence affected everyone.

Contarini's tolerant attitude, so striking in 1541, remained unchanged. Even as the inquisition was being reorganized in Rome, he remained extremely wary of labeling someone's views as heretical. When the Augustinian hermit Giuliano da Colle, who preached the Lenten sermons of 1542 in Parma, was accused of spreading heresy, Contarini warned that "great caution is necessary before [articles of faith] are condemned as heretical."[104] At a time when the curia was becoming increasingly suspicious of the Capuchine general Bernardino Ochino, the legate invited the friar to Bologna and expressed his pleasure at the thought of being in Ochino's company.[105] Another

101. Ibid., 118 (no. 68): "Non vogliamo commandarvi, desiderando che la vostra riformatione sia in tutta voluntaria et che venga da voi come vedemo che desiderate et noi più che voi desideriamo che sia più che voluntaria, chè niuno puote essere buono se non è buono per voluntà."

102. Ibid., 129 (no. 90): "Vediamo chiaramente che il vivere di noi religiosi ha dato grande scandolo al populo christiano, donde sono nasciuti tanti tumulti et travagli come toccamo con mano. Nostro debito è di ricognoscerci et redurci ad una vita in edificatione del populo con lo exempio nostro che ricompensi al scandolo già dato."

103. Ibid., 96 (no. 24).

104. Letter of 18 April 1542 to Badia: "Et circa questo io sono del'istesso parer vostro, ciò è che ci bisogni gran consideratione prima che si dannino [gli articoli] per hereticj" (ibid., 105 [no. 42]). For da Colle, see Pietro Tacchi-Venturi, *Storia della Compagnia di Gesù in Italia*, 2d ed. (Rome: Civiltà Cattolica, 1950), 1(1):465–66.

105. Casadei, "Lettere," 93 (no. 18).

suspect of heresy, Filippo Valentini, was appointed Contarini's auditor and therefore a member of his household. These instances confirm his openness to theological questions that were being discussed with passion on all sides, as well as his sympathy with the thought of *spirituali* more radical than himself, some of whom later embraced Protestantism.

Daily involvement in government affairs left Contarini little time for literary activities during the months in Bologna. Beccadelli mentions that the legate "wrote for his private study many beautiful annotations to all the epistles of St. Paul, and the Catholic epistles, on which he was still at work when death supervened."[106] These annotations were included in Contarini's collected works as *Scholia in epistolas Divi Pauli*.[107] It is not possible to establish when he began the *Scholia* or commented on specific epistles, since so far no manuscript of this work has come to light. Judging from internal evidence, it was probably composed gradually as the result of his reading and meditation on the letters of St. Paul. It is tempting to examine above all his comments on Romans, and to read them in the light of the discussions about article 5 in Regensburg, though at present to do so would be methodologically indefensible. The only support for such a reading is tenuous at best: a sentence in a letter of Cristoforo Madruzzi, prince-bishop of Trent, mentioning that Contarini had written about healing his wound caused by the emperor's defeat in Africa with study of the Bible.[108] Nothing else supports the supposition that this study was focused on St. Paul, or that its result was the *Scholia*.

There is little secondary literature on this work and its sometimes contradictory theological ideas. Dittrich surmises that Contarini's purpose was "to highlight the rich content of the Pauline epistles and make it accessible to wider circles," adding that "therefore he purposely omits the learned apparatus, strives for the greatest possible brevity, clarity, and comprehensibility, and avoids almost all references

---

106. Beccadelli, "Vita," 59: "Scrisse anchora per suo studio particolare molte belle Annotationi sopra tutte le Epistole di San Paolo, et Catholiche, le quali tuttavia haveva in mano, quando della morte sopravenuto fu." Pole's friend Alvise Priuli in a letter to Beccadelli dated from Viterbo, 13 March 1542, refers to Contarini's "brief exposition" on the epistles of St. Paul. See Maria Cristina Pauselli, "Note sugli *Scholia* di Gasparo Contarini ad Efesini e Galati," *Archiv für Reformationsgeschichte* 83 (1992): 132 n. 18.

107. *Opera*, 435–530.

108. " . . . Et quum in calce litterarum suarum D. V. Rma. scribat, se huic vulneri, quando tempus supersit, studio sacrarum litterarum mederi, non opus est, ut multa verba consolatoria in medium afferam" (Trent, 22 Dec. 1541, in *Monumenti Beccadelli* 1[2]:210). Dittrich, *GC*, 839, suggests without any further evidence that the result of these studies might be the *Scholia*.

to the theological movements and disputes of his time."[109] If Contarini meant to help readers without a theological education, he fulfilled his intention very imperfectly, since his choice of verses to be annotated reflects the flow of his own ideas rather than an attempt at a systematic explanation of the main themes found in the epistles. In the absence of other information, we are left with Beccadelli's statement that the *Scholia* was the result of Contarini's private study, meant primarily for himself.

What insistently occupied his thoughts was justification, about which he did not change his mind after Regensburg. Dittrich has singled out the many passages of the *Scholia* where this topic is mentioned,[110] and even a casual reading of the text shows Contarini returning to it again and again. The annotations of Romans, as might be expected, contain repeated statements about our justification by faith (*per fidem*, 1:6), through faith in the blood of Christ (*per fidem in sanguine Christi*, 3:24), and through the imputation of Christ's justice and his merits (4; 5:12). Sometimes Contarini summarizes an entire epistle or a chapter, as, for example, 2 Corinthians 5: "Christ's justice is given to us and imputed to us. That is the essence";[111] or in his introduction to Hebrews (which he accepts as Pauline): "All saints were wholly justified by faith and through faith. That is the essence."[112] In Ephesians 1:3 we read: "Everywhere Paul tries to show that we are grafted into Christ through faith and charity."[113] Such statements abound in the *Scholia*, tantalizing the reader. But they are disembodied, as it were, since we lack any information about their context. They remain pieces of a puzzle still to be assembled and understood.[114]

If the genesis of the *Scholia* and the exact time of its composition are not known, the contrary is true for a small work written in June 1542, the *Catechesis sive Christiana instructio*.[115] An abundance of precise information about its context exists, beginning with the letters of Mo-

109. *GC*, 839.   110. Ibid., 840–42.   111. *Opera*, 469.
112. Ibid., 515.   113. Ibid., 483.
114. Hünermann, *Theologische Entwicklung*, uses the *Scholia* cautiously for the same reason: its relation with Contarini's other works is unclear, as is its chronology. Pauselli, "Note sugli *Scholia*," is the most recent and detailed examination of Contarini's annotations to Ephesians and Galatians. It compares his exegesis with those of some of his contemporaries, both Catholic and Protestant, as well as with selected patristic sources, especially St. Augustine, without, however, establishing lines of dependency, and concludes that he was eclectic (pp. 152–53).
115. *Opera*, 533–545, now superseded by the edition in Firpo and Marcatto, *Processo* 3:190–221. The printed editions are discussed on pp. 47–61, and the manuscripts on pp. 61–70.

rone's vicar in Modena, Giovanni Domenico Sigibaldi, who reported the spread of heretical ideas in his diocese to the absent bishop.[116] While Morone was on his diplomatic missions in Germany, Sigibaldi worried already in 1540 that the whole city was infected with heresy, like Prague, and that "in shops, on street corners, in houses, and so forth, everyone (as I hear) disputes about faith, free will, purgatory, the Eucharist, and predestination."[117] Controversies among preachers contributed to the volatile religious atmosphere in Modena; Augustinians were especially suspected of introducing "novelties" such as doubt about the existence of purgatory.[118] In the winter of 1540–41 conflicts between various groups in the city intensified, the secular authorities now becoming involved.[119] Morone's vicar was not the man to deal firmly with an increasingly complex problem as the circle of men suspected of heresy grew wider. It came to include the so-called Academy of Modena, an informal group of intellectuals who met for common reading of classical texts and discussions of scientific and philosophical subjects that of course included the religious issues of the day. Among these men the writer Ludovico Castelvetro, the physician Giovanni Grillenzoni, the priest Giovanni Bertari, and Contarini's auditor Filippo Valentini stand out.

Massimo Firpo has discussed the growing religious tensions in Modena in some detail and shown that Morone repeatedly counseled patience, charity, and humanity in dealing with those suspected of unorthodox views in general, and with members of the Academy in particular.[120] When he was finally able to return to his diocese in May 1542, he was shocked to find not only that heresy had made serious inroads among the people, but also that the Academy had played an important role in the spread of heterodox ideas. "In this the common opinion of the entire city concurs," he reported to Cardinal Farnese.[121]

Against this background Morone conceived the idea of requesting members of the Academy to draw up a confession of faith. After they sought various pretexts for avoiding to do so, Morone tried to

116. The most recent and fullest examination of the background to the *Catechesis* is by Firpo, "Spirituali."

117. Ibid., 47.

118. Susanna Peyronel Rambaldi, *Speranze e crisi nel Cinquecento modenese* (Milan: Franco Angeli Editore, 1979), 212–22, discusses the religious unrest due to preachers.

119. Firpo, "Spirituali," 48–50.

120. Ibid., 55–57. Morone's attitude toward those suspected of heresy was very similar to that of Contarini.

121. Quoted in ibid., 59n.58.

convince them to subscribe to a catechism that had been printed on Giberti's order in Verona in 1541. That attempt proved unsuccessful, and the *accademici*, in turn, suggested texts that Morone found unacceptable.[122] Eventually he turned to Contarini for help and counsel on how to ascertain what the members of the Academy actually believed "concerning purgatory, the sacrifice of the mass, the real presence of Christ in the sacrament of the altar, adoration of the host, auricular confession, the legislative authority of the church, intecession and invocation of saints, and the glory of the blessed."[123] The friendship, closeness, and even affection that had developed between the two men made it easy for Morone to confide in Contarini, and for the latter to take a sincere interest in the affairs of his younger, always deferential, but also more practical colleague.[124] Morone paid a brief visit to Bologna during the first week of June, bringing Contarini information in person about the situation in Modena. Within a few days Contarini completed and sent to Morone a confession of faith, the "Articuli orthodoxae professionis," which appeared under the title *Catechesis sive Christiana instructio* in Contarini's collected works of 1571.

Although this little work, consisting of forty-one questions and answers, was ostensibly written for general use and even translated into German,[125] it was actually intended for the Modenese *accademici*. They are not mentioned in the work, for Contarini did not want to single them out for censure and so alienate them further. Instead he adopted the transparent strategy of addressing the issues they had raised and giving broad definitions of articles of faith in the hope that the *accademici* would accept them, remain in the church, and make interference in Modena by Roman authorities unnecessary .

The first question asks what it is to be a Christian, and Contarini offers a very simple reply: "To be a Christian is to be a member of Christ, incorporated into him through faith and the sacraments

122. Ibid., 62–64.

123. Morone's detailed letter to Contarini of 21 May 1542 is printed in *Ep. Poli* 3:cclxvii–cclxxi; and in part in Firpo, "Spirituali," 60–61n.63; and Fragnito, "Gli 'spirituali,'" 268n.41.

124. The growth of their friendship and the changes in Morone due to Contarini's influence are remarkable. The solicitous and kind tone Contarini adopted in his correspondence with Morone is exemplified in Casadei, "Lettere," 113 (no. 57), 120–21 (no. 73), and 224 (no. 100). In writing to his friend Ermolao Barbaro on 5 July (ibid., 256 [no. 166]), Contarini mentioned Morone, "with whom I am joined by a love and affection as great as it is possible to express."

125. Christoph Monfang, *Katholische Katechismen des sechzehnten Jahrhunderts in deutscher Sprache* (Mainz, 1881), includes this version.

of faith."[126] From the beginning, the necessity of the sacraments is stressed. The definition of the term *sacraments* is entirely traditional: they are "visible signs of invisible grace." Contarini refers to the authority of St. Paul and Thomas Aquinas,[127] affirms the existence of seven sacraments, and proceeds to define each. He treats the Eucharist extensively, linking its discussion with that of the mass. As he had done in Regensburg, so he now also upholds the teaching of the Fourth Lateran Council: "After the consecration there is not the substance of bread and wine under the visible signs, but the true body and blood of Christ, as is manifest by the opinion of the entire church and all the doctors."[128] What is immediately striking here, of course, is the omission of the word *transubstantiation*, on which Contarini had insisted so vehemently in Germany. There he had defended a solemnly promulgated dogma which the Lutherans denied. Now he was addressing men whom he regarded as fellow Catholics in the hope of keeping them in the fold despite their mistaken ideas. He presumed the existence of a broad consensus between himself and them, and therefore made his formulations as noncontroversial as possible, consistent with his preference for gentle persuasion instead of coercion.

The Modenese are further instructed about the nature of the Eucharist as Contarini takes on specifically Protestant tenets. He affirms the presence of Christ's body and blood in the host, deriving from this the necessity of its adoration;[129] states that "the mass, as all ancient and modern doctors teach, is a sacrifice"; and emphasizes the utility of offering the mass for the living and the dead.[130] As he had done with the Eucharist, however, so now in discussing the mass Contarini gives a definition into which it was possible to read a number of meanings. To the question concerning the manner in which the mass is a sacrifice, he replies that

the mass is a sacrifice of praise, a sacrifice of thanksgiving: it is a sacrifice because it is the remembrance of that unique sacrifice by which Christ offered himself to the father for us through the Holy Spirit; it is also a sacrifice because it is the oblation through which we offer Christ and his sufferings (as Augustine says in Book Ten of *The City of God*), and by which we offer the entire

---

126. Firpo and Marcatto, *Processo* 3:190.   127. Ibid., 192 (question 5).

128. Ibid., 196 (question 11): "Post consecrationem non est sub sensibilibus illis signis substantia panis seu vini, sed verum corpus Christi et eius sanguis, quod perspicuum est et sensu totius ecclesiae et doctorum omnium."

129. Ibid., 198 (question 15).

130. Ibid., 199 (question 16), 200–202 (questions 18–20).

church through Christ to almighty God, in order that through Christ we may draw close to Him, the supreme good of all goods.[131]

Obviously, this politic if diffuse statement avoided forcing the reader to choose between the mass as sacrifice or as memorial service.

Seven articles are devoted to the sacrament of penance. The Modenese *accademici* were familiar with the sharp differences in the views of Catholic and Protestant theologians on this subject. Contarini is seeking to base his explanation on an uneasy blend of elements from the New Testament, Thomas Aquinas, and canon law. Beginning with the lapidary definition of penance as the sacrament "whose form and perfection is the absolution by the priest,"[132] he goes on to instruct the reader that it derives its power "from faith in the sufferings of Christ, as St. Thomas says. For, as the Apostle [Paul] says in several places (as in Eph. 1:7), the remission of sins and reconciliation with God does not happen except through Christ and his merits, to whom we are joined through faith as we accept the spirit by whom we are either made a new creation, as in baptism, or raised again and given new life, as in the sacrament of penance."[133] Neither Romans 1:17, the great Protestant proof-text for justification by faith, nor Contarini's own unchanged views of twofold justification are mentioned. Clearly, he was steering the Modenese away from the controversies about justification by referring to the views of St. Thomas. But in the very next sentence faith in the merits of Christ as the keystone in reconciling man and God appears, opening the possibility for the Modenese to accept Contarini's formulation.

He also insists, however, on the juridical character of penance when he defines the priest as judge in article 25, or discusses satisfaction in a remarkably diffuse article 26. His conception of the church as a visible community governed in an orderly fashion by law can be seen in the

131. Ibid., 199–200 (question 17): "Missa est sacrificium laudis, est sacrificium gratiarum actionis, est sacrificium quia est memoria unici illius sacrificii quo Christus se pro nobis obtulit patri per spiritum sanctum; est etiam sacrificium quia est oblatio qua offerimus Christum eiusque passionem, ut inquit Augustinus in decimo De civitate Dei, et totam ecclesiam per Christum Deo omnipotenti, ut ei inhaereamus per Christum tanquam supremo omnium bono."

132. Ibid., 204 (question 23): "Sacramentum poenitentiae, cuius forma et perfectio est absolutio sacerdotis."

133. Ibid., 204 (question 24): "Unde vim habet sacramentum poenitentiae? Responsio. A fide passionis Christi, ut dicit beatus Thomas. Nam, sicuti dicit Apostolus in pluribus locis ut in epistola ad Ephesios c. I, [7], remissio peccatorum et reconciliatio cum Deo non fit nisi per Christum et eius merita, cui coniungimur per fidem ut accipiamus spiritum per quem vel nova creatura efficiamur, ut in baptismate, vel resurgamus et reviviscamus, ut in sacramento poenitentiae."

next few articles, which clarify such issues as the validity of confession made to a layman or to a priest other than one's own parish priest, absolution given by a sinful and personally unworthy priest, or the existence of purgatory. In each case straightforward and traditional answers are given, as might be expected of a man for whom the necessity of institutions to guide and supervise human society was self-evident and beyond doubt.

Contarini the former Venetian statesman did not deny his deep respect for a hierarchically ordered society when discussing ritual, ceremonies, and manmade regulations. While acknowledging that Christ gave his followers no rules on these matters, Contarini derives their necessity from reason. Article 35 explains that proper order and obedience to authority must exist in the church for the good of all its members, and article 37 makes reference to an array of patristic writers and doctors of the church in support of the Christian hierarchy and the monastic life. But Contarini is careful not to define the latter as a good work. The monk is likened to a traveler who strains all his forces in the ascent toward his goal, which is the perfection of charity.[134]

The cult of the saints, "the most living and noblest members of Christ,"[135] is endorsed, with the veneration of their images justified by reference to the decrees of the Seventh Ecumenical Council in 787, which declared them to be "as the books of the uneducated"[136] because they move believers to the veneration and imitation of those depicted. This article contains a rare mention of art by Contarini. Indeed, his attitude toward art generally is almost puritanical and makes one wonder what he thought about the great artists of his time, about Raphael or Michelangelo, whose works he had certainly seen: "We cannot approve of the practice of those who use pictures and images of the saints to set off the skill of the artist and offer vain or even base delight to those who look on the images, and do not have a basis in the church's teaching for allowing these images but in fact abuse the church's teaching in order to give lascivious or secular delight."[137]

134. Ibid., 216 (question 37).
135. Ibid., 218 (question 38): "Sancti sunt viventia et nobilissima membra Christi. . . ."
136. Ibid., 219 (question 39): "In septima Synodo, sub Constantino et Hyrene, decretum fuit imagines tanquam libros idiotarum esse, ut aspectu etiam doctos moveant et excitent ad venerationem et imitationem optimorum hominum, in ecclesia admittendas et venerandas, non quidem ut eis veneratio defferatur, sed sanctis per eas."
137. Ibid.: " . . . non probandum censemus eorum usum qui in picturis et imaginibus sanctorum, ut artificis peritia ostendatur et delectatio vel vana vel turpis ex earum aspectu videntibus offeratur, nullam habent rationem institutionis ecclesiae in imaginibus admittendis, immo ea abutuntur in lasciviam vel inanem oblectationem."

Two articles address specific matters that had been disputed in Modena. Article 31 concerns whether Christians who have died rise up to heaven immediately or wait until the resurrection of their bodies. Contarini answers that those who have died "freed from the bonds of sin and washed in the blood of Christ from the stains of sin" immediately reached blessedness in soul and spirit.[138] The mention of this esoteric issue indicates that he knew the opinions of Camillo Renato, a Sicilian Franciscan who preached in Modena in 1540 before his imprisonment and trial for heresy and eventual escape to Switzerland. Among Renato's teachings was that physical death is followed by "the provisional death or sleep of the soul" until the last judgment and the resurrection of the body (psychopannychism),[139] which Contarini considered erroneous.

The final article was probably written against the opinion of the Modenese priest Giovanni Bertari, who held that someone who prays without understanding what he is saying sins and blasphemes.[140] Contarini recognizes that praying in a language which is not understood shows good intentions, and that the simple people should be encouraged to say prayers even if they do not understand them—meaning, of course, prayers in Latin. Still, he makes the commonsense statement that it is preferable and more useful to comprehend the prayers one recites.[141] A heartfelt "The end. Praise be to God!" concludes this work.

The history of Contarini's articles leading to their acceptance and signing by the Modenese *accademici* after the cardinal's death has been told expertly and in detail by Massimo Firpo.[142] Our concern here is with the significance of the articles for understanding Contarini's thought. Besides furnishing yet another proof of his irenic and conciliatory approach to dissenters or doubters, they offer evidence of his political sensitivity in the extremely delicate situation of the *spirituali* at almost the precise moment when the Roman Inquisition was

138. Ibid., 209 (question 31): "Qui ex hac vita decedunt soluti a vinculis peccati et abluti in sanguine Christi peccatorum maculas . . . confestim ad beatitudinem perveniunt animo et spiritu . . . "

139. See George Huntston Williams, "Camillo Renato (c. 1500–?1575)," in *Italian Reformation Studies in Honor of Laelius Socinus (1562–1962)*, ed. John A. Tedeschi, *Proceedings of the Unitarian Historical Society* 14, pts. 1 and 2 (1962–63): 133; according to Williams, Renato presumably held before his trial "that the souls of the saints and the others justified have not yet entered heaven and will not enter in fact until after the last judgment . . . and do not yet enjoy the delights of paradise nor the vision of the highest God."

140. Firpo and Marcatto, *Processo* 3:220n.171.

141. Ibid., 221.   142. Firpo, "Spirituali," 80–111.

being organized. Both he and Morone tried by all means possible to avoid a major eruption of heresy-hunting in Modena, and they were aided in this by two prominent Modenese, Cortese and especially Sadoleto, who ultimately played a key role in persuading the *accademici* to sign the articles.[143]

In his dealings with the Academy, Contarini assumed the role of mediator rather than that of its protector. On several occasions his patience was tried, as when he wrote to Morone: "It seems to me that I see in them [the *accademici*] such an arrogance and pride, mother of all evil, joined to great ignorance, that I think very ill of them. . . . I do not believe that they can be brought back by humanity and courtesy."[144] Another time, when he was irritated by what he considered their quibbling over the fine points of Latin instead of engaging in discussion of substantial issues, he burst out: "I care little about being censured, especially in what concerns the Latin and Ciceronian language, which I have forgotten already many years [ago], and I do not think any more about it."[145] Despite these annoying instances, though, his basic aim remained unaltered: to keep in the Catholic church a troubling and troubled group of intellectuals who were attracted to Protestant ideas.

This episode depicts where Contarini stood in 1542. His attitude toward the *accademici* was in conformity with the more inclusive Catholicism of Renaissance prelates rather than that of the men who became champions of the Counter-Reformation. The church to him was a mother, "mater ecclesia," able to encompass an enormous variety of people and opinions provided they agreed with broad, comprehensive articles of faith that left many specific questions open. His mentality was not that of the inquisitor or the intolerant guardian at the gate, scrutinizing the minutiae of a man's convictions. Contarini the aristocrat persisted in his assumption that there was such a thing as a common ethos among the educated elite of Italy. To its members, including the Modenese *accademici*, he attributed the same goodwill that he himself brought to discussions of religious issues. But as had happened in Regensburg, so now, too, he was mistaken in thinking

143. *GC*, 809–10, 816–17; Douglas, *Sadoleto*, 165–67; Firpo, "Spirituali," 100–102.

144. Letter of 13 July 1542, *Reg.*, 353 (Inedita, no. 89); text corrected by Firpo, "Spirituali," 84: " . . . a me pare vedere in costoro una tale arrogantia et superbia, madre di ogni male, adiuncta cum grande ignorantia, che penso di loro ogni male; . . . né penso che per via de humanità et gentilezza si possino raquistare."

145. Firpo, "Spirituali," 83: "Poco mi curo d'essere censurato, massime nella lingua latina et ciceroniana, che già molti anni mi ho scordato né più vi penso."

that men would be willing to stop arguing about doctrine for the sake of peace and concord. Ironically, this attitude separated him not only from the conservative members of the curia and the college of cardinals, but also from the more radical *spirituali*, whether in Modena or in Viterbo with Pole.

Less than a decade after Contarini's death Francesco Negri, a Protestant exile from Italy, wrote bitingly about men "who seem to have founded a new school of Christianity arranged according to their fashion, where they do not deny that justification of man is through Jesus Christ but then do not want to admit the consequences that necessarily follow from this."[146] Negri's criticism goes to the heart of what troubled some of the *spirituali* about Contarini. There is no doubt that Pole, while continuing to profess his friendship and devotion, tried to avoid a showdown over theological questions. Instead he repeatedly turned a deaf ear to Contarini's requests for replies to his writings, especially those dealing with justification and related issues. How do we interpret Pole's unwillingness to support Contarini or to debate his ideas? Why did he retreat to bland phrases about his hope to discuss the issues orally at some other time?[147]

One modern answer, given with verve by Paolo Simoncelli, posits a breakup of the *spirituali* after Regensburg into a moderate wing led by Contarini and a radical one with Pole at its head. In this view, an ever-widening rift developed between the two groups with every new doctrinal challenge, from the article on justification to the catechism for the Modenese in 1542, and finally to the thorny issues of penance and atonement.[148] Contarini is presented as a figure increasingly isolated between the intransigent curialists on the one hand and the radical *spirituali* on the other, a man of moderation when such a stance was no longer possible in the charged religious atmosphere following his "defeat" of 1541. Although he supposedly tried to draw nearer the group of Viterbo both politically and doctrinally, he ultimately proved to belong to the orthodox rather than the radical side, since unlike the radical *spirituali* he accepted Lutheran premises without their conclusions.[149] Basically, we are back to Negri's statement.

146. Francesco Negri, *Della tragedia . . . intitolata Libero arbitrio*, 2d ed. (n.p., 1550 [actually 1551]); cited by Firpo and Marcatto, *Processo* 1:248n.13.

147. Simoncelli, *Evangelismo italiano*, 105–6, 120, 122–23.

148. Ibid., 113–24.

149. Ibid., 126. For a somewhat different view, see Tommaso Bozza, *Nuovi studi sulla riforma in Italia*, vol. 1: *Il Beneficio di Cristo* (Rome: Edizioni di Storia e Letteratura, 1976), 80, who thinks that Contarini belonged "to the left wing of the church."

I would like to argue for a somewhat different interpretation of the evidence by positing greater closeness between Contarini and Pole, as well as a less sharp division of the *spirituali* into the two groups described by Simoncelli. My evidence will be Contarini's last treatise, "Cardinali Polo de paenitentia" (To Cardinal Pole Concerning Penance), written the month before his death.[150] In this short work he "admitted" the consequences mentioned by Negri, and tried to explain his views. Contarini was neither stuck in some "moderate" position from which he was unable to budge, nor did he think of himself and Pole as moving along such different theological tracks that a gap had opened between them which he had to bridge by seeking to draw closer to the English cardinal. In Pole he continued to see a kindred spirit whom he believed to share identical concerns for reform of the church. Because he died unexpectedly after a brief illness, he had no time to give his ideas definitive shape. Although his last little work can in no sense be considered his testament, it is emblematic of the views he held at the end of his life, in the particularly delicate situation of the summer of 1542, and deserves closer examination.[151]

The occasion for the composition of "De poenitentia" were the queries and reservations Pole had expressed about the articles touching on penance, apparently above all article 25,[152] of the catechism for the Modenese which Contarini had sent to Viterbo. Pole returned his comments and annotations to Bologna, together with the request for a fuller explanation of Contarini's ideas about penance. Unfortunately, this letter of Pole's is lost, as is his reply to "De poenitentia."[153] The relation between the two cardinals during these months has to be reconstructed for the most part from Contarini's treatise. He addresses Pole as a friend who, like himself, accepts justification by faith and is facing the necessity of deciding what the implications of this belief are on the pastoral level. Unlike his previous retreat into exclamations about the riches of the wisdom of God, Contarini now is at pains to work out a coherent and convincing position. He stresses his closeness

150. The treatise was written after 22 July 1542; see *GC*, 820. Pole acknowledged its receipt on 8 August; *Ep. Poli* 3:60; and Firpo, "Spirituali," 75.

151. Text in *Reg.*, 353–61 (Inedita, no. 90). Contarini's autograph in ASV, A.A., Arm. I–XVIII, 6461, fols. 132r–144r, is used here to correct the printed version, which has *paenitentia* rather than *poenitentia* as in the manuscript.

152. Firpo, "Spirituali," 74.

153. In a letter of 27 August, three days after Contarini's death, Pole's friend Alvise Priuli asked Beccadelli to keep the last letters of Pole and Vittoria Colonna to Contarini; cited by Firpo, "Spirituali," 76n.113.

to Pole, whom he sees struggling with problems that both would like to discuss further: "I see that Your Reverence wishes a fuller explanation from me, which I likewise would like from you about that which you say concerning satisfaction toward God, the church, and one's neighbor."[154]

Contarini begins by stating that the Lutherans have built everything on the foundation of their faith, which is the belief that Christ by his passion has given full satisfaction to God for all our sins: "Whoever is grafted into Christ through faith has remission of his sins and full satisfaction for them, because that [the satisfaction] of Christ becomes his." From this the Lutherans deduced that no other satisfaction was necessary; all else, like purgatory or indulgences, they considered only as means of exacting money from the people, and saw religious vows as mere hypocrisy.[155] As this teaching spread to Italy, it met with two different reactions. Those who defended the church opposed this doctrine and stressed the necessity of works to such an extent that they contradicted the very basis of Christian belief, while those who accepted it became Lutherans and presumptuously abandoned the teaching of the Catholic church, "believing their wits more than the opinion of all modern theologians as well as the ancient authors." Contarini and Pole should flee these alternatives: "I exhort both of us to steer clear of this Scylla and Charybdis, and to pass safely between them without abandoning the teaching of the church, but believing in it more than in our own wits."[156]

This is a reiteration of the same principle Contarini had embraced in Regensburg, that the *magisterium* of the church must take precedence over personal opinions. But what did the church teach about penance that Christians must believe? This tract includes one of the most frequently cited passages in all of Contarini's writings, one that has often been lifted out of context and used as evidence for his full agreement with the key Lutheran doctrine of justification by faith alone: "The foundation of the Lutheran edifice is most true, and we must not contradict it in any way, but must accept it as true and catholic, indeed as the basis of the Christian religion."[157] Yet upon reading further we find his affirmation that the doctrine of justification *sola fide*, the basis of not just the Lutheran but the Christian edifice, is solidly rooted in Catholic theology, especially that of St. Thomas. The Lutherans have done nothing more than dress this ancient teaching of the church in

154. *Reg.*, 354.   155. Ibid.   156. Ibid., 355.   157. Ibid., 358.

new words and boast that they alone have understood correctly what St. Paul wrote.[158]

Because he did not consider justification by faith a Lutheran innovation but rather an ancient doctrine, Contarini saw no dilemma for the Catholic who held fast to it, as he himself did without uncertainty or doubt. But Pole realized what some of the attendant problems for Catholics were, if Contarini's summary correctly represents what Pole wrote: "I see that you say that the sinner is completely reconciled with God by Christ, and that there is no need to add anything of ours, and then you say that he has offended the church and himself; the offense against himself is nothing other than the offense against natural law written by God in our hearts. Strengthened by the words of Your Reverence I have undertaken to elucidate [further] what you have said and what I have."[159] Judging from this passage, Pole raised the question of how far sin was an offense not only against God, but also against the church and one's own nature.

Having decided against employing the language of scholastic philosophy,[160] maybe because he knew that Pole did not like to use it, Contarini in his treatise nevertheless adheres to the substance if not the terminology of Thomistic doctrine. He explains that because sin is a threefold transgression, it requires more than one kind of satisfaction. The sinner can simultaneously offend against divine, natural, and human law. The benefit of Christ's suffering on the cross has given satisfaction for transgressions against divine law, but what about transgressions against the the others? For example, adultery offends against all three kinds of law, as does murder.[161] Contarini considers a most significant divergence of Protestantism from Catholicism to be the Protestant teaching that stops short of requiring appropriate satisfaction for sins. While recognizing the right of civil authorities to impose punishment, the Protestants have skipped over the norms of natural law and all that follows from them, including the doctrine of purgatory. The mistake of the Protestants distorts the ancient and accepted doctrine of

158. Ibid., 354.

159. Ibid., 360–61: " . . . vedo, ch'ella dice, che il peccatore per Christo e perfectamente reconciliato cum dio, ne vi bisogna che vi pongamo del nostro, poi dice che ha offeso la chiesia et se stesso; l'offensione di se stesso non è altra che l'offensione della lege naturale scritta nelli nostri cuori da dio, pero confirmato io dalle parole di V.S. mi son posto a fare questa dechiaratione delli sui detti et delli mei."

160. "Io riferiro la doctrina di San Thomaso, ma non usero gia il modo suo di parlare, et la dilatero piu di quello che e stato facto da lui" (ibid., 356).

161. Ibid., 358.

penance in the Christian church, which has always taught that only God forgives our sins through the merits of Christ but that punishment due to sin remains. The sinner must render satisfaction for the transgressions of the positive law of church and state and for offenses against his neighbor. This is necessary because of God's justice.[162]

Repeating his conviction that Catholics and Lutherans shared the crucial doctrine of justification by faith, Contarini ultimately finds the Catholic answer to its consequences in a Thomistic view of atonement. He plainly states toward the end of his treatise where he stands: "We have explained how to guide ourselves in accepting and rejecting the Lutheran structure by basing our treatise on the doctrine of St. Thomas, that is, by following his guidance."[163]

He was not "stranded intellectually" because of his inability to "bridge the gap between two doctrines which led in contrary directions," as a sensitive and thoughtful scholar maintained.[164] To him, the two doctrines were compatible. Contarini was schooled in the theology of St. Thomas, but also in the political world of Venice, and in "De poenitentia" he combined categories of ideas drawn from both spheres. We have repeatedly seen his conviction that a hierarchical order was necessary for all aspects of human society, whether religious, ecclesiastical, or civil. Applying this thinking to sin, he had no difficulty conceiving it as an act that simultaneously offended a number of norms in descending order of gravity. On the highest level, that of Christian reality, sin was an offense against God for which no human action could merit God's forgiveness. The sinner's hope was in the benefits of Christ's death rather than in any action he could perform himself.[165]

But as one descended from that level to the realms of ecclesiastical and civil society and the moral universe of each individual, sin assumed a different import, depending on its context. As a matter of justice,

162. "Questa paena l'homo reconciliato cum Dio per li meriti della passione di Christo et per virtu della absolutione del sacerdote resuscitato in Christo per il spirito de Christo, che ha de novo recevuto, la patisse o qui over in purgatorio, patientemente laudando dio et amando piu la iustitia de dio, che il suo commodo" (ibid., 359, corrected with ASV, A.A., Arm. I–XVIII, 6461, fol. 114v).

163. "Hor dechiarato che habiamo, a quale modo ci devemo governare in acettare et reiicere questo aedificio luterano, fundando questo nostro discorso sopra la doctrina di San Thomaso, cioe prendendo lo indice da lui" (ibid., 360).

164. Fenlon, *Heresy and Obedience*, 65.

165. *Reg.*, 358: "Per Christo perfectamente etiam siamo liberati dalla obligatione et reato della paena aeterna, ne qui ci bisogna opere nostre ne compagno alcuno, a solo Christo havemo questa obligatione, da lui solo devemo cognoscere questo beneficio."

divine and secular, satisfaction had to be made at each level of transgression. This was a matter not of theology but of equity. Contarini's
categories of thought were scholastic, even if his language was not, but
they were also political. As a Venetian magistrate, he had dealt with
criminal transgressions without doubting that they required satisfaction if the authority of the state was to be preserved. So, too, atonement for breaking the norms of natural law to him was a self-evident
necessity. Men were not free to disregard the laws of reason and society
because Christ died for all on the cross; forensic justification of the sinner still required that the demands of justice be met.

Pole understood this argument. But he did not think in scholastic
terms, and he was obviously loath to engage in a debate that would call
his friend's intellectual assumptions into question. Maybe Pole could
intuit that Contarini's explanation was not only intellectual but deeply
personal as well, combining the thoughts of a Catholic and a Venetian
statesman. Pole's unwillingness to explain his views fully might be attributed to his realization that he and Contarini, whom he did not
want to alienate, quite literally spoke different theological languages.
Pole was not interested in his friend's hierarchical ordering of the consequences of sin or his entire logical and Thomistic argumentation. He
offered another way, that of applying "two rules, of Scripture and
of experience,"[166] to the questions under discussion. It is obvious that
his ideas pointed to a much greater scriptural orientation and subjec-
tivism than did Contarini's—a fact that later on did not escape the
inquisition.[167]

It would be a mistake to view Pole in the summer of 1542 as some
sort of crypto-Protestant who distanced himself from the "moderate"
Contarini because of doctrinal disagreements. Both men, after all, remained in the church and submitted themselves to its teaching. Their
differing ways of dealing with the implication of *sola fide* had a great
deal to do with their political aims as proponents of reform and their
respective temperaments. Contarini was more open, direct, and anxious for consensus among the *spirituali*, while Pole was more subtle,
circumspect, and even enigmatic. When he became the leading figure
among the *spirituali* after Contarini's death and curial conservatives
came increasingly to mistrust him and his circle, these qualities stood
him in good stead. He was also the better theologian of the two. If

166. To Contarini, Viterbo, 1 May 1542, in *Ep. Poli* 3:53.
167. Fenlon, *Heresy and Obedience*, 67–68.

one accepted the structure of Contarini's argument, which moved from theology to philosophy through reasoning by analogy, then it was possible to agree that he had reconciled the necessity of penance with justification by faith alone. But Pole was more aware than Contarini of the theologically unsystematic way in which this reconciliation was accomplished. His criteria of "Scripture and experience," although not spelled out, ultimately offered more intellectual freedom to the Christian than Contarini's uneasy alliance of *sola fide* and scholastic reasoning.

Contarini's biographer Franz Dittrich, an apologist for Catholicism in the *Kulturkampf* of nineteenth-century Germany,[168] throughout his volume insists on the absolute Catholic orthodoxy of his subject. In discussing "De poenitentia," however, he is constrained to admit that Contarini's explanation of satisfaction "does not entirely agree with Catholic dogma."[169] Dittrich's reason for this statement lies in Contarini's "protestantizing conception of justification," which downplays human cooperation with divine grace, and his continued use of such phrases as "per fidem in sanguine suo," which are open to misunderstanding.[170] Dittrich measures Contarini's orthodoxy by the standards of Tridentine decrees, which is methodologically inappropriate. "De poenitentia," which satisfied neither Protestants nor Catholics, is a signal example of Contarini's religious thought. He had found a personally acceptable solution that because of its hybrid nature could not be transposed to the pastoral level. Here, maybe better than in any other single piece of writing, we see the Achilles' heel of the *spirituali*. Not of the "radical" or "moderate" *spirituali*, but of all those *spirituali* who did not want to break with the Catholic church.

Contarini's reputation has stood high ever since his death 450 years ago. Contemporaries eulogized him as a virtuous and learned man,[171]

168. Kurt-Victor Selge, "Conclusione del convegno," in Cavazzana Romanelli (ed.), *Gaspare Contarini e il suo tempo*, 243–44.

169. *GC*, 822.

170. Ibid., 823: "Erscheint schon diese unhaltbare Begründung der katholischen Satisfactionstheorie als die Folge einer zu grossen Annäherung an den protestantischen Rechtfertigungsbegriff, so beweist auch im übrigen diese Abhandlung, daß Contarini trotz aller Erfahrungen, die er gemacht, trotz alles Widerspruches, den er gefunden hatte, seinen protestantisirenden [*sic*] Rechtfertigungsbegriff in nichts geändert hat."

171. The early eulogy by the Venetian patrician Michele Barozzi (1535–59), in VBC, Cod. Cicogna 2978/28-I, was an extravagant humanistic piece "in praise of famous men" and gives little idea of how precisely Contarini was remembered by men who knew him. It is doubtful that it was delivered before the Venetian Senate, as Hackert thinks (*Staatsschrift*, 1). For other early mentions of Contarini, see Giancarlo Morel, "Gasparo Contarini negli appunti del Mazzuchelli," *Atti dell'Accademia delle scienze di Torino* 108 (1968–69): 279–303.

while later historians, both Catholic and Protestant, developed the image of the cardinal as a spiritual, serious, and irenic churchman intent on healing the schism in Western Christianity. In a nineteenth-century novel we find him in the character of a wise but crafty Catholic who almost succeeds in converting the young German Protestant hero;[172] in another guise he appears, unexpectedly enough, in a forgotten, or at least hitherto unrecorded, opera entitled *Contarini*.[173] The most recent Italian scholarly works interpret him, as we have seen, as the leader of the *spirituali*, whose unsuccessful mission to Regensburg supposedly marked his personal defeat together with that of the moderate and conciliatory proponents of reform at the papal court. A recent American work, by contrast, goes so far as to state that his appointment in 1535 marked the beginning of the Counter-Reformation.[174]

In these pages, another image of Contarini has emerged. First, he should not be cast in the mold of a major theoretician of Catholic reform. An examination of his writings shows that he was not an original thinker in either philosophy or theology. His most characteristic theological insight about the centrality of justification by faith had its basis not in theory but in his personal experience. Although he never wavered in this belief, he did not succeed in expressing it in such language and with such reasons as to convince those who did not share his deeply personal theological ideas. Most of his writings were *pièces d'occasion* rather than carefully crafted works, and they failed to sway readers who began with different theological premises.

Second, the "defeat" of Contarini as the result of the colloquy of Regensburg has been overdramatized. Had his mission been perceived in purely negative terms by Pope Paul III, it would be very difficult to explain the appointment of not just one but three *spirituali* cardinals in June 1542, all of them friends of Contarini. Morone, Badia, and Cortese were men whose voices strengthened the politically liberal element in the college of cardinals. It is inconceivable that a pontiff as

172. Friedrich von Uechtritz, *Albrecht Holm: eine Geschichte aus der Reformationszeit* (Berlin: Verlag von Alexander Duncker, 1852–53). "Contarini" is the the title of chap. 3, 1(3):231–71. At the end Contarini, although a powerful cardinal of the Roman church, trembles at the thought of being suspect to the inquisition.

173. By Henry Hugo Pierson (1815–73), in *Chambers's Biographical Dictionary*, ed. Wm. Geddie and J. Liddell Geddie (Edinburgh and London: W. & R. Chambers, 1931), 743.

174. John C. Olin, *Catholic Reform from Cardinal Ximenes to the Council of Trent, 1495–1563: An Essay with Illustrative Documents and a Brief Study of St. Ignatius Loyola* (New York: Fordham University Press, 1990), 19: "It is at this point in 1535 when Paul III brought Gasparo Contarini to Rome that the Counter-Reformation in one sense of the word may be said to have begun."

shrewd as Paul III would add to the college at this crucial juncture men whose views had been totally discredited. Cardinal Farnese, the pope's alter ego in the conduct of politics, remarked to Pole that if Contarini could have picked cardinals himself, he certainly would have made the same choices.[175] Contarini added to the almost extravagant expression of his joy at the appointment of his friends an affirmation of his confidence that the pope was executing God's design for the good of the church. "My pen is carried away by my emotion," he concluded.[176] Hardly the sentiments of a bitter or isolated man!

Finally, the significance of the unsuccessful colloquy of Regensburg for the history of Italian Evangelism has been exaggerated. After July 1542, the pope and his advisors quite deliberately and realistically abandoned a course of action that they had adopted under pressure from the emperor and that had led nowhere. But there was no sudden change of attitude at the papal court toward the *spirituali*, nor did they abruptly fall from favor. Contarini was appointed legate to Charles V in August 1542. According to one report, Paul III, in conversation with Cardinal Sadoleto, spoke about Contarini and said "so many good things about his goodness and virtue, that it seemed as if he were speaking about St. Augustine. He added that the court was greatly mistaken in reputing Msgr. Contarini as pro-imperial, for in his embassy to Germany he had sufficiently demonstrated where his sympathies lay, and whether he was a pro-imperial or a true churchman. He even said that this last was Contarini's true title."[177] Ironically, it was not the pope but the emperor who in the end repudiated Contarini: Charles V did not accept him as legate, probably because of his firm stand on transubstantiation in Regensburg.

The main reason the *spirituali* initially lost ground and influence was not their "defeat" by ideological opponents, but the fact that their ideas on how to solve the crisis in the church had not worked. Moreover, once the reorganized Roman Inquisition began to function, their religious views became increasingly suspect. This suspicion naturally grew stronger after a number of them fled to Protestant states or cities. Another important factor was the death during the 1540s of some of their most conspicuous members: Fregoso died in 1541, Contarini in 1542, Giberti in 1543, Sadoleto, Bembo, and Badia in 1547, and

175. Pole to Contarini, Rome, 2 June 1542, in *Reg.*, 234 (no. 895).
176. *Reg.*, 234 (no. 896).
177. Carlo Gualteruzzi to Ludovico Beccadelli, Rome, 7 Aug. 1542, quoted in Fragnito, "Evangelismo e intrasigenti," 27–28n.26.

Cortese in 1548. Church leaders of the next generation were men of the Counter-Reformation whose outlook was quite different. By and large they shared a militant attitude toward Protestantism and considered its adherents as heretics to be combated rather than as Christian brethren with whom Catholics could or should discuss their faith. The old church of the Renaissance was about to disappear, and with it the religious openness that had characterized many of its leading figures, including the *spirituali* cardinals. It was not a matter of fanatics replacing proponents of toleration, but of legalistic bureaucrats succeeding more latitudinarian prelates who had been educated in the spirit of Renaissance humanism.

Contarini died in Bologna on 24 August 1542. Before long a mythology grew up around the visit to the dying cardinal of Bernardino Ochino, general of the Capuchins, who a few days later defected to Calvin's Geneva, and maintained that Contarini had encouraged him to flee from Italy. But the shape of Contarini's whole life and thought makes this improbable. He died as he had lived, as a Christian, a Venetian, and a cardinal. The government, society, and political world of Venice in which he was formed gave his ideas their distinctive character and defined the categories into which he ordered reality. He can best be understood as a *zentiluomo veneziano*, a Venetian gentleman, who had internalized and idealized the traditional values of his homeland so that they became the filter through which he saw the great political and religious issues of his time. He was a Venetian patrician first, and a Roman cardinal second. Most of all, he held a view of the church and embodied in his person ideals of *civilitas* and *humanitas* that became irrelevant in the fast-approaching age of religious wars. Contarini can be a wonderful partner in a dialogue with modern interlocutors who care about questions of political and religious order, of liberty and authority. His thought still invites them to meditate on unresolved issues and on thinkable alternatives to the course of events in church and state, then and now.

Appendixes

1 Genealogy of the Contarini della Madonna dell'Orto, 14th–17th centuries

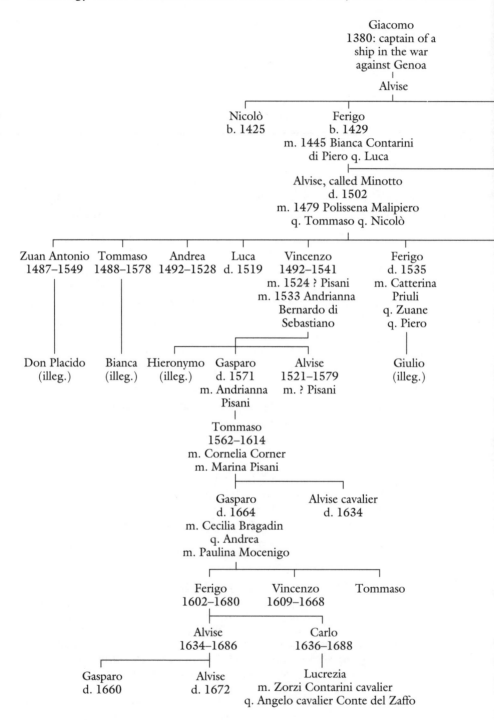

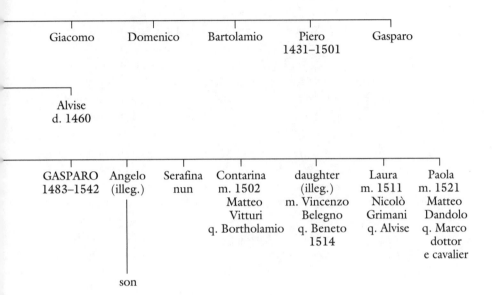

Giacomo   Domenico   Bartolamio   Piero   Gasparo
                                   1431–1501

Alvise
d. 1460

GASPARO   Angelo   Serafina   Contarina   daughter   Laura   Paola
1483–1542 (illeg.)   nun   m. 1502   (illeg.)   m. 1511   m. 1521
                                Matteo   m. Vincenzo   Nicolò   Matteo
                                Vitturi   Belegno   Grimani   Dandolo
                                q. Bortholamio q. Beneto   q. Alvise q. Marco
                                             1514   dottor
                                                                      e cavalier

son

2 Structure of the Venetian Government

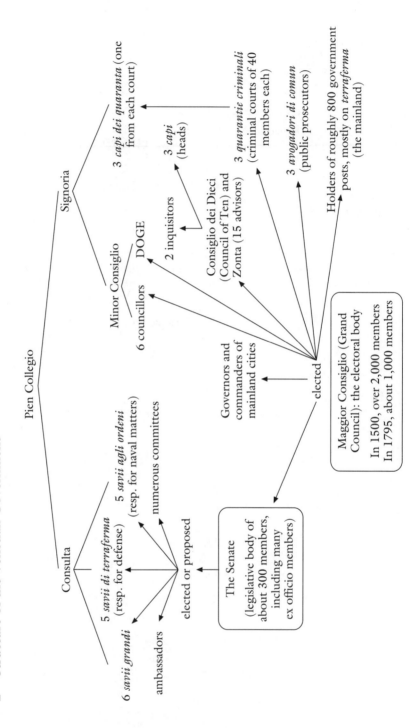

Pien Collegio (initiative and executive body): consulta + signoria
Consulta: 6 *savii grandi* + 5 *savii di terraferma* + 5 *savii agli ordeni*
Signoria: minor consiglio + 3 *capi dei quaranta*

Works Cited

Abbondanza, M. "Federico Fregoso nella storia della diocesi di Salerno e la visita pastorale del 1510–11." *Quaderni contemporanei* (Salerno) 4 (1971): 7–19.

Albèri, Eugenio. *Relazioni degli ambasciatori veneti al Senato.* 14 vols. and Appendix. Florence, 1839–63.

Alberigo, Giuseppe. *I vescovi italiani al Concilio di Trento (1545–1547).* Florence: Sansoni, 1959.

——"Vie active et vie contemplative dans une expérience chrétienne du XVIᵉ siècle." In *Théologie: le service théologique dans l'église. Mélanges offertes à Yves Congar pour ses soixante-dix ans,* 287–321. Paris: Cerf, 1974.

——"Vita attiva e vita contemplativa in un'esperienza cristiana del XVI secolo." *Studi veneziani* 16 (1974): 177–225.

Allport, Gordon W. *Becoming: Basic Considerations for a Psychology of Personality.* New Haven: Yale University Press, 1955.

——*The Individual and His Religion.* New York: Macmillan, 1950.

Ambrosini, Federica. "Echi della conquista del Messico nella Venezia del Cinquecento." In *L'impatto della scoperta dell'America nella cultura veneziana,* edited by Angela Caracciolo Aricò, 7–23. Rome: Bulzoni Editore, 1990.

——"Immagini dell'impero nell'ideologia del patriziato veneto del '500." In *I ceti dirigenti in Italia in età moderna e contemporanea: atti del Convegno Cividale del Friuli, 10–12 settembre 1983,* edited by Amelio Tagliaferri, 67–80. Udine: Del Bianco, 1984.

——*Paesi e mari ignoti: America e colonialismo europeo nella cultura veneziana (secoli XVI–XVII).* Venice: Deputazione Editrice, 1982.

Anderson, H. George, T. Austin Murphy, and Joseph A. Burgess, eds. *Justification by Faith.* Lutherans and Catholics in Dialogue 7. Minneapolis: Augsburg Publishing House, 1985.

Arnaldi, Girolamo, and Manlio Pastore Stocchi, eds. *Storia della cultura veneta*. Vol. 3, in 3 pts. Vicenza: Neri Pozza Editore, 1980.

Aubert, Alberto. "Alle origini della Controriforma: studi e problemi su Paolo IV." *Rivista di storia e letteratura religiosa* 22 (1986): 303–55.

——*Paolo IV Carafa nel giudizio della età della Controriforma*. Città di Castello: Stamperia Tiferno Grafica, 1990.

Augustijn, Cornelis. "De gesprekken tussen Bucer en Gropper tijdens het godsdienstgesprek te Worms in December 1540." *Nederlands archief voor kerkgeschiedenis*, n.s., 47 (1965–66): 208–30.

——*De godsdienstgesprekken tussen rooms-katholieken en protestanten van 1538 tot 1541*. Haarlem: De Erven F. Bohn, 1967.

——"The Quest of Reformatio: The Diet of Regensburg as a Turning-Point." Paper presented at the conference "The Reformation in Germany and Europe: Interpretations and Issues," Washington, D.C., 25 September 1990.

——"Die Religionsgespräche der vierziger Jahre." In *Die Religionsgespräche der Reformationszeit*, edited by Gerhard Müller, 43–53. Gütersloh: Mohn, 1980.

Bataillon, Marcel. *Erasme et l'Espagne*. Paris: Droz, 1937. The Spanish translation is also a revised edition: *Erasmo y España. Estudios sobre la historia espiritual del siglo XVI*. Translated by Antonio Alatorre. 2d ed. Mexico City: Fondo de Cultura Económica, 1966.

Bauer, Clemens. "Die Epochen der Papstfinanz: ein Versuch." *Historische Zeitschrift* 138 (1927): 457–503.

Bäumer, Remigius. "Johannes Cochlaeus und die Reform der Kirche." In *Reformatio ecclesiae: Beiträge zu kirchlichen Reformbemühungen von der Alten Kirche bis zur Neuzeit. Festgabe für Erwin Iserloh*, edited by Remigius Baümer, 333–54. Paderborn: Schöningh, 1980.

Baumgarten, Paul Maria. *Von den Kardinälen des sechzehnten Jahrhunderts*. Krumbach: F. Aker, 1927.

Belladonna, Rita, and Andrea Del Col. "Per una sistemazione critica dell' evangelismo italiano e di un'opera recente." *Critica storica* 17 (1980): 266–76.

Bennato, F. "La partecipazione militare di Venezia alla Lega di Cognac." *Archivio veneto*, 5th ser., 58 (1956): 70–87.

Bigaglia, Giuseppe. *La chiesa della Madonna dell'Orto in Venezia*. Venice: A. Vidotti, 1937.

Boas, George. "Nature." In *Dictionary of the History of Ideas*, edited by Philip R. Wiener, 3:346–51. New York: Scribner, 1973.

Bouwsma, William J. *Venice and the Defense of Republican Liberty*. Berkeley and Los Angeles: University of California Press, 1968.

——"Venice and the Political Education of Europe." In *Renaissance Venice*, edited by J. R. Hale, 45–66. London: Faber & Faber, 1973.

Bozza, Tommaso. *Nuovi studi sulla riforma in Italia*. Vol. 1: *Il Beneficio di Cristo*. Rome: Edizioni di Storia e Letteratura, 1976.

Brandi, Karl. *The Emperor Charles V*. Translated by C. V. Wedgwood. London: Jonathan Cape, 1939.

Brieger, Theodor. "Contarini's Begleitschreiben zu der Formula Concordiae de iustificatione." *Zeitschrift für Kirchengeschichte* 5 (1882): 591–95.

———"Nic. Ardinghelli im Namen des Papstes an Contarini, Rom, 15. Juni 1541: die beiden ersten Entwürfe dieser Depesche, vom 10. Juni." *Zeitschrift für Kirchengeschichte* 5 (1882): 595–604.

———"Zur Correspondenz Contarini's während seiner deutschen Legation: Mitteilungen aus Beccadelli's Monumenti." *Zeitschrift für Kirchengeschichte* 3 (1878–79): 492–523.

Brown, Horatio. *Studies in the History of Venice.* 2 vols. London: John Murray, 1907.

———*The Venetian Printing Press.* London, 1891.

Brown, Rawdon, ed. *Calendar of State Papers and Manuscripts Relating to English Affairs Existing in the Archives and Collections of Venice, and in Other Libraries of Northern Italy.* Vols. 3–4. London, 1869–71.

Brucker, Gene A. "Religious Sensibilities in Early Modern Europe: Examples from the Records of the Holy Penitentiary." *Historical Reflections/Réflexions historiques* 15 (1988): 13–25.

Buck, August. "Laus Venetiae." *Archiv für Kulturgeschichte* 57 (1975): 185–94.

Burrows, Mark. "Converging Themes in a 'Counter-Reformation' Debate: A Study of the Pastoral Foundations of Contarini's *Confutatio articulorum seu quaestionum Lutheranorum* and the *Confessio Augustana.*" Paper presented at Princeton Theological Seminary, September 1984.

Cairns, Christopher. *Domenico Bollani, Bishop of Brescia: Devotion to Church and State in the Republic of Venice in the Sixteenth Century.* Nieuwkoop, Neth.: B. De Graaf, 1976.

Calvin, Jean. *Ioannis Calvini opera quae supersunt omnia.* Vol. 11. Braunschweig, 1872.

Campeggio, Tommaso. *Opus Thomae Campegii Bononiensis, Episcopi Feltrensis, de auctoritate et potestate Romani Pontificis. . . .* Venice, 1555.

Canal, Bernardo. "Il Collegio, l'ufficio e l'archivio dei Dieci Savi alle Decime di Rialto." *Nuovo Archivio Veneto* 16 (1908): 115–50, 279–310.

Canons and Decrees of the Council of Trent. Translated by H. J. Schroeder, O.P. St. Louis: Herder, 1941.

Cantimori, Delio. "Le idee religiose del Cinquecento: la storiografia." In *Storia della letteratura italiana,* edited by Emilio Cecchi and Natalino Sapegno, vol. 5: *Il Seicento,* 7–87. Milan: Garzanti, 1967.

Capasso, Carlo. *Paolo III.* 2 vols. Messina: Principato, 1923–24.

Caracciolo Aricò, Angela, ed. *L'impatto della scoperta dell'America nella cultura veneziana.* Rome: Bulzoni Editore, 1990.

Cardauns, Ludwig. *Zur Geschichte der kirchlichen Unions- und Reformbestrebungen von 1538 bis 1542.* Rome: Loescher, 1910.

Cargnoni, Costanzo, ed. *I frati Cappuccini: documenti e testimonianze del primo secolo.* 3 vols. to date. Perugia: Edizioni Frate Indovino, 1988–.

Casadei, Alfredo. "Lettere del Cardinale Gaspero Contarini durante la sua legazione di Bologna (1542)." *Archivio storico italiano* 118 (1960): 77–130, 220–85.

Cassirer, Ernst, and John Herman Randall, Jr., eds. *The Renaissance Philosophy of Man*. Chicago: University of Chicago Press, 1948.

Cavazzana Romanelli, Francesca, ed. *Gaspare Contarini e il suo tempo: atti convegno di studio*. Venice: Comune di Venezia, Assessorato Affari Istituzionali, and Studium Cattolico Veneziano, 1988.

Célier, Léonce. *Les dataires du XVIᵉ siècle et les origines de la Daterie apostolique*. Paris: Fontemoing, 1910.

————"L'idée de réforme à la cour pontificale du Concile de Bâle au Concile de Latran." *Revue des questions historiques* 86 (1909): 418–35.

Celsi, Mino. *In haereticis coërcendis quatenus progredi liceat*. Edited by Peter G. Bietenholz. Corpus Reformatorum Italicorum. Naples: Prismi Editrice/Chicago: Newberry Library, 1982.

Cervelli, Innocenzo. *Machiavelli e la crisi dello stato veneziano*. Naples: Guida, 1974.

————"Storiografia e problemi intorno alla vita religiosa e spirituale a Venezia nella prima metà del '500." *Studi veneziani* 8 (1966): 447–76.

Cesareo, Francesco C. *Humanism and Catholic Reform: The Life and Work of Gregorio Cortese (1483–1548)*. New York and Bern: Peter Lang, 1990.

Cessi, Paolo. "Paolinismo preluterano." *Rendiconti dell'Accademia dei Lincei: classe di scienze morali, storiche e filologiche* 12 (1957): 3–30.

Chamberlin, Eric R. *The Sack of Rome*. London: Batsford, 1979.

Chambers, David S. "The Economic Predicament of Renaissance Cardinals." *Studies in Medieval and Renaissance History* 3 (1966): 287–313.

Chastel, André. *The Sack of Rome, 1527*. Princeton: Princeton University Press, 1983.

Chiacchella, Rita. "Per una reinterpretazione della 'guerra del sale' e della costruzione della Rocca Paolina a Perugia." *Archivio storico italiano* 145 (1987): 3–60.

Chiari, Isidoro. *Ad eos qui a communi ecclesiae sententia discessere, adhortatio ad concordiam*. Milan, 1540.

Chojnacki, Stanley. "La posizione della donna a Venezia nel Cinquecento." In *Tiziano e Venezia: convegno internazionale di studi*, 65–70. Vicenza: Neri Pozza, 1976.

Cian, Vittorio. "A proposito di un'ambasceria di Pietro Bembo (dicembre 1514)." *Archivio veneto* 30 (1885): 355–81.

Cicogna, Emmanuele Antonio. *Delle inscrizioni veneziane*. 6 vols. Venice, 1824–53.

Cintio, Alvise. *Libro della origine delli volgari proverbi*. Venice, 1526.

Clarke, Ashley, and Philip Rylands, eds. *Restoring Venice: The Church of the Madonna Dell'Orto*. London: Elek, 1977.

Cochlaeus, Johannes. *Aequitatis discussio super Consilio delectorum cardinalium (1538)*. Edited by Hilarius Walter, O.S.B. Corpus Catholicorum 17. Münster i.W.: Aschendorff, 1931.

Collett, Barry. *Italian Benedictine Scholars and the Reformation*. Oxford: Clarendon Press, 1985.

Colliva, Paolo. "Bologna dal XIV al XVIII secolo: 'governo misto' o signoria senatoria?" In *Storia dell'Emilia Romagna*, edited by Aldo Berselli, 2: 13–34. Bologna: University Press of Bologna, 1977.

Concilium Tridentinum: diariorum, actorum, epistularum, tractatuum nova collectio. Edited by Societas Goerresiana. 13 vols. Freiburg i.B.: Herder, 1901–38; reprint 1963–67.

Contarini, Gasparo. *Gegenreformatorische Schriften (1530c.–1542).* Edited by Friedrich Hünermann. Münster i.W.: Aschendorff, 1923.

———*Quattro lettere di monsignor Gasparo Contarino.* Florence, 1558.

Corazzol, Gigi. *Fitti e livelli di grano: un'aspetto del credito rurale nel Veneto del '500.* Milan: Franco Angeli, 1980.

Cortese, Gregorio. *Gregorii Cortesii omnia quae huc usque colligi potuerunt sive ab eo scripta, sive ad illum spectantia.* 2 vols. Padua, 1774.

Cortese, Paolo. *De cardinalatu, libri tres.* Rome, 1510.

Cozzi, Gaetano. "Authority and the Law in Renaissance Venice." In *Renaissance Venice,* edited by J. R. Hale, 293–345. London: Faber & Faber, 1973.

———"I rapporti tra stato e chiesa." In *La chiesa di Venezia tra riforma protestante e riforma cattolica,* edited by Giuseppe Gullino, 11–36. Venice: Edizioni Studium Cattolico Veneziano, 1990.

———*Repubblica di Venezia e stati italiani: politica e giustizia dal secolo XVI al secolo XVIII.* Turin: Einaudi, 1982.

———"Lo stato veneziano nell'opera politico-religiosa di Gasparo Contarini a cavallo degli anni '30." Paper presented at the meeting commemorating the five-hundredth anniversary of the birth of Gasparo Contarini, Venice, 2 March 1986.

Cracco, Giorgio. Review of "Lettere del Cardinale Gaspero Contarini durante la sua legazione di Bologna (1542)," by Alfredo Casadei. *Bollettino dell'Istituto di storia della società e dello stato veneziano* 3 (1961): 305–13.

Cuthbert, Father, O.S.F.C. *The Capuchins: A Contribution to the History of the Counter-Reformation.* 2 vols. New York and Toronto: Longmans, Green, 1929.

D'Amico, John F. "Papal History and Curial Reform in the Renaissance: Raffaele Maffei's *Breuis Historia* of Julius II and Leo X." *Archivum historiae pontificiae* 18 (1980): 157–210.

Davis, James C. *A Venetian Family and Its Fortune, 1500–1900.* Philadelphia: American Philosophical Society, 1975.

De Leva, Giuseppe. "La concordia religiosa di Ratisbona e il Cardinale Gasparo Contarini." *Archivio veneto,* 1st ser., 4 (1872): 5–36.

———"Della vita e delle opere del Cardinale Gasparo Contarini." *Rivista periodica dei lavori della I. R. Accademia di scienze, lettere ed arti in Padova* 12 (1863): 47–97.

———*Storia documentata di Carlo V in correlazione all'Italia.* 5 vols. Venice, 1863–94.

Delph, Ronald. "From Venetian Visitor to Curial Humanist: The Development of Agostino Steuco's Counter-Reformation Thought." Paper read at the Sixteenth-Century Studies Conference, St. Louis, October 1990.

Del Re, Niccolò. *La curia romana.* 3d ed. Rome: Edizioni di Storia e Letteratura, 1970.

Denzinger, H. *Enchiridion symbolorum.* 33d ed. Freiburg i.B.: Herder, 1965.

Desroussilles, François Dupuigrenet. "L'Università di Padova dal 1405 al Concilio di Trento." In *Storia della cultura veneta,* edited by Girolamo

Arnaldi and Manlio Pastore Stocchi, 3(2):607–47. Vicenza: Neri Pozza Editore, 1980.

de Vocht, H. *History of the Foundation and Rise of the Collegium Trilingue Lovaniense, 1517–1550.* 3 vols. Louvain: Bibliothèque de l'Université, 1951–54.

Di Napoli, Giovanni. *L'immortalità dell'anima nel Rinascimento.* Turin: Società Editrice Internazionale, 1963.

———*Studi sul Rinascimento.* Naples: Giannini, 1973.

Dionisotti, Carlo. "Chierici e laici nella cultura italiana del primo Cinquecento." In *Problemi di vita religiosa in Italia nel Cinquecento: atti del Convegno di storia della chiesa in Italia (Bologna, 2–6 settembre 1958),* 167–85. Padua: Antenore, 1960.

———*Geografia e storia della letteratura italiana.* Turin: Einaudi, 1967.

———"Monumenti Beccadelli." In *Miscellanea Pio Paschini,* edited by A. Casamassa, 2:251–68. Rome: Facultas Theologica Pontificii Athenaei Lateranensis, 1949.

Dittrich, Franz. *Gasparo Contarini, 1483–1542: eine Monographie.* Braunsberg, 1885.

———"Nachträge zur Biographie Gasparo Contarinis." *Historisches Jahrbuch der Görresgesellschaft* 8 (1887): 271–83.

———*Nuntiaturberichte Giovanni Morones vom deutschen Königshofe, 1539–1540.* Paderborn, 1892.

———"Die Nuntiaturberichte Giovanni Morone's vom Reichstage zu Regensburg 1541." *Historisches Jahrbuch der Görresgesellschaft* 4 (1883): 395–472, 618–73.

——— ed. *Regesten und Briefe des Cardinals Gasparo Contarini (1483–1542).* Braunsberg, 1881.

Dorez, Léon. *La cour du Pape Paul III d'après les registres de la Trésorerie secrète.* 2 vols. Paris: E. Leroux, 1932.

Douglas, Richard. *Jacopo Sadoleto, 1477–1547: Humanist and Reformer.* Cambridge, Mass.: Harvard University Press, 1959.

Eck, Johann Mayer von. *Apologia pro Reverendiss. se. ap. Legato et Cardinale Caspare Contareno.* Cologne, 1542.

———*Enchiridion locorum communium adversus Lutheranos.* Cologne, 1526.

Eells, Hastings. "The Origin of the Regensburg Book." *Princeton Theological Review* 26 (1928): 355–72.

Ehses, Stephan. "Ein Gutachten zur Reform des päpstlichen Gnadenwesens aus dem Jahre 1538." *Römische Quartalschrift* 14 (1900): 102–19.

———"Johannes Groppers Rechtfertigungslehre auf dem Konzil von Trient." *Römische Quartalschrift* 20 (1906): 175–88.

———"Kirchliche Reformarbeiten unter Papst Paul III. vor dem Trienter Konzil." *Römische Quartalschrift* 15 (1901): 153–74.

———"Zu den kirchlichen Reformarbeiten unter Paul III.: der deutsche Kardinal Nikolaus von Schönberg." *Historisches Jahrbuch der Görresgesellschaft* 29 (1908): 597–603.

Elliott, John H. *The Old World and the New, 1492–1650.* Cambridge: Cambridge University Press, 1970.

Erasmus, Desiderius. *Inquisitio de fide*. Edited by Craig Thompson. New Haven: Yale University Press, 1950.

Erikson, Erik H. *Young Man Luther: A Study in Psychoanalysis and History.* New York: W. W. Norton, 1962.

Fanti, Mario. "Le classi sociali e il governo di Bologna all'inizio del secolo XVII in un'opera inedita di Camillo Baldi." *Strenna storica bolognese* 11 (1961): 133–79.

Fasoli, Gina. "Nascita di un mito." In *Studi storici in onore di Gioacchino Volpe per il suo 80 compleanno* 1:447–79. Florence: Sansoni, 1958.

Favaro, A. "Lo studio di Padova al tempo di Niccolò Copernico." *Atti del R. Istituto Veneto di scienze, lettere ed arti* 6 (1880): 285–356.

Fenlon, Dermot. *Heresy and Obedience in Tridentine Italy: Cardinal Pole and the Counter Reformation.* Cambridge: Cambridge University Press, 1972.

Ferrara, Orestes. *Gasparo Contarini et ses missions.* Paris: A. Michel, 1956.

Ferrero, Ermanno, and Giuseppe Müller, eds. *Carteggio delle lettere di Vittoria Colonna.* 2d ed. Turin, 1892.

Fink, Zera S. *The Classical Republicans.* 2d ed. Evanston, Ill.: Northwestern University Press, 1962.

Finlay, Robert. "Politics and Family in Renaissance Venice: The Election of Doge Andrea Gritti." *Studi veneziani*, n.s., 2 (1978): 97–117.

———*Politics in Renaissance Venice.* New Brunswick, N.J.: Rutgers University Press, 1980.

———"The Venetian Republic as a Gerontocracy: Age and Politics in the Renaissance." *Journal of Medieval and Renaissance Studies* 8 (1978): 157–78.

Firpo, Luigi, ed. *Relazioni di ambasciatori Veneti al Senato.* Vol. 2: *Germania, 1506–1554.* Turin: Bottega d'Erasmo, 1970.

Firpo, Massimo. "Juan de Valdés e l'evangelismo italiano: appunti e problemi di una ricerca in corso." *Studi storici* 26 (1985): 733–54.

———"Gli spirituali, l'Accademia di Modena e il formulario di fede del 1542: controllo del dissenso religioso e nicodemismo." *Rivista di storia e letteratura religiosa* 20 (1984): 40–111.

———*Tra alumbrados e "spirituali": studi su Juan de Valdés e il valdesianesimo nella crisi religiosa del '500 italiano.* Florence: Olschki, 1990.

Firpo, Massimo, and Dario Marcatto. "Il primo processo inquisitoriale contro il cardinal Giovanni Morone (1552–1553)." *Rivista storica italiana* 93 (1981): 71–142.

———*Il processo inquisitoriale del Cardinal Giovanni Morone.* 5 vols. in 6. Rome: Istituto Storico Italiano per l'Età Moderna e Contemporanea, 1981–89.

Flaminio, Marcantonio. *Lettere.* Edited by Alessandro Pastore. Rome: Edizioni dell'Ateneo & Bizzarri, 1978.

Foffano, Francesco. "Marco Musuro, professore di greco a Padova ed a Venezia." *Nuovo Archivio Veneto* 3 (1892): 453–73.

Fontana, Bartolomeo. "Documenti vaticani inediti contro l'eresia luterana in Italia." *Archivio della R. Società romana di storia patria* 15 (1892): 71–165, 365–474.

Forget, Mireille. "Les relations et les amitiés de Pierre Danès (1497–1577)."

Bibliothèque d'humanisme et renaissance 3 (1936): 365–83; 4 (1937): 59–77.

Foscari, Antonio, and Manfredo Tafuri. *L'armonia e i conflitti: la chiesa di San Francesco della Vigna nella Venezia del '500.* Turin: Einaudi, 1983.

Fraenkel, Pierre. *Einigungsbestrebungen in der Reformationszeit.* Mainz: Institut für europäische Geschichte, 1965.

———"Les Protestants et le problème de la transubstantiation au Colloque de Ratisbonne: documents et arguments du 5 au 10 mai 1541." *Oecumenica* 3 (1968): 70–115.

Fragnito, Gigliola. "Aspetti della censura ecclesiastica nell'Europa della Controriforma: l'edizione parigina delle opere di Gasparo Contarini." *Rivista di storia e letteratura religiosa* 21 (1985): 3–48.

———"Il Cardinale Gregorio Cortese e la crisi religiosa del Cinquecento." *Benedictina* 30 (1983): 129–71, 417–59; 31 (1984): 79–134.

———"Cultura umanistica e riforma religiosa: il 'De officio boni viri ac probi episcopi' di Gasparo Contarini." *Studi veneziani* 11 (1969): 75–189.

———"Evangelismo e intransigenti nei difficili equilibri del pontificato farnesiano." *Rivista di storia e letteratura religiosa* 25 (1989): 20–47.

———*Gasparo Contarini: un magistrato veneziano al servizio della cristianità.* Florence: Olschki, 1988.

———*In museo e in villa: saggi sul Rinascimento perduto.* Venice: Arsenale, 1988.

———*Memoria individuale e costruzione biografica: Beccadelli, Della Casa, Vettori alle origini di un mito.* Pubblicazioni dell'Università di Urbino, Serie di lettere e filosofia. Urbino: Argalìa, 1978.

———"'Parenti' e 'familiari' nelle corti cardinalizie del Rinascimento." In *"Famiglia" del principe e famiglia aristocratica,* edited by Cesare Mozzarelli, 565–87. Rome: Bulzoni, 1988.

———"Per lo studio dell'epistolografia volgare del Cinquecento: le lettere di Ludovico Beccadelli." *Bibliothèque d'humanisme et renaissance* 43 (1981): 61–87.

———"Gli 'spirituali' e la fuga di Bernardino Ochino." *Rivista storica italiana* 84 (1972): 777–813.

Friedensburg, Walter. "Der Briefwechsel Gasparo Contarini's mit Ercole Gonzaga." *Quellen und Forschungen aus italienischen Archiven und Bibliotheken* 2 (1899): 161–222.

———"Das Consilium de emendanda ecclesia, Kardinal Sadolet und Johannes Sturm von Strassburg." *Archiv für Reformationsgeschichte* 33 (1936): 1–69.

———*Kaiser Karl V. und Papst Paul III. (1534–1549).* Leipzig: M. Heinsius Nachfolger, 1932.

———"Zwei Aktenstücke zur Geschichte der kirchlichen Reformbestrebungen an der römischen Kurie (1536–1538)." *Quellen und Forschungen aus italienischen Archiven und Bibliotheken* 7 (1904): 251–67.

Fulin, Rinaldo. "Gli inquisitori dei Dieci." *Archivio veneto* 1 (1871): 1–64, 298–313; 2 (1871): 357–91.

Gaeta, Franco. "Alcune considerazioni sul mito di Venezia." *Bibliothèque d'humanisme et renaissance* 23 (1961): 58–75.

————"L'idea di Venezia." In *Storia della cultura veneta*, edited by Girolamo Arnaldi and Manlio Pastore Stocchi, 3(3):565–641. Vicenza: Neri Pozza Editore, 1980.

————*Un nunzio pontificio a Venezia nel Cinquecento (Girolamo Aleandro).* Venice and Rome: Istituto per la Collaborazione Culturale, 1960.

————"Storiografia, coscienza nazionale e politica culturale nella Venezia del Rinascimento." In *Storia della cultura veneta*, edited by Girolamo Arnaldi and Manlio Pastore Stocchi, 3(1):1–91. Vicenza: Neri Pozza Editore, 1980.

————ed. *Nunziature di Venezia*. Vol. 1: *12 marzo 1533–14 agosto 1535*; vol. 2: *9 gennaio 1536–9 giugno 1542*. Rome: Istituto Storico Italiano per l'Età Moderna e Contemporanea, 1958–60.

Ganzer, Klaus. "Zum Kirchenverständnis Gasparo Contarinis." *Würzburger Diözesangeschichtsblätter* 35–36 (1974): 241–60.

Geanakoplos, Deno J. *Greek Scholars in Venice: Studies in the Dissemination of Greek Learning from Byzantium to the West.* Cambridge, Mass.: Harvard University Press, 1962.

Gerbi, Antonello. *The Dispute of the New World: The History of a Polemic, 1750–1900.* New, enlarged ed. Translated by Jeremy Moyle. Pittsburgh: Univerity of Pittsburgh Press, 1973.

Giacon, Carlo. "L'aristotelismo avicennistico di Gasparo Contarini." In *Atti del XII Congresso internazionale di filosofia* 9:109–19. Florence: Sansoni, 1960.

Gilbert, Felix. "Contarini on Savonarola: An Unknown Document of 1516." *Archiv für Reformationsgeschichte* 59 (1968): 145–50.

————"Cristianesimo, umanesimo e la bolla 'Apostolici regiminis' del 1513." *Rivista storica italiana* 79 (1967): 976–90.

————"The Date of the Composition of Contarini's and Giannotti's Books on Venice." *Studies in the Renaissance* 14 (1967): 172–84.

————"Gasparo Contarini as a Venetian Gentleman." Paper presented at the XVIII International Congress of Medieval Studies, Kalamazoo, Michigan, May 1983.

————*History: Choice and Commitment.* Cambridge, Mass.: Belknap Press of Harvard University Press, 1977.

————*The Pope, His Banker, and Venice.* Cambridge, Mass.: Harvard University Press, 1980.

————"Religion and Politics in the Thought of Gasparo Contarini." In *Action and Conviction in Early Modern Europe: Essays in Memory of E. H. Harbison*, edited by T. K. Rabb and J. E. Seigel, 90–116. Princeton: Princeton University Press, 1969.

————"The Venetian Constitution in Florentine Political Thought." In *Florentine Studies*, edited by Nicolai Rubinstein, 463–500. London: Faber & Faber, 1968.

————"Venice in the Crisis of the League of Cambrai." In *Renaissance Venice*, edited by J. H. Hale, 274–92. London: Faber & Faber, 1973.

Gilmore, Myron. "Myth and Reality in Venetian Political Theory." In *Renaissance Venice*, edited by J. R. Hale, 431–44. London: Faber & Faber, 1973.

Gilson, Etienne. Appendix 1 to "L'affaire de l'immortalité de l'âme à Venise au début du XVIe siècle." In *Umanesimo europeo e umanesimo veneziano*, edited by Vittore Branca, 31–36. Civiltà europea e civiltà veneziana, Aspetti e problemi 2. Florence: Sansoni, 1963.

————"Autour de Pomponazzi: problématique de l'immortalité de l'âme en Italie au début du XVIe siècle." *Archives d'histoire doctrinale et littéraire du moyen âge* 28 (1961): 163–279.

Giuliani, Innocenzo. "Genesi e primo secolo di vita del Magistrato sopra monasteri (Venezia, 1519–1620)." *Venezie francescane* 28 (1961): 42–68, 106–69.

Giustiniani, Paolo. *Trattati, lettere e frammenti.* Edited by Eugenio Massa. 2 vols. to date. Rome: Edizioni di Storia e Letteratura, 1967–74.

Gleason, Elisabeth G. "On the Nature of Italian Evangelism: Scholarship, 1953–1978." *Sixteenth Century Journal* 9 (1978): 3–25.

————"Reading Between the Lines of Contarini's Treatise on the Venetian State." *Historical Reflections/Réflexions historiques* 15 (1988): 251–70.

————*Reform Thought in Sixteenth-Century Italy.* Chico, Calif.: Scholars Press, 1981.

Gléz, G. "Pouvoir du pape dans l'ordre temporel." In *Dictionnaire de théologie catholique* 12(2), cols. 2670–2772.

Gnoli, D. "Un censimento di Roma sotto Clemente VII." *Archivio della R. Società romana di storia patria* 17 (1894): 375–520.

Göller, Emil. *Die päpstliche Pönitentiarie von ihrem Ursprung bis zu ihrer Umgestaltung unter Pius V.* 2 vols. Rome: Loescher, 1907–11.

Gothein, Eberhard. *Ignatius von Loyola und die Gegenreformation.* Halle, 1895.

Gramsci, Antonio. *Selections from the Prison Notebooks of Antonio Gramsci.* Edited and translated by Quintin Hoare and Geoffrey Nowell Smith. New York: International Publishers, 1971.

Grendler, Paul. *The Roman Inquisition and the Venetian Press, 1540–1605.* Princeton: Princeton University Press, 1977.

Grillo, Luigi. *Elogi di Liguri illustri.* 2d ed. 3 vols. Genoa, 1846.

Grubb, James S. "When Myths Lose Power: Four Decades of Venetian Historiography." *Journal of Modern History* 58 (1986): 43–94.

Guidiccione, Giovanni. *Le lettere.* Edited by Maria Teresa Graziosi. 2 vols. Rome: Bonacci, 1979.

Gullino, Giuseppe, ed. *La chiesa di Venezia tra riforma protestante e riforma cattolica.* Venice: Edizioni Studium Cattolico Veneziano, 1990.

Hackert, Hermann. *Die Staatsschrift Gasparo Contarinis und die politischen Verhältnisse Venedigs im sechzehnten Jahrhundert.* Heidelberg: Winter, 1940.

Hale, J. R. "Terra Ferma Fortifications in the Cinquecento." In *Florence and Venice: Comparisons and Relations* 2:169–87. Florence: La Nuova Italia, 1980.

————ed. *Renaissance Venice.* London: Faber & Faber, 1973.

Hall, Basil. "The Colloquy Between Catholics and Protestants, 1539–41." *Studies in Church History* 7 (1971): 235–66.

Hallman, Barbara McClung. *Italian Cardinals, Reform, and the Church as*

Property. Berkeley and Los Angeles: University of California Press, 1985.

——"Practical Aspects of Roman Diplomacy in Germany, 1517–1541." *Journal of Medieval and Renaissance Studies* 10 (1980): 193–206.

Headley, John. *The Emperor and His Chancellor: A Study of the Imperial Chancellery Under Gattinara.* Cambridge: Cambridge University Press, 1983.

Heer, Friedrich. *Die dritte Kraft: der europäische Humanismus zwischen den Fronten des konfessionellen Zeitalters.* Frankfurt: S. Fischer, 1959.

Herlihy, David. *Cities and Society in Medieval Italy.* London: Variorum Reprints, 1980.

——"Vieillir à Florence au Quattrocento." *Annales: E.S.C.* 24 (1964): 1338–52.

Hirsch, Elisabeth Feist. *Damião de Gois: The Life and Thought of a Portuguese Humanist, 1502–1574.* The Hague: Martinus Nijhoff, 1967.

Hocquet, Jean-Claude. "Monopole et concurrence à la fin du moyen âge: Venise et les salines de Cervia (XIIe–XVIe siècles)." *Studi veneziani* 15 (1973): 21–133.

——*Le sel et la fortune de Venise.* 2d ed. 2 vols. Lille: Publications de l'Université de Lille, 1982.

Hofmann, Walther von. *Forschungen zur Geschichte der kurialen Behörden vom Schisma bis zur Reformation.* 2 vols. Rome: Loescher, 1914.

Hollerbach, Marion. *Das Religionsgespräch als Mittel der konfessionellen und politischen Auseinandersetzung im Deutschland des 16. Jahrhunderts.* Frankfurt: Lang, 1982.

Hook, Judith. *The Sack of Rome, 1527.* London: Macmillan, 1972.

Hudon, William V. *Marcello Cervini and Ecclesiastical Government in Tridentine Italy.* De Kalb: Northern Illinois University Press, 1992.

——"Papal, Episcopal, and Secular Authority in the Work of Marcello Cervini." *Cristianesimo nella storia* 9 (1988): 493–520.

——"Two Instructions for Preachers from the Tridentine Reformation." *Sixteenth Century Journal* 20 (1989): 457–70.

Hünermann, Friedrich. "Die Rechtfertigungslehre des Kardinals Gasparo Contarini." *Theologische Quartalschrift* 102 (1921): 1–22.

Hurtubise, Pierre. "Familiarité et fidélité à Rome au XVIe siècle: les 'familles' des cardinaux Giovanni, Bernardo et Antonio Maria Salviati." In *Hommage à Roland Mousnier: clientèles et fidélité en Europe à l'époque moderne,* 335–50. Paris: Presses Universitaires Françaises, 1981.

——"La table d'un cardinal de la renaissance: aspects de la cuisine et de l'hospitalité à Rome au milieu du XVIe siècle." *Mélanges de l'Ecole Française de Rome, moyen âge–temps modernes* 92 (1980): 249–82.

Iserloh, Erwin, Josef Glazik, and Hubert Jedin, eds. *Handbuch der Kirchengeschichte.* 7 vols. in 10. Freiburg i.B.: Herder, 1963–79.

James, William. *The Varieties of Religious Experience.* New York: New American Library, 1958.

Jedin, Hubert. "Analekten zur Reformtätigkeit der Päpste Julius III. und Pauls IV." *Römische Quartalschrift* 42 (1934): 305–32; 43 (1935): 87–156.

————"An welchen Gegensätzen sind die vortridentinischen Religionsge-spräche zwischen Katholiken und Protestanten gescheitert?" *Theologie und Glaube* 48 (1958): 50–55.

————"Das Bischofsideal der katholischen Reformation: eine Studie über die Bischofsspiegel vornehmlich des 16. Jahrhunderts." In *Kirche des Glaubens—Kirche der Geschichte: ausgewählte Aufsätze und Vorträge* 2:75–117. Freiburg i.B.: Herder, 1966.

————"Eine bisher unbekannte Denkschrift Tommaso Campeggios über die Reform der römischen Kurie." In *Festgabe Joseph Lortz*, edited by Erwin Iserloh and Peter Manns, 1:405–17. Baden-Baden: Bruno Grimm, 1958.

————"Concilio e riforma nel pensiero del Cardinale Bartolommeo Guidiccione." *Rivista di storia della chiesa in Italia* 2 (1948): 33–60.

————"Contarini und Camaldoli." *Archivio italiano per la storia della pietà* 2 (1959): 59–118. (Also published separately as a preprint: Rome: Edizioni di Storia e Letteratura, 1953.)

————"Gasparo Contarini e il contributo veneziano alla riforma cattolica." In *La civiltà veneziana del Rinascimento*, 105–24. Florence: Sansoni, 1958.

————*Geschichte des Konzils von Trient.* 4 vols. in 5. Freiburg i.B.: Herder, 1951–75.

————*Kardinal Contarini als Kontroverstheologe.* Münster i.W.: Aschendorff, 1949.

————"Ein Streit um den Augustinismus vor dem Tridentinum (1537–1543)." *Römische Quartalschrift* 35 (1927): 351–68.

————*Tommaso Campeggio (1483–1564): tridentinische Reform und kuriale Tradition.* Münster i.W.: Aschendorff, 1958.

————"Ein 'Turmerlebnis' des jungen Contarini." *Historisches Jahrbuch der Görresgesellschaft* 70 (1951): 115–30.

————"Vincenzo Querini und Pietro Bembo." In *Kirche des Glaubens—Kirche der Geschichte: ausgewählte Aufsätze und Vorträge* 1:153–66. Freiburg i.B.: Herder, 1966. Originally published in *Miscellanea Giovanni Mercati* 4:407–24. Vatican City: Biblioteca Apostolica Vaticana, 1946.

Jung, Eva-Maria. "On the Nature of Evangelism in Sixteenth-Century Italy." *Journal of the History of Ideas* 14 (1953): 511–27.

Kalkoff, Paul. "Zur Charakteristik Aleanders." *Zeitschrift für Kirchengeschichte* 43 (1924): 209–19.

King, Margaret L. *Venetian Humanism in an Age of Patrician Dominance.* Princeton: Princeton University Press, 1986.

Korte, August. *Die Konzilspolitik Karls V. in den Jahren 1538–1543.* Halle a.d.S.: E. Karras, 1905.

Kretschmayr, Heinrich. *Geschichte von Venedig.* 3 vols. Gotha: Perthes, 1905–34.

Kristeller, Paul Oskar. *Eight Philosophers of the Italian Renaissance.* Stanford: Stanford University Press, 1964.

————"A New Manuscript Source for Pomponazzi's Theory of the Soul from His Paduan Period." *Revue internationale de philosophie* 5 (1951): 144–57.

————"Two Unpublished Questions on the Soul of Pietro Pomponazzi."
Medievalia et humanistica 9 (1955): 76–101.

La Clavière, R. de Maulde. *S. Gaetano da Thiene e la riforma cattolica italiana (1480–1527)*. Rome: Desclée, 1911.

Laemmer, Hugo. *Die vortridentinisch-katholische Theologie des Reformationszeitalters*. Berlin, 1858.

Lane, Frederic C. "Family Partnerships and Joint Ventures." In *Venice and History*, 36–55. Baltimore: Johns Hopkins University Press, 1966.

————*Venice, a Maritime Republic*. Baltimore: Johns Hopkins University Press, 1973.

Lauchert, Friedrich. *Die italienischen literarischen Gegner Luthers*. Freiburg i.B.: Herder, 1912.

Leclercq, Jean. *Un humaniste érémite: le bienheureux Paul Giustiniani (1476–1528)*. Rome: Edizioni Camaldoli, 1951.

Le Plat, Jodocus. *Monumentorum ad historiam Concilii Tridentini potissimum illustrandam spectantium amplissima collectio*. 7 vols. Louvain, 1781–87.

Lepori, Fernando. "La scuola di Rialto dalla fondazione alla metà del Cinquecento." In *Storia della cultura veneta*, edited by Girolamo Arnaldi and Manlio Pastore Stocchi, 3(2): 537–605. Vicenza: Neri Pozza Editore, 1980.

Lettere di principi. Vol. 3. Venice, 1570.

Libby, Lester J., Jr. "Venetian History and Political Thought After 1509." *Studies in the Renaissance* 20 (1973): 7–45.

Lipgens, Walter. *Kardinal Johannes Gropper (1503–1559) und die Anfänge der katholischen Reform in Deutschland*. Münster i.W.: Aschendorff, 1951.

Litva, Felice, S.J. "L'attività della Dataria durante il periodo tridentino." *Archivum historiae pontificiae* 5 (1967): 79–174.

Loewenich, Walther von. *Duplex iustitia: Luthers Stellung zu einer Unionsformel des 16. Jahrhundert*. Wiesbaden: Franz Steiner, 1972.

Logan, Oliver. *Culture and Society in Venice, 1470–1790*. London: Batsford, 1972.

————"The Ideal Bishop and the Venetian Patriciate: c. 1430–c. 1630." *Journal of Ecclesiastical History* 29 (1978): 415–50.

Lorenzetti, Giulio. *Venice and Its Lagoons*. Trieste: Edizioni LINT, 1975.

Lortz, Joseph. *Die Reformation in Deutschland*. 2 vols. Freiburg i.B.: Herder, 1940.

————"Wert und Grenzen der katholischen Kontroverstheologie in der ersten Hälfte des sechzehnten Jahrhunderts." In *Um Reform und Reformation*, edited by A. Franzen, 9–32. Münster i.W.: Aschendorff, 1968.

Lowry, Martin. *The World of Aldus Manutius*. Ithaca, N.Y.: Cornell University Press, 1979.

Luther, Martin. *The Career of the Reformer*. Vol. 34 of *Luther's Works: American Edition*. Philadelphia: Muhlenberg Press, 1960.

————*Werke. Briefwechsel*, vol. 9. Weimar: Hermann Böhlaus Nachfolger, 1941.

Lutz, Heinrich. "Kardinal Morone: Reform, Konzil und europäische Staatenwelt." In *Politik, Kultur und Religion im Werdeprozess der frühen Neuzeit*, edited by M. Csàky, 183–92. Klagenfurt: Universitätsverlag Carinthia, 1983.

————*Reformation und Gegenreformation.* 2d ed. Munich and Vienna: R. Oldenbourg, 1982.

Maccagni, Carlo. "Le scienze nello studio di Padova e nel Veneto." In *Storia della cultura veneta,* edited by Girolamo Arnaldi and Manlio Pastore Stocchi, 3(3):135–71. Vicenza: Neri Pozza Editore, 1980.

McCue, James F. "Double Justification at the Council of Trent: Piety and Theology in Sixteenth-Century Roman Catholicism." In *Piety, Politics, and Ethics: Reformation Studies in Honor of George Wolfgang Forell,* edited by Carter Lindberg, 39–56. Kirksville, Mo.: Sixteenth Century Journal Publishers, 1984.

McGinness, Frederick J. "Of 'Vices and Virtues, Punishment and Reward': Authentic Preaching, Reform, and a Counter-Reformation Riddle." Paper read at the Sixteenth-Century Studies Conference, St. Louis, October 1990.

Mackensen, Heinz. "Contarini's Theological Role at Ratisbon in 1541." *Archiv für Reformationsgeschichte* 51 (1960): 36–57.

————"The Diplomatic Role of Gasparo Contarini at the Colloquy of Ratisbon of 1541." *Church History* 27 (1958): 312–37.

McNair, Philip. *Peter Martyr in Italy: An Anatomy of Apostasy.* Oxford: Clarendon Press, 1967.

McPherson, David. "Lewkenor's Venice and Its Sources." *Renaissance Quarterly* 41 (1988): 459–66.

Mahoney, Edward P. "Nicoletto Vernia on the Soul and Immortality." In *Philosophy and Humanism: Renaissance Essays in Honor of Paul Oskar Kristeller,* edited by Edward P. Mahoney, 144–63. New York: Columbia University Press, 1976.

Mansi, Johannes Dominicus. *Sacrorum Conciliorum nova et amplissima collectio.* Edited by J. B. Martin and L. Petit. 60 vols. Paris: Welter, 1899–1927.

Marchetti, Valerio. *Gruppi ereticali senesi del Cinquecento.* Florence: La Nuova Italia, 1975.

Marmion, J. P. "Cardinal Pole in Recent Studies." *Recusant History* 13 (1975–76): 56–61.

Martin, John. "Salvation and Society in Sixteenth-Century Venice: Popular Evangelism in a Renaissance City." *Journal of Modern History* 60 (1988): 205–33.

Massa, Eugenio. *L'Eremo, la Bibbia e il medioevo in umanisti veneti del primo Cinquecento.* Naples: Liguori Editore, 1992.

————"Gasparo Contarini e gli amici, fra Venezia e Camaldoli." In *Gasparo Contarini e il suo tempo: atti convegno di studio,* edited by Francesca Cavazzana Romanelli, 39–91. Venice: Comune di Venezia, Assessorato Affari Istituzionali, and Studium Cattolico Veneziano, 1988.

————"Paolo Giustiniani." In *Bibliotheca Sanctorum* 7, cols. 2–9. Rome: Istituto Giovanni XXIII della Pontificia Università Lateranense, 1966.

————"Paolo Giustiniani e Gasparo Contarini: la vocazione al bivio del neoplatonismo e della teologia biblica." *Benedictina* 35 (1988): 429–74.

Matheson, Peter. *Cardinal Contarini at Regensburg.* Oxford: Clarendon Press, 1972.

Mehlhausen, Joachim. "Die Abendmahlsformel des Regensburger Buches." In *Studien zur Geschichte und Theologie der Reformation: Festschrift für Ernst Bizer*, edited by Luise Abramowski and J. F. Gerhard Goeters, 189–211. Neukirchen-Vluyn: Neukirchener Verlag, 1969.

Melanchthon, Philip. *Opera.* Vol. 4 of *Corpus Reformatorum*, edited by Carl Gottlieb Bretschneider. Halle, 1837.

Merzbacher, Friedrich. "Wandlungen des Kirchenbegriffs im Spätmittelalter." *Zeitschrift der Savigny-Stiftung für Rechtsgeschichte* 39 (1953): 274–361.

Miccoli, Giovanni. "La storia religiosa." In *Storia d'Italia* 2(1):431–1079. Turin: Einaudi, 1974.

Mildonian, Paola. "La conquista dello spazio americano nelle prime raccolte venete." In *L'impatto della scoperta dell'America nella cultura veneziana*, edited by Angela Caracciolo Aricò, 115–33. Rome: Bulzoni Editore, 1990.

Minnich, Nelson H. "Concepts of Reform Proposed at the Fifth Lateran Council." *Archivum historiae pontificiae* 7 (1969): 163–252.

Minnich, Nelson H., and Elisabeth G. Gleason. "Vocational Choices: An Unknown Letter of Pietro Querini to Gasparo Contarini and Niccolò Tiepolo (April, 1512)." *Catholic Historical Review* 75 (1989): 1–20.

Mittarelli, Johannes Benedictus, and Anselmus Costadoni, eds. *Annales Camaldulenses Ordinis Sancti Benedicti.* 9 vols. Venice, 1755–73.

Mollat, Guillaume. "Contributions à l'histoire du Sacré Collège de Clément V à Eugène IV." *Revue d'histoire ecclésiastique* 46 (1951): 22–112.

Monfang, Christoph. *Katholische Katechismen des sechzehnten Jahrhunderts in deutscher Sprache.* Mainz, 1881.

Morel, Giancarlo. "Gasparo Contarini negli appunti del Mazzuchelli." *Atti dell'Accademia delle scienze di Torino* 108 (1968–69): 279–303.

Moretti, Lino. *La chiesa della Madonna dell'Orto in Venezia.* Turin: Scaravaglio, 1981.

Müller, Gerhard, ed. *Die Religionsgespräche der Reformationszeit.* Gütersloh: Mohn, 1980.

Nardi, Bruno. "Letteratura e cultura veneziana del Quattrocento." In *La civiltà veneziana del Quattrocento*, 101–45. Florence: Sansoni, 1957.

———"La scuola di Rialto e l'umanesimo veneziano." In *Umanesimo europeo e umanesimo veneziano*, edited by Vittore Branca, 93–139. Civiltà europea e civiltà veneziana, Aspetti e problemi 2. Florence: Sansoni, 1963.

———*Studi su Pietro Pomponazzi.* Florence: F. Le Monnier, 1965.

Negri, Francesco. *Della tragedia ... intitolata Libero arbitrio.* 2d ed. N.p., 1550 [actually 1551].

Negri, Girolamo. *Epistolarum orationumque liber.* Padua, 1579.

Neuser, Wilhelm H. "Calvins Beitrag zu den Religionsgesprächen von Hagenau, Worms und Regensburg (1540/41)." In *Studien zur Geschichte und Theologie der Reformation: Festschrift für Ernst Bizer*, edited by Luise Abramowski and J. F. Gerhard Goeters, 213–37. Neukirchen-Vluyn: Neukirchener Verlag, 1969.

———*Die Vorbereitung der Religionsgespräche von Worms und Regensburg 1540/41.* Neukirchen-Vluyn: Neukirchener Verlag, 1974.

Nussdorfer, Laurie. "Civic Institutions and Papal Control in Sixteenth-Century

Rome and Bologna." Paper read at the Sixteenth Century Studies Conference, St. Louis, October 1986.

Oberman, Heiko. "Wir sein pettler. Hoc est verum: Bund und Gnade in der Theologie des Mittelalters und der Reformation." In *Die Reformation: von Wittenberg nach Genf,* 90–112. Göttingen: Vandenhoeck & Ruprecht, 1986.

Olin, John C. *Catholic Reform from Cardinal Ximenes to the Council of Trent, 1495–1563: An Essay with Illustrative Documents and a Brief Study of St. Ignatius Loyola.* New York: Fordham University Press, 1990.

Oliva, Cesare. "Note sull'insegnamento di Pietro Pomponazzi." *Giornale critico della filosofia italiana* 7 (1926): 83–103, 179–90, 254–75.

Partner, Peter. "Papal Financial Policy in the Renaissance and Counter-Reformation." *Past and Present,* no. 88 (1980): 17–62.

———*The Pope's Men: The Papal Civil Service in the Renaissance.* Oxford: Clarendon Press, 1990.

Paschini, Pio. *Un amico del Cardinale Polo: Alvise Priuli.* Rome: Pontificio Seminario Romano Maggiore, 1921.

———"I monasteri femminili in Italia nel Cinquecento." In *Problemi di vita religiosa in Italia nel Cinquecento: atti del Convegno di storia della chiesa in Italia (Bologna, 2–6 settembre 1958),* 31–60. Padua: Antenore, 1960.

Pasolini, Pietro Desiderio. *Delle antiche relazioni fra Venezia e Ravenna.* Florence, 1874.

Pastor, Ludwig von. "Die Correspondenz des Cardinals Contarini während seiner deutschen Legation (1541)." *Historisches Jahrbuch der Görresgesellschaft* 1 (1880): 321–92, 473–501.

———*Geschichte der Päpste seit dem Ausgang des Mittelalters.* 16 vols. Freiburg i.B.: Herder, 1909–33.

———*Die kirchlichen Reunionsbestrebungen während der Regierung Karls V.* Freiburg i.B., 1879.

Pastore, Alessandro. *Marcantonio Flaminio.* Milan: Franco Angeli, 1981.

Pásztor, Lajos. "Histoire de la curie romaine, problème d'histoire de l'église." *Revue d'histoire ecclésiastique* 64 (1969): 353–66.

Patrides, C. A. "Hierarchy and Order." In *Dictionary of the History of Ideas,* edited by Philip P. Wiener, 2:434–49. New York: Scribner, 1973.

Pauselli, Maria Cristina. "Note sugli *Scholia* di Gasparo Contarini ad Efesini e Galati." *Archiv für Reformationsgeschichte* 83 (1992): 130–53.

Paz, P. "La doctrine de la double justice au Concile de Trente." *Ephemerides theologicae Lovanienses* 30 (1954): 5–53.

Pesch, Otto Hermann. *Die Theologie der Rechtfertigung bei Martin Luther und Thomas von Aquin.* Mainz: Matthias-Grünewald Verlag, 1967.

Peyronel Rambaldi, Susanna. "Ancora sull'evangelismo italiano: categoria o invenzione storiografica?" *Società e storia* 5, no. 18 (1982): 935–67.

———*Speranze e crisi nel Cinquecento modenese.* Milan: Franco Angeli Editore, 1979.

Pfeilschifter, George, ed. *Acta Reformationis Catholicae Ecclesiam Germaniae concernentia saeculi XVI.* Vol. 6. Regensburg: F. Pustet, 1974.

Pfnür, Vinzenz. "Die Einigung bei den Religionsgesprächen 1540/41: eine Täuschung?" In *Die Religionsgespräche der Reformationszeit,* edited by Gerhard Müller, 55–88. Gütersloh: Mohn, 1980.

Pieper, Anton. *Zur Enstehungsgeschichte der ständigen Nuntiaturen.* Freiburg i.B., 1894.

Pieri, Piero. *Il Rinascimento e la crisi militare italiana.* 2d ed. Turin: Einaudi, 1971.

Pine, M. "Pomponazzi and the Problem of 'Double Truth.'" *Journal of the History of Ideas* 29 (1968): 163–76.

Pocock, J.G.A. *The Machiavellian Moment.* Princeton: Princeton University Press, 1975.

Poppi, Antonino. "Il prevalere della 'vita activa' nella paideia del Cinquecento." In *Rapporti tra le università di Padova e Bologna: ricerche di filosofia, medicina e scienza,* edited by Lucia Rossetti, 97–125. Trieste: Edizioni LINT, 1988.

———*Saggi sul pensiero inedito di Pietro Pomponazzi.* Padua: Antenore, 1970.

———"La teologia nell'Università e nelle scuole." In *Storia della cultura veneta,* edited by Girolamo Arnaldi and Manlio Pastore Stocchi, 3(3): 1–33. Vicenza: Neri Pozza Editore, 1980.

Preto, Paolo. *Venezia e i Turchi.* Florence: Sansoni, 1975.

Prodi, Paolo. "I colloqui di Ratisbona: l'azione e le idee di Gaspare Contarini (tavola rotonda)." In *Gaspare Contarini e il suo tempo: atti convegno di studio,* edited by Francesca Cavazzana Romanelli, 207–22. Venice: Comune di Venezia, Assessorato Affari Istituzionali, and Studium Cattolico Veneziano, 1988.

———*The Papal Prince.* Cambridge: Cambridge University Press, 1987.

———"The Structure and Organization of the Church in Renaissance Venice: Suggestions for Research." In *Renaissance Venice,* edited by J. R. Hale, 409–30. London: Faber & Faber, 1973.

Prosperi, Adriano. "Di alcuni testi per il clero nell'Italia del primo Cinquecento." *Critica storica* 7 (1968): 137–68.

———"Intellettuali e chiesa all'inizio dell'età moderna." In *Storia d'Italia, Annali 4: Intellettuali e potere,* edited by Corrado Vivanti, 159–252. Turin: Einaudi, 1981.

———*Tra evangelismo e controriforma: G. M. Giberti (1495–1543).* Rome: Edizioni di Storia e Letteratura, 1969.

Pullan, Brian. "The Occupations and Investments of the Venetian Nobility in the Middle and Late Sixteenth Century." In *Renaissance Venice,* edited by J. R. Hale, 379–408. London: Faber & Faber, 1973.

———"The Significance of Venice." *Bulletin of the John Rylands University Library of Manchester* 56 (1973–74): 443–62.

Puppi, Leonardo, ed. *Architettura e utopia nella Venezia del Cinquecento: catalogo della mostra.* Milan: Electa, 1980.

Queller, Donald E. "The Civic Irresponsibility of the Venetian Nobility." In *Economy, Society, and Government in Medieval Italy: Essays in Memory of Robert L. Reynolds,* edited by David Herlihy, Robert S. Lopez, and Vsevolod Slessarev, 223–36. Kent, Ohio: Kent State University Press, 1969.

———"The Development of Ambassadorial Relazioni." In *Renaissance Venice,* edited by J. R. Hale. London: Faber & Faber, 1973.

———*The Venetian Patriciate: Reality Versus Myth.* Urbana: University of Illinois Press, 1986.

Quirini, Cardinal Angelo Maria. *Tiara et purpura veneta*. Venice, 1761.

Randall, John H., Jr. "The Development of Scientific Method in the School of Padua." *Journal of the History of Ideas* 1 (1940): 177–206.

———"Paduan Humanism Reconsidered." In *Philosophy and Humanism: Renaissance Essays in Honor of Paul Oskar Kristeller*, edited by Edward P. Mahoney, 275–82. New York: Columbia University Press, 1976.

———*The School of Padua and the Emergence of Modern Science*. Padua: Antenore, 1961.

Ranke, Leopold von. *Die römischen Päpste in den letzten vier Jahrhunderten*. 4 vols. 9th ed. Leipzig, 1889.

Reinhard, Wolfgang. "Ämterhandel in Rom zwischen 1534 und 1621." In *Ämterhandel im Spätmittelalter und im 16. Jahrhundert*, edited by Ilja Mieck. Berlin: Colloquium Verlag, 1984.

———"Ämterlaufbahn und Familienstatus: der Aufstieg des Hauses Borghese." *Quellen und Forschungen aus italienischen Archiven und Bibliotheken* 54 (1974): 328–427.

———"Finanza pontificia e stato della chiesa nel XVI e XVII secolo." In *Finanze e ragion di stato in Italia e in Germania nella prima età moderna*, edited by Aldo De Maddalena and Hermann Kellenbenz, 353–87. Bologna: Il Mulino, 1984.

———"Finanza pontificia, sistema beneficiale e finanza statale nell'età confessionale." In *Fisco religione stato nell'età confessionale*, edited by Hermann Kellenbenz and Paolo Prodi, 459–504. Bologna: Il Mulino, 1989.

———"Kardinalseinkünfte und Kirchenreform." *Römische Quartalschrift* 77 (1982): 157–94.

———"Nepotismus: der Funktionswandel einer papstgeschichtlichen Konstanten." *Zeitschrift für Kirchengeschichte* 86 (1975): 145–85.

———"PAPA PIUS: Prolegomena zu einer Sozialgeschichte des Papsttums." In *Von Konstanz nach Trient: Beiträge zur Geschichte der Kirche von den Reformkonzilien bis zum Tridentinum. Festgabe für August Franzen*, edited by Remigius Bäumer, 262–99. Munich: Schöningh, 1972.

———*Papstfinanz und Nepotismus unter Paul V. (1605–1621)*. 2 vols. Stuttgart: Hiersemann, 1974.

———"Reformpapsttum zwischen Renaissance und Barock." In *Reformatio ecclesiae: Beiträge zu kirchlichen Reformbemühungen von der Alten Kirche bis zur Neuzeit. Festgabe für Erwin Iserloh*, edited by Remigius Baümer, 779–96. Paderborn: Schöningh, 1980.

Ribier, Guillaume. *Lettres et memoires d'estat, des roys, princes, ambassadeurs, et autres ministres, sous les regnes de François premier, Henry II et François II*. Paris, 1666.

Robey, Daniel, and John Law. "The Venetian Myth and the 'De Republica Veneta' of Pier Paolo Vergerio." *Rinascimento*, 2d ser., 15 (1975): 3–59.

Rodenwaldt, Ernst. "Untersuchungen über die Biologie des venezianischen Adels." *Homo: Zeitschrift für die vergleichende Forschung am Menschen* 8 (1957): 1–26.

Romano, G. *Cronaca del soggiorno di Carlo V in Italia*. Milan, 1892.

Roosen, William. "Early Modern Diplomatic Ceremonial: A Systems Approach." *Journal of Modern History* 52 (1980): 452–76.

Rosand, Ellen. "Music in the Myth of Venice." *Renaissance Quarterly* 30 (1977): 511–37.

Ross, James Bruce. "The Emergence of Gasparo Contarini: A Bibliographical Essay." *Church History* 41 (1972): 1–24.

———"Gasparo Contarini and His Friends." *Studies in the Renaissance* 17 (1970): 192–232.

———"Venetian Schools and Teachers, Fourteenth to Sixteenth Century: A Survey and a Study of Giovanni Battista Egnazio." *Renaissance Quarterly* 39 (1976): 521–60.

Rossetti, Lucia. [Bibliography of Studies Concerning the University of Padua]. *Quaderni per la storia dell'Università di Padova* 1 (1968): 179–311; 2 (1969): 109–88.

Rückert, Hanns. *Die theologische Entwicklung Gasparo Contarinis.* Arbeiten zur Kirchengeschichte. Bonn: A. Marcus & E. Weber, 1926.

Rusconi, Roberto. "Predicatori e predicazione." In *Storia d'Italia, Annali 4: Intellettuali e potere,* edited by Corrado Vivanti, 951–1035. Turin: Einaudi, 1981.

Sambin, Paolo. "Altre testimonianze (1525–1540) di Angelo Beolco." *Italia medioevale e umanistica* 7 (1964): 221–47.

Sanuto, Marin. *Chronachetta.* Edited by R. Fulin. Venice, 1880.

———*I diarii.* 58 vols. Venice, 1879–1903.

Sarpi, Paolo. *Istoria del Concilio Tridentino.* 2 vols. Bari: Laterza, 1935.

Schottenloher, Karl. *Bibliographie zur deutschen Geschichte im Zeitalter der Glaubensspaltung.* 2d ed. Vol. 3. Stuttgart: Hiersemann, 1957.

Schultze, Victor. "Aktenstücke zur deutschen Reformationsgeschichte." *Zeitschrift für Kirchengeschichte* 3 (1878–79): 609–53.

———"Dreizehn Depeschen Contarini's aus Regensburg an den Cardinal Farnese (1541)." *Zeitschrift für Kirchengeschichte* 3 (1878–79): 150–84.

Schutte, Anne Jacobson. "The *Lettere volgari* and the Crisis of Evangelism in Italy." *Renaissance Quarterly* 28 (1975): 639–88.

———*Pier Paolo Vergerio: The Making of an Italian Reformer.* Geneva: Droz, 1977.

Schweitzer, Vinzenz. "Beiträge zur Geschichte Pauls III." *Römische Quartalschrift* 22 (1908): 132–42.

———"Kardinal Bartolommeo Guidiccione (1469–1549)." *Römische Quartalschrift* 20 (1906): 27–53, 142–61, 189–204.

Seidel Menchi, Silvana. *Erasmo e l'Italia, 1520–1580.* Turin: Bollati Boringhieri, 1987.

Selge, Kurt-Victor. "Conclusione del convegno." In *Gaspare Contarini e il suo tempo: atti convegno di studio,* edited by Francesca Cavazzana Romanelli, 243–54. Venice: Comune di Venezia, Assessorato Affari Istituzionali, and Studium Cattolico Veneziano, 1988.

Simoncelli, Paolo. *Il caso Reginald Pole: eresia e santità nelle polemiche religiose del Cinquecento.* Rome: Edizioni di Storia e Letteratura, 1977.

———*Evangelismo italiano del Cinquecento: questione religiosa e nicodemismo*

politico. Rome: Istituto Storico Italiano per l'Età Moderna e Contemporanea, 1979.

——"Pietro Bembo e l'evangelismo italiano." *Critica storica* 15 (1978):
1–63.

Solmi, Edmondo. "La fuga di Bernardino Ochino secondo i documenti
dell'Archivio Gonzaga di Mantova." *Bullettino senese di storia patria* 15
(1908): 23–98.

——"Gasparo Contarini alla Dieta di Ratisbona secondo i documenti
inediti dell'Archivio Gonzaga di Mantova." *Nuovo Archivio Veneto* 13
(1907): 5–33, 69–93.

——"Lettere inedite del cardinale Gasparo Contarini nel carteggio del cardinale Ercole Gonzaga." *Nuovo Archivio Veneto* 7 (1904): 245–74.

Spitzer, Leo. *Classical and Christian Ideas of World Harmony.* Baltimore:
Johns Hopkins University Press, 1963.

Stella, Aldo. "La lettera del Cardinale Contarini sulla predestinazione." *Rivista di storia della chiesa in Italia* 15 (1961): 411–41.

——"Spunti di teologia contariniana e lineamenti di un itinerario religioso." In *Gaspare Contarini e il suo tempo: atti convegno di studio*, edited
by Francesca Cavazzana Romanelli, 147–66. Venice: Comune di Venezia,
Assessorato Affari Istituzionali; and Studium Cattolico Veneziano; 1988.

——"Die Staatsräson und der Mord an Michael Gaismair." *Der Schlern* 58
(1984): 307–10.

Storti, Nicola. *La storia e il diritto della Dataria Apostolica dalle origini ai
nostri giorni.* Naples: Athena Mediterranea, 1969.

Stupperich, Robert. *Der Humanismus und die Wiedervereinigung der Konfessionen.* Leipzig: M. Heinsius Nachfolger, 1936.

Suquìa, Angel. "Las reglas para sentir con la iglesia en la vida y en las obras del
Cardenal Gaspar Contarini (1483–1542)." *Archivum historicum Societatis
Iesu* 25 (1956): 380–95.

Tacchi-Venturi, Pietro. *Storia della Compagnia di Gesù in Italia.* 2d ed. Rome:
Civiltà Cattolica, 1950.

Tafuri, Manfredo. "'Renovatio urbis Venetiarum': il problema storiografico."
In *"Renovatio urbis": Venezia nell'età di Andrea Gritti (1523–1538)*,
edited by Manfredo Tafuri, 9–55. Roma: Officina Edizioni, 1984.

——*Venezia e il Rinascimento: religione, scienza, architettura.* Turin: Einaudi, 1985.

Tellechea Idigoras, J. I. "Contarini, Pole, Morone, denunciados por el Cardenal Francisco de Mendoza (1560)." In *Fray Bartolomé Carranza y el Cardenal Pole: un navarro en la restauración católica de Inglaterra*, 283–302.
Pamplona: Deputación Foral de Navarra, 1977.

Thorndike, Lynn. *A History of Magic and Experimental Science.* 8 vols. New
York: Columbia University Press, 1923–58.

Tiezza, Nilo. "I vescovi di Belluno Giulio e Gaspare Contarini e il Concilio di
Trento." *Dolomiti* 2, no. 6 (1979): 7–10.

Tramontin, Silvio. "Il 'De officio episcopi' di Gaspare Contarini." *Studia
Patavina* 12 (1965): 292–303.

Tucci, Ugo. "Pesi e misure nella storia della società." In *Storia d'Italia* 5(1):585–612. Turin: Einaudi, 1973.

———"The Psychology of the Venetian Merchant in the Sixteenth Century." In *Renaissance Venice*, edited by J. R. Hale, 346–78. London: Faber & Faber, 1973.

Uechtritz, Friedrich von. *Albrecht Holm: eine Geschichte aus der Reformations- zeit*. 3 pts. in 7 vols. Berlin: Verlag von Alexander Duncker, 1852–53.

Ulianich, Boris. "Scrittura e azione pastorale nelle prime omelie episcopali di Isidoro Chiari." In *Reformata reformanda: Festgabe für Hubert Jedin zum 17. Juni 1965*, edited by Erwin Iserloh and Konrad Repgen, 1:610–34. Münster i.W.: Aschendorff, 1965.

Urbani, Domenico. "Lettere ducali a Gasparo Contarini." *Raccolta veneta* 1 (1886): disp. 1, 19–34; disp. 3, 7–25.

"U.S. Lutheran-Roman Catholic Dialogue: Justification by Faith." *Origins: NC Documentary Service* 13, no. 17 (6 October 1983).

Valier, Agostino. *Memoriale … a Luigi Contarini Cavaliere sopra gli studi ad un senatore veneziano convenienti*. Edited by G. Morelli. Venice, 1803.

Vendramini, Ferruccio. *Tensioni politiche nella società bellunese della prima metà del '500*. Belluno: Tarantola, 1974.

Ventura, Angelo. "Scrittori politici e scritture di governo." In *Storia della cul- tura veneta*, edited by Girolamo Arnaldi and Manlio Pastore Stocchi, 3(3):513–63. Vicenza: Neri Pozza Editore, 1981.

Vetter, Paul. *Die Religionsverhandlungen auf dem Reichstage zu Regensburg 1541*. Jena, 1889.

Vogelsänger, Peter. "Ökumenismus im 16. Jahrhundert: zur Geschichte des Religionsgesprächs von Regensburg 1541." In *Unterwegs zur Einheit: Fest- schrift für Heinrich Stirnimann*, edited by Johannes Brantschen and Pietro Selvatico, 631–48. Freiburg, Switz., and Freiburg i.B.: Herder, 1980.

Walz, Angelus, O.P. "La giustificazione tridentina." *Angelicum* 28 (1951): 97–138.

Watts, Pauline Moffitt. *Nicolaus Cusanus: A Fifteenth-Century Vision of Man*. Leiden: E. J. Brill, 1982.

Weil, Erich. "Die Philosophie des Pietro Pomponazzi." *Archiv für Geschichte der Philosophie* 41 (1932): 127–76.

Weil-Garris, Kathleen, and John F. D'Amico. *The Renaissance Cardinal's Ideal Palace: A Chapter from Cortese's "De Cardinalatu."* Rome: Edizioni dell'Elefante, American Academy in Rome, 1980.

Welti, Manfred. *Kleine Geschichte der italienischen Reformation*. Gütersloh: Mohn, 1985.

Williams, George Huntston. "Camillo Renato (c. 1500–?1575)." In *Italian Reformation Studies in Honor of Laelius Socinus (1562–1962)*, edited by John A. Tedeschi, 104–83. *Proceedings of the Unitarian Historical Society* 14, pts. 1 and 2 (1962–63).

Wright, A. D. Review of *Gasparo Contarini*, by Gigliola Fragnito. *Journal of Modern History* 63 (1991): 405–7.

Zanetti, V. *La chiesa della Madonna dell'Orto in Venezia*. Venice, 1870.

Zarri, Gabriella. "Monasteri femminili e città (secoli XV–XVIII)." In *Storia d'Italia, Annali 9: La chiesa e il potere politico dal medioevo all'età contemporanea*, edited by Giorgio Chittolini and Giovanni Miccoli, 357–429. Turin: Einaudi, 1986.

zur Mühlen, Karl-Heinz. "Die Einigung über den Rechtfertigungsartikel auf dem Regensburger Religionsgespräch von 1541—eine verpasste Chance?" *Zeitschrift für Theologie und Kirche* 76 (1979): 331–59.

Index

Compositor:	G & S Typesetters
Text:	10/13 Galliard
Display:	Galliard
Printer and Binder:	BookCrafters